The United States Army War College

The United States Army War College educates and develops leaders for service at the strategic level while advancing knowledge in the global application of Landpower.

The purpose of the United States Army War College is to produce graduates who are skilled critical thinkers and complex problem solvers. Concurrently, it is our duty to the U.S. Army to also act as a "think factory" for commanders and civilian leaders at the strategic level worldwide and routinely engage in discourse and debate concerning the role of ground forces in achieving national security objectives.

The Strategic Studies Institute publishes national security and strategic research and analysis to influence policy debate and bridge the gap between military and academia.

The Center for Strategic Leadership contributes to the education of world class senior leaders, develops expert knowledge, and provides solutions to strategic Army issues affecting the national security community.

The Peacekeeping and Stability Operations Institute provides subject matter expertise, technical review, and writing expertise to agencies that develop stability operations concepts and doctrines.

The School of Strategic Landpower develops strategic leaders by providing a strong foundation of wisdom grounded in mastery of the profession of arms, and by serving as a crucible for educating future leaders in the analysis, evaluation, and refinement of professional expertise in war, strategy, operations, national security, resource management, and responsible command.

The U.S. Army Heritage and Education Center acquires, conserves, and exhibits historical materials for use to support the U.S. Army, educate an international audience, and honor soldiers—past and present.

STRATEGIC STUDIES INSTITUTE

The Strategic Studies Institute (SSI) is part of the U.S. Army War College and is the strategic-level study agent for issues related to national security and military strategy with emphasis on geostrategic analysis.

The mission of SSI is to use independent analysis to conduct strategic studies that develop policy recommendations on:

- Strategy, planning, and policy for joint and combined employment of military forces;

- Regional strategic appraisals;

- The nature of land warfare;

- Matters affecting the Army's future;

- The concepts, philosophy, and theory of strategy; and,

- Other issues of importance to the leadership of the Army.

Studies produced by civilian and military analysts concern topics having strategic implications for the Army, the Department of Defense, and the larger national security community.

In addition to its studies, SSI publishes special reports on topics of special or immediate interest. These include edited proceedings of conferences and topically oriented roundtables, expanded trip reports, and quick-reaction responses to senior Army leaders.

The Institute provides a valuable analytical capability within the Army to address strategic and other issues in support of Army participation in national security policy formulation.

Strategic Studies Institute
and
U.S. Army War College Press

THE HUMAN TERRAIN SYSTEM:
OPERATIONALLY RELEVANT SOCIAL
SCIENCE RESEARCH
IN IRAQ AND AFGHANISTAN

Christopher J. Sims

December 2015

*****

Comments pertaining to this report are invited and should be forwarded to: Director, Strategic Studies Institute and U.S. Army War College Press, U.S. Army War College, 47 Ashburn Drive, Carlisle, PA 17013-5010.

*****

All Strategic Studies Institute (SSI) and U.S. Army War College (USAWC) Press publications may be downloaded free of charge from the SSI website. Hard copies of this report may also be obtained free of charge while supplies last by placing an order on the SSI website. SSI publications may be quoted or reprinted in part or in full with permission and appropriate credit given to the U.S. Army Strategic Studies Institute and U.S. Army War College Press, U.S. Army War College, Carlisle, PA. Contact SSI by visiting our website at the following address: *www.StrategicStudiesInstitute.army.mil.*

*****

The Strategic Studies Institute and U.S. Army War College Press publishes a monthly email newsletter to update the national security community on the research of our analysts, recent and forthcoming publications, and upcoming conferences sponsored by the Institute. Each newsletter also provides a strategic commentary by one of our research analysts. If you are interested in receiving this newsletter, please subscribe on the SSI website at *www.StrategicStudiesInstitute.army.mil/newsletter.*

*****

Scholarship is a collective enterprise, yet, its production is often undertaken in seclusion. The resulting research process is precariously balanced between isolated periods of introspective writing on the one hand, and networking aimed at greater comprehension of the subject on the other. The historian Edward Gibbon delineated this dichotomy when arguing that "conversation enriches understanding, but solitude is the school of genius." While the ideal equilibrium between network and separation remains unresolved here, this book only exists because of the generosity of a number of individuals who gave selflessly of their time and expertise. Professor Greg Kennedy and Professor Thomas Rid were always on hand to offer any or all aspects of their broad expertise; they are both noteworthy mentors. Professor Anthony King and Dr. Robert Johnson gave invaluable comments which have shaped the book's content and character; for that, and for showing me the wider possibilities of the research, I am extremely grateful. Robert Holliday and Patrick McGrann also deserve special mention. Kelly Collis and Patrick Bauer provided all logistical support, encouragement, and ethnographic expertise in Washington, DC; without their immense kindness, there would be no book.

Michael Davies at the U.S. National Defense University, Dr. Nicholas Krohley at King's College London, and Dr. Paula Holmes-Eber at the U.S. Marine Corps University provided critical feedback and offered selflessly their own research and expertise solely to augment my own studies; I have learned from them that scholarship is, indeed, a collective enterprise. Dr. Martin Bayly, Dr. Aliki Karapliagou, Andrea Coles, Terry Sims, Stefan Sabo-Walsh, James Appleyard, Dr. Alison Hawks, and Dr. Nina Musgave offered advice and assistance whenever and wherever I sought their counsel. Dr. Ben Rockett's inspiring erudition ensured my continued motivation for the task at hand. Gregory Mueller at the U.S. Army Training and Doctrine Command went far beyond any expectations I may have had of him; his is a significant contribution. Colonel Cindy Jebb, Ph.D., at the School of Social Sciences, U.S. Military Academy, West Point, New York, and Dr. Walt Perry at the RAND Corporation also gave noteworthy assistance to this research project, with the sole aim of improving understanding of the Human Terrain System.

The final academic year of study (2013-14) was partially funded by a generous grant from the Allan and Nesta Ferguson Charitable Trust. During periods of writing this book, first Google and then Maplecroft Consultancy offered flexible employment and professional encouragement for which I am immeasurably grateful. My family provided welcomed perspective, insights, and support throughout; their lives continue to enrich my own. I also detail my grateful acknowledgement of all those individuals unnamed here that relinquished their time to contribute to this effort. Simultaneously humbling and illuminating, it was these encounters which taught me that the research process is to be enjoyed as much as the outcome; unknown to me at the beginning of the journey was that it would excavate so many priceless treasures. If I have accomplished to any degree improving knowledge of the Human Terrain System, it is the result of these individuals' expertise and patience.

Any errors that remain herein are entirely my own.

ISBN 1-58487-717-0

CONTENTS

FOREWORD

The announcement that the Human Terrain System (HTS) was brought to a close in the fall of 2014 met with a flurry of responses. Commentators assessed the character and content of the social science research program and several identified plausible legacies that it may bequeath U.S. Armed Services. Often the conclusions therein were mixed, hinting instructively at the absence of a strong empirical record of the program. Therefore, this book is a welcomed larger study of the HTS, one of the first investigations to delineate the experiences of former program members, chart the stance of the American Anthropological Association, and gain engagement both from the U.S. Training and Doctrine Command, and a manager from the first primary contractor, BAE Systems.

As a scholarly assessment of the complex interplay of these perspectives, the book becomes part of an attempt to find a platform for collaboration and discussion on what has become a profoundly polarizing subject. In so doing, the author links the strategic, operational, and tactical arenas of the campaigns in Iraq and Afghanistan. This is both an examination of the organizational origins of the HTS, and a tactical history delineated through the experiences and insights of former Human Terrain Team social scientists, set against the backdrop of a wider debate in the academy and media on the efficacy and ethicality of the program. These are important issues, both for the program as a historical object of study and the wider agenda of the military's engagement with social science research and researchers.

To engage these issues, this book commences with an overview of the program and proceeds to examine the wider debate around social science and the military. It subsequently charts the origins of the program and the experiences and insights of former Human Terrain Team social scientists in both Iraq and Afghanistan, exploring common themes which emerge from accounts of these embedded civilians. Through these accounts, the book exposes us to war at the most intimate and challenging level, delineating contours of two conflicts that have been characterized by deep military footprints, fought among civilian populations.

This seminal study of the U.S. Army HTS by the Strategic Studies Institute is an illuminating story of civilians conducting social science research in conflict in order, as one former social scientist notes in the book, to help "win a war."

DOUGLAS C. LOVELACE, JR.
Director
Strategic Studies Institute and
    U.S. Army War College Press

ABOUT THE AUTHOR

CHRISTOPHER J. SIMS has presented research on the Human Terrain System at various international conferences, as well as being an invited speaker on the subject. His examination of the U.S. Army program is part of broader interests in anthropology and insurgencies. Dr. Sims is committed to open access outputs and virtual academies on the principle that making research and teaching freely available enhances the global exchange of knowledge by enabling equal access to scholarship. His work has been published in several journals, including *Foreign Affairs* and *Small Wars Journal*. Dr. Sims holds a Ph.D. from King's College London.

INTRODUCTION

To avoid the footpaths which may have been mined with improvised explosive devices (IEDs), Ryan Evans, a U.S. federal civilian, was walking across a wheat field in Babaji, Helmand Province, in the spring of 2011. Evans was attached to the Royal Highland Fusiliers (2 Scots), C Company, a heavy infantry patrol tasked with providing security in the vicinity. Begun 2 years earlier, the Helmand Food Zone Program was a form of development intervention which offered subsidies, seed, and fertilizers to farmers who replaced lucrative opium cultivation from poppies with growing and harvesting wheat and vegetable crops. Babaji had been in the control of insurgents until a few months earlier and had not received any assistance from the program during the previous year; consequently, there were tensions between the community and British forces. As Evans and the patrol emerged from the field, an Afghan man sitting nearby, clearly irate, shouted in Pashto that the British soldiers had wanted the farmer to grow wheat instead of poppy, and then the same British soldiers walked through their fields.

At the immediate level, the encounter demonstrated the direct link between conflict, food security, and local trade, but conflict has many interrelated and mutual dependencies such that the anecdote is instructive on myriad broader milieus. Where, for example, is the tipping point that makes a civilian value creating an expression of discontent to a heavily armed patrol above his immediate physical security? Do livelihoods and cultures affect military strategies? Are there interdependencies between insurgencies, societies, and economies? Does the language of war require a sociological grammar in order to be understood?

1

Armed conflict is a human enterprise such that, by extension, understanding of the human dimension in a given area of operations should be thought integral to planning successful operations.[1]

Evans was part of a U.S. Army program whose field component had commenced 4 years earlier. On February 7, 2007, a five-person military-civilian Human Terrain Team (HTT) embedded with the U.S. Army 4th Brigade Combat Team (BCT), 82nd Airborne Division, at Forward Operating Base (FOB) Salerno in Khost province, Afghanistan. Designated AF1, this experiment in hybridized civil-military relations was the first embedded team in the Human Terrain System (HTS), an ambitious proof-of-concept program managed by the U.S. Army Training and Doctrine Command (TRADOC).

The team's mission was to provide BCT — approximately 3,000 personnel — commanders:

> with operationally relevant, sociocultural data, information, knowledge and understanding, and the embedded expertise to integrate that understanding into the commander's planning and decisionmaking process.[2]

This embedded expertise was borne in part from an identified need to fuse focused social science scholarship to military instruments in Iraq and Afghanistan so as to wage more effective population-centered counterinsurgency (COIN) campaigns in and among the population.[3] Teams were to be geographically located, to develop understanding of a particular area in order to "preserve and share sociocultural knowledge" across unit rotations.[4]

The requirement for an HTS was not straightforward, however. Some levels of sociocultural capability already existed with the BCTs, including, for example, Civil Affairs teams and tactical Psychological Operations detachments. Civil Affairs teams were configured as a project management function to assess, repair, or build infrastructure, and evaluate agricultural practices per requirements. They were therefore an evaluation and monitoring asset that, while in theory was grounded in sociocultural analysis of the area of operations to prioritize requirements and efficacy, in practice was largely assessment conducted at a more abstract level. In part, this refracted analysis may explain the poor return on the substantial funds invested in development projects and tangentially why more detailed research is required in the future.[5] Conversely, Psychological Operations teams worked at a tactical level, delivering messages to the population but did not gather information in a concerted manner to influence BCT thinking, planning, or action. It was therefore the development of Courses of Action (COAs) beyond their own element which would create a higher level of sociocultural capability than that provided by existing functions.[6]

HTS promised a different and therefore unique sociocultural capability. The teams would conduct granular social science research among the civilian population and report directly to the brigade staff. Thus they were plugged in to the highest levels of planning on the ground with the ability to influence all aspects of the brigade based on their findings. As a former HTT member observed, while other brigade elements "directly engage the people on a continual basis" focusing on development projects and influencing the local population, the HTT's unique contribution was in "understanding the people."[7] In Iraq and Afghanistan, in complex COIN campaigns, understanding the people required fluent language skills, robust knowledge of research methods, and field experience. Such skills, meaning that the team could influence BCT staff products in the provision of sociocultural research, required social science expertise identified as only available in the U.S. civilian reservoir.

As the Afghanistan campaign drew down in early-2014, plans to transition the program to a postwar capability took shape. The HTS program was transitioned on September 30, 2014, into the residual organization at TRADOC called the Global Cultural Knowledge Network. The network is composed of a commissioned officer, three social scientists, a geospatial specialist, and a knowledge manager.[8] Quoted in *The New York Times* in 2015, an intelligence officer at the command noted that the remaining organization was a "nucleus" capable of rapid expansion if required, but that TRADOC lacked the administrative and support infrastructure to embed social scientists in the future.[9] Thus the fall of 2014 brought to a close one of the most ambitious and compelling social science experiments conducted by the U.S. military, and its character and content deserves investigation.

In this book, I examine this fusion of civilian expertise and military operations in the HTS. I investigate the HTS, initially from a review of secondary sources and then from interviews, Freedom of Information Act request material, and program documents, in order to understand the contribution of social science research to brigades in Iraq and Afghanistan. I answer the broad question: Why did the U.S. Army embed social scientists in Iraq and Afghanistan? The initial hypothesis is that HTS was created in response to, and facilitated by, a technological crisis in the U.S. Department of Defense (DoD). This hypothesis, in part, supports the view which sees the program as part of the COIN turn which stressed understanding culture as a necessary element of overall victory in Iraq and Afghanistan. In that definition, overall victory would be defined as popular endorsement of government efforts and loss of support for the insurgent elements. But I argue also that it was the impoverished understanding of the societal network behind the IEDs which facilitated the introduction of the program. Existing notions of the program as a creation of the COIN turn in military thinking curtails an important understanding of the way in which technological crises bring forth myriad urgent solutions in a febrile atmosphere in the U.S. military enterprise.

The hypothesis is tested in three steps. First, I examine the technological crisis which befell U.S. forces in Iraq and Afghanistan as attempts were made to mitigate the effects of the IED and the creation of the HTS from that perfect storm. Second, I examine the evolution of the program as it consolidated feedback from embedded and returning social scientists, affording insight into the character of the program. Third, and forming the core of the analysis, I assess experiences of former program social scientists that embedded with military units in Iraq or Afghanistan, principally through interviews. Interviewing social scientists who have deployed on HTTs in Iraq or Afghanistan across a significant time period lends substantial understanding of why social scientists were embedded in combat brigades. As former HTT social scientist Marcus Griffin has noted, a combat brigade "is nothing more than an information-consuming machine" and thus having "a social scientist on their staff helps them make sense of all the information coming at them."[10] I therefore investigate the information required by the brigade and the ability of the social scientists to deliver products based on that requirement, thus I contribute to the emerging corpus of scholarship detailing the program and the experiences of social scientists in HTTs.[11] A limitation of the work is that it does not interview whole teams, which would provide valuable feedback of social scientist research. It was team leaders, for example, that were the military bridge between the team and the brigade staff and would have added insight into the operational relevance of the research conducted.

Embedding civilians to practice academic skill sets in order to influence military thinking, planning, and action in combat zones led to disproportionate scrutiny of the program. The historically brittle synthesis between academia and the military ensured that the HTS captured and maintained media interest. The program was at once a compelling and divisive endeavor, and it crystallized sustained opposition from a number of anthropologists within the academy whose primary fear was the appropriation of their principled expertise for military purposes. In their reading, information gathered on the population could be used by the brigade to target insurgent networks with lethal effect, placing the population in harm as a result of the embedded team activities. This was an anathema to the academic anthropologists. It was also a debate conducted from irreconcilable platforms. As the first HTS program manager notes, "The standard they gave HTS to meet was to show that nothing produced by HTS could ever be used by anyone to target individuals. Most major works of anthropology in the past and present cannot meet that standard."[12] Examining the program is therefore a further opportunity to investigate the sociocultural dimension of military operations through the lens of ethics.

Despite its relatively small size in the U.S. Department of the Army in terms of both personnel and budget, the importance of the HTS as a subject of study is marked. As a 2008 West Point study on the program notes:

> It is important to revisit this study in the changing military context as the Army continues to learn how best to conduct operations that will not only help secure the country, but also help shape the conditions that will promote state capacity and legitimacy.[13]

At a more abstract level, the book informs debate concerning the investigation, distillation, and retention of scholarship in its myriad forms beyond the university, speaking to the way in which military agents seek to extract, collate, and apply academic methods of inquiry and accumulate knowledge. It is the author's intention that the analysis resonate beyond the permeable boundaries of the academy; social science is the study of social structure to inform society, a point which can often be obfuscated in the rush for scholarly profundity.

Operational Planning.

Conflicting and superficial accounts from both media and scholars have complicated attempts to understand the character of the HTS. The problem has been exacerbated by the story of the program being so compelling to the extent that, paraphrasing Mark Twain, truth has never stood in the way of telling it. As an American Anthropological Association assessment indicates of the program's early years, existing journalistic accounts provide multiple and often contrasting points of view on what HTS is basically about, how it works, and its implications for anthropology and for the new counter-insurgency doctrine.[14]

The program, as noted by a professor of ethics and a professor of anthropology in an edited volume on the program, was "hardly immune from a variety of legitimate and justifiable concerns," but they further argue that the HTS was placed by anthropologists within a historical narrative of anthropology's fraught engagement with the military, "pre-empting any impartial assessment of its legitimacy or effectiveness."[15]

In order to proceed from this uncertain platform, I first consolidate and examine existing literature on the program in a review chapter. In the second chapter, I assess the dimensions of the military's engagement with anthropology, for which the HTS served as a specific site for sustained debate. The third chapter examines the sense of crisis in military operations in Iraq which allowed the controversial program to cohere and evolve. The fourth chapter assesses elements within the training cycle of relevance to understanding the role of the social scientist in Iraq and Afghanistan. The fifth chapter investigates the experiences of social scientists when embedded, and the sixth chapter follows on from these experiences, observing limitations in social science research in contested spaces. In conclusion, I highlight the limiting factors of social science research in such insecure environments as Iraq and Afghanistan, and suggest possibilities for future applications of the program.

This analysis requires a broad framework for conceptualizing the levels of violence in Iraq and Afghanistan where the social science research took place. I follow the approach of political scientist Stathis N. Kalyvas in modelling areas of violence in intrastate wars. Usefully, Kalyvas has shown the complexity of the situation on the ground, which harbors deep, often fluid mixtures of identities and actions:

> Civil wars are not binary conflicts, but complex and ambiguous processes that foster the 'joint' action of local and supralocal actors, civilians, and armies, whose alliance results in violence that aggregates, yet still reflects, their diverse goals.[16]

Instructive in the need for detailed research at the very granular level, war generates "new local cleavages because power shifts at the local level upset delicate arrangements."[17] In theory, then, the unique social situation encountered by each brigade in their Area of Responsibility, and its inevitable change over time, meant that there was a requirement for a permanent element on staff, assessing this sociocultural element of the terrain.

Beneath that nuanced conceptualization of intrastate conflict, where "behavior, beliefs, preferences, and even identities" can be altered, Kalyvas models the intensity of structured violence between actors.[18] Irregular war fought between the incumbent and insurgent is split into five zones, where the first and fifth zones are conceptualized as total sovereign and insurgent control, respectively, but hegemonic, though incomplete control in Zone 2 and Zone 4 leads to high levels of selective, discriminate violence against adversaries.[19] The third zone, depicted as where opposed forces are present in similar arrangements, contains less selective violence.

Beyond those areas where actors exercise complete or equal control, there are contested spaces characterized by selective violence. It is in these contested spaces where insecurity is relatively high, and military forces are specifically and systematically targeted. In reference to Iraq and Afghanistan, it is in those contested spaces where there is the least security for coalition forces and insurgents exercise hegemonic control, the physical danger and methodological difficulties inherent in social science research modes are the greatest. At the time of this writing, a proposal for a 12-person proof-of-concept HTT in the U.S. Pacific Command (PACOM) was awaiting authorization by the U.S. Congress (see Appendix B).[20] Program management of the HTS visited PACOM in late-2008 to explore possibilities for the combatant command, with the theoretical recommendation for an 11-person team.[21] Based on the Kalyvas model, this team would probably conduct research in areas of complete or hegemonic control by incumbents where insurgent violence is negligible. Therefore, ascertaining why the HTS should evolve into this social science asset conducting research in less contested, more secure spaces is a contribution of this book.

Methods.

From its physical origins within the Joint Improvised Explosive Device Defeat Organization (JIEDDO) landscape, the HTS evolved into a U.S. Army program which, by Fiscal Year 2012, commanded a budget of U.S.$135 million; a more than six-fold increase on its original U.S.$20.4 million funding in 2006.[22] The program expanded despite journalistic and academic criticism, congressional inquiry, and a budget freeze, demonstrating merit in the Army's use of nonorganic additions to augment social science research in its ranks. Previous academic assessments of the program, however, have suffered because the program has been entrenched in the conflicts in Iraq and Afghanistan. Despite the plausibility of considerable engagement with the program and possible release of unclassified documents, there nevertheless has been a paucity of information regarding the program. The last HTT departed Iraq in 2011, and in 2014, the last teams departed Afghanistan. As a consequence, there are now many HTT social scientists departing the program such that there is a reasonable expectation of balanced assessments of team-level experiences and insights gleaned from interviews.

This research process is inductive, a method that has been used in previous examination of the program.[23] I generate research which lends itself to observations and findings in order to make comment on existing theory. Deconstructing the research question into sequential steps creates a clear framework for progression. Within the research, interviews are semi-structured such that, in accordance with existing social science guidelines, "topics are pre-specified and listed on an interview protocol, but they can be reworded as needed and are covered by the interviewer in any sequence or order."[24] Interviews have been chosen as a technique because they provide in-depth information and high interpretive validity. Moreover, interviews historically have a high response rate and can be used both for exploratory aspects of the thesis and confirmatory aspects. Interview questions have been formulated using rules for designing interview questions drawn from prevailing social research frameworks methods.[25]

To develop a holistic assessment of the program, I move beyond previous examinations that focused exclusively on current or former members of the program. I interview a spectrum of stakeholders, draw from a pool including academia — principally the chair of the American Anthropological Association's commission investigating the program — a moderating voice on the commission — professional military anthropologists, and, serving staff within TRADOC Intelligence Staff G-2. In addition, to gain insight from the perspective of the contractor, I interview the HTS program director for the BAE Systems contract, 2008-09, and use contracting material not previously in the public domain to augment the study. These interviews are valuable in placing the program within the larger trajectory of the U.S. Army's engagement with the social sciences for the purposes of informing operational planning. This is important because the program represents a rare opportunity for the academic community to investigate why this social science expertise became integrated into tactical planning.

Parameters of the Study.

This book is a narrow analysis insofar as it is an assessment of why the U.S. Army came to use social scientists on the front line of conflict. This precise investigation removes from the investigation larger issues such as the differing approaches to cultural warfighting developed by the U.S. Army and the U.S. Marine Corps (USMC). The USMC, for example, due to its original expeditionary nature, has had protracted experience fighting small wars in the past; hence the publishing of the *Small Wars Manual* and development of the Combined Action Program in Vietnam, although that small wars mentality appears elided in its current trajectory toward a heavy amphibious force. In contrast to the Army, however, the USMC incorporated culture and language into its operations by establishing the Center for Advanced Operational Culture Learning, a culture and language training center. The HTS was funded by the DoD and the Army, but support to the USMC, however, was a requirement of the program. The HTS was directed to support all BCTs and USMC regional command teams (RTCs) in theater.

Sample and Research Pool.

There are more than 20 interviews with people who have worked on or with the HTS or critiqued it in a professional capacity. These interviews range from approximately 30 to 120 minutes in length and include social scientists that have been embedded in Iraq or Afghanistan, or in both countries. To develop a broad cross-sectional representation of the program, I interviewed the first Program Manager, the first Director of the Social Science Directorate, and the subsequent Acting Director of the Social Science Directorate, social scientists that embedded in Iraq between 2008 and 2009 and in Afghanistan between 2008 and 2012. I interviewed other members of the HTS management, including members of the Program Development Team, Operational Planning Team, and Training Directorate. The majority of interviews were conducted in Virginia, Rhode Island, Maryland, and Washington, DC, in 2013. I have at least one interview with former members from all levels of field HTS teams, HTTs, Human Terrain Analysis Teams, and Theater Coordination Elements (TCEs). Social scientists that were interviewed have embedded with a range of military units; U.S. Army Combat Brigades, USMC Regimental Brigades, British, Polish, and Danish units, and other smaller units such as those comprised of U.S. Special

Operations Forces, and in both Iraq and Afghanistan, that supported a range of activities, including but not limited to Village Stability Operations in Afghanistan.

In order to gain a holistic analysis of the range of social sciences represented in the field, and not limit the analysis to those trained anthropologists, I interviewed former HTT social scientists who have undergraduate or postgraduate degrees in political science, geography, theology, archaeology, international relations, war studies, and anthropology. This cross-section of intellectual origins is an important methodological element: Limiting the study to one area of the social science spectrum would present skewed qualitative data. Participation is marked in all instances by in-depth, semi-structured, qualitative interviews by telephone or in person, and thematic coding is used for interview transcript analysis. One characteristic of the cross-sectional interview design is that it is applicable when there is interest in capturing a snapshot of thematic interests for the given population for which data is being collated. At the same time, data can be collated on individual characteristics, to enhance analysis. Therefore, it is useful for deductive research methodologies of the type adopted for this analysis.

I consider that the former program personnel interviewed were afforded enough temporal and professional distance to evaluate critically the spectrum of their experiences, from recruitment, training, and pre-deployment, to embedded research and expertise retention after their return to the United States. All former HTT social scientists interviewed offer enough criticism to suggest sufficient detachment from the program to lend the necessary objectivity for validity in their observations. Moreover, when analyzed as a corpus, the close thematic correlation of their experiences strongly suggests legitimacy.

It is the interviews with social scientists that have departed the program that form the core of this thesis. Unencumbered by any residue of responsibility and having been embedded for at least 9 months, these men and women are eloquent, articulate, and thoughtful about the nature of their experiences in Iraq and Afghanistan. Echoing Paul Joseph of Tufts University, in his 2014 study that included interviews from teams in Afghanistan, it is best practice to let the social scientists' experiences remain whole in the text wherever possible.[26] Moreover, their competencies show that many of them earned distinguished records of service, meaning that they are best placed to answer why they were embedded in combat brigades. Interviewing social scientists that embedded across different time periods affords the opportunity to draw out common themes experienced by embedded team members, across different periods of time, and in cases where experiences may be idiosyncratic to countries, regions, or even towns of cities. Conflict is, after all, about change over time, about the drawing and redrawing of boundaries, both geographical and human, and about growth and decay.

To prevent missed differences or similarities between female and male perspectives, of the nine former HTS social scientists interviewed, three are female, a statistically significant 33 percent of the sample. Interviewing both genders allows examination of any differences or similarities between the sexes regarding recruitment, training, integration into the military unit, and interaction with the host population and relationships with indigenous translators. Particularly in Afghan society, female social scientists would have greater access to women in the country, and thus the experiences of these social scientists is important in any attempt to understand the role, if any, of gender in attempts by military units to interact and understand local populations.

Assistance and engagement from TRADOC G-2 differentiates this book from other recent volumes of note. Any holistic study of the HTS requires input from the parent organization of the program. Previous studies' difficulty in engagement is a consequence of the politicization of the program, criticism from the academic community, and media portrayals. The effect, as Christopher Lamb *et al.* note, is that:

> Requests for assistance with external studies of HTS are routinely turned down. TRADOC also avoids publicity and help from interested outside parties. It provided minimal cooperation for the CNA [Center for Naval Analyses, 2010] report, and none at all for this and other studies it did not commission.[27]

Engagement from the TRADOC Intelligence Staff is therefore important, but there are limitations. The G-2 now differs in personnel from the staff that existed in the early years of the HTS, and the emphasis is on institutional training as opposed to support of field units.

To strengthen the research design, I introduce a control group into the study of the HTS, a technique which has been utilized before to important effect: Cindy Jebb *et al.* conducted interviews with combat commanders in Iraq that did not have HTTs in their units in order to include a control group in their investigation of HTT effectiveness.[28] To differentiate from that control group, I interview at least one individual that has worked with the U.S. Agency for International Development (USAID) and the U.S. Department of State, familiar with HTT products, to ask why these civilian entities did not create their own embedded teams. Thus, in asking why the U.S. Army chose to embed civilian social scientists in combat brigades, I also ask explicitly why USAID and the U.S. Department of State did not choose to embed social scientists, despite the professional gap between USAID and the U.S. Department of State, and that of civilian social scientists being less pronounced and thus easier to navigate than the military and the social scientists.

This book does not examine the views of commanders of units in which teams embedded. Myriad studies in the public domain have been conducted that include interviews with commanders, for example, Jebb *et al.* and Lamb *et al.* Moreover, it has been argued persuasively that commanders are less critical of HTT performance than are team members.[29] Ultimately, it is enough to say that many commanders interviewed assessed the embedded teams as being useful.[30] Sample sizes for commanders have varied (nine for instance, in the case of the Lamb *et al.*, a study that also included 19 commanders from the Institute for Defense Analyses study, by far the largest group), and this book would not improve on these sample sizes nor enjoy similar levels of access to high-level military commanders. Moreover, because the program was supported by officials such as Secretary of Defense Robert Gates and General David Petraeus, there is inevitably a political dimension to consider in responses from senior commanders, which would color any utilization of their responses.

Finally, the character of this book is shaped with specific intent to generate a work which scholars can utilize as a platform for future avenues of study. The longitudinal and latitudinal dimensions of HTS extend far beyond the program itself, meriting myriad opportunities for deep, objective examination. It is probable that, in the immediate future, a social science capability will be produced as a long-range planning asset of the U.S. Army, informing the strategic direction of planning by identifying at-risk societies where insurgencies may develop. From that mission, I envisage that small teams of expert social scientists will conduct research in regions of burgeoning interest to the U.S. Army for 12 to 24 months before returning to staff to write detailed products of utility to the combatant commands. This analysis, in part, then answers why that transformation may occur.

ENDNOTES - INTRODUCTION

1. For recent identification of this requirement, see Raymond Odierno, James F. Amos, and William H. McRaven, *Strategic Landpower: Winning the Clash of Wills*, Fort Leavenworth, KS: U.S. Army Training and Doctrine Command (TRADOC), 2013.

2. Nathan Finney, *The Human Terrain Team Handbook*, Fort Leavenworth, KS: TRADOC, 2008, p. 35.

3. Jacob Kipp *et al.*, "The Human Terrain System: A CORDS for the 21st Century," *Military Review*, Vol. 85, No. 5, 2006, pp. 8-15.

4. Montgomery McFate and Janice H. Laurence, "Introduction: Unveiling the Human Terrain System," in Montgomery McFate and Janice H. Laurence, eds., *Social Science Goes to War: The Human Terrain System in Iraq and Afghanistan*, London, UK: Hurst, p. 11.

5. See, for example, Sharon Behn, "US Watchdog Slams Afghanistan Aid Waste," *Voice of America*, August 12, 2013.

6. The Human Terrain System program management visited U.S. Army Civil Affairs and Psychological Operations Command multiple times to try and build a partnership, without success. Steve Fondacaro, personal communication with author, September 15, 2015.

7. Jonathan D. Thompson, "Human Terrain Team Operations in East Baghdad," *Military Review*, Vol. 90, No. 4, 2010, p. 77.

8. Justin Doubleday, "Controversial Army Social-Science Program Morphs Into 'Reach-Back' Office," *Inside the Army*, Vol. 27, No. 27, 2015.

9. Vanessa Gezari, "The Quiet Demise of the Army's Plan to Understand Afghanistan and Iraq," *The New York Times*, August 18, 2015, available from *www.nytimes.com/2015/08/18/magazine/the-quiet-demise-of-the-armys-plan-to-understand-afghanistan-and-iraq.html?_r=0*, accessed September 10, 2015.

10. Marcus Griffin, quoted in Nathan Swire, "McFate Explains Human Terrain Teams," *The Dartmouth*, September 26, 2008.

11. Christopher J. Lamb *et al.*, *Human Terrain Teams: An Organizational Innovation for Sociocultural Knowledge in Irregular Warfare*, Washington, DC: Institute of World Politics Press, 2013; Nicholas Krohley, *The Death of the Mehdi Army: The Rise, Fall and Revival of Iraq's Most Powerful Militia*, London, UK: Hurst, 2015; Paul Joseph, *"Soft" Counterinsurgency: Human Terrain Teams and US Military Strategy in Iraq and Afghanistan*, New York: Palgrave Pivot, 2014; Montgomery McFate and Janice H. Laurence, eds., *Social Science Goes to War: The Human Terrain System in Iraq and Afghanistan*, London, UK: Hurst, 2015.

12. Steve Fondacaro, personal communication with author, September 15, 2015.

13. Cindy R. Jebb, Laurel J. Hummel, and Tania M. Chacho, *Human Terrain Team Trip Report: A "Team of Teams,"* West Point, NY: Unpublished report for TRADOC, 2008, p. 8. Copy held by author.

14. Commission on the Engagement of Anthropology with the U.S. Security and Intelligence Communities, *Final Report on the Army's Human Terrain System Proof of Concept Program*, Arlington, VA: American Anthropological Association, October 14, 2009, p. 11.

15. Carolyn Fluehr-Lobban and George R. Lucas Jr., "Assessing the Human Terrain Teams: No White Hats or Black Hats, Please," in Montgomery McFate and Janice H. Laurence, eds., *Social Science Goes to War: The Human Terrain System in Iraq and Afghanistan*, London, UK: Hurst, p. 241.

16. Stathis N. Kalyvas, "The Ontology of 'Political Violence': Action and Identity in Civil Wars," *Perspectives on Politics*, Vol. 1, No. 3, 2003, p. 475.

17. *Ibid.*, p. 480.

18. Stathis N. Kalyvas, "Promises and Pitfalls of an Emerging Research Program: The Microdynamics of Civil War," in Stathis N. Kalyvas, Ian Shapiro, and Tarek Masoud, eds., *Order, Conflict, and Violence*, Cambridge, UK: Cambridge University Press, 2008, p. 403.

19. *Ibid.*, p. 407.

20. I am indebted to Michael Davies for highlighting this redirection.

21. Steve Fondacaro, personal communication with author, September 15, 2015.

22. Montgomery McFate and Steve Fondacaro, "Reflections on the Human Terrain System during the First 4 Years," *PRISM*, Vol. 2, No. 4, 2011, p. 63.

23. For example, Julia Page, "Human Terrain Teams," unpublished master's thesis, Blacksburg, VA: Virginia Polytechnic and State University, February 3, 2012.

24. Abbas Tashakkori and Charles Teddlie, eds., *Handbook of Mixed Methods in Social and Behavioral Research*, Thousand Oaks, CA: Sage, 2003, p. 306.

25. Alan Bryman, *Social Research Methods*, Oxford, UK: Oxford University Press, 2004, pp. 152-156.

26. Joseph, p. 10.

27. Lamb *et al.*, p. 80.

28. Jebb, Hummel, and Chacho, p. 2.

29. Lamb *et al.*, p. 169.

30. *Ibid.*

CHAPTER 1

CAPABILITY GAP

There is enough variation in accounts of the Human Terrain System's (HTS's) origin that the precise character of the program's early development may remain unresolved. Too many people, both protagonists and peripheral actors, relate the story differently for there to emerge a single unifying narrative. However, the program's physical origins lay firmly in the counter-improvised explosive device (C-IED) enterprise conducted by the Department of Defense (DoD). Within this enterprise, technological efforts to mitigate the effect of improvised explosive devices proved largely futile. As part of an effort to examine the sociocultural fabric behind the IED's human networks, a proof-of-concept program, the Cultural Preparation of the Environment, was created in April 2005. The program's testing phase focused on Diyala province, Iraq, and was aimed at developing taxonomies for sociocultural data gathered in the field. In practice, the program proved unworkable because the Iraqi researchers involved did not accurately portray their findings.[1] The Joint IED Defeat Task Force-Iraq leader at that time also notes that the brigade commander was "already overwhelmed with a multitude of information input capabilities in his headquarters (HQ) from all levels of military intel in DoD" and that the staff "had no capability or time to sit with a laptop with yet another unique database with its own protocol and data fish."[2] Specialist researchers embedded with combat brigades would be necessary to collect information and produce reports related to combatting the social network behind the IEDs.

23

Nevertheless, there was significant knowledge borne from this attempt to extract and visualize sociocultural data from Iraq, and it should be properly considered the first fragile iteration of an HTS. This program also helped to create a network of individuals, most importantly, DoD cultural anthropologist, Dr. Montgomery McFate, and then-U.S. Army Colonel Steve Fondacaro, both of whom would become synonymous with HTS content and character as Director of the Social Science Directorate and Program Manager, respectively. Many other personnel within the HTS *zeitgeist* would also be borne from this network, such that the human capital of the HTS emerged definitively from the fight against the IED. The Cultural Preparation of the Environment (CPE) had been developed by a task force at DoD level led by Hirar Cabayan who engaged anthropologists Andrea Jackson and Montgomery McFate to assist. Andrea Jackson, at that time working for the Lincoln Group as a contractor, was with Fondacaro in Baghdad during the implementation of the CPE.[3] Fondacaro had previously met both of them in 2005 during a conference in Tampa, Florida.

At the CPE outbrief, the requirement for sociocultural knowledge expertise to influence Courses of Action for brigade combat teams (BCTs) was highlighted. As Fondacaro explains, that briefing from Baghdad was given to General Montgomery Miegs, commander of JIEDDO and Maxie McFarland in 2005. McFarland took the findings to TRADOC after departing a short-term position in the Joint IED defeat enterprise and tasked the Foreign Military Studies Office (FMSO) with finding a possible solution, based on Fondacaro's recommendation that experts be deployed to theater.[4] The FMSO was a small staff, and the capability of deployed experts was one topic of study; the staff had sat in on the weekly video conferences which CPE had held while it was active and so were versed on the possible requirement for team structure.

The FMSO staff members were researchers rather than field personnel, although already known to Fondacaro: Jacob Kipp, Director of FMSO, was with him at the School of Advanced Military Studies; Karl Prinslow had been at West Point with him; and Lester Grau, a Central Asia expert, had taught him at the U.S. Command and General Staff College.[5] Already briefed on the requirement for field personnel, FMSO had written an article for *Military Review* which made analogous the requirement in Iraq to that in Vietnam. As Fondacaro explains, the FMSO article, published before he returned from Iraq, "compared HTS to the CORDS [Civil Operations and Revolutionary Development Support] program late in the Vietnam conflict" and the HTS later:

> spent years trying to overcome, unsuccessfully, the impression created by this article that HTS was designed to support kinetic targeting like the Phoenix Program. The comparison, while interesting from a compare and contrast approach, was inaccurate in that we were not a 21st Century CORDS by any stretch. Everyone is entitled to his opinion, but, as the Director of FMSO, everyone reading this accepted this as the HTS mission statement.[6]

When Fondacaro returned from Iraq, only Don Smith, a military reserve officer, was working on the HTS concept. Smith was serving his annual active duty tour with FMSO at the time.[7]

The model for the program moved forward in tandem with an Army Operational Needs Statement

(ONS) for cultural knowledge from the 10th Mountain Division in late-2005.[8] The ONS was not urgent, however, and there was no requirement for the Army to act on it. The FMSO, however, lacked funds to embed a team in a combat theater, and the HTS was still an idea held loosely at FMSO. When the Joint Improvised Explosive Device Defeat Organization—the joint C-IED organization in DoD—authorized the HTS concept on June 12, 2006, and provided U.S.$20.4 million, McFarland, a retired Army officer who was then Deputy Chief of Staff for Intelligence, G-2, at TRADOC, appointed Fondacaro head of a Cultural Operations Research–Human Terrain System (COR-HTS) steering committee and program manager.[9] Fondacaro, who had been assigned to the HTS project in May, had made the earlier funding request brief to Dr. Robin Keesee, Deputy Director, JIEDDO, earlier in the month, and half of the amount was received in August.[10] This fund was built on a U.S.$1.12 million loan that Don Smith had secured from the Counter Terrorist Advisory Group on the DoD staff.[11]

In 2004, Fondacaro had been a TRADOC assigned officer assigned to TRADOC HQ staff and then selected to lead the Joint Improvised Explosive Device Defeat Task Force-Iraq (JIEDDTF-Iraq) in early-2005 until April 2006 when the mandatory 30-year retirement commenced, but he had already been approached by McFarland during that period to return to TRADOC to initiate the HTS capability outlined as part of the CPE.[12] The HTS was to remain part of FMSO until April 2007, when the rapid expansion of the program meant that the FMSO research capability was no longer appropriate to house an operational training program.[13] The FMSO had emphasized testing and collating results carefully over a period of years.[14] The request and approval for JIEDDO in the initial funding request was for a 2-year proof of concept, consisting of five teams, of which two would be in Afghanistan and three in Iraq. As Fondacaro notes:

> We needed this 2-year period to study and discover how to recruit, train, integrate and deploy a team like this. Nothing like it had been ever done before. We had no development and training model to borrow from. So we needed the time and experience to discover how to do it right.[15]

The FMSO had wanted the teams to collect long-term research which could be used to populate their open-source database, the World Basic Information Library.[16] Fondacaro, however, wanted teams to support units in Iraq and Afghanistan directly, using their accrued research to influence brigade planning.[17] This changed leadership thus transitioned the mission of teams and thus altered the character of the embedded researchers. As Fondacaro explains it, FMSO saw the capability as a team that would occasionally deploy and conduct research, but that level of superficial engagement would "only be one more distraction interfering with tactical operations in the same way many other programs were already confusing the BCT's battlespace."[18] Funding for a World Basic Information Library project was unlikely to have gained traction from JIEDDO; as such, the program as it evolved was to support BCT staff directly.

As the program concept was created as the result of JIEDDO funding, the components became divided into two: the deployed teams and the continental U.S.-based components that supported them with administration, support, training, and an information reservoir of the operating environments designated reach-back analysis. These deployed teams that embedded with military units were the program's signature apparatus, integrating the expertise of civilian social scientists into BCTs in order to "research, interpret, archive, and provide cultural data, information, and knowledge to optimize operational effectiveness by harmonizing courses of action within the cultural context of the environment," going beyond the CPE tool in providing the requisite additional human dimension to military evaluation of the sociocultural layer of the terrain.[19] While these Human Terrain Teams (HTTs) would be varied in precise composition, in the ideal format, the initial model planned for five roles; team leader, cultural analyst, regional studies expert, research manager, and human terrain analyst.[20] The cultural analyst was to be an anthropologist or sociologist fluent in the local language; the regional studies expert would possess similar skills without specific disciplinary social sciences background; both were to hold a master's degree or above.[21] The other three team members were to be former or military reservists.

Gaining such a totality of social science skill sets proved difficult, hampered principally by the esoteric sociocultural aspects of Iraq and Afghanistan. Bluntly, the military sought area experts with granular knowledge of regions within Iraq and Afghanistan, and methods experts who were not simply theorists but possessed abundant field experience, in order to provide practical, operational value to BCT operations. Even considering the entire academic pool available at that time, personnel with these skill and knowledge sets (coupled with the physical demands of the environment) were in extremely short supply. This muddies the view of contractor failings in recruitment; the requisite skills did not reside in the academy, and, as a consequence, there was inevitably a shortage of specific expertise combined with practical experience that the Department of the Army sought through the

HTS. In actuality, the HTS embedded teams actually created the skill sets and practical experience that the program sought in the first place and was the basis for the request to JIEDDO to field five teams on a 2-year trial basis. The only blueprint for team composition was Project Jedburgh in the Office of Strategic Services in World War II and shows the extent to which the HTS management was conducting a novel experiment.[22]

In addition to the academic knowledge deficit, funding constraints had limited the initial roll-out to the single team, AF1, embedded in February 2007, in Khost province, Afghanistan. While AF1 was in Afghanistan, the U.S. Central Command (CENTCOM) requested five teams be sent to Baghdad by August 2007 as part of the surge of troops to quell the escalating insurgency, and requested subsequent team placement with every brigade and division in Iraq and Afghanistan, for a total of 26 teams.[23] The pair of phases must be considered in separation; the request for JIEDDO to field five teams over 2 years and a second phase which asked for rapid deployment of five teams to Iraq in a short time frame. The personnel with the requisite skill and knowledge sets for an expansion to 26 teams did not exist in the U.S. military. At this time also, integrating into the intellectual military *zeitgeist*, the HTS evolved away from the C-IED enterprise. The program became identified as a tool for population-centered counterinsurgency (COIN) operations that attempted to combat the adversary not through overwhelming application of force, but by disenfranchising the insurgent from its support in and among the population.

The first team, AF1 in Khost, received praise from its brigade staff. Commander of the 4th BCT, 82nd

Airborne Division Colonel Martin Schweitzer's initial positive assessment of AF1 in October 2007 (quoted by *The New York Times*) credited the team with reducing the need for kinetic activity by 60 percent in his brigade's area of operations and led to the rapid expansion of the program.[24] AF1's more granular understanding of tribal dynamics had helped to diffuse complex feuds. As a consequence, Schweitzer argued, his soldiers had more scope for 'improving security, health care and education for the population.'[25] Social science expertise resident in AF1, particularly in the form of a West Point-trained officer, who also had master's-level anthropology training, had catalyzed the development of a process to engage and win over the local communities.[26]

The military elements which ensured operational relevance and integration into the BCT were team leader Rick Swisher, Robert Holbert (a convert to Islam), and Roya Sharifsoltani, a female Army captain who was an Iranian and native Dari speaker. Additionally, in the summer of 2007, AF1's team members conducted interviews with the population that had been valuable in planning Operation MAIWAND, a military offensive to remove the Taliban presence from the Andar district of Ghazni. Underlining Schweitzer's assessment was a classified Combined Joint Task Force-82 Joint Urgent Operational Needs Statement (JUONS) in April 2007, which mirrored the earlier ONS, and which created a requirement for sociocultural awareness in Afghanistan, 2 months after AF1 had embedded.

The JUONS is an official request by a combatant commander for an urgently required capability deemed necessary for combat or contingency operations and is employed where failure to field the capability could result in an inability to complete the mission or increase loss of life. The statement thus allows a critical capability to be fielded rapidly and is the central method for combat commanders to interdict the standard bureaucracy of acquisitions procedures. A CENTCOM JUONS consolidated that Afghanistan JUONS and a similar Multi-National Corps-Iraq JUONS from 2007, leading to a later request by DoD for 26 teams across Iraq and Afghanistan.

That proof-of-concept team, AF1, used reservists with the relevant language capabilities and knowledge of social science research methods feasible for a single team. But as noted, with the subsequent enlargement required by DoD, the requisite number of personnel with the required skills did not exist in the military enterprise.[27] Originally, in 2005-06, FMSO thought it would be able to find 10 Ph.D.-level social scientists, five experienced regional experts on either Iraq or Afghanistan, and five social scientists with DoD to staff the first five proof-of-concept teams. However, as a United States House Armed Services Committee-directed assessment by the Center for Naval Analyses indicated, the:

> skills needed for HTTs do not appear to be resident in sufficient numbers in the DoD civilian workforce or in the military to staff the program. HTS therefore must hire from the general pool available to academia and business to source their personnel requirements.[28]

Inevitably, recruiting from the civilian sector as well-remunerated private contractors to embed in combat brigades failed to earn unequivocal and unilateral support in the Armed Services. The program came into existence because of an identified capability gap in the military component of government. No entity was performing the HTS function before the program was created. As a nonorganic addition, it thus highlighted the absence of sociocultural expertise resident in DoD. Despite the capability gap, Ben Connable, a retired Marine Intelligence Officer and head of the Marine Corps Cultural Intelligence Program from 2006-07, wrote in *Military Review* in 2009 of the problematic contours encountered in outsourcing cultural awareness to the civilian sector. Contextually, as Fondacaro explains, he visited the U.S. Marine Corps Center for Advanced Operational Culture Learning (CAOCL) in 2006, meeting with the Director, Jeffrey Bearor, and Major Connable of the Marine Corps Intelligence Activity (MCIA): there had already been important and far-reaching work produced on the importance of operational cultural knowledge at MCIA, particularly by Arthur Speyer and Connable, but the result of the meeting was that the idea of a partnerships which would have turned HTS into a joint program and led to a departure from TRADOC was rejected.[29] Connable in the 2009 article questioned the necessity of embedding academics in Iraq and Afghanistan when military officers could be trained in the social sciences. To do so would not be without its problems, however. Culturally oriented intelligence assets already existed in the military structure, for instance, the Foreign Area Officers, but their positions required intensive 3-year training processes. As is seen by the powerful sense of crisis, immediate solutions were favored. Such immediate solutions, however, could be considered detrimental to the military; for example, Connable noted that the:

> practice of deploying academics to a combat zone may undermine the very relationships the military is trying

to build, or more accurately rebuild, with a social science community that has generally been suspicious of the U.S. military since the Vietnam era.[30]

Positively, civilians embedded in the military offer the chance for effective collaboration. Fondacaro notes that embedding teams of former military and social scientists together in the combat zone may "actually work to achieve consensus" because of the "shared experience."[31] Iraq and Afghanistan did have high operational tempos which required significant and arduous integration into the decisionmaking cycle. But in longer-range research in regions of high incumbent control on the ground, military logistical reach and civilian expertise can expand to encompass remote regions and offer ultimately contributions both to the military and to scholarship. HTS is not simply a program for Iraq and Afghanistan, but a tool for all regions of strategic interest to the U.S. Army. Wedding academic knowledge and military practicality may produce new avenues of exploration for ethnography in the future particularly in regions less contested than those that teams were to experience in Iraq and Afghanistan.

HUMAN TERRAIN SYSTEM AND COUNTERINSURGENCY

The concerns raised by Connable frame the core of this analysis. While there is a robust case to be made for social science expertise within a COIN framework, why did that expertise manifest as embedded academics rather than teaching and training of existing military personnel? The answer may be a complex one, intrinsic to the nature of the unfolding stabilization and enabling operations. Writing in 2007, the former director of the British Defence Academy, Sir John Kiszely argued broadly that soldiers find it difficult to transition to engaging elements of the population having pejoratively framed them in battle sequences, therefore soldiers inevitably return to a default setting where they exercise hard power when they should be exercising soft power; as he calls it, "fighting small wars with big war methods."[32] These complexities are exacerbated by the absence of any overarching principles for conducting COIN, rather "all counterinsurgencies are *sui generis*—of their own kind—making problematic the transfer of lessons from one to another."[33] As such, there is a strong case for the application of expert culture-specific knowledge, both to counter prevalent problems associated with ethnocentrism, and also because Iraq and Afghanistan presented two different—*sui generis*—social science knowledge requirements.[34]

Understanding and influencing local civilians— something considered necessary for a successful population-centered COIN campaign—required socially astute engagement. Writing in 2004, Lieutenant Colonel James S. Corum observed that a COIN campaign required human intelligence; an "inexact art" necessitating the development of taxonomies for amorphous sociocultural data, detailed and transparent methodologies, prolonged relationships with the population and detailed profiles of the insurgents; an "intelligence picture" inevitably built from "unreliable sources and partial data combined with the analyst's intuition."[35] *U.S. Army Field Manual* (FM) 3-24, *Counterinsurgency*, published in December 2006, went further, stating that COIN is an "intelligence-driven endeavor" requiring understanding of the operational environment in which the population is a critical part.[36]

To understand all facets of a population, tactical units at the brigade level and below were required to conduct research in areas such as economics, anthropology, and governance that may be "outside" the expertise of existing intelligence personnel, such that "drawing on the knowledge of nonintelligence personnel and external subject matter experts with local and regional knowledge are critical to effective unit preparation."[37] Against the backdrop of this culture-inflected COIN doctrine, societal awareness to understand the population was of such import that the civilian social scientists and their expertise were considered an important addition to the military architecture. David Kilcullen, Australian COIN expert and special advisor to General David Petraeus, argued in 2007 that "ethnographic knowledge" in population-centered COIN operations was a critical component for success.[38]

COIN inverts the traditional modality of intelligence gathering, generating data from the bottom and filtering up through a unit. Societal analysis, production, and dissemination required expert distillation in order to provide a coherent data bridge between the tactical operations and brigade command. In addition to that structural difficulty, effective knowledge transfer between departing and relieving units during transition into and out of an area of operations was often lost, a disconnect amplified by a rapidly changing security environment and competition between brigades and armed service components. In effect, this meant that the incoming unit would have to commence baseline assessments based on relearning knowledge which had already been to some extent incorporated in the departing unit and lost in the transition.[39] A bridge to ensure effective knowledge transfer between units was part of the remit of the HTS, and the reason many teams embedded during a tour, which was to ensure continuity between departing and incoming units.

Why must this bridge be in the form of civilian academics, when the structure is a military one? In her nuanced evaluation of the program, Jennifer Greanias identifies McFate's assertion that Ph.D.-level academics are not necessary for the program's success, carrying it forward. From the contracting job information, if "4 years of appropriate experience that demonstrates that the applicant has acquired knowledge of one or more of the behavioral or social sciences equivalent to the field" is all that is needed to qualify as an HTT social scientist, Greanias asks what the value is in outsourcing the function of ethnographic research to the civilian sector and housing this mission outside of military or government channels.[40] In answering, Greanias finds that the distance afforded civilian social scientists to the military structure, to operate and present information free from hierarchical obligation:

> may be overstated in light of the many advantages afforded by HTT members who have military experience and who thus understand military planning, language, and culture, an asset to military commanders.[41]

Finding a Home.

The COIN modality is prominent in the secondary sources. One former HTT member has argued that, in a COIN environment, it is "just as — if not more — important to know and understand the cultures of those noncombatants living in an area of operations, even if they are not an enemy."[42] The influential West Point study led by Colonel Cindy Jebb notes the myriad organizations that were "trying to leverage or capture nonlethal effects," including the Iraqi Advisor Task Force, which had a mission to "capture environmental atmospherics" and embedded Provincial Reconstruction Teams (PRTs), which attempted to provide a bridge to the local/central governance structure.[43] That West Point study was directed by TRADOC as an external, objective inquiry of the program and begun in 2008, with West Point faculty and students traveling first to Fort Leavenworth, Kansas, and then to Iraq.[44] Ultimately, the authors argued, these teams together "provide the commander with the necessary critical mass that allows him to adapt to the situation," but that different organizations have "different organizational personalities, and bring different skill sets and focus to the operation."[45] Problematic was the character of HTS in that the teams, when operational, were under the control of the BCTs. The BCTs had little training on how to use the teams; as one former HTT social scientist notes: "Despite HTS products like the conveniently labeled 'Commanders Handbook' and the countless capability briefs our team delivered, HTTs were sometimes nevertheless viewed as external, unknown, and unproven entities."[46]

Here is the first identified problem in the existing literature. There are myriad organizations in an area of operations providing societal investigation. The Iraqi Advisor Task Force leveraged domestic expertise led by former U.S. Special Operations Forces to investigate societal elements. The PRTs in Afghanistan from 2003, and later in Iraq, were composed of approximately 50 to 100 personnel led by a military officer and composed of personnel from Department of State, U.S. Agency for International Development (USAID), the Department of Agriculture, and the Department of Justice, as well as other agencies. In the British model, the government's aid agency, the Department for International Development, attached personnel to leverage the PRT capabilities. According to one former HTT social scientist, however, the PRTs do not fall under the control of the BCT commander and "can lead to frustrations if the commander and embedded PRT leader have different priorities."[47]

The Iraqi Advisor Task Force and PRTs were already assembled models for societal investigation and evaluation and were led by military officers. The Task Force, however, was not focused on enhanced understanding of the population in order to augment the knowledge of the brigade staff, and the PRTs did not fall under the BCT command. Still, the aperture for the HTS to show a unique capability was relatively small. From the existing literature, it was doctrine which promoted the requirement for nonorganic additions to address a critical capability gap. The 2006 *Counterinsurgency* FM foregrounded a need for sociocultural awareness in a COIN campaign. To paraphrase Voltaire, if HTS had not already existed, it would have been necessary to invent it.

If the COIN push highlighted the immediate need for the HTS, why was the program to encounter such controversy? Sociocultural research of the type envisaged by the program management to plug a capability gap was going to be difficult. Embedding civilians to do the job for the military exacerbated the complexities of the task. For the research itself in conflict zones, there was going to be difficulty in establishing significant and enduring relationships with the population. But the promise of the capability explains to some extent the introduction of HTTs. This was a research capability which could provide deeper expert analysis than existing vehicles available to the brigade.

Existing Civil Affairs capabilities, resident in the PRTs for example, were relatively superficial, focused on aid and reconstruction, rather than purposeful interaction based around a research methodology to achieve products useful for the commander at the granular level.

Audrey Roberts has written eloquently on social science application in COIN environments. Roberts was a human terrain analyst and social scientist with AF1 in eastern Afghanistan, and had benefitted from working with the country and stabilization operations expert Michael Bhatia. In Roberts' subsequent role as the program's outreach coordinator, she identified two specific knowledge and capability deficiencies which led to the creation of the HTS: first, an existing inability in the military to exploit cultural data; and second, the ability to conduct research or tap into the reservoir of academic expertise relevant to their environments on the ground.[48]

Examining the first assertion; the military could attempt to integrate exploitation of cultural data if it wanted to do so, but the military exists because of a requirement to apply force, such that there was probably little appetite for doing so. The second assertion requires more granular analysis; academic expertise on contemporary Iraq and Afghanistan existed, but areas changed so quickly that any nonresident expertise was quickly dated. Of these assertions, then, it is that ability to conduct research which was the core of the skills which HTTs could bring to the brigade. In addition, the HTT would be enhanced by the Research Reachback Centers (RRCs) and "a contracted Social Science Research and Analysis (SSRA) capability to conduct primarily quantitative research in areas where the teams could not travel."[49]

Externally, a congressionally directed assessment of the program observed that the "HTT assists commanders in understanding the operational relevance, or the 'so what?' of sociocultural information as it applies to the military decisionmaking process."[50] Program efforts can be distilled as involving background research (including open-source and classified information), creating a research plan, conducting research, and analyzing and reporting findings.[51] A paucity of language skills indigenous to teams meant that they travel with interpreters who are hired and vetted by other commands in the area of operations, and should not be considered "a component of HTS" despite being "vital for successful interactions with the local population."[52] In part, this drives again at the contracting issue, which for Fondacaro was "the key program failure" and "the source of the most heated arguments and controversy between TRADOC G-2 and HTS."[53]

Confirmation of the unique bridge which the HTS provided between the brigade and the population it was tasked with protecting came from the highest levels of government. While acknowledging the "attendant growing pains" of a program still in its infancy, U.S. Secretary of Defense Robert M. Gates used an April 2008 speech delivered to the American Association of Universities to stress the value of the work done by embedded teams. Echoing the earlier identification of a deficiency in the research capabilities which existed in the two theaters, HTS filled a capability gap because the operations performed by military personnel in Iraq and Afghanistan:

> have at times been undercut by a lack of knowledge of the culture and people they are dealing with every-

day [sic]—societies organized by networks of kin and tribe, where ancient codes of shame and honor often mean a good deal more than 'hearts and minds.'[54]

According to Gates, who could draw on feedback from Colonel Schweitzer and other BCT commanders by this time, active HTTs resulted often in "less violence across the board, with fewer hardships and casualties among civilians as a result."[55]

View from the Ground.

According to the attendant literature, then, HTTs existed because civilian experts were required to fill a capability gap in military forces. That is the "why," but "how" were social scientists filling that esoteric void? There are some clues in the literature, but they are largely skewed by being defenses or critiques of the program. Indubitably, once embedded, the onus was on the HTTs to prove their usefulness to the brigade commander. But, being useful to the brigade in practice meant a wide spectrum of possibilities for conducting research when the team embedded. Former team leader Peter W. Pierce and senior social scientist Robert M. Kerr were part of IZ3, a team embedded in Baghdad in 2008 as part of the surge of forces begun the previous year as part of the population-centered COIN transition. The pair saw that the problems in the city for coalition forces were:

> cultural misunderstandings and failure to understand how the society functioned in this area had the potential to turn neutral (or even supportive) groups of people against the coalition and to the side of the insurgents.[56]

Pierce and Kerr argued that societal expertise could help facilitate the Iraqi surge tactic of moving troops out of larger bases into smaller forward operating bases, even into smaller combat outposts and smaller still joint security stations.[57] Therefore, it was not just a knowledge gap the team could bridge, but a logistical problem which embedded teams could solve.

The work of the HTTs outlined in these sources was so broad that any focused answer as to the work of the embedded teams is problematic. Pierce and Kerr give some clue as to the problem with secondary sources concerning the HTS. Many HTTs—in both Iraq and Afghanistan—operated in close concert with PRTs: to be effective, these teams required information on the local politics and culture which were best undertaken by the unique skill sets and function generated by teams.[58] In addition, in Iraq, an embedded team could focus on propagating key leader engagements (KLEs) with district advisory councils and neighborhood area councils—pseudo-elected bodies created by the coalition forces to perform administrative duties at district and neighborhood levels, respectively, and which would occur on a weekly, sometimes daily basis—local government managers, and sheikh councils.[59] The latter engagement was necessary because the tribal system in Iraq "remained robust and important, and Sheikh Councils dated back to the old Ba'ath Party Regime."[60] Kerr and Pierce conclude that 80 percent of their BCT's civil engagement reports originated with HTT IZ3 and that in terms of their achievements, they assert a "strategic role in that success" by HTTs due to facilitating comprehension of the human terrain.[61]

Such an account hints at what British philosopher of metaphysics F. H. Bradley, in his investigation of abstract notions of reality in Hegelian scholarship, called the "unearthly ballet of bloodless categories."[62] There are such a broad number of roles the HTTs perform under the remit of providing sociocultural knowledge to the BCT that we are left none the wiser about what the HTTs actually provided that was of value, and what was prized by the commanders on the ground. These sociocultural provisions and their effects on the BCTs may be difficult to measure qualitatively, and quantitative examinations may never exist for the program. This goes to the heart of the relationship between the social sciences and the military enterprise in areas experiencing high levels of insurgent violence. Despite multiple investigations of the HTS by different entities, there is no definitive quantitative way to measure the effectiveness of social research on military operations.

Individual team experience of the type elucidated here by IZ3 was valuable in 2008. However, each team, and iteration of the team as it was backfilled by new personnel, was *sui generis*. As such, a singular problem is that the experience of an individual team is not necessarily relevant to any other team at any other time. Every moment for HTTs in every location was unique, requiring different skills, strategies and *foci*. This complicates examination of the secondary sources since there is a spectrum of analyses determined by the variety of unique settings. A social scientist in Afghanistan will have had an incomparable set of challenges to a social scientist in Iraq.

Each team and each individual performed differently and had different experiences. For example, Zenia Helbig, a graduate student at the University of Virginia, joined the program in April 2007 but was eventually suspended on tendentious security breach allegations amid concerns regarding her professionalism. Helbig remained sure of the program's worth and a supporter of what Fondacaro was trying to achieve. Initially a human *cause célèbre* for critics of the program, speaking at the annual American Anthropological Association conference, Helbig became outspoken of many of the critiques levelled at the program by the association, and she was effectively marginalized.[63] Helbig's greatest concerns had been at the management failing writ large, rather than the goals of the program. A different example is that of Marcus Griffin, Professor of Anthropology and Sociology at Christopher Newport University, Virginia, whose published writing on the program offered robust endorsements and catalogued success. Second, there were different challenges in different areas of operations. Third, teams were of different composition, hence suitable for different roles and, indeed, often fractured along the lines of best fit for tasks confronting the brigade.

Further complicating the picture of the program are existing accounts of the evaluation of the function of the embedded teams by other social scientists. Marcus Griffin deconstructed the role of the Human Terrain team into five different but related elements.

1. To provide descriptions and analyses of civil considerations (community profiles and studies);

2. To maintain an understanding of local leadership, how they interact with each other;

3. To provide assistance to projects to facilitate completion, efficiency, and social impact;

4. To provide guidance to soldiers regarding how to collect human terrain information to improve their intelligence preparation of the battlefield and reporting efforts; and,

5. To respond to requests for information from elements within the brigade.[64]

This lack of focus and broad remit makes any granular knowledge of the work of HTT social scientists impossible without deeper examination through interviews and examination of actual team documents. The experience of social scientists is a significant aspect of the thesis, and a part of this book examines motivations of HTT personnel because of the paucity of scholarship on this sphere of the program.

Clarity and Planning.

Clarity is fundamental to actionable planning in complex conflict zones. Yet, in planning, clarity and detail clash. That dichotomy would necessarily manifest in the research conducted by the HTTs. The de facto requirement for the embedded team was at the tactical level:

> In many cases, despite the majority of the operational capability serving as assets on HTTs at the brigade level, teams operate predominately at even lower (i.e., battalion and company) levels due to the nature of the conflicts in Iraq and Afghanistan.[65]

Emphasizing the difficulty of making social science research relevant at the tactical level, Audrey Roberts emphasizes, "The planning process is incremental. Sociocultural reality is not."[66]

Additional detail of an aspect of the population can generate a confusing picture about the entire population; making heterogeneous the homogeneous, added variables at the granular level muddy attempts to homogenize the human terrain; HTTs emphasize interactions, myriad variables, "grass root" engagement, whereas the military seek uniformity and coherence for comprehension and execution. The dichotomy is evident in Roberts' evaluation of the bounded units being largely unrepresentative of the reality to the point that seeking such clarity of comprehension over detail jeopardizes lives.

How, then, can culture, critical to understanding the society, be modeled? Culture as a complex, malleable identity matrix has broad precedent in existing literature. In 1945, cultural anthropologist Bronislaw Malinowski asserted that cultures are composed of interrelated patterns of organization, which is a dynamic tool for societal survival and, as such, subject to change over time as human needs change.[67] Eminent international relations scholar Alexander Wendt has stressed the prominence of cultures in modeling the global political arena and argued that state identities are constantly subjected to structural changes generated by changing national interests.[68]

In her edited volume of case studies, Barbara Shaffer noted that cultural constraints are often bypassed when political crises dictated the necessity to change, or suffer deleterious impact.[69] Similarly, military historian Patrick Porter, in his examination of several examples, observes that "no war culture is an island," and that the symbols and practices of a culture are a reservoir from which to draw discriminately in order to adapt practices to achieve victory.[70] In presenting his case, Porter also cites Indian economist and philosopher Armatya Sen, who argued that ideas of fixed cultures encoding human practise makes us slaves to an "illusory force."[71]

In practice then, it is no surprise that in Iraq and Afghanistan, despite the emphasis in doctrine, this amorphous and indistinct notion of "culture" did not resonate with the spectrum of a field commander's concerns:

Interestingly, 'culture' in the broad anthropological sense (for example, as defined in *Army Culture and Foreign Language Strategy* as 'the set of distinctive features of a society or group and that drives action and behaviour') has less salience than might have been anticipated. Despite the frequent use of the term in doctrine and by policymakers in Washington, D.C., 'culture' appears to be less relevant than social structure, political and economic systems, and the grievances of the population in the context of the conflicts in Iraq and Afghanistan.[72]

Thus there is a discrepancy not only between the tactical and policymaking levels, but more broadly between the military executioner and the political narrative. This observation carries weight because it is a product of lessons learned in the field conducting COIN operations in two different countries. At the tactical level in a COIN campaign, the collection of information saw no value in the assessment and evaluation of culture as a unit to integrate into planning considerations. The reality was in stark contrast to the theory and the practice of teams was to research those units — economy, agriculture, political — which were, to some extent, comprehensible.

Arguably, therefore, the notion of cultures as units with intrinsic worth held greatest value in the evaluation of the relationship of the two cultures where these social science methods and conceptualizations were contained. The HTS was one of many forms of social science research in DoD, but it took civilians into combat units to conduct research among local populations using anthropological and sociological methods. In Chapter 2, therefore, I first examine the broad strokes of the historical relationship between the academy, social science research, and the U.S. military enterprise to provide context for a nuanced examination of the critiques from the professional anthropological community regarding the program, the ultimate purpose of which was to produce effective reactions within the population in the areas where BCTs operated.

ENDNOTES - CHAPTER 1

1. Christopher J. Lamb *et al.*, *Human Terrain Teams: An Organizational Innovation for Sociocultural Knowledge in Irregular Warfare*, Washington, DC: Institute of World Politics Press, 2013, p. 29.

2. Steve Fondacaro, personal communication with author, September 15, 2015.

3. *Ibid.*

4. Steve Fondacaro, telephone interview with author, September 15, 2015.

5. *Ibid.*

6. Steve Fondacaro, personal communication with author, September 15, 2015.

7. *Ibid.*

8. Lamb *et al.*, p. 32.

9. *Ibid.*, pp. 31-32.

10. Steve Fondacaro, personal communication with author, September 15, 2015.

11. *Ibid.*

12. *Ibid.*

13. Steve Fondacaro, telephone interview with author, September 15, 2015.

14. Lamb *et al.*, pp. 32-33.

15. Steve Fondacaro, personal communication with author, September 15, 2015.

16. Lamb *et al.*, p. 33.

17. *Ibid.*

18. Steve Fondacaro, personal communication with author, September 15, 2015.

19. Nathan Finney, *The Human Terrain Team Handbook*, Fort Leavenworth, KS: TRADOC, 2008, p. 35.

20. Jacob Kipp *et al.*, "The Human Terrain System: A CORDS for the 21st Century," *Military Review*, Vol. 85, No. 5, 2006, p. 12.

21. *Ibid.*, p. 13.

22. Steve Fondacaro, personal communication with author, September 15, 2015.

23. Yvette Clinton *et al.*, *Congressionally Directed Assessment of the Human Terrain System*, Arlington, VA: Center for Naval Analyses, 2010, p. 128.

24. David Rohde, "Army Enlists Anthropology in War Zones," *The New York Times*, October 5, 2007.

25. *Ibid.*

26. *Ibid.*

27. See Vanessa Gezari, *The Tender Soldier: A True Story of War and Sacrifice*, New York: Simon and Schuster, 2013, p. 316. Gezari makes the point that it was difficult to find the academics.

28. Clinton *et al.*, p. 7.

29. Steve Fondacaro, telephone interview with author, September 15, 2015. The MCIA had been developing a concept for

"cultural intelligence" independently, including through Ben Connable, Arthur Speyer, and the Hicks and Associates analyst, Job Henning. Henning possessed impeccable credentials, having worked on the broader development of cultural intelligence as part of a research program at the Office of Net Assessment at the Pentagon, propagating the idea in respect to U.S. involvement in Asia. The HTS management again asked for "formal partnership" with the USMC at a USMC Intelligence Community Conference in September 2009.

30. Ben Connable, "All Our Eggs in a Broken Basket: How the Human Terrain System is Undermining Sustainable Military Cultural Competence," *Military Review*, Vol. 89, No. 2, 2009, p. 58.

31. Steve Fondacaro, telephone interview with author, September 15, 2015.

32. John Kiszely, "Learning about Counterinsurgency," *Military Review*, Vol. 87, No. 2, 2007, p. 9.

33. *Ibid.*

34. Following Lamb *et al.*, I define sociocultural knowledge as "knowledge pertaining to society and culture that has been synthesized and had judgement applied to a specific situation to comprehend the situation's inner relationship." Lamb *et al.*, p. 7.

35. James S. Corum, "Fighting Insurgents—No Shortcuts to Success," Carlisle, PA: United States Army War College, 2004, p. 1.

36. Headquarters, Department of the Army, and Head-quarters, U.S. Marine Corps, *Field Manual* (FM) *3-24/Marine Corps Warfighting Publication* (MCWP) *3-33.5, Counterinsurgency*, Washington, DC: U.S. Government Printing Office, December 2006, p. 3-1.

37. *Ibid.*, p. 3-2.

38. David Kilcullen, "Comment: Ethics, Politics, and Non-State Warfare," *Anthropology Today*, Vol. 23, No. 3, 2007, p. 20.

39. Nathan Hodge, *Armed Humanitarians: The Rise of the Nation Builders*, New York: Bloomsbury, 2011, p. 242.

40. Jennifer Greanias, "Assessing the Effectiveness of the US Military's Human Terrain System," unpublished master's thesis, Washington, DC: Georgetown University, 2010, p. 23.

41. *Ibid.*

42. Peter W. Pierce and Robert M. Kerr, "The Human Terrain System in Northeast Baghdad: The View from the Team Level," *E-International Relations*, August 20, 2012, available from *www.e-ir.info/2012/08/20/the-human-terrain-system-in-northeast-baghdad-the-view-from-the-team-level/*, accessed on August 17, 2014.

43. Cindy R. Jebb, Laurel J. Hummel, and Tania M. Chacho, *Human Terrain Team Trip Report: A 'Team of Teams'*, West Point, NY: Unpublished report for TRADOC, 2008, p. 5. Copy held by author.

44. Lamb *et al.*, p. 70.

45. Jebb, Hummel, and Chacho, p. 5.

46. Brian G. Brereton, "Tangi Valley: The Limitations of Applied Anthropology in Afghanistan," in Montgomery McFate and Janice H. Laurence, *Social Science Goes to War: The Human Terrain System in Iraq and Afghanistan*, London, UK: Hurst, p. 285.

47. Katherine Blue Carroll, "What do You Bring to the Fight? A Year in Iraq as an Embedded Social Scientist," in Montgomery McFate and Janice H. Laurence, *Social Science Goes to War: The Human Terrain System in Iraq and Afghanistan*, London, UK: Hurst, p. 138.

48. Audrey Roberts, "'Embedding with the Military in Eastern Afghanistan: The Role of Anthropologists in Peace and Stability Operations," Walter E. Feichtinger, Ernst M. Felberbauer, and Erwin A. Schmidl, eds., *International Crisis Management: Squaring the Circle*, Vienna, Austria, and Geneva, Switzerland: National Defense Academy and Austrian Ministry of Defense and Sports in cooperation with Geneva Centre for Security Policy, 2011, pp. 83-84.

49. Montgomery McFate and Janice H. Laurence, "Introduction: Unveiling the Human Terrain System," in Montgomery McFate and Janice H. Laurence, *Social Science Goes to War: The Human Terrain System in Iraq and Afghanistan*, London, UK: Hurst, p. 14.

50. Clinton *et al.*, p. 17.

51. *Ibid.*, p. 18.

52. *Ibid.*, p. 19; See also Roberts, p. 90.

53. Steve Fondacaro, personal communication with author, September 15, 2015.

54. United States Department of Defense, *Speech as Delivered by Secretary of Defense Robert M. Gates*, Washington, DC: Association of American Universities, April 14, 2008.

55. *Ibid.*

56. Pierce and Kerr.

57. *Ibid.*; Hodge, p. 248.

58. Pierce and Kerr.

59. *Ibid.*

60. *Ibid.*

61. *Ibid.*

62. F. H. Bradley, *Principles of Logic*, Oxford, UK: G. E. Stechert, 1912, p. 533.

63. Zenia Helbig, "Personal Perspective on the Human Terrain System Program," Paper presented to the American Anthropological Association's Annual Conference, Washington, DC, November 29, 2007; Zenia Helbig, "Memorandum: Human Terrain System Program; U.S. Army Training and Doctrine Command," letter to Representative Ike Skelton, chairman of the House Armed Services Committee, and Representative Henry Waxman,

chairman of the House Committee on Oversight and Government Reform, September 13, 2007.

64. Marcus Griffin, An Anthropologist among the Soldiers: Notes from the Field," John D. Kelly *et al.*, eds., *Anthropology and Global Counterinsurgency*, Chicago, IL: University of Chicago Press, 2010, p. 218.

65. Roberts, p. 84.

66. *Ibid.*, p. 86.

67. Bronislaw Malinowski, *The Dynamics of Culture Change*, New Haven, CT: Yale University Press, 1945.

68. Alexander Wendt, *Social Theory of International Politics*, Cambridge, UK: Cambridge University Press, 1999.

69. Barbara Shaffer, ed., *Islam and the Limits of Culture*, Cambridge, MA: Massachusetts Institute of Technology Press, 2006.

70. Patrick Porter, *Military Orientalism: Eastern War through Western Eyes*, London, UK: Hurst and Company, 2009, p. 2.

71. Armatya Sen, *Identity and Violence: The Illusion of Destiny*, New York: W. W. Norton, 2006, p. 103, cited in Porter, *Military Orientalism*, p. 83.

72. Montgomery McFate, Britt Damon, and Robert Holliday, "What do Commanders Really Want to Know? U.S. Army Human Terrain System Lessons Learned from Iraq and Afghanistan," Janice H. Laurence and Michael D. Matthews, eds., *The Oxford Handbook of Military Psychology*, Oxford, UK: Oxford University Press, 2012, p. 111.

CHAPTER 2

TWO CULTURES

The historical dimensions of the engagement of anthropology with the U.S. military enterprise inform the discussion of the confrontational atmosphere which would come to characterize debate upon the Human Terrain System (HTS).[1] At times, professional anthropology and anthropologists tessellated with the strategic requirements of the U.S. military posture; in other periods, the discipline and the military enterprise were in opposed tangents. This fractious relationship results from the fact that war is an extension of politics. The political element of warfighting necessarily lends controversial dimensions to each martial endeavor. It is accurate to write that, where the controversial political character of warfighting was greatest, there, too, could be found the most tense and sustained opposition to the military enterprise from sections of the academic community. Anthropology and archaeology historically have been particularly entwined with the long-range lens of protracted armed conflict. Where conflict has most explicitly impacted and is impacted by society, the call to the social sciences becomes loudest. This historical tail is important as both context and as a repository for analogous activities in the conversation regarding the HTS.

Anthropology "crystalized in the context of war. In the United States, anthropology emerged as the state sought to understand and administer native populations in the Indian Wars."[2] This was in the middle of the 19th century. Cultural anthropologist and museum professional Dustin M. Wax argued that the Bureau of Ethnology created by the U.S. Department

55

of Interior in 1879 afforded one such case.[3] A staunch critic of the HTS, Roberto González has gone further, arguing for a direct link between work undertaken by anthropologists during the European colonial era, as information gatherers for indirect rule, and those actions of the Human Terrain Teams (HTTs). González, in his historical reference, singled out the interwar work of British anthropologist C. K. Meek, who was "charged with helping colonial administrators fine-tune a system of indirect rule" among Nigerian Igbo following the Women's Riots.[4]

War and anthropology have always existed in a curious symbiosis. Anthropology's "signature methodology of extended participant observation" in the field—which would make its academic experts so appealing to the HTS—was forced upon the Polish-born British anthropologist Bronislaw Malinowski by the onset of World War I.[5] There has been "a long history of entanglement between archaeology and anthropology on the one hand and political interests and the intelligence and military establishment on the other."[6] With the onset of that Great War, anthropologists and scholars of related disciplines in possession of such obvious and invaluable regional expertise found themselves as "key players in the new game in town—espionage."[7] In 1914, T. E. Lawrence, later to be popularized as "Lawrence of Arabia," conducted geographical surveys for the British military forces in the Negev under the auspices of an archaeological expedition. Dr. Montgomery McFate would later assert that his seminal account of that period, the *Seven Pillars of Wisdom*, is "essentially an ethnographic text, concerned with the customs and conventions of desert dwellers."[8]

In the U.S. military enterprise, McFate cites Harvard-trained archaeologist Sylvanus Morley, discoverer of the Mayan city of Naachtun, who was considered the "best secret agent the United States produced during World War I."[9] The application of ostensibly peaceful scholarship for military activities aroused an ethical debate, however. The nature of Morley's work for the Office of Naval Intelligence, much of which was conducted under the cover of fieldwork, was rebuked by Franz Boas in late-1919; at that time arguably the preeminent figure in the field of anthropology. Boas' letter to the *The Nation* suggested that unnamed anthropologists "have prostituted science by using it as a cover for their activities as spies."[10] But little came from the letter and Boas' other criticisms of the war, save that he was censured "quickly and publicly" by the American Anthropological Association in 1919.[11]

The military interest in anthropological expertise did not abate after World War I. According to historian Priya Satia, between the two world wars, there was a preoccupation in imperial security with the accumulation of knowledge of foreign societies.[12] The use of airpower by the British in Arabia to subdue the population did not depend solely upon economic or strategic reasons, but was based on ethnological perceptions of the inhabitants, such that agents involved developed an "intuitive intelligence epistemology modelled on their understanding of the Arabian population."[13] The ethnographic work of those in possession of anthropological expertise could influence policy in the regions in which they operated and assisted the exercise of military power, deciphering the social and historical dimensions of foreign nations.

The existential threat posed to the United States by World War II enabled a systematic adoption of the discipline of anthropology to the U.S. military enterprise for the first time.[14] The scale and scope of the threat posed by her foes necessitated a proportionate amplification of military intelligence in the United States. Increasing the size of the intelligence apparatus allowed the structured and sustained application of a wider range of tools to problem solving than had previously been the case. For the first time, there was "the organized use of social science for understanding the knowledge of war; that is, the systematic deployment of social sciences to collect and analyze information necessary for strategic military ends."[15] In 1941, the American Anthropological Association passed a resolution placing its resources and skill sets in the service of the country.[16]

In mid-1941, the U.S. Office of the Coordinator of Information (OCI) was created by Presidential Order—a civilian agency charged with centralizing the existing intelligence architecture. The OCI was restructured and renamed the Office of Strategic Services (OSS) in mid-1942.[17] The charter of the OSS was "to collect and analyze all information and data which may bear upon national security," reporting directly to the President and the Office of the Joint Chiefs of Staff.[18] The OSS was divided into two broad sections. The first, the Research and Analysis section, analyzed and produced information pertaining to the war effort. The second section used field operatives to procure actionable information that could assist in military planning.

This immense war effort saw myriad academic disciplines involved in the fight. For example, the OSS was the single largest government institution in which geographers worked during World War II, with 129 employed at the same time at its peak.[19] But the profession did not only impact war, it was also impacted by its focus of study:

> The very experiences of some of the geographers at R&A [Research and Analysis section of the OSS] as they tried to apply their geographical training to war altered their conception of geographical research, helping to propel the discipline to a different form.[20]

Yet, the OSS had a number of systemic issues, including the often indecipherable effect from their products, which meant that the motivation to create them inevitably diminished over time; and also among the military, "A deep suspicion that academics cannot contribute to war."[21]

Such was the broad utility of anthropology during a global war that a report by American Anthropological Association Secretary Fred Eggan to the American Association for the Advancement of Science in 1943 noted that more than 50 percent of professional anthropologists in the United States were engaged directly in the war effort and "most of the rest are doing part-time work."[22] But not all anthropologists embraced using their expertise to assist the war effort; echoing Boas' concern during the Great War, Melville Herskovits considered the ethical dilemma posed by using ethnographic knowledge gained from a society against that society.[23] The end of the war led to departures from the military enterprise. In part, this was a diminished need for expertise after the triumph of the Allied Powers, but also it was in part because, in the aftermath of the Hiroshima and Nagasaki, Japan, atomic detonations, the ethical implications of what had just been done in the name of freedom made many social scientists seek immediate egress from the military enterprise.[24]

SOCIETY AT WAR

The strength of the Soviet Union as a rival to U.S. hegemony in the immediate post-war period maintained a need for social science expertise in the military enterprise. After the collapse of a crucial U.S.-Soviet Union summit in Paris on May 17, 1960, U.S. Senator John F. Kennedy was moved to outline a new approach to foreign policy based on a 12-point agenda in which he argued the necessity to "increase the strength of the non-Communist world."[25] It was necessary, Kennedy observed, to act against a "lack of long-range preparation, the lack of policy-planning, the lack of coherent and purposeful national strategy backed by strength."[26] The perceived threat to the United States and her allies by the uptake of Communism was exacerbated by the end of the colonial era. In January 1961, Soviet premier Nikita Khrushchev had pledged his support for wars of national liberation around the world. Insurgencies on different continents threatened American interests and strategic projection of power.

The relationship of anthropology to the Cold War fighting, according to Seymour Deitchman, who was involved on military research programs at this time, grew generally from "America's increasing involvement, after the Second World War, in the affairs of the former European colonial empires" and more explicitly from Vietnam—a "long and difficult war in a strange and far-off corner of the world."[27] America was involved in multiple theaters in which its influence and therefore its ultimate survival were at stake.[28] By necessity, given the spectrum of threats faced, a broad array of military plans was undertaken; from nuclear strategy to irregular warfighting: at President

Kennedy's request in 1961, Congress appropriated approximately U.S.$120 million for "expansion of research and development programs having to do with limited war."[29]

There are three facets to the application of social science techniques to warfighting which arise time and again. The first is that there must arise a crisis in conventional military planning which necessitates social science tools; second, that there is a common consensus on a specific research field in which social sciences will be useful; third, that in that research field, social sciences will be able to contribute meaningfully in the search for a solution to the problem. That third aspect — proving useful to the production of a military solution — has been consistently difficult to prove, both historically and in the contemporary military setting, with the result that soldiers continue to wrestle with attempts to resolve the discrepancies between promise and delivery. When social science is unpackaged from the box and presented to the military enterprise, measuring the effect of social science expertise is problematic.[30] Social science can be used to explain cause or predict effect, but both human spheres are subject to myriad variables and the study of human environments situates researchers as a variable in the very domain they study. This phenomenon whereby social science affords a promise which is difficult to measure in terms of actual utility has been an unresolved problem at the heart of the complex historical relationship between the military and the discipline of anthropology.

The promise of social science as an aid to deciphering the complexities of the post-colonial world was important to the U.S. military enterprise. A Defense Science Board report published January 30, 1965, recommended the foundation of the social and behavioral sciences geared toward national security be built up through multidisciplinary centers for basic research in selected universities.[31] In 1964, the U.S. Army developed a specific project to examine how communist-driven insurgencies might take root and spread. Named Project Camelot, its mission was to examine "the feasibility of developing a general social-systems model that would make it possible to predict and influence politically significant aspects of social change in the developing nations of the world."[32] It was Camelot's work in Chile which broke the project to the media; in June 1965, Chilean newspaper *El Siglo* ran the headline, "Yankees Study Invasion of Chile."[33] Even though Camelot was subsequently terminated, it was seized upon as evidence by Senators Joseph McCarthy, J. William Fulbright, and Michael Mansfield of an improper and expanding grasp of Department of Defense (DoD) on foreign affairs, and social sciences funding was imperiled as a consequence. Indeed, more generally, Fulbright considered that counterinsurgency (COIN) techniques suppressed valid national aspirations toward legitimate independence.[34]

Camelot has been of signal import in the divergence of academia and the military enterprise after the Vietnam War. Professor Hugh Gusterson, placing the HTS within a wide historical arc, has compared it directly to the Camelot project, the latter he labelled, a "lavishly funded initiative to mobilize anthropologists and other social scientists to investigate the origins of peasant radicalism and insurgency and devise strategies to pre-empt, contain, and repress revolutionary movements."[35] Therefore, Gusterson saw Camelot as an important historical precedent which legitimated the evolution of the HTS; a powerful analogous model promising to decode cultures. Maja Zehfuss suggests that the controversy over the HTS recalls Camelot in two ways:

> First, anthropologists are again embroiled in controversy over a project that involves few of them but may have serious ramifications for their discipline. Second, in objecting to HTS, anthropologists have again framed the problem in terms of professional ethics, now armed with an ethics code which has been revised since its initial formulation (AAA [American Anthropological Association], 1998).[36]

That first code of ethics by the American Anthropological Association had been created by anthropology's relationship with the military: the use of anthropologists as advisors to DoD in Southeast Asian villages led to adoption of a code in 1971.[37] This code reaffirmed that the primary obligation of anthropologists is to protect the subjects of their studies. The strong reaction from anthropologists resulted from possible violations of this obligation by anthropologists who may not have protected those that they studied.[38]

Dr. Robert Albro, a moderating voice in the anthropologists' critique and chair of the American Anthropological Association's commission investigating the HTS has argued that "Camelot is often cited as Exhibit A in why we don't want to do these things."[39] Albro points out anomalies in attempts at comparison. First, Camelot did not employ anthropologists. Instructively, Albro observes that:

> This means that there is something we have to notice about the way that conversation has gone within the community of anthropologists, which is that there is a narrative about anthropology's engagement, that is slightly mythologised, a kind of a *Just-So Story*. We

are not altogether critically grounded about our own stories in this matter. This is a pity because what our stock and trade would seem to be among other things is ethnographic, grounded methodologies in all areas of our work.[40]

This febrile atmosphere generated by periods of protracted crises coupled to the mythologized character of Camelot and comparable Cold War programs makes their invocation frequent.[41]

THE LONG SHADOW OF VIETNAM

While Camelot was the most high profile social science-related project by the Army, there were other projects at that time. The RAND Corporation had conducted a study upon the motivation of Vietnamese insurgents, *VC Motivation and Morale*, the nature of which was raised in questioning by a congressional subcommittee in 1965.[42] Project Agile coordinated the Advanced Research Projects Agency's social science work; Agile's social science projects fared better than Camelot, avoiding the scrutiny of Congress such that, during 1966-69, its small-survey work was allowed to continue. So too, Project Themis, a program to enhance the research of smaller universities by government funding led to research submissions for foreign area work to DoD.[43]

By the mid-1960s, U.S. involvement in Vietnam was becoming increasingly complex, and organizations on the ground now included the State Department and the Central Intelligence Agency (CIA). Therefore, it was inevitable that, as part of a rising commitment to be seen to understand the intricacy of the situation, in May 1967 the Civil Operations and Revolutionary

Development Support (CORDS) was created and "unambiguously placed the military in charge of pacification."[44] CORDS was placed directly under the command of General William C. Westmoreland. One of the programs under its umbrella was the Intelligence Coordination and Exploitation Program, created in July 1967 and in December 1967 it was renamed as Phoenix. By 1970, there were 704 U.S. Phoenix advisors in South Vietnam.[45] Deployed segments were divided into two broad units: Provincial Reconstruction Units and regional interrogation centers. The program was part of a counterterror strategy in Vietnam and targeted the human infrastructure considered responsible for perpetrating the insurgency. At heart, Phoenix was a targeted killing program to disrupt important nodes within an insurgent network.[46] Its structure was proposed as the model for a contemporary program by COIN expert David Kilcullen. To counter what he saw as an emerging global Islamic insurgency, in a 2004 paper, Kilcullen proposed a Global Phoenix Program.[47] Kilcullen saw the future as using covert operations, small footprints, and highly specialized forces to disrupt the nodes. Anthropologists and behavioral scientists could be used; for example, to "exploit the physical and mental vulnerabilities of detainees."[48]

Instructively, Kilcullen identifies a mythology arisen from scholarly attempts to characterize Phoenix:

> Contrary to popular mythology, this was a largely civilian aid and development program supported by targeted military pacification operations and intelligence activity to disrupt the Viet Cong Infrastructure. A global Phoenix program (including the other key elements that formed part of the successful Vietnam CORDS system) would provide a useful starting point to consider how disaggregation would develop in practice.[49]

Each separate national insurgency—part of a complex whole:

> demands intelligence collection and analysis capability at the lowest possible tactical level. Local commanders must have the means to analyze and understand their own environment, diagnose key local system elements and the best means of attacking them, and communicate this understanding across the force.[50]

Against the backdrop of Project Camelot and Vietnam, anthropology's relationship with the military has been fraught. Presciently, writing in 1966 on the Malayan Emergency, Robert Tilman argued that:

> While anthropological knowledge is now necessary to national security, the ethics of anthropologists must be taken into account. In addition to direct discussion and debate on using ethnographic information, policymakers and military personnel must be trained to apply anthropological and social knowledge effectively, appropriately, and ethically.[51]

Explaining the shift from a largely consensual academy in World War II to a divided Cold War camp, Gusterson views the change as a generational one. Whereas the "good fight" against fascism was a relatively unproblematic ethical enterprise, the Vietnam War saw a young generation of anthropologists invoke the stance of Franz Boas in 1919, questioning the myriad "private bargains" undertaken between anthropologists and the U.S. military enterprise.[52]

Beneath the long shadow cast by the Vietnam War, the relationship between the academy and national security has been eroded. It shows starkly how the context of the moral dimensions of wars flavors the tension regarding anthropological engagement with the military enterprise. After the Vietnam War, there followed a period of introspection on the nature of the activities previously undertaken. Dustin M. Wax has argued that anthropology's segregation from the military during the Cold War heralded a rapid ascent to maturity as a discipline; that emancipation during this period from its martial shackles allowed anthropology to develop "an understanding of transnational flows of goods, money, people, and ideas; finally moved past the obsession with assimilation to discover nuanced interplays between cultures even in the face of massive power imbalances."[53]

This period consistently has been depicted in severe terms. Albro argues that it presented a:

> wholesale change in the relationship of the academy particularly the social sciences, specifically the social sciences, with some obvious exceptions such as ecology primarily, with regard to the military as a social institution, as a public institution in American society from the Vietnam era to the present.[54]

Thus, in Albro's view, there subsequently has been generations in which there have existed:

> virtually no relationship, no personal connection to the military as a social institution, amongst anthropologists, at least among those that form the professional voice that shapes agendas around what it is should quote unquote as a pronoun or shouldn't be doing, how we need to be thinking about these things and what our reasoning is around it and our ethical frames for going forward.[55]

It was thus that when the HTS was created against the backdrop of severe objection to the invasions of Iraq and Afghanistan, the discipline of anthropology was poised to afford severe critiques of the military's interest in their signature methodologies and ethnographies.

These broad strokes delineating aspects of the historical tail of the story of the HTS serve a purpose. As Albro argues, the relationship between anthropologists and the military enterprise has "been a very persistent intergenerational story and a dilemma that anthropology has wrestled with."[56] Yet, while these strokes show the baggage of history with which the HTS was reluctantly but inevitably encumbered, the program has no perfect historical analogy. For that reason, to paraphrase Mark Twain, the HTS is not a repetition of history, but a rhyme. The program is the latest in an often awkward dance between the military enterprise and the academy, and expanded beneath the still long shadow cast by the war in Vietnam.

THE WEIGHT OF HISTORY

Given the historical tail therefore, the HTS was a compelling story colored by the recent past. The earliest media reports framed the program as the acme of an academic approach to military operations required for successful COIN operations in Iraq and Afghanistan. The expanded HTS depended, at least in part, upon developing the program's profile in the academic community and public sphere in order to both attract applicants and buttress funding justifications. To raise its head above the parapet, however, was a double-edged sword: increasing general awareness of the program—being a controversial collaboration between civilians and soldiers in a time of war—subjected the HTS to scrutiny. Using anthropological methods led to consideration of the program within a historical trajectory, characterized as the latest in a series of difficult military engagements with the academy. In addition, the nature and efficacy of embedded teams were questioned. González has been critical of the HTS claims of reducing civilian casualties, and more widely critical of the Iraq and Afghan wars, which he saw as colonial enterprises.[57] González called the favorable press reports that emerged concerning HTTs a carefully choreographed public relations campaign.[58]

Indicative of the ease with which conflicting assessments of the program could proliferate, González also labelled the HTS a secretive organization wedded to the covert national security state.[59] Objectively, the HTS is one of the most public-oriented programs in the U.S. Department of the Army. It was a prominent program in the nascent COIN modality of military operations and recruited civilian academics through an open process. There was no covert element in its creation or propagation, as seen by the myriad accounts relating to it, and the Department of the Army has continued to engage researchers of the program in the hope of better understanding its optimum function. Unlike covert elements of the national security state, its former members publish widely on their research in academic journals, doing so originally largely as part of an outreach program, and latterly as part of neutral contributions to scholarship.

The ambiguous initial assessments from academics lacking deep research of their subject makes the HTS such a pertinent subject to study. Its profile, disproportionate to its small size, is a result of its compelling character and its ability to polarize opinion. Few commentators on the program were to emerge apathetic. American anthropologist David Price, who became a key critic of the program, made a Freedom of Information Act request for the assessment which led to Colonel Martin Schweitzer's claim in congressional testimony concerning the quantitative reduction in kinetic activity. In February 2008, after recalibrating the initial praise, the U.S. Army admitted that no such records existed. It is difficult to overstate the damage caused by this admission, demonstrating as it did that the capabilities of the HTS were being praised for results that did not exist. The only positive outcome was that the Department of the Army was transparent enough to return the inquiry. This admission fueled criticism and entrenched each side in the debate, making collaboration more difficult. In defense, and to his credit, Schweitzer composed a personal reply to Price, stating that the HTT under his command had focused his operations on the population, not the enemy, and further that the team operationalized the *Pashtunwali* code—an orally communicated ethical template governing social norms among Pashto speakers—assisting the armed forces in application of a specialized COIN methodology.[60]

While the admission from the Department of the Army exacerbated the criticism, the core of the problem in the debate remained that the professional academic anthropologists were not using their own signature methodology—ethnography—in their examination of the program. Instead, examination was often cursory and superficial, with material extracted from newspaper articles. These expert ethnographers were failing to conduct ethnographies of the HTS. As a consequence, their findings were often generalized and served only to obfuscate understanding of the program.

The outside-in-perspective further served to distance not only the American Anthropological Association from the military, but distance the military from the American Anthropological Association. What could have been an exercise in collaboration, conciliatory research, and cross-cultural communication instead quickly degenerated into entrenched defensive positions, from which occasional salvos were fired from each side. This was greatly to the detriment of each enterprise, for the HTS posed no threat to the American Anthropological Association. In addition, the HTS was a broad church of social scientists such that critique from a small section of expert anthropologists ultimately could not terminate the program. Ultimately these agendas, one of practicality, the other of ethicality, existed on divergent platforms such that throughout the lifetime of the program in Iraq and Afghanistan, the discourse between the two entities was irreconcilable.

Academic interrogation of the program was complicated by the domestic U.S. political setting at this time. There was significant opposition to the U.S. military presence in Iraq and Afghanistan. Invasion of the former was seen in many spheres as the action of an imperial power, and many of the detractors of the HTS were staunch critics of the wider U.S. military activities. The HTS public profile was thus hamstrung before it started the race; being a high-profile civil-military hybrid program focused opposition to the wars on a single entity. Criticism was not simply about the quagmire of deciphering ethical boundaries in conflict zones; it was also tied to the concern that here was a program which required civilian academic expertise and was fielded in support of a controversial occupation.

Of the program itself, academic critique crystalized into three distinct categories; debate concerning the ethics of the program; efficacy of the embedded teams; and the place of the program in the larger historical context of military engagement with the social sciences. The debate emerged on myriad platforms: the program has been the subject of a poem, a documentary, two plays, popular and scholarly books, as well as articles in academic scholarly journals including *Security Dialogue*, *Anthropology News*, and *Anthropology Today*, and military ones such as *Joint Force Quarterly*, *Small Wars Journal*, and *Military Review*.[61] Both staunch criticism and robust defense of the program were characterized by a degree of hostility because of the perceived stakes—literally life and death—such that there emerged a difficulty in developing constructive scholarship on this historically important program. This hostility ties back to the broad context of the perceived illegality of the Iraq occupation and the HTS as performing a core function in that occupation. Public opinion was turning against the military enterprise by late-2006, and many polls showed that the majority of the U.S. population were against the war in Iraq. Focused critique served only to make the HTS more opaque to scrutiny. Indeed:

> the effects of the polarization of the 'debate' surrounding the HTS probably made it more difficult for structural problems inside the program to be fixed while it was on the road from a proof-of-concept program to a program-of-record.[62]

Media and academic focus narrowed on the program and its processes as a result of the deaths of three HTT social scientists in separate incidents between 2008 and 2009. These high profile fatalities (Michael

Bhatia's life and death formed part of the 2009 documentary, *Human Terrain: War Becomes Academic*; Nicole Suvege's death was delineated in Nathan Hodge's *Armed Humanitarians*; and Paula Loyd's death was the focus of Vanessa Gezari's 2013 book, *A Tender Soldier*) amplified scrutiny of the program. The result was the retrenching of the HTS management to external inquiry exacerbating the outside-in-perspective. Subsequent analyses inevitably oversimplified the program and skewed analyses because of the complications in garnering a spectrum of interviews and gaining access to program documentation.

What is required, however, is that a social science research program's development not take place in a vacuum, entrenched against outside critique. The program suffered to some extent from focused criticism in this early period. Yet, the goals and processes of the program were so novel that collaboration and nuanced analysis and review from academics would have been invaluable. Neither did the program's detractors emerge unscathed. The academics suffered from examinations of the program which were colored by the backdrop of the U.S.-led invasions of Iraq and Afghanistan, the countries where HTTs embedded. As a result, the character of social science research by these novel HTTs has been largely obscured in literature.

THE "JAUNDICED EYE"

Members of the professional anthropological community were concerned at appropriation of their discipline for military utility, although there was little clear evidence about who owned the origins of these social science tools that they fought over. In addition, the unearthly ballet of research meant that the program remained largely unintelligible. Aware of this tension between the academy and military for which the HTS had become a focal point, in 2008, Secretary of Defense Robert Gates placed the problem within a historical trajectory, arguing that each enterprise:

> continues to look on the other with a jaundiced eye. These feelings are rooted in history — academics that felt used and disenchanted after Vietnam, and troops who felt abandoned and unfairly criticised by academics during the same time. And who often feel that academia does not support their efforts.[63]

Gates ultimately conceded that at least some of the blame fell at the feet of DoD, because it fails to explain fully the functions of many of its elements in language which is accessible outside of the profession: "Like academia, the Pentagon has its own, shall we say, unique approach to the English language."[64]

This language gap complicated expression of the character and content of the program successfully bridging military and academic languages. This is not a facile bridge to cross. The term "human terrain" does not appear in nonmilitary academic literature prior to the program's inception. Gates argued in that speech that the program's name "appears almost designed to induce maximum paranoia."[65] This evaluation is borne out by the evidence. However, existing scholarship currently identifies the first use of "human terrain" as being in 1968.[66] Reporting on the threat of social disaggregation from militant groups such as the Black Panthers, the United States House Un-American Activities Committee concluded that domestic guerrilla forces, while asymmetric in their material and logistical support, nevertheless "possess the ability to seize and retain the initiative through a superior control of the human terrain."[67]

In fact, the first instance when the term was used was in a 1967 memorandum from then-Director of the CIA Richard Helms to National Security Advisor Walt Rostow.[68] In the memorandum on the situation in Vietnam, Helms wrote of the requirement of forces aligned with U.S. interests to dominate political influence of the local population, and that, to achieve that goal, it was necessary to target the "Human Terrain."[69] This human terrain, the "target of pacification," was regarded as "highly fragmented by race, regionalism, religion, politics, and an inherent mistrust of 'outside' influence and authority."[70] The term resurfaced 4 decades later in 2000 when retired Army officer and military analyst Ralph Peters considered the human terrain of a city as being the dominant factor in urban COIN operations.[71] Montgomery McFate and Janice H. Laurence, in their co-edited volume on the program, identify that true credit for the term "human terrain system" belongs to Colonel Joseph Celeski, who McFate had referenced in an earlier article.[72]

Use of the term "human terrain" for a military project led to criticism from academics because of that disconnect between the discourses of the military and the academy. Roberto González suggested that the phrase will have objectifying and dehumanizing effects," although no examples of how that might be in practice were provided.[73] For Price, the U.S. Army "does not just want to understand the cultural environment it is working in, it wants to change it to its liking, and anthropologists are to be the tools leveraging needed cultural knowledge."[74] These critiques were augmented by the public articulation of the military customer of the program. In the words of

Schweitzer, brigade staffs were motivated by a desire to reduce kinetic activity, and, in doing so, better achieve national objectives: "Ultimately, success will require us to change the environment and to do that will require a continued deliberate focus on the culture and population of Afghanistan."[75] This reduction in kinetic activity would reduce collateral damage, affording improved security and engender increased relations of trust with the population. Armed violence in these settings has a deleterious impact on attempts to communicate with the population.

Such scrutiny of a relatively small piece of the U.S. Army enterprise occurred because the HTS served as a focal mechanism for a more diffuse debate being held in the academy over the appropriation of social science knowledge and anthropological methodologies more specifically by DoD to assist in the conduct of the military. In 2002, Price warned that America's challenges in Iraq and Afghanistan raised:

> numerous ethical issues that must be confronted by anthropologists and their colleagues—especially those concerning the integrity of the discipline of anthropology, as pressures to harness anthropological knowledge of other societies for military purposes and other objectives re-emerge.[76]

Price argued that a clash between the ethical guidelines of anthropology and the strong desire to serve the interests of one's country would be inevitable, as had been observed in recent history.[77]

The perilous historical trajectory of anthropology's relationship with the military was invoked by those scholars concerned at their discipline's relationship with DoD. Stressing the gravity of the evolving situation, Price cautioned that:

wars raise the stakes for anthropologists, exposing the nature of our commitments and principles, and, as past wars and colonial campaigns have shown, anthropologists as a group have served both the oppressed and the oppressors. Many aspects of our field's relationship with power remain unresolved.[78]

This meant that as the conflicts in Afghanistan and Iraq became more complex and the apparent anthropological character of military operations burgeoned, each side in the encounter refused to offer a conciliatory stance. Under the FMSO initial plan to make the program conduct research which was then logged in an open-access database, the relationship between the program and academia would have been less treacherous, but would also have created data which was of little operational relevance to the BCT. Fondacaro's plan to use embedded teams directly to influence brigades on the ground in Iraq and Afghanistan amplified the stakes and made the possibility of appropriating the discipline a matter of existential concern. Fondacaro's position was formed from his experience as a battalion and brigade commander, and then as JIEDDTF-Iraq leader; that more data or tools would be irrelevant, and that the only solution would be embedded human operators working with the BCT staff.[79] Embedded expertise enduring beyond a unit rotation would prevent the 10-year war being fought 1 year at a time.

The recruitment of social scientists for warfighting was seen as part of a wider securitization of public life and hence a necessary site for concerted critiques of the developments.[80] Elements within the social science community, which Dan G. Cox, Assistant Professor of Political Science at the United States Army School of

Advanced Military Studies, labeled a "small but vociferous chorus of pundits and academics," argued
that anthropology's re-engagement with the military
risked changing the character of the discipline.[81]

HTS thus served as a principal site for the anthropological debate on the wars in Iraq and Afghanistan.
The program placed academic experts in roles designed to directly influence the direction of conflict.
There was a notable lack of abundant and systematically analyzed evidence to support these claims
against the program, and, because the two sides had
now become entrenched in defensive positions, there
was difficulty in gaining access to the program to create new information based on interviews or program
documents.

Anthropology as a discipline existed in tension
with the program because the idea of the HTS under Fondacaro, if not execution on the ground, was
spun from an appropriation of the discipline's signature methodology, ethnography, for a purpose of
national security. To some within the anthropological community, this was unacceptable. As Lamb *et al.*,
note, anthropology as a social scientific discipline is
relatively small in size; there are only approximately
11,000 members of the America Anthropological Association, compared to for example, 137,000 members of the American Psychological Association.[82]
In focusing on the HTS, the criticism by a relatively
small academic community concentrated on a single
program in the U.S. military enterprise. The criticism
made the concerted arguments against the program
more pronounced than had been the case against the
broader military ventures in Iraq and Afghanistan
precisely because it engaged anthropology's signature
characteristics.

For its proponents, defending both the concept of the program and the execution of the idea was more than the protection of the HTS; it was rather the defense of population-centered COIN as a whole. The HTS and COIN became linked such that it was necessary in defense of COIN to defend the work of the program and flaws were covered up. Supporters and proponents of the program considered it ethical, that it helped to save lives through more focused and effective operations, was not involved in collecting intelligence that led to kinetic targeting of individuals, and was a key way for anthropology to become relevant to the shaping of operations in the field, and eventually policy back home. In doing so, the discipline could move away from the abstract field it had become in the wake of its retreat from government after the U.S. ended its military involvement in Vietnam.[83]

The wide parameters of the debate hinted at the program becoming the focal mechanism for a generational debate on anthropology's engagement with the military. But larger still, and with important implications for the durability of the discussion, it could be seen as a conversation regarding the application of scholarship to any and all exploitative ventures, especially those with national security implications. As such, it posed a question: should the demarcation between the academy and the nonacademy be distinct and impermeable? This was a conversation with a lineage; most recently regarding the use of anthropologists in corporate contexts in the 1990s.[84] There, too, concerns were voiced regarding the use of data, and the possible exploitation of research subjects and degree of transparency in the context of corporate competitiveness.[85] That period of anthropology's tense engagement with corporate America was linked explicitly when accusations of McFate having at one time been a corporate spy emerged in 2008.[86]

The focus anthropology as a discipline exerted on the HTS has parallels, even within the Iraq conflict. The American Psychological Association had earlier focused on the Abu Ghraib controversy as a catalyst for concern, allowing discussion of the utilization of academic knowledge in intelligence interviewing techniques as they were being integrated into a broader spectrum of torture.[87] That central concern and alarm about its situation within the national intelligence architecture broadly paralleled anthropology and the HTS, taking ethnography and situating its use within the national intelligence architecture. This debate was not new to the field, only to the field's current generation of scholars.

Collaboration or Confrontation?

From the academic side, the debate surrounding the program should have been nuanced and deeply researched, as befitting the program. Social science is the deep study of society not for the benefit of social sciences, but for society. Instead, the examination was superficial and the language inflammatory. As much as there was cause to evaluate the program, the magnitude of the attacks and the core use of newspaper articles devalued what could have been a chance to move forward collaboratively with the military. Instead of collaboration, the site of the HTS debate unfortunately was one of confrontation. This friction had the added consequence of making intricate academic research of the program more arduous as fragile bridges of trust between the sections of the anthropological community in the academy and DoD were unceremoniously burnt.

The core space for that vociferous debate was the American Anthropological Association's Commission on the Engagement of Anthropology with the U.S. Security and Intelligence Communities. There were two phases to the commission's life which were associated with two broad studies: The first, published on November 4, 2007, was chaired by James Peacock, Emeritus Professor at the University of North Carolina, and developed from concern at the CIA posting an employment advertisement on the American Anthropological Association's website for professional vacancies and the Pat Roberts Intelligence Scholars Program.[88] This first phase attempted to delineate the contemporary engagement between anthropology and the national security structure in the United States.

The HTS was included in the report as the public discussion around the program was escalating.[89] In the report, a peripheral but emerging debate among the panel was the extent to which HTT fieldwork could be conducted in alignment with the American Anthropological Association Code of Ethics or a generic review board, given that the research would be for a military customer among a population in a contested space.[90] Importantly, the commission identified a primary issue with embedded teams regarding the primary obligation of anthropologists to "do no harm." Seeking to answer if the teams were used "for" or "against" the population, the panel wrote that team research is "framed by the military as undertaken to 'protect' studied populations, but HTS studies also present risks of using cultural research against studied populations."[91]

The peripheral examination of the U.S. Army program compared to its high profile necessitated a second phase of the commission beginning in December

2008, when the American Anthropological Association asked the Commission to review specifically the HTS in order to develop a concerted stance regarding members' participation in the program's activities.[92] This review was chaired by Albro, Professor of Anthropology at American University, based on his position in the first phase.

The priorities of the commission changed between the phases.[93] The second report was preempted by the American Anthropological Association Executive Board's statement censuring the HTS on October 31, 2007, which was not entirely aligned with the broader conclusions of the American Anthropological Association committee.[94] While that committee in the second phase was consulted by the executive board, there was pressure from the rank and file to make a statement on the HTS, and they went ahead and did that at that time without engagement with the program and relied instead upon journalistic accounts of the program, as they termed it "information in the public record."[95]

The executive board methodological shortcomings and its terse 800-word indictment against the program exacerbated the deepening divide between DoD and the discipline of anthropology, and, more broadly, degraded the way in which the military perceived academia because of the board's absence of evidence. As much as this quickly released statement served to highlight the concerns on the American Anthropological Association's Executive Board, it would also alienate sympathetic elements in the military enterprise that would, as a consequence of the absence of research, be dismissive of the critique. The board expressed grave concerns that responsibilities of HTT members might lie with their units, and that they could fail to identify themselves as anthropologists rather than military personnel; concerns identified in "the context of a war that is widely recognized as a denial of human rights and based on faulty intelligence and undemocratic principles."[96] In addition, the board noted the difficulty of getting informed consent in contested spaces, the use of information for targeting and the toxic spillage for non-HTS anthropologists of anthropology's association with the military in this instance.[97]

The executive board statement gave superficial indictments of the program's activities, despite the profound questions posed by the first phase of the commission. In this regard, the board's assessment served to detract from the ongoing investigation which was later led by Albro. The board made the statement without contacting the U.S. Army program and relied on journalistic accounts. Thus, that hastily erected position contributed to entrenching the polarization of the debate because it could so readily be dismissed by proponents of the program as an inquiry using existing journalistic accounts. In addition, the board noted explicitly the illegality of the conflicts in which the program teams operated, such that the broader context colored the assessment of the program activities. In that regard, the HTS was a focal mechanism for a much larger debate. Also — as has been seen in the historical assessment — the greater the controversy of the conflict, then the greater tension that exists in the relationship between professional anthropology and the military.

The second commission's report was notable in that participants did interview HTS administrators at that time, including Senior Social Scientist and Director of the Social Science Directorate McFate, and asked the program management a set of questions and requested a formal response, which they received, with the answers included in the commission report appendix. That second commission was composed of members from both academic and nonacademic arenas, as well as being composed of academics from different disciplinary commitments.[98] These commission members arrived at the discussion from different viewpoints and with different priorities.[99]

The broad character meant that other members of the commission focused on the questionable ability of embedded team members to get documented, informed consent in a conflict zone—another key component of the Association's ethics code. But the core conversation within the commission centered on the distancing of the HTS from any institutional review board, the application of outmoded theory, and the perceived absence of organizational transparency and of the research itself. The commission's report suffered from the inevitable clash of multiple viewpoints and priorities, as well as a lack of solid, aggregated, and mutually reinforcing evidence about the specific activities of different teams. The report offered the broad conclusion that HTT work in the field was not professional anthropology and was in contravention of "disciplinary ethics."[100] The crux of the commission's assessment was:

> When ethnographic investigation is determined by military missions, not subject to external review, where data collection occurs in the context of war, integrated into the goals of counterinsurgency, and in a potentially coercive environment—all characteristic factors of the HTS concept and its application—it can no longer be considered a legitimate professional exercise of anthropology.[101]

The commission was correct: In these contested spaces, this was a different form of interaction with the population, distinct and different from engagement with the population in an ethnographic sense.

In contrast to the short assessment from the executive board, the commission was tasked with formulating a consistent and explicit stance on participation in the HTS for the American Anthropological Association's members but spoke more widely to "any social science organization or federal agency that expects its members or its employees to adhere to established disciplinary and federal standards for the treatment of human subjects."[102] The commission was therefore widening the lens of the debate from the narrow discipline of anthropology to a broader discussion of the use of any of the myriad forms of social science in research involving human subjects. The HTS was therefore the principal site in the Iraq and Afghanistan wars for renewed debate on the appropriation of a spectrum of academic expertise in order to influence or shape foreign populations.

As a principal site for scholarly debate of the ongoing population-centered COIN effort, the commission asserted that gathering sociocultural information to aid commanders' planning on the ground risked the program being able to single-handedly define "anthropology" for DoD.[103] This is a conclusion cloaked in the dramatic context of a divisive war; a conclusion which was unrepresentative of the reality on the ground and the research being conducted and the position of the program in the DoD enterprise. As the commission itself notes, the program was "one development among many."[104]

The HTS as a social science program implemented rapid assessments of local populations where high levels of selective violence inhibited the ability to conduct traditional ethnographies. Conflict forces rapid change of populations over time. For the HTS in practice to influence the planning cycle of a brigade, a team would need to conduct rough and ready operationally relevant reporting of the host society in ways that were distanced from professional anthropology. This could be understood by detailed analysis of research products from the field. The problem in 2008 and 2009 when the commission was conducting its assessment, however, was that despite the "extensive body of information about HTS in the public domain," the "vast majority has been generated not by HTS employees, or academics, but rather by journalists."[105] It is the journalistic accounts which have exacerbated the level of uncertainty over the research conducted by HTTs, and the character of the program. The commission was thus forced to sidestep the bulk of the existing material on the program. As the program was ongoing and without complete access to HTT research, despite many interviews with HTT social scientists, the commission's assessments can only be, as noted, tentative.[106] The core problem identified by the commission is a perpetual symptom of study of the program; that there are conflicting viewpoints on the nature of the program and the experiences of the fieldwork, and the sources are often contradictory.[107] In addition, its wider relationship with the military enterprise of which it was, unquestionably, a small, esoteric part was uncertain.

The program's direct relationship to professional anthropology is largely tangential. The commission notes that the 2008 *Human Terrain Team Handbook* describes how research methods for embedded teams could "include classic anthropological and sociological methods such as semi-structured and open-ended interviews, polling and surveys, text analysis, and participant-observation."[108] This is a broad attempt to reference the sociological character of the program, but certainly does not risk defining "anthropology" for DoD, or appropriating professional anthropological practices for the program or professional anthropology's signature methods, for instance ethnography and core concepts, for example, culture.[109] "Culture" was an abstract concept without resonance in the practical requirements of HTTs, while "ethnography" as a professional practice requiring hegemonic control by the incumbent to ensure security on the ground and 12 to 24 months among the population was, by definition, impossible circumstances for HTTs in Iraq and Afghanistan. The commission quotes an unnamed HTT social scientist thus: "This is not ethnography. It is translating abstractions into actionable recommendations."[110]

The core concern was on the fidelity of the data gained from working in a contested space in the presence of a military force. These concerns are well founded, and an unnamed U.S. Marine Corps commander stated that in such environments, interviews could be considered that the research "looks more like push polling."[111] This unwittingly strikes at the heart of a much larger tension in DoD and data analytics more generally between qualitative and quantitative data signals. The honesty of the data derived from qualitative assessments in areas experiencing high levels of violence is questionable. That must be compared to the absolute values in quantitative assessments of human centers, such as the price of foodstuffs or illicitly traded weapons. This concern thus resonates because it is part of a broader debate in which quantitative assessments are likely to win out over qualitative research modalities. Qualitative uncertainty is proportional to physical insecurity.

On the issue of the HTS as an intelligence asset, the commission observed with some explicit uncertainty that there is "significant likelihood that HTS data will in some way be used as part of military intelligence, advertently or inadvertently."[112] In part, the ambiguity is a product of the uncertain nature of what "intelligence" entails. Evaluating Joint doctrine, the commission observes that "intelligence is pretty much any form of knowledge production."[113] That all-encompassing definition raises larger, potentially discomforting questions about all knowledge, even professional scholarship in the public sphere, being employed in intelligence production. But, in part, also this question regarding the uncertainty on information and intelligence was also due to the commission's conclusion that: "There is significant variation in the ways that HTTs interact with the intelligence elements in their area. This seems to rely, at least to some extent, on the inclination of the people filling social scientist roles."[114] The ethical character of the research lay at the heart of this argument. Research guarantees both anonymity and the safety of participants, or it does not.[115] It is a clear binary state. Teams could choose to cross over the line or not, with the ability to choose being facilitated, if not dictated, by the *laissez-faire* freedoms experienced in these contested spaces found in Iraq and Afghanistan.

The commission foregrounded the ethical character of the program and ethics dominate the broader professional discussion.[116] The commission observed that, in the creation of the HTS, the American Anthropological Association's Code of Ethics, which identifies the need for "the establishment of voluntary informed consent, taking care to insure that no harm comes to research participants as a result of HTS research, and full disclosure to research participants what will be done with collected data," appears to have been ignored.[117] This is largely anticipated, given the applied nature of the research: McFate has observed that in developing the research modalities for the team, she consulted the Society for Applied Anthropology's Code of Ethics.[118]

The character of this applied social science research being developed by the HTS was unique and posed problems in relation to standardized professional practice. The American Anthropological Association in its close inspection of the program in relation to ethics concluded that "so far as we can tell, HTS does not currently use an IRB [Institutional Review Board]."[119] At the level of the combat brigade, where there was high operational tempo in areas experiencing high levels of selective violence by insurgents, this was likely unfeasible in these contested spaces. Research was often dictated by the transport available; where the military logistics determine the opportunity for research—for example, route clearance or resupply convoys. An IRB would thus have to have been staffed 7 days a week, for every hour of each day, and had a panel available to assess the research proposals in the U.S. and send them back to each team; in the rapid evolution of the program, this type of novel IRB system seems unlikely to be able to implement. With longer research modes in regions where there are less pronounced insurgencies, the IRB seems not just feasible, but a prerequisite for the HTS were it to continue to evolve beyond the conflicts in Iraq and Afghanistan.

The American Anthropological Association chose the ethical dimensions of the research to critique most heavily rather than the value of the work done. Albro, consistently eloquent and considered on the conversation between the profession of anthropology and the military enterprise, voices concern about the discipline's persistent use of ethics "as its stock in trade, to talk about where anthropologists should be, what anthropologists should and shouldn't be doing and to define the lines between academic anthropology and mostly everything else."[120] Moreover, the American Anthropological Association and senior professional anthropologists in the United States were not united in their broad assessment. The Network of Concerned Anthropologists, a group of professional anthropologists that included members of the commission and executive board, gave a petition to the U.S. Congress in 2010 in a bid to halt funding of the program. The petition was signed by six of nine living former presidents of the American Anthropological Association, meaning that a third chose not to take an explicit stance against the program in this manner.[121] This absence of a concerted stance; the different investigative modes of the board statement and the commission; the varied concerns of those members of the commission; and the rapidly evolving nature of the program being studied each contributed to ameliorating the impact of these fundamentally important concerns of professional anthropology.

Effectiveness, however, rather than ethics, arguably mattered most to the military customer. On the back of Schweitzer's estimated quantitative assessment of his embedded team's contribution to a reduction in kinetic activity, which was presented as fact, the need for careful investigation of the program was implicit. Indeed, the trenchant position of the Network of Concerned Anthropologists arguably hindered equitable discourse, but their point that there is no evidence that HTTs are effective points to the singular problem in appropriating social science research modalities for combat zones. How do you measure success? The arguments of the professional anthropologists were further hindered by the difficulty in offering homogeneous assessment of the program when there was a spectrum of voices in the critique and a spectrum of voices from the program itself, often generating conflicting viewpoints, was pronounced.

In 2012, Albro and Gusterson wrote that they stood by the 2009 conclusions of the commission, specifically that the program contravenes anthropological ethics and falls short of professional standards for ethnography.[122] Based on the commission's findings, Albro and Gusterson also expressed concern at possible plans to reconfigure the program to a shaping tool in regions where insecurity may prove to be problematic to U.S. interests, noting that research conducted in a military setting lacks the integrity to be considered professional anthropology and that compared to other engagements between the military enterprise and anthropology, "HTS is different because it threatens the integrity of that core relationship between anthropologists and their subjects."[123]

This dominant theme regarding the ethics of the profession stems from a larger concern which is grounded in the historical military engagement with the social sciences, namely, the actual utility of academic knowledge which was used to defeat insurgencies. This is why Albro is right to identify the particular emphasis placed on ethical research forms as an issue of importance in and of itself. Historically, social science research methods and theoretical conceptual-izations are integrated into military epistemologies for actionable benefit. But the relationship has not been continual or one of constant progress or evolution. In-stead, the complex discrepancy between expectation and reality regarding what social science research can offer the military enterprise has meant the historical encounter has been wrought by opaque experiments often curtailed by consistently uncertain ends. The overarching question when the engagement between anthropology and war is taken as a whole is: To what extent does social science research augment the op-erational picture?[124] Across generations, that question has never been adequately answered, and it is for that reason that we find this intergenerational story con-tinuing. Surrounding the detailed assessments by the American Anthropological Association's commission and the statement of the board, the specter of the op-position to the Iraq and Afghan wars inevitably hangs heavily over the existing debate on the HTS.

Toward Pragmatism.

Packaging anthropological knowledge in a form which was both comprehensible and actionable re-quired the use of parsimonious frameworks for mod-eling the operating environment. Presciently, Price had suggested there would be a selective uptake of anthropological methods when he wrote:

> There is much of anthropology that the military does not want: the military does not want anthropologi-cal critiques of power, imperialism, or neocolonial-ism. It does not want empathetic understandings of 'the other' unless this can be used as an 'asset' for 'leveraging'.[125]

What was taking place in the crisis of Iraq was a rapid and selective uptake of social science. As part of that selective uptake and a site for sustained debate was the program's utilization of structural functionalism. This theoretical construct was a social model of the environment which had been fashionable in the 1950s but was now perceived as being outmoded.[126] For HTS, however, there was significant utility in the theoretical framework because it models society as symbiotic elements which aggregate to a single organism. In this model, propagated by American sociologist Talcott Parsons, culture, traditions, and institutions are organs within the societal body, the function of each impacting the viability of the whole. Addressing one to the detriment of any other would distort the fragile equilibrium, generating imbalance such that the societal structure is disturbed.

These anthropomorphic and reifying tendencies of the theory were attractive to a military enterprise modeling insurgencies in a resonant manner. The model utilizes a consensus theory in which a coherent society is developed through the architecture of order, a balancing of interest in those interrelated macroscopic elements upon which the society functions. Pertinent to the COIN doctrine being propagated, structural functionalism had the added advantage of foregrounding the role of culture in shaping the societal edifice; values, norms, ideas, and beliefs are all causally relevant. Culture is the binding force to the extent that it "is seen as a patterned, ordered system of symbols that are objects of orientations to actors, internalized aspects of the personality system, and institutionalized patterns in the social system."[127]

The contemporary position of the academic discipline of anthropology with regard to this model was at odds with its renaissance in the military, however. The academy had consigned this system to possessing largely historical significance, comparative to its situation in the 1950s and 1960s as the "primary organizing paradigm for most of American sociology."[128] As a criticism, using the model decades later fundamentally misrepresented the intellectual moment of the discipline of anthropology. Instructively, in her 1994 doctoral dissertation, McFate had already noted that there lay a discrepancy between the scholarly discipline of anthropology and military application of its models, but argued for its relevance to the military as a simplistic model encouraging understanding and constructing an intellectual bridge between the military and academia:

> Although structural-functionalist methodology has long been unfashionable within anthropology, the oscillating equilibrium model (with the addition of population dynamics and catastrophe theory) is now being used in military operational research for predicting the oscillating force-structure patterns in counterinsurgency.[129]

It demonstrates an aspiration within the military for modeling the character of warfare in complex environments; in this instance, the variation of force-size around a central value with respect to time.

Moreover, as Gezari notes in her examination of the program, as a student, McFate "wrote papers arguing that structural functionalism was invalid because it objectified and dehumanized the subjects of anthropological observation. But the pragmatist in her rejected this argument."[130] Pragmatism in stabilization and enabling operations is paramount in successful planning and execution of plans; where decisiveness, assertiveness, and clarity by necessity win out over uncertainty, deference, and detail.

Structural functionalism can be viewed as a stepping stone for military engagement with sociocultural expertise resident in the academy; a tentative step toward collaboration between two poles; one emphasizing the production of knowledge for unity of purpose, the other, granular exposition of knowledge for no particular end. This theoretical model thus served as a platform for the military to move ahead in their conceptualization of the human terrain. Indeed, as Gezari notes, rather than a traditional military predisposition to amalgamating disparate elements such as "politics, economics, social organization or the ideas that people have in their heads," unhelpful in explaining tribal systems, kinship organizations, religion, and the fact that "not all tribal systems are Islamic and not all of Islamic societies are tribal," there was the necessity to make a distinction in order to "clearly explain to people in uniform what is going on downrange [in Iraq and Afghanistan]."[131] Structural functionalism therefore offered an accessible academic language that could clarify the embedded work conducted by the HTTs, as well as engaging existing conceptual frameworks which the military enterprise was utilizing for assessment of social environments in which it operated.

The bridge between theory and practice may require compromise. Teaching structural functionalism to model and make resonant the human environment in complex contested spaces is one such compromise. As McFate explains, structural functionalism "is predicated on looking at society as a holistic entity and the view that all parts are all elements of the society at some function" but importantly, it must be thought of as "a heuristic model, not as an accurate description. Some way in which to capture a bit of social reality and make it explicable to people who do not know what these words mean, it is not such a bad approach."[132] As much as a model is a compromise between clarity and detail, so the teaching of the model itself is a compromise.

Social scientists on embedded teams thus represented a first attempt to bridge the gap between the academy and the military in person, albeit functioning amidst the high operational tempo of stabilization operations. To enable conversation and collaboration, HTS taught its recruits basic social theory, and tracked with structural functionalism by making "society" analytically distinct from "culture," something which the military historically had not tended to do.[133] Struggling to comprehend the character of the insurgencies developing in Iraq and Afghanistan, a structural functionalist interpretation of culture was the de facto lens through which to identify and understand societal constituents. Perhaps the model's single greatest limitation was an absence of quantitative methods which allowed the statistical representation of data. This approach therefore foregrounded qualitative assessments of the environment in training which were subsequently brought into the field environments. Ultimately, however, a model is an abstraction of reality according to a certain conceptualization and that model can facilitate communication, learning, and analysis about relevant aspects of the underlying terrain provided that the categorization of that terrain is expressed in a language which enables understanding.

The model shows the divide between the contemporary academic setting and aspects of the teaching and training in the HTS program despite the possibility that structural functionalism may experience an evolving renaissance in scholarship more broadly, even beyond the confines of DoD. As shown by Mc-Fate, there is value in its application in a military setting. But as a misrepresentation of the contemporary paradigms of the discipline, the concerns of the American Anthropological Association's commission regarding the narrative that the HTS is able to direct in DoD have some resonance:

> The potential problem here is that, despite the fact that HTS is just one modest program, among many, to which anthropology might contribute in DoD—and in the security sector broadly conceived—its notoriety is shaping prevailing wisdom about what anthropology is and what the role of anthropology should be among military and security policymakers, in ways that might very well be to the detriment of everyone else, or other more constructive arrangements, collaborations, and ethical applications of anthropological practice and knowledge.[134]

Despite this tense historical engagement and contemporary setting against the backdrop of controversial conflicts, the program gained funding and expanded rapidly. Given the controversial nature of its existence and the granular critique from the American Anthropological Association, I ask why the U.S. Army embedded civilians in military units in Iraq and Afghanistan to conduct research using social science methods. In Chapter 3, I examine the origins of the program and its evolution into a proof-of-concept entity with a physical home at the U.S. Army Training and Doctrine Command (TRADOC).

ENDNOTES - CHAPTER 2

1. I am indebted to Professor Anthony King for comments on an earlier draft of this chapter.

2. Cited in Hugh Gusterson, "Anthropology and Militarism," *Annual Review of Anthropology*, Vol. 36, 2007, p. 156.

3. Dustin M. Wax, "The Uses of Anthropology in the Insurgent Age," John D. Kelly *et al.*, eds., *Anthropology and Global Counterinsurgency*, Chicago, IL: University of Chicago Press, 2010, p. 154.

4. Robert J. González, "Indirect Rule and Embedded Anthropology: Practical, Theoretical, and Ethical Concerns," in *Anthropology and Global Counterinsurgency*, John D. Kelly *et al.*, eds., *Anthropology and Global Counterinsurgency*, Chicago, IL: University of Chicago Press, 2010, p. 236.

5. Gusterson, "Anthropology and Militarism," p. 156.

6. Geoff Emberling, "Archaeologists and the Military in Iraq, 2003-2008: Compromise or Contribution?" *Archaeologies*, Vol. 4, No. 3, 2008, p. 448.

7. Montgomery McFate, "Anthropology and Counterinsurgency: The Strange Story of their Curious Relationship," *Military Review*, Vol. 85, No. 2, 2005, p. 29.

8. Montgomery Cybele Carlough, "Pax Britannica: British Counterinsurgency in Northern Ireland,1969-1982," unpublished Ph.D. dissertation, New Haven, CT: Yale University, 1994, p. 28.

9. Cited in McFate, "Anthropology and Counterinsurgency," p. 29.

10. *Ibid.*

11. Vanessa Gezari, *The Tender Soldier: A True Story of War and Sacrifice*, New York: Simon and Schuster, 2013, p. 122.

12. Priya Satia, *Spies in Arabia: The Great War and the Cultural Foundations of Britain's Covert Empire in the Middle East*, New York: Oxford University Press USA, 2008.

13. *Ibid.*, p. 5. See also Priya Satia, "The Defense of Inhumanity: Air control and the British idea of Arabia," *American Historical Review*, Vol. 111, No. 1, 2006, pp. 16-51.

14. David Price, "Lessons from Second World War Anthropology: Peripheral, Persuasive and Ignored Contributions," *Anthropology Today*, Vol. 18, No. 3, 2002, p. 14.

15. Trevor J. Barnes, "Geographical Intelligence: American Geographers and Research and Analysis in the Office of Strategic Services 1941-1945," *Journal of Historical Geography*, Vol. 32, 2006, p. 150.

16. Gezari, p. 122.

17. Barnes, p. 150.

18. *Ibid.*

19. *Ibid.*

20. *Ibid.*, p. 162.

21. *Ibid.*, p. 157.

22. Cited in Price, "Lessons from Second World War Anthropology," p. 16.

23. *Ibid.*

24. John D. Kelly, Beatrice Jauregui, Sean T. Mitchell, and Jeremy Walton, "Culture, Counterinsurgency, Conscience," in John D. Kelly, Beatrice Jauregui, Sean T. Mitchell, and Jeremy Walton, eds., *Anthropology and Global Counterinsurgency*, Ann Arbor, MI: University of Chicago Press, 2010, p. 1.

25. Allan Nevins, ed., *The Strategy of Peace by John F. Kennedy*, New York, Evanston, IL, and London, UK: Harper & Row, 1960.

26. *Ibid.*

27. Seymour J. Deitchman, *The Best-Laid Schemes: A Tale of Social Research and Bureaucracy*, Cambridge, MA: Massachusetts Institute of Technology Press, 1976, p. 2.

28. *Ibid.*, pp. 2-3.

29. *Ibid.*, p. 26.

30. I thank Dr. Robert Johnson for making this argument so eloquently.

31. Deitchman, p. 117.

32. Sharon Weinberger, "The Pentagon's Culture Wars," *Nature*, Vol. 455, 2008, p. 585.

33. Deitchman, p. 158.

34. *Ibid.*, pp. 240-245.

35. Hugh Gusterson, "'Militarizing knowledge,' in Union [sic] of Concerned Anthropologists," *The Counter-Counterinsurgency Manual*, Chicago, IL: Prickly Paradigm Press, 2009, p. 48, cited in Maja Zehfuss, "Culturally Sensitive War? The Human Terrain System and the Seduction of Ethics," *Security Dialogue*, Vol. 43, No. 2, 2012, pp. 175-190.

36. Zehfuss, "Culturally Sensitive War?" p. 179.

37. Gusterson, "Militarizing knowledge," pp. 48-49, cited in Zehfuss, "Culturally Sensitive War?" p. 179.

38. Zehfuss, "Culturally Sensitive War?" pp. 179-180. A fuller examination of codes of ethics as they related to historical events is in Carolyn Fluehr-Lobban and George R. Lucas Jr., "Assessing the Human Terrain Teams: No White Hats or Black Hats Please," in Montgomery McFate and Janice H. Laurence, *Social Science Goes to War*, London, UK: Hurst, 2015, pp. 237-264.

39. Robert Albro, interview by author, Washington, DC, August 14, 2013; Gezari, pp. 122-125.

40. Albro interview.

41. *Ibid.*

42. Deitchman, pp. 234-235.

43. *Ibid.*, p. 336.

44. Dale Andrade and James H. Willbanks, "CORDS/Phoenix: Counterinsurgency Lessons from Vietnam for the Future," *Military Review*, March-April, 2006, p. 14.

45. *Ibid.*, p. 18.

46. *Ibid.*, p. 20.

47. David Kilcullen, "Countering Global Insurgency," *Small Wars Journal*, November 30, 2004.

48. Tom Hayden, "Meet the New Dr. Strangelove," *The Nation*, July 7, 2008.

49. Kilcullen, p. 40.

50. *Ibid.*

51. Robert O. Tilman, "Non-lessons of the Malayan Emergency," *Military Review*, 1966, p. 46, cited in Montgomery McFate, "The Military Utility of Understanding Adversary Culture," *Joint Force Quarterly*, Vol. 38, 2005, p. 48.

52. Gusterson, "Anthropology and Militarism," p. 157.

53. Wax, p. 163.

54. Albro interview.

55. *Ibid.*

56. *Ibid.*

57. Roberto J. González, "'Human Terrain': Past, Present and Future Applications," *Anthropology Today*, Vol. 24, No. 1, 2008, pp. 21-26.

58. González, "Indirect Rule and Embedded Anthropology," p. 231.

59. Roberto J. González, "Anthropology and the Covert: Methodological Notes on Researching Military and Intelligence Programmes," *Anthropology Today*, Vol. 28, No. 2, 2012, p. 24.

60. David H. Price, "Soft Power, Hard Power, and the Anthropological 'Leveraging' of Cultural 'Assets': Distilling the Politics and Ethics of Anthropological Counterinsurgency," John D. Kelly *et al.*, eds., *Anthropology and Global Counterinsurgency*, Chicago, IL: University of Chicago Press, 2010, p. 249.

61. See Maximilian C. Forte, "The Human Terrain System and Anthropology: A Review of Ongoing Public Debates," *American Anthropologist*, Vol. 113, No. 1, 2011, p. 150.

62. Marc W. D. Tyrrell, "The Human Terrain System: Clashing Moralities or Rhetorical Dead Horses," *E-International Relations*, February 5, 2012, available from *www.e-ir.info/2012/02/05/the-human-terrain-system-clashing-moralities-or-rhetorical-dead-horses/*, accessed August 12, 2014.

63. Robert M. Gates, *Speech to the Association of American Universities*, Washington, DC, DoD.

64. *Ibid.*

65. *Ibid.*

66. For erroneous identification of 1968 as the first instance, see, for example, Richard M. Medina, "From Anthropology to Human Geography: Human Terrain and the Evolution of Operational Sociocultural Understanding," *Intelligence and National Security*, 2014, p. 4.

67. Cited in González, "Indirect Rule," p. 223.

68. I am indebted to Andrew Gawthorpe of the Defence Studies Department at King's College London for pointing out this 1967 use of the term and for providing a citation for the document. Both Helms and Rostow had worked for the Office of Strategic Services in World War II.

69. Memorandum, Helms to Rostow, February 17, 1967, folder "Vietnam memos, A. Vol. 66," Box 41, National Security File: Vietnam, Lyndon B. Johnson Library, Austin, Texas, p. 5.

70. *Ibid.*

71. Ralph Peters, "The Human Terrain of Urban Operations," *Parameters*, Vol. 30, No. 1, 2000, pp. 4-12.

72. Montgomery McFate and Janice H. Laurence, "Introduction: Unveiling the Human Terrain System," in Montgomery McFate and Janice H. Laurence, eds., *Social Science Goes to War: The Human Terrain System in Iraq and Afghanistan,*London, UK: Hurst, 2015, p. 5.

73. González, "Indirect Rule," p. 223.

74. Price, "Soft Power, Hard Power," p. 250.

75. *Ibid.*

76. David Price, "Past Wars, Present Dangers, Future Anthropologies," *Anthropology Today*, Vol. 18, No. 1, 2002, p. 3.

77. *Ibid.*, p. 4.

78. David Price, "Lessons from Second World War Anthropology," p. 19.

79. Steve Fondacaro, personal communication with author, September 15, 2015.

80. *Final Report on the Army's Human Terrain System*, Arlington, VA: American Anthropological Association, October 14, 2009, p. 5; Zehfuss, "Culturally Sensitive War?" p. 177.

81. Dan G. Cox, "Human Terrain Systems and the Moral Prosecution of Warfare," *Parameters*, Vol. 41, No. 3, 2011, p. 20; see, for example, Josef Ansorge, "Spirits of War: A Field Manual," *International Political Sociology*, Vol. 4, No. 4, 2010, p. 372.

82. Christopher J. Lamb *et al.*, *Human Terrain Teams: An Organizational Innovation for Sociocultural Knowledge in Irregular Warfare*, Washington, DC: Institute of World Politics Press, 2013, p. 119.

83. Forte, "The Human Terrain System and Anthropology," p. 149; McFate, "Anthropology and Counterinsurgency," pp. 24-38.

84. See, for example, Timothy de Waal Malefyt and Robert J. Morais, *Advertising and Anthropology: Ethnographic Practice and Cultural Perspectives*, New York: Berg, 2012.

85. I am indebted to Dr. Robert Albro for providing this important context on the aspects of the debate.

86. Maximilian Forte, "A SPY IN OUR MIDST: Montgomery Sapone/Montgomery McFate," *Zero Anthropology*, January 15, 2013, available from *zeroanthropology.net/2008/07/31/a-spy-in-our-midst-montgomery-saponemontgomery-mcfate/*.

87. Bronwen Lichtenstein, "Beyond Abu Ghraib: The 2010 APA Ethics Code Standard 1.02 and Competency for Execution Evaluations," *Ethics and Behavior*, Vol. 23, No. 1, 2013, pp. 67-70.

88. David Price, "America the Ambivalent: Quietly Selling Anthropology to the CIA," *Anthropology Today*, Vol. 21, No. 5, 2005, p. 1; Roberto J. González, "We Must Fight the Militarisation of Anthropology," *The Chronicle of Higher Education*, February 2, 2007.

89. Albro interview.

90. *Commission on the Engagement of Anthropology with the US Security and Intelligence Communities: Final Report*, Arlington, VA: American Anthropological Association, November 4, 2007, p. 10.

91. *Ibid.*, p. 20.

92. *Ibid.* I am indebted to Dr. Robert Albro for providing this detailed account of the American Anthropological Association's engagement with the HTS through this period.

93. *Ibid.*

94. *Ibid.*

95. Albro interview; *Executive Board Statement on the Human Terrain System Project,* Arlington, VA: American Anthropological Association, October 31, 2007.

96. American Anthropological Association, *Executive Board Statement on the Human Terrain System Project.*

97. *Ibid.*

98. Albro interview.

99. *Ibid.*

100. American Anthropological Association, *Final Report on the Army's Human Terrain System,* p. 3.

101. *Ibid.,* p. 4.

102. *Ibid.,* p. 3.

103. *Ibid.*

104. *Ibid.,* p. 6.

105. *Ibid.,* p. 8.

106. *Ibid.,* pp. 7-8.

107. *Ibid.,* p. 11.

108. Nathan Finney, The Human Terrain Team Handbook, Fort Leavenworth, KS: TRADOC, 2008, p. 4, cited in American Anthropological Association, *Final Report on the Army's Human Terrain System,* p. 19.

109. American Anthropological Association, *Final Report on the Army's Human Terrain System*, p. 6.

110. *Ibid.*, p. 30.

111. *Ibid.*, p. 24.

112. *Ibid.*, p. 3.

113. *Ibid.*, p. 36.

114. *Ibid.*

115. I am indebted to Dr. Nicholas Krohley for highlighting this point.

116. Albro interview.

117. American Anthropological Association, *Final Report on the Army's Human Terrain System*, p. 42.

118. Montgomery McFate, interview with author, August 1, 2013.

119. *Ibid.*, p. 48.

120. Albro interview.

121. Robert Albro and Hugh Gusterson, "Commentary: 'Do No Harm'," *C4ISR Journal*, April 25, 2012, available from *www.defensenews.com/article/20120425/C4ISR02/304250001/Con*, accessed March 16, 2015.

122. *Ibid.*

123. *Ibid.*

124. I thank Dr. Robert Johnson for highlighting this issue.

125. Price, "Soft Power, Hard Power," p. 258.

126. For a broad but excellent analysis of U.S. military engagement with sociology, see Chris Paparone, *The Sociology of Military Science: Prospects for Postinstitutional Military Design*, New York: Continuum, 2012.

127. Talcott Parsons, *The Structure of Social Action*, New York: Free Press, 1937, p. 77.

128. Peter Hamilton, *Talcott Parsons*, Chichester, UK: Ellis Horwood, 1983, p. 45.

129. J. T. Dockery and A. E. R. Woodcock, eds., *The Military Landscape: Mathematical Models of Combat*, Cambridge, UK: Woodhead Publishing, 1993, cited in Carlough, pp. 21-22. The oscillating equilibrium model proposed by Edmund Leach is based on the structural functionalist approach in assessing society as composed of functional constituents prone to flux.

130. Gezari, p. 114.

131. *Ibid.*

132. McFate interview.

133. *Ibid.*

134. American Anthropological Association, *Final Report on the Army's Human Terrain System*, p. 51.

CHAPTER 3

FROM A MILITARY CRISIS

The prevailing orthodoxy asserts that Human Terrain System (HTS) is a counterinsurgency (COIN) tool created to provide sociocultural knowledge in that capacity. From the outside-in perspective, it is easy to link the social science research program to requirements for military forces in Iraq and Afghanistan, outlined explicitly in *Field Manual* (FM) *3-24*. Bluntly, the American Anthropological Association argued that the program performs a "tactical function in counterinsurgency warfare."[1] In their authoritative study, Lamb *et al.* argued that the population-centric approach to COIN required "protecting and eliciting cooperation from the population" and that "the principal instruments for delivering this understanding to [General David] Petraeus' military forces in the field were Human Terrain Teams" (HTT).[2] The problem in this reading is that if COIN was the solution, we must search for the problem to understand why the HTS was considered valuable. Examining only the solution will do nothing to inform evaluation of future contours in military planning.

Searching for the problem, we run into difficulty. COIN is a diffuse concept, and there is no identified *casus belli* for the social sciences uptake, other than a general reading of two wars gone awry. Professor Hugh Gusterson, a critic of the conflicts, wrote that the national security apparatus took a "cultural turn" after "deciding that anthropology might be to the 'war on terror', what physics was to the cold war."[3] The introduction of the COIN FM, suggests another scholar, was:

a response to the near-implosion of Iraq, where an insurgency mutated into horrific communal violence, while the North Atlantic Treaty Organization (NATO) tries to navigate the tribal world of Afghanistan and a resurgent Taliban.[4]

Eminent political geographer Derek Gregory's paper on the cultural turn, what he terms "the rush to the intimate," notes that the interim COIN *FM 3.07-22* released in 2004 was an "attempt to shore up the rapidly deteriorating situation" in Iraq.[5] For Gregory, the ensuing cultural turn was "a heterogeneous assemblage of discourses and objects, practices, and powers distributed across different but networked sites: a military *dispositif* if you prefer."[6]

By the end of 2006, the George Bush administration simply ran out of ideas, according to a leading critic of the handling of the Iraq occupation that had supported the initial invasion.[7] Fred Kaplan suggests it was driven by Petraeus and his "cabal" or "mafia"; graduates from the West Point Department of Social Sciences who adapted their enemies' tactics to overhaul their own military and reorganize it for small wars.[8] While critical of COIN doctrine, retired U.S. Army officer Ralph Peters notes that it is part of "a growing sense that the reality on the ground in Iraq and elsewhere contradicts the theories we were fed."[9] Theory driven approaches to this renewed emphasis on cultural understanding have been employed but produce different conclusions. Janine Davidson, writing as a leading author of the COIN FM, argued not for the why but for the how; employing organization theory to argue that there was a remarkable flexibility within the U.S. Armed Forces to respond to novel threats which enabled victory in Iraq and Afghanistan.[10]

Seen as a novel threat, it is unsurprising that deterioration in security in Iraq generated specific calls for a paradigm shift in military thinking to circumvent an apparent Cold War conventional warfighting paradigm which had proved unable to counter the insurgency patterns in the country. In 2004, COIN expert David Kilcullen called for "a new paradigm, capable of addressing globalized insurgency."[11] In 2005, Montgomery McFate placed the need for a transition into a historical trajectory, arguing that the end of the Cold War had altered the "nature of the enemy" and that globalization, failed states, and small arms proliferation required, "An immediate transformation in the military conceptual paradigm."[12] In 2006, Petraeus echoed earlier calls for a paradigm shift in thinking to combat the deleterious situation in Iraq.[13] These calls built on identified requirements in the field: Major Michael S. Patton, speaking to *The Washington Post* from Baghdad in 2003 argued that the Iraq conflict was a new form of war where "Everyone is an intelligence officer—that's sort of our theme. If you're talking about a paradigm shift, this is it: You have to see everyone you come into contact with as having intelligence value."[14]

Seen as part of this trend for cultural awareness, Human Terrain System was thus part of a cultural turn in the wars in Iraq and Afghanistan. Paul Joseph, Professor of Sociology at Tufts University, in his 2014 account asserts that the "very existence of the program' reflected a trend in the Department of Defense for deeper understanding of operations "among people whose reactions to those operations will significantly influence, if not ultimately determine, success or failure."[15] For Joseph, it was part of a culture wave, during which "HTS emerged during this recognition of the need for greater cultural sophistication."[16] Other studies arrive at similar conclusions. The Center for Naval Analyses assessment of the HTS argued that the program was "intended to provide military decisionmakers in Iraq and Afghanistan with greater understanding of the local population's cultures and perspectives."[17]

In this chapter, I argue against the cultural turn in the Iraq and Afghanistan conflicts catalyzing formation and of the HTS. Instead, I assert that the military crisis created by the improvised explosive device (IED), primarily in Iraq, engendered an "anything goes" approach to combatting the insurgency. I use Freedom of Information Act requests to obtain elements of the Joint Urgent Operational Needs Statements (JUONS) (see Appendix D for explicit linkage of HTS to the IED defeat fight) in order to deepen understanding of this evolution. Understanding of the character of this particular military crisis and the clamor for novelty it engendered is useful. It informs discussion on the manner in which peripheral ideas and projects can rapidly become the normal and accepted modes of thought in periods of military fragility.

The remaining piece of the puzzle is why the HTS departed the counter-IED (C-IED) enterprise and emerged into the broader COIN realm concerned with understanding the population. The answer is threefold; idealism, pragmatism, and pecuniary motives all contributed. First, the ascendant COIN theory in the Department of the Army allowed the HTS to develop as a nonkinetic asset which sat more comfortably with McFate's vision for the future of the program than as a primarily C-IED tool. Second, the move was pragmatic; it fell into line with the work McFate was doing with Petraeus on the FM 3-24, which, especially in

Chapter 3 (part of which had been written by McFate) could then be used to highlight to brigades what HTTs could offer.[18] It was also easier to recruit civilians through a COIN narrative than a C-IED narrative, the latter being the largest cause of U.S. casualties in Iraq.

Third, by mid-2007, when the U.S. Central Command JUONS was drafted by the program management, COIN doctrine, which sought a high profile in the U.S. media and received it, had emerged with powerful fathers. Petraeus, then commander of the Multi-National Corps-Iraq and General James N. Mattis, commander of 1 Marine Expeditionary Force were staunch advocates. With the HTS set for Iraq after a surge replaced the penciled draw-down of forces, linking the program to a scholarly, nonkinetic dimension of the COIN operations was the only game in town and in a crisis, "anything goes." Begun in late-2005, HTS preceded the COIN push, but as it burgeoned, it became easy to transition the HTS, a C-IED tool, to the COIN fight.

REVOLUTION AND EVOLUTION

HTS evolved to such an extent that by 2010 the Outreach Coordinator for the program stated that it was not in the program's mandate "to pursue information related to insurgents, improvised explosive devices or other weapons employed by insurgent elements" but insecurity and its attendant manifest elements arise frequently in interviews with the local population, such that, ambiguously, "HTS teams only provide their unit with information related to IEDs and insurgent activity, if this information is provided to them, *unsolicited* [my italics], by the people they are interviewing."[19] It is the argument made in this chapter that the IED was the lodestone which catalyzed need, funding, and ability to create the HTS.

Given the controversy surrounding it and the many individuals involved in its genesis, the origins of the program are difficult to capture. Vanessa Gezari has made this assessment eloquently in writing:

> The roots of the Human Terrain System are ambiguous and contested, stained with bad blood and accusations of impure motives, its origin myths embellished by ambitious and therefore potentially unreliable narrators who, nevertheless, each holds a piece of the story. Its elements evolved simultaneously and organically from various corners of the defense establishment and flourished in the atmosphere of ferment that grew out of the Army's realization that it was losing the war in Iraq.[20]

Nevertheless, I use primary and secondary sources, including interviews with McFate and documentation obtained from Freedom of Information Act requests to construct a trajectory of the origin of the program and its relationship with the C-IED landscape.

The crisis generated by the IEDs in Iraq created rich funding opportunities for myriad initiatives designed to counter the threat.[21] In keeping with the military preference for technological solutions to mitigate emerging threats, there was an initial focus on technological solutions to combat IEDs; products which would fight, if not negate, the effects of the device itself. By 2006 with key personnel changes in the C-IED landscape and as the limitations of applying technological alone solutions became obvious, there was a shift in emphasis, if not focus, from combatting the device to attacking the network behind it, with consequentially increased importance placed on intelligence and social science research techniques in order to better understand the nature of the social networks in Iraq and Afghanistan. This shift is explored in two steps: first, an investigation of the evolution of attempts to combat the IED; second, an examination of the development of the HTS from the C-IED architecture.

LETHAL AMBUSH

Giving a historical trajectory to the problem of the IED in Iraq and Afghanistan, Lieutenant General Thomas Metz told the House Armed Services Committee: "In its most fundamental form, the IED is a lethal ambush, and men have been ambushing their enemies for thousands of years."[22] Within the ambush, the IED has proliferated to become the weapon of choice to implement the tactic in Iraq and Afghanistan. The problems posed by IEDs today are six-fold: first, they require little or no physical confrontation with opposed forces; second, they are difficult to detect or counter with current technologies and their improvised nature means that they can be quickly modified to overcome countermeasures defined to defeat them; third, they prevent security on the ground and therefore inhibit reconstruction efforts; fourth, they do not require military hardware, instead often being assembled from nonmilitary products such as fertilizer; fifth, the inability to retaliate against the opponent responsible has a deleterious effect upon soldiers' morale; and sixth, events against coalition forces appear on insurgent and terrorist websites. As such, the IED is a weapon that can have strategic impact, possessing the ability to deliver the goals of an insurgency by exerting considerable influence on popular perceptions of the conflict.

Following the U.S.-led invasion of Iraq, the IED was immediately the weapon of choice for insurgents because of the abundance of deteriorated munitions throughout Iraq following the fall of Saddam's regime and its ease of manufacture, cost-effectiveness, and brutal effects. Its use evolved to such an extent that, by late-2003, there was already a crisis in military operations and only the first and second battles of Fallujah in 2004 — in which there was small arms fire and close quarter combat — temporarily lessened the IED casualty rate as a percentage of overall fatalities. By December 2004, IED casualties accounted for half of all U.S. military casualties, and, by the following year, all major forms of IED were apparent in Iraq.[23] Road side bombs had evolved early in the Iraq campaign as a way to exploit the relatively unprotected underside and lower sides of armored vehicles, especially the Humvee, and were conducted against the spectrum of coalition vehicles, including Abrams tanks.[24] The explosively formed penetrator, which received particular media coverage as a technology possibly having been "brought" to Iraq by Iranian actors, was present as early as 2004.[25] One study suggested that the explosively formed penetrator never accounted for more than 5 to 10 percent of the total number of IEDs detonated, but accounted for 40 percent of the casualties. Although the study does not define the time period, it demonstrates the capacity for the IED to cause widespread casualties.[26]

An absence of deep planning for the post-invasion scenarios meant that the IED threat was not provisioned for in the equipment spectrum of coalition forces. Without any specific C-IED technologies, U.S. troops improvised by "hanging armored vests on the doors of vehicles and placing sand bags on the floors of Humvees to absorb blasts."[27] Troops also began to use scrap metal to up-armor the vehicles for enhanced survivability. In June 2003, General John P. Abizaid, who had taken over from General Tommy Franks as Commander of United States Central Command, declared IEDs his "number one threat."[28] Franks had failed to envisage the rise of militias antagonistic to coalition forces and had appeared disconnected from the rapidly changing events on the ground.

The powerbrokers in Iraq remained the Coalition Provisional Authority and Multi-National Force-Iraq, but Abizaid's observations are valuable in being the distilled analyses from the situation in Iraq. Implicit in the appointment was a changing emphasis where intent lay less in coercing the population than winning them over. Abizaid was a fluent Arabic speaker who combined military experience with scholarly learning, and he had already indicated his desire for greater training for troops engaged in peacekeeping. Showing the awareness at the highest levels of the evolving insurgency, in a statement to the Senate Armed Services Committee in September 2003, Abizaid considered that U.S. forces in Iraq were already engaged in "a wide range of activities" including "counterinsurgency, counterterrorist, stability, and civil-affairs operations."[29]

The primary modality of the evolving and increasingly violent insurgency was the IED. It was inevitable, given the scramble for additional armor being sought by military personnel, that the ensuing push for C-IED projects was orientated toward finding technological solutions. In October 2003, the United States Congress approved U.S.$572 million for more armored Humvees and U.S.$100 million for bolt-on-armor retrofits to existing vehicles.[30] Yet armored

Humvees provided only a minimal increase in protection because they had been designed to combat land mines, not the lateral blasts from many of the IEDs.[31] The problem, however, was more than a technological one, as an unnamed senior Army officer noted; if the armor was increased, the insurgents would just build bigger and better IEDs.[32] The admission hints at the psychological effects of the ubiquitous device in Iraq, as well as the ability of the insurgents to adapt to U.S. innovation with ease and develop cost-effective solutions to mitigate vastly superior U.S. technology.[33]

In parallel with the escalating IED crisis was an emerging identity to the campaign in Iraq. By March 2004, Abizaid considered that U.S. forces were "waging a counterinsurgency against an enemy hiding within the population and operating without rules."[34] Explicit now was the military's preoccupation with the IED, and Abizaid considered at this time that the central element of the COIN effort would be human intelligence collected through myriad initiatives, which would include the cultivation of the populace and its leaders.[35] Yet, Abizaid did not link the IED to the COIN campaign; in combatting the former, he was a staunch advocate of rapidly deployed technological approaches to fight the device. At this stage and under this leadership, COIN and the IED were discussed largely in separation.

An absence of a single joint instruction to produce a blanket, unified C-IED strategy meant that units on the ground produced ad hoc tactics, techniques, and procedures as insurgent tactics evolved.[36] Organizationally, the U.S. Army relied on the Rapid Equipping Force created in 2002 and the Operational Needs Statement which enabled combat commanders to bypass standard acquisition channels for materiel solutions by creating an urgent need. At this early stage, C-IED was still oriented toward materiel solutions aimed at defeating the device itself. The variation was most obvious between Armed Service components.

Within the Marine Corps, initial C-IED efforts were based at the Marine Corps Combat Development Command, responsible for developing material needs.[37] Requests for C-IED material to the Command accelerated from two in 2002 to eight in 2003 and 26 in 2004. Of all requests to the Command during 2002-04, 13 percent were for C-IED material.[38] Conscious of the rising requests, in 2004 the Marine Corps established a C-IED cell which was later transferred to the Marine Corps Warfighting Laboratory, and during this period, the Urgent Universal Needs Statement was developed to allow rapid fielding of critical technologies.

Given the crisis unfolding and the lack of direction from the top of planning, myriad C-IED initiatives proliferated at the component services level. The Combined Explosives Exploitation Cell, established by the U.S. Army in 2003, performed physical, biometric, and tactical exploitation of evidence from IED attack scenes.[39] The cell included early attempts to acquire biometric data and analysis of enemy tactics. In 2004, the Naval Explosive Ordnance Disposal Technology Division served as an administrative sponsor to the cell. The Technical Support Working Group was also involved in fielding technologies as part of the Combating Terrorism Directorate at the Joint Staff Operations Center. The Terrorist Explosive Device Analytical Center was formed in 2003 to investigate recovered IED components in order to provide actionable intelligence to coalition forces. According to officials, the center "focused on higher-level strategic issues rather than tactical ones" and thus shows the tactical and strategic threat posed by IEDs in Iraq.[40]

119

With the Army bearing the brunt of the IED fight, in October 2003, Lieutenant General Richard Cody, the Army's Vice Chief, created the Army IED Task Force. Cody was acutely aware of the danger posed by the IED to coalition forces, calling the IED the "poor man's cruise missile."[41] Cody nominated Brigadier General Joseph L. Votel, then Army Deputy Director for Information Operations, to head the nascent task force. With a budget of only U.S.$20 million allotted, this task force focused primarily on the cultivation of intelligence and, to that end, deployed small numbers of contractors (former Special Operations Forces) and officers to the field to investigate the IED landscape and make recommendations for best practices in the light of their findings.

These suggested revisions to operational and training methods were sent back as lessons learned from field teams to a coordinating cell in Washington and relayed to the Army Center for Lessons Learned.[42] The first team deployed to Iraq in December 2003, and in April 2004, another team went to Iraq and a first team was sent to Afghanistan. In addition, the organization communicated across the Armed Services and Department of Defense (DoD), finding some islands of technological expertise already in the structure, for example, at the U.S. Army Engineer School.[43] An IED cell was established at the Army center for incorporating lessons into the training of outgoing troops in Iraq and deployed a very limited amount of C-IED technology.[44] But with such a limited budget and no interservices authority, there was no scope beyond the relatively narrow remit afforded to it; its only option was to continue its major initiative to train soldiers on how to detect or avoid IEDs.

At this time, Colonel Steve Fondacaro, who would later become the driving force behind development of the HTS, joined the Army IED Task Force headed by Votel. Fondacaro had known Votel from his time at the Army Rangers.[45] Fondacaro was one of the officers sent to Iraq to head the field-deployed projects against IEDs which Lamb *et al.* note in their study, "were by far the largest cause of U.S. casualties in Iraq and the most prominent operational problem confronting U.S. forces there."[46] During his time in Iraq, Fondacaro was working in close proximity with Andrea Jackson, who had been assigned by the now-defunct Washington, DC-based public relations firm, the Lincoln Group, to work for Multi-National Corps-Iraq headquarters on the Cultural Preparation of the Environment (CPE) project.[47]

Diyala province was chosen for the proof-of-concept in part because prior research had been undertaken there for the Iraq Training Program. The project's aim was to:

> provide commanders on the ground with a tool that will allow them to understand operationally relevant aspects of local culture; the ethno-religious, tribal, and other divisions within Iraqi society; and the interests and leaders of these groups.[48]

It was thus through the C-IED architecture that key relationships in the HTS network began to develop. In addition, at a Booz Allen Hamilton event held in Tampa, Florida, in early-2005 that focused on how sociocultural knowledge could be employed to defeat the IED, McFate met Fondacaro, and they would begin to sketch the first outlines of what would become ultimately the HTS.[49] The aim was to depart the C-IED landscape and to examine and understand the underpinning of the conflict, the "reason why the population were silent witnesses, passive and sometimes active supporters."[50] From Fondacaro's experience in Iraq, notably with the JIEDDTF, focusing on the IEDs themselves "resulted only in minor incremental advantages that were very temporary, while the problem continued endlessly."[51]

As the task force showed, there was an increasing need for information on the character of asymmetric threats and to deploy specialists to acquire the specific knowledge from the theater. Therefore, in order to advise commanders on methods for combatting irregular arranged adversaries, at the request of Army Operations staff engaged with the IED Task Force, an Asymmetric Warfare Group was nominally created in April 2004. The group was termed the Asymmetric Warfare Regiment at conception, and was then redesignated the Asymmetric Warfare Group (AWG) in April 2006. In reality, the Army began organizing the AWG in January 2005 to be operational by the middle of that year.[52] As early as March 2005, a part of the group already involved "Linkages to the warfighter [which] will be established through dedicated liaison teams to functional and geographic combatant commanders."[53] The model for the organization of the group included an operations squadron, the job of which was to "provide the trained and ready teams that deploy forward to collect, develop, and disseminate tactics, techniques, and procedures and observations."[54] Further, "The operations squadron will be able to provide liaison and staff integration with supported commands and will be *capable of assisting deployed units in the integration and training of rapidly fielded countermeasures* [my italics]."[55] A U.S. located training and assessment team trained personnel prior to their deployment into theater, and incorporated feedback from the forward-deployed operations squadron into that training.

These AWG teams consisted of military personnel and contractors, and deployed typically for periods of 90-120 days. The establishment of the AWG indicated an important juncture had been reached in the fight against IED networks. The Army had decided that as well as a technological approach, there was clearly the necessity for specific expertise to low-intensity kinetic environments, and that it would go to some lengths to develop that capability. In a 2005 article, Brigadier General Votel and Lieutenant General James J. Lovelace concluded that conventional U.S. warfighting methods and technological solutions to the violent insurgency had been overrun in Iraq:

> Every new or improved capability, however, no matter how dominant, brings with it a whole new set of inherent vulnerabilities. A smart, resourceful enemy will seek out those chinks in his adversary's armor and attack them with asymmetric means.[56]

Tellingly, the authors note that "A stark example of this is the current threat posed by improvised explosive devices (IEDs) in Iraq."[57] Among the required initiatives to fill existing gaps at this time was "adequate knowledge of indigenous cultures and availability of skilled linguists."[58]

The task force and the AWG were Army-only solutions and did not capitalize on the strengths of all the services which were pursuing their own C-IED programs independently. The need for a coordinated department-wide effort led Deputy Secretary of Defense Paul Wolfowitz on July 12, 2004, to establish the Joint Integrated Process Team (JIPT) in a 1-paragraph memorandum. The team would be the core of DoD efforts to combat the IED threat and would be led by the Army. As a consequence of this action, the Army IED Task Force became a Joint IED Task Force. The team was organized around and incorporated the existing Army IED Task Force but also pulled together the myriad existing initiatives within DoD, academy, and the private sector; the primary focus was on technology-based solutions.[59]

CULTURAL PREPARATION
OF THE ENVIRONMENT

In 2004, Lieutenant Colonel William Adamson returned from Diyala province, Iraq, to serve a joint tour in the Pentagon, having been a strong advocate for better understanding of the population in an area of operations. Adamson believed that military comprehension of civilian networks had been fundamental to securing local support among the population but that after leaving the area of operations, this knowledge had not been stored in a way that could be easily accessed by relief forces.[60] Adamson and Dr. Hriar Cabayan, Chief Science Advisor for the Joint Chiefs of Staff J-3, thus worked at the Pentagon on development of a methodology to solve that problem across different areas of operations. At the same time, McFate had undertaken a project for Marine Corps Brigadier General Thomas D. Waldhauser, based on a need to understand the cultural environment in an area of operation, and which centered on interviewing Marines returning from Iraq and Afghanistan. Waldhauser had participated in combat operations in southern Afghanistan and Iraq before returning to serve as Commanding General, Marine Corps Warfighting Laboratory, and Deputy Commander, Marine Corps Combat Development Command, and thus was well-placed to sponsor small-scale investigations into the application of cultural layers to aid warfighting.

When the project finished during 2004, McFate briefed the assessment around the Pentagon framed as a problem with the requirement to understand better the population in order to mitigate insurgent activity. It was this networking which brought McFate to the attention of Hriar Cabayan, as a suitable person for the project being developed with William Adamson. At that first meeting with Cabayan, Adamson, and project manager Nancy Chesser, the plan unveiled was the creation of a database called Cultural Preparation of the Environment, which would be designed by the MITRE Corporation.[61] Significantly, the funding source was from the C-IED architecture; the Joint IED Task Force provided U.S.$1.2 million for the creation and testing of the device between 2004 and 2006.

The network behind the IED was at this point unintelligible to U.S. forces operating in Iraq. The use of IEDs had proliferated as an effective ambush weapon, causing significant physical injury and impact upon morale. Any tool that promised to decipher these networks and decode the population was of immense utility in such an atmosphere. In 2005, Abizaid was given a demonstration of the Cultural Preparation of the Environment platform and observed that, with it, "we would know more about Iraq than we do the US."[62] As part of this database drive, McFate and Jackson wrote a briefing with notes which was sent to numerous individuals as part of the networking push, including the then-editor of the *Military Review*, on how to solve the sociocultural operational problems. The briefing was published as an article in the July-August 2005 edition of that journal.[63]

It was that article which laid out the organizational dimensions for an HTS capability. In the words of McFate speaking retrospectively: "You need to have an entity that can do research in a war zone, that can advise military forces, that can conduct independent research, that can train," and stressing the importance of historical models, McFate notes that she "was reading a lot at that time about the OSS [Office of Strategic Services] and the OSS structure" which influenced the thinking regarding structure.[64] McFate and Jackson were tasked with developing taxonomies and ontologies for the data, and, to begin this process, McFate noted that it was necessary to "try to go back and not start from scratch; somebody, somewhere must have done something similar to this in the dim, distant past."[65] The research that was conducted was focused on templates in the civil affairs communities, organization in historically relevant models such as the Human Relation Area Files, because McFate could find no analogical models in existence after 1945. There were further complications because those files were organized differently as they concerned comparative analysis. McFate was not concerned with comparative analysis in an area of operations, but instead emphasized that the program envisaged "quick and dirty presentation of data in a way that a military officer could understand; not for social scientists."[66]

McFate had already written about the organizational context of the IED social network. In the May-June 2005 issue of *Military Review*, she painted the security landscape of the IED problem, noting their ubiquity and lethality, it was argued that while "U.S. defense science and technology communities have focused on developing technical solutions to the IED threat," it must also be considered that:

IEDs are a product of human ingenuity and social organization. If we understand the social context in which they are invented, built, and used we will have an additional avenue for defeating them.[67]

For McFate, a "shift in focus from the IED technology to IED makers requires examining the social environment in which bombs are invented, manufactured, distributed, and used."[68] Focusing on the bomb maker and their enabling social network would then require four areas of evaluation of the organization, the material procurement, and the surrounding population.

The IED network, shadowy and indistinct, was thus the terrain on which McFate could launch the need for an HTS capability. Based on sources, McFate argued in the article that IED production in Iraq stems from an Iraqi Intelligence Service (part of Saddam Hussein's toppled regime) unit called M-21 (also known as the A1 Ghafiqi Project). In short, McFate concludes, "The ISS M-21 unit is a key reason the Iraqi insurgency is so adept at constructing IEDs," providing a skeleton of the body of the nascent post-war insurgency.[69] At this juncture, a specific date is highlighted — September 2003 — when the IED threat escalated because "IEDs became more sophisticated, evolving from simple suicide attacks to more complex remote-control, vehicle-borne IEDs and daisy-chain IEDs using trip-wires."[70] The increasing sophistication over time indicated "that their design and construction has become a specialized function within the insurgency, rather than a dispersed function."[71]

Thus September 2003 became a temporally identifiable crisis point in the escalation of IED use to which no solution had yet been created. This meant in conclusion that "identifying the bombmakers must be an absolute priority."[72] To that end, the bomb making organization must be analyzed because, "Members of insurgent cells operate part-time and blend back into the civilian population when operations are complete."[73] The presence of foreign fighters aside, McFate argues that the "majority of insurgents are native Iraqis connected to each and to the general population by social networks and relationships. The most important social network in Iraq is the tribe." Indeed, "The tribes provide money, manpower, intelligence, and assistance in escape and evasion after an attack."[74]

But theory was complicated by practice; work on the taxonomy for the Cultural Preparation of the Environment tool designed to identify the tribal network behind the bomb maker was complicated by the nascent networks being developed which were essentially alien to those involved; at that time, the Tactical Ground Reporting System was being developed by the Defense Advanced Research Projects Agency; the Combined Information Data Network Exchange, a tactical reporting database, which would become critical to the proliferation of HTS products in the field had not yet been created, while Palantir and the Distributed Common Ground System-Army were not widely utilized.

The result was that the project managers were "operating blind" in the creation of categories for the data, after which the MITRE Corporation, the contractors for Cultural Preparation of the Environment, created the interface.[75] The data call for that system was unsuccessful, with requests from different agencies on number and structure of tribes in Diyala province bringing wide variation in answers. The absence of deep, robust information about the province was indicative of a wider problem in the intelligence community, to which, as McFate explains, the solution was to:

> do the research on the ground. And when you are talking about Iraq and Afghanistan these are societies that have been closed to social science research for about 30 years, more or less and mostly it has never been done at the very granular level that we were being asked to look at.[76]

These closed societies would also mean finding subject matter experts to deploy later in the HTS was an extremely arduous, if not impossible, task.

As this Cultural Preparation of the Environment tool was beginning to be field tested, the pronounced impact of the IED was foregrounded in the American media sphere. By the end of 2004, there were detailed reports of the IED crisis; a prominent *Chicago Tribune* article in October noted that over half of the more than 8,600 war casualties were caused by the "low-tech" IED threat.[77] In public, Votel conceded that there was a lack of intelligence about how the adversaries' IED network was structured. Asked in a National Public Radio interview if the threat originated from a unified command structure, Votel responded that there were probably different groups which were united only in a common goal to oust U.S. forces, and he could only assume that these disparate elements were sharing intelligence with each other.[78]

This is the military problem that we have been searching for in this chapter, for which the C-IED was the ascendant solution. In identifying the trajectory of the expanding problem, we are able to chart the rise of the nontechnological solutions to the IED threat, of which the HTS was to become a high-profile example. The stark gap in knowledge about the insurgents that were escalating their use of the device was pronounced. It was also difficult to cover up. In 2005, Votel conceded that predicting the number of attacks by the enemy in the following year would be difficult, because he was "not sure he knows enough about their capabilities."[79] Votel obscured discussions that the use of technology might defeat the IED blasts in Iraq because they had so far proved ineffective. Instead, Votel asserted that greater efforts must be made to track the perpetrators and cells behind the atrocities.[80] A *World Tribune* article from the same month observed: "Officials said the army appears to have reached a stalemate in the war against IEDs."[81]

Without obvious solutions to the IED, Gordon England, Deputy Secretary of Defence, who had replaced Paul Wolfowitz in June 2005, recommended evolving Wolfowitz' Joint IED Task Force into a Joint IED Defeat Task Force. The difference between the two entities is a small but important one for identification of the evolution of the C-IED enterprise as the latter now assimilated the Force Protection Working Group and the Joint Integrated Process Team. England formerly had been Secretary of the Navy and in that capacity in 2004 had met with senior government scientists, agreeing upon the need for a comprehensive approach to combat the IED threat. In the new iteration of the C-IED enterprise, a spectrum of solutions would be sought, and, because of the existential threat to the military venture posed by the crisis, funding could circumvent traditional DoD bureaucracy.

Retired General Montgomery Meigs was appointed the first director of the new task force, reporting directly to Deputy Director England. Meigs held a doctorate in history from the University of Wisconsin-Madison and had been an International Affairs Fellow at the Massachusetts Institute of Technology; therefore, he was ideally suited to fuse an academic approach with practical approaches to warfighting. His academic work had focused on the hybridization of civilian expertise and military initiatives. Meigs' 1982 doctoral thesis was titled "Managing Uncertainty: Vannevar Bush, James B. Conant, and the Development of the Atomic Bomb, 1940-1945." In the thesis, Meigs argued that civilian expertise had been vital to solving complex military problems which threatened national security.

In 2003, Meigs published an article on asymmetric warfare in the U.S. Army journal, *Parameters*, in which he noted that to "isolate al-Qaeda's true advantage, we should begin with a look at the historical roots of asymmetric warfare."[82] Framing the current confrontation as one of permanent ambush, Meigs argued that, in Afghanistan, the situation now resembled one which is characteristic of the situation faced by Afghan fighters throughout the centuries: "a relatively conventional military force on the ground attempting to chase down groups and individuals almost invisible in the native culture and terrain."[83] On beginning his appointment with the Joint IED Task Force on December 12, 2005, Meigs brought with him Maxie McFarland, the Deputy Chief of Staff, G-2, at the Training and Doctrine Command (TRADOC), with an immediate but temporary responsibility to increase the intelligence capability of the task force. In 2005, McFarland had authored an influential article in *Military Review* entitled "Military Cultural Education," which stressed the need for lessons learned to be transported back to the United States. As part of his remit, Meigs travelled to Iraq and Afghanistan, and McFarland travelled with him. Earlier, Meigs had expressed the need to develop investigative skills in forward operating roles.[84]

Fondacaro was head of the JIEDDTF-Iraq. At the time of his deployment there, he considered that an information technology revolution of the past 30 years meant that narratives rather than technology were key to victory; "Perception truly now is reality, and our enemies know it. We have to fight on the information battlefield."[85] He considered himself a "radical" who, in revolutionizing the way the war in Iraq would be conducted, required the help of academics, specifically, social scientists because it was necessary to go beyond incremental gains which could be made against the effects of violence and look closely at the causes, the "human terrain" as he termed it.[86] Yet, Fondacaro identified problems with the Cultural Preparation of the Environment capability: brigade staffs were already overloaded with technologies for which they had no time to learn how to utilize; there was also a lack of sufficient baseline knowledge allowing the military to most efficiently use the information; and there was a marked absence of social scientists to produce valuable cultural knowledge.[87] It was to address these shortcomings that McFate and Jackson produced their briefing published in the *Military Review*. The result of the field test, however, was that the CPE tool was returned to the C-IED enterprise and as a tool the conclusion was that it lacked utility. As Fondacaro explains, "It was not granular enough, was not timely, the information sources for its content varied wildly. It was clear the unit had to do its own research, in its own AOR [Area of Responsibility] for the content to be relevant and usable."[88]

Despite the increased budget and raised profile, a DoD official interviewed by the Government Accountability Office (GAO) suggested that, by 2006, the temporary status of the Joint IED Task Force made attracting and retaining qualified personnel difficult.[89] This meant that working for the organization was fraught with professional uncertainty, making it difficult to recruit experienced personnel with the desired expertise. A temporary status for an organization which was central to combatting the crisis in Iraq was clearly unacceptable. Plans were already underway at the Office of the Deputy Secretary of Defense in late-2005 to make the organization permanent, which was achieved in February 2006 with *DoD Directive 2000.19E*, turning the task force into a permanent entity and jointly manned activity of the department. Renamed the Joint Improvised Explosive Device Defeat Organization (JIEDDO), the permanent structure now had a budget of U.S.$3.7 billion. This budget was delivered, according to one official, "with the intention to provide the institutional stability necessary to attract and retain qualified personnel."[90]

The establishment of that new organization was arranged in the absence of DoD having formal guidance for establishing joint organizations but rather developed through conversations between high-level officials in various departments and services. The ad hoc construction of the new organization, JIEDDO, along with its considerable budget, undertaken through informal channels and without official guidelines to implement a joint organization, demonstrated the fly-by-wire nature of the C-IED project and the ample resources allocated to it because of the nature of the IED crisis. That its *sui generis* procurement system was necessary also more broadly highlighted existing difficulties in the acquisition system which were not solved during the Iraq and Afghanistan conflicts. Importantly for the development of HTS, programs seeking JIEDDO funding were likewise largely configured without official oversight. In addition, Fondacaro had finished a tour for the organization and thus had credibility for program funding based on findings in the field. For funding, to rapidly field capabilities, only programs requiring over U.S.$25 million required annual briefings to the Deputy Secretary of Defense's Senior Resource Steering Group.[91] (See Figure 3-1.)

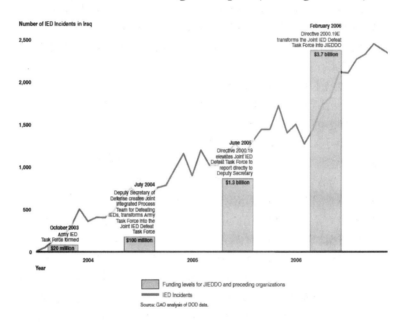

Source: Government Accountability Office, Washington, DC.

Figure 3-1. Evolution of C-IED Organizations Versus IED incidents in Iraq.

The organization had specific instruction from DoD to sponsor a spectrum of potential capabilities. While focus was on technology-based solutions, it could approve "some counter-IED initiatives without vetting them through the appropriate service counter-IED focal points because the process allows the organ-

134

isation to make exceptions if deemed necessary and appropriate."[92] In practice, this meant that the Director of JIEDDO C-IED training center could "make exceptions when training requirements and training support activities need to be accelerated to meet pre-deployment training requirements."[93] Such was the parallel importance of knowledge in the C-IED landscape that the organization bypassed its acquisition process by working directly with individual service units and organizations to address specific capability gaps.[94]

According to Vincent T. Clark of the U.S. Navy, JIEDDO was specifically created to "circumvent the bureaucratic processes of the Services."[95] Clark wrote of a "paradigm shift" in bureaucratic procedure, particularly in budgeting, allowing previous obstacles to be surmounted.[96] The organization worked with TRADOC to establish the Joint Training Counter-Improvised Explosive Device Operations and Integration Center. Although this went ahead without input from the Army's Asymmetric Warfare Office and sat uneasily with the Army's existing C-IED initiatives, it demonstrates the broad and strong development of a doctrinal aspect to counter the threat. McFarland had brought the idea for the center back from his work with the JIEDDTF, but it struggled for funds, as Fondacaro notes.[97]

In early-2006, Abizaid conceded in testimony before the House Appropriations Subcommittee on Defense that the IED was the "perfect asymmetric weapon" and "the single greatest source of our casualties," being "the enemy's most effective weapon."[98] The insurgency, however, was not easily defined, and, consequently, knowledge about the nature of the adversary in Iraq remained acutely inchoate. IEDs, Abizaid continued, were a "strategic threat," seemingly ubiquitous, adaptable, and continually augmented in their lethality.[99] At this point the U.S. Central Command focused its intelligence efforts on the IED challenge.[100] So great was the crisis that Abizaid stressed it was necessary to "mobilize our country's resources, *both military and civilian* [my italics], to better understand the region and the extremist enemies we face."[101] In a prepared statement before the House Armed Services Committee in November 2006, Abizaid emphasized the need in Iraq to invest in "more manpower and resources into the coalition military transition teams, speed the delivery of logistics, and mobility enablers."[102] Echoing the need for nonorganic additions to the military enterprise to assist in understanding, General Michael Maples, Director of the Defense Intelligence Agency, in a Senate hearing on Iraq and Afghanistan in that same month, described the situation in Iraq as "unquestionably complex and difficult."[103]

FOREIGN MILITARY STUDIES OFFICE

With Cultural Preparation for the Environment running into problems both with information and data presentation at TRADOC, Maxie McFarland, who both McFate and Andrea Jackson had known previously, asked McFate to participate in Unified Quest, the Army wargame run at the command. McFate and McFarland also met with John Agoglia, Director of the U.S. Army Peacekeeping and Stability Operations Institute at the U.S. Army War College, Carlisle, Pennsylvania, in Fort Monroe, Virginia, to discuss the basic idea of an HTS-type capability. With Andrea Jackson, McFate followed up with McFarland at Fort Leavenworth, Kansas, and McFarland noted that TRADOC was well-placed to develop an HTS capability within the Foreign Military Studies Office (FMSO).

Dr. Jacob Kipp, Karl Prinslow, Lester Grau, and Captain Don Smith, members of the FMSO, were then directed by McFarland to audit the weekly video teleconferences for the CPE capability where Fondacaro was briefing for small teams of experts to be embedded with brigades to offer a solution, instead of the tool which had notable shortcomings. All four men possessed expert knowledge of the Soviet experience with fighting Afghan and Chechen warriors, and the problems the Russians encountered fighting irregular conflicts in both countries.[104] Indicative of these professionals' expertise in identifying military capability gaps, in 1987, Lester Grau quoted Soviet General Shkirko on their Chechen experience, that the Soviets:

> did not have a war which had been expected, for which the troops and staffs were preparing, which had been studied in academies and planned accordingly, and which would have complied with regulations and field manuals.[105]

Don Smith, in particular, was enthusiastic about the idea of an HTS capability and met with McFate at Fort Leavenworth, where Smith expressed interest in taking the idea forward, which seemed logical to McFate, "Because this is something that has to happen in the military," and he was a uniformed military officer.[106] Cultural Preparation of the Environment was drawing to a conclusion, absent requisite funding and posting results of no value from the field.

The CPE tool, one of the many technologies Fondacaro oversaw in Iraq, was "chewed and regurgitated" data when what was required was "information that was a couple of days old."[107] The CPE, basically a laptop with data entered, was irrelevant, because the brigade commanders were already "drinking from a firehose turned on full blast" with databases and technologies from the PRT, the CIA, and myriad other entities, when what the commander needed was:

> living people, humans, on my staff, on my team . . . I need someone on my team doing research, going out on operations every day, explaining the granular problems I have and then telling me the recommendations they have in terms of Courses of Action. I need them to do all this work.[108]

As interest moved to an HTS capability of deployed social scientists as a successor to the poorly performing Cultural Preparation of the Environment, there were questions as to where it would sit in the military architecture, as the Joint Chiefs of Staff, J-3, home to Hriar Cabayan, lacked the ability to run joint programs. Personnel who worked on the CPE were meeting with different entities which possessed the capability to stage the HTS prototype, including the State Department Humanitarian Information Unit in March 2005, the Army Civil Affairs and Psychological Operations Command in June 2005, and the Marine Corps Intelligence Activity in July 2005, all of which refused. The FMSO then suggested that the capability could be housed with them at TRADOC.[109] Cabayan was sceptical of the FMSO arrangement, considering the office to be best suited to long-range analysis.[110] In addition, the most enthusiastic member of the FMSO, Don Smith, was only a captain, and it was uncertain if he possessed the stature to consolidate the program. However, Cabayan's Strategic Multi-Layer Assessment Group at the Pentagon agreed to transition the Cultural Preparation of the Environment capability to the FMSO for further development into an HTS prototype in February 2006; the CPE capability was the hardware which would come to form mapping the human terrain (MAP-HT).[111] Fondacaro, who had been a Joint IED Defeat Task Force commander in Iraq from 2005-06 and thus well known to McFarland, was transitioning to retirement when the HTS capability came up. This was also a meeting of minds; McFarland had been brought into the task force when Meigs began his appointment on December 12, 2005 — while retaining his role at TRADOC — and with an immediate responsibility to increase the intelligence capability of the task force. McFarland had also been present at the Baghdad briefings to Meigs by Fondacaro and Jackson.[112]

McFarland could act in a supervisory capacity for the FMSO program, and lacking viable, funded alternatives for the program as envisaged, the idea of developing a possible HTS prototype became integrated into the remit of the office. If the COIN requirement was so pronounced, there would have been a clamor from different entities in the Department of State and DoD to fund the program. There was no clamor, but at the FMSO, the particular areas of expertise of the staff gave them a heightened awareness of culture and sociocultural knowledge in stabilization operations, and:

> how it impacts not just decision-making at the highest levels, but down to the tactical level. And we saw this in Afghanistan in the [19]80s. That knowledge bled through everything the Foreign Military Studies Office did in the creation of HTS in the beginning — those guys' ability to understand different how perspectives impacted on warfighting was vitally important to where the programme came from.[113]

By April 2006 the FMSO team had a draft design for the HTS program, which was published in *Military Review*.[114]

Through his work with the C-IED initiatives, McFarland had seen firsthand in Iraq the necessity to move "left of bang," and to do that would require enhancing cultural awareness not only on the ground but in a pedagogic capacity.[115] McFarland was uniquely placed within the architecture of TRADOC as its G-2 Intelligence chief, and had seen firsthand the requirements for sociocultural information on the ground to enable such a transformation. McFarland created a steering committee for what was now termed the Cultural Operations Research-HTS prototype in July 2006. Smith and Fondacaro continued to attempt to procure funding for the program now that it had a physical home, but, as McFate explains of DoD budget allocation:

> it's not like venture capital in the civilian world where you've got a widget and you're going to go out and meet some guys in the Silicon Valley, and they are going to pony up $2 million. There is no one place in the Pentagon to go if you want to raise money so basically you just have to go meet as many people as you can, and this is what they were doing.[116]

In addition, as Fondacaro explains, at this point there was a "solid plan to operationalize HTS," and Dr. Robin Keesee, the Deputy JIEDDO Director, who approved the initial funding, was a human dynamics engineer that Fondacaro had previously employed on his team when he was running the Objective Force Soldier Study for General Eric Shinseki, Chief of Staff of the Army, when Fondacaro was a brigade commander in 2002.[117] Being the end of the Fiscal Year also worked in their favor; with unspent money in departments which could be spent quickly on unfulfilled requirements.[118] At the same time, they made a proposal for funds to JIEDDO for a U.S.$20.4 million five-team proof of concept and, with neither permanent office space nor training facilities, began the first HTT training with those funds.[119] The funding proposal for Cultural Operations Research-HTS therefore came from the C-IED enterprise. During this time and as part of this process, while expecting the proposal to move forward, the FMSO developed the prototype at TRADOC. They used reservists to assemble two field teams and two research teams, spending an estimated U.S.$700,000 in salaries and materiel. While the office lacked sufficient funds to deploy a team, training could begin.[120] It is unclear, however, where the U.S.$700,000 came from and may have formed part of the standard assigned salaries to the reservists as part of their active duty tour, paid wherever they deployed and thus not part of an HTS project per se but part of a budget which already existed.

Instructively, it was also JIEDDO which set the original proof-of-concept objectives in 2007: to provide brigade information and knowledge; to minimize loss in continuity between incoming and departing units; to archive cultural information to enhance operational effectiveness; and to maximize effectiveness of operational decisions by harmonizing courses of action with target area cultural knowledge.[121] In this original iteration for the proof-of-concept, there was no mention of interaction with the host population, and no allusion to COIN doctrine, despite it being an ascendant trope in policy. JIEDDO wanted the capability to provide cultural expertise to enhance operational effectiveness. But the physical home at TRADOC, cautioned against by Cabayan, was still problematic. Ultimately, in retrospect, Fondacaro observes that TRADOC "doesn't operationalize anything" and had no existing funds to develop the HTS concept itself, so that the priority for the longevity of the idea was:

> to get it started, because if you gain credibility, if you gain support, then you figure out where it is supposed to go. But there is no Department of Good Ideas in the Pentagon; there's no place like that. JIEDDO was as close as you could get to a new ideas funding source. And I had credibility there.[122]

Within a very short period after AF1 deployed to Afghanistan, The Multi-National Corps-Iraq JUONS was generated. This statement created a requirement for five teams to deploy to Iraq by mid-2007, the refreshing of AF1 as an enduring team, and 13 further teams and four Human Terrain Analysis Teams, the latter serving at the division level. This statement effectively jettisoned the original blueprint for a 2-year proof-of-concept program. The HTS was always an ad hoc program "to see what works, so we had, it was like 'It's an experiment, it's an in-situ experiment, I love grounded theory. Let us see what works'."[123] But after the JUONS, the HTS, instead of testing, experimenting, and analyzing these teams over time would be forced to create an entirely new enduring capability and thrust them into the field. In the words of Fondacaro: "We were building this plane in flight, that is what the JUONS did to us."[124] This new requirement marked a distinct evolution in the program; from the experimental, ad hoc nature of AF1, to a deliberate effort to replicate AF1 with the five teams in Iraq, as well as backfilling people into AF1.

The creation of the JUONS meant that Fondacaro, as program manager, met with the Joint Rapid

Acquisition Cell (JRAC) to determine whether to "fill or kill" the HTS capability; to designate it as an Immediate Warfighter Need.[125] The JRAC is instructive in the sense of building innovation through crisis; established in September 2004, it was, in Fondacaro's words as someone who briefed successfully to it, one of the "rapid workarounds created by the war."[126] The brief had to explain that without the capability there was risk of mission failure and put soldiers' lives at stake. As a result of the meeting, Fondacaro was promised U.S.$16 million, which was later expanded substantially, as part of organizations making surplus budgets available to the proof-of-concept program.

A program brief from May 2007 notes that the Under Secretary of Defense for Intelligence had developed a Surge Support Initiative in February 2007 that "recommended redirecting and expanding HTS to support operations in Iraq (Baghdad)" and that requests for HTTs had come from Command Groups of the 10th Mountain Division; II Marine Expeditionary Force; 1 Cavalry Division/III Corps; 82nd Airborne Division; Special Operations Command, Pacific; and the 4th Infantry Division.[127] At the same time as this rapid expansion into the combat brigades, Fondacaro had an ongoing, broader plan to transition the capability into a strategic one, housed at the Humanitarian Information Unit at the Department of State. The program creators initially had funding for the HTS capability turned down by the unit, but maintained engagement with the Department of State for funding and integration.

The briefing for CENTCOM and Multi-National Corps-Iraq in mid-2007 also included the raw results of two 10-person focus groups conducted by the Lincoln Group in Baghdad in June 2006, which "resulted in an increased understanding of opinion in Baghdad about several of the main issues facing the Coalition in Iraq" and the "participants expressed the opinion that the Iraqi government is weak or non-existent."[128] It was this understanding of the popular perception in the areas in which coalition forces fought that was seen as pivotal to winning against the insurgency. The briefing was also to include raw results from 34 interviews entitled "Mahdi army" which asked unnamed cases 77 questions ranging from demographics to perception of the insurgency.

In addition, a "Social Science Research and Analysis: Implementation Plan for Baghdad" presentation from Andrea V. Jackson, who had been Director of Research at the Lincoln Group and was a consultant to the HTS, proposed conducting in eight districts of Baghdad 1,500-person random sample surveys; 40 interviews with members of each militia; 40 interviews with members of each ethno-religious group; one set of two focus groups (one male, one female); and observational research based on a research question.[129] It was this aspect of the presentation from the work done by the Lincoln Group, which created the Social Science Research and Analysis (SSRA) element of the HTS program and which commenced in both Iraq and Afghanistan in 2008, subcontracted to Glevum Associates by BAE Systems. The SSRA Research and Analysis Management Team used indigenous contractors to conduct polling, surveys, focus groups and semi-structured interviews of the population on a variety of issues which could be useful in understanding and countering insurgencies, conducting quantitative and qualitative analysis of the results.

Against the backdrop of this initial and detailed assessment of what could be provisioned in order to fill a capability gap, the concept and the program developed robust support. As the teams were sent to Iraq and Afghanistan, their positive and negative effects on the brigades could be assessed, and also briefed. It was this ongoing, iterative process which allowed feedback on outcomes. On January 8, 2009, for example, Congressman Tim Baird, Chairman of the Science and Education Committee, set up a meeting which included Ike Skelton, Chairman of the Armed Service Committee; Tim McClees, Staff Director for the Subcommittee on Terrorism; and Mike Warren, an HTT leader. The meeting was a chance to outline the capabilities of an HTT to Skelton as well as existing shortcomings, and Skelton highlighted that, in his opinion, the capability should be expanded to Combatant Commands beyond CENTCOM, and that he wanted to assist with resourcing, when the Army identified requirements.

The solution to the capability gap offered by the HTS resonated further; across coalition partners in Afghanistan, where the complex social patterns required intricate understanding of the population in order to engage it effectively. From January 8 to January 9, 2009, Fondacaro and McFate met with representatives from the North Atlantic Treaty Organization's Joint Force Command, and the Strategic Communications Advisor, Supreme Headquarters Allied Powers Europe, to discuss integrating an HTS capability into the command structure in Afghanistan. The Joint Force Command were "unclear exactly what they desire" and ultimately for the HTS, it was "not clear what the support expectation from ISAF [International Security Assistance Force] actually is."[130] Additionally, the HTS program also engaged with the NATO Tiger Team to examine ways in which the role of culture could be integrated into interagency intelligence procedures.

CONCLUSIONS

Speaking in the throes of revolution, Abraham Lincoln observed:

> The dogmas of the quiet past are inadequate to the stormy present. The occasion is piled high with difficulty, and we must rise with the occasion. As our case is new, so we must think anew and act anew. We must disenthrall ourselves.[131]

Crises are existential threats which exert intolerable pressures upon the status quo. There is a necessity in the throes of a crisis to think anew and act anew. After the U.S.-led invasion of Iraq in 2003, military resistance proliferated to the extent that an examination of the enemy and the population in which they operated could not be ignored.

Despite its immense size, the intellectual tools and the experts necessary to understand the character of the human terrain at the granular level on the ground were absent from the military enterprise. That capability gap required prompt action: as Robert Gates argued at the National Defense University on September 29, 2008, "No one should ever neglect the psychological, cultural, political, and human dimensions of warfare."[132] To that end, the expertise found in the intellectual reservoir of the academy was considered a necessary and immediate addition to the warfighting effort because the military structure did not possess a:

> deeply rooted constituency inside the Pentagon or elsewhere for institutionalizing the capabilities necessary to wage asymmetric or irregular conflict—and to quickly meet the ever-changing needs of forces engaged in these conflicts.[133]

Future planning for irregular warfare had been proceeding in the periphery of military thought throughout the post-Vietnam era, but by 2006, Petraeus could suggest that the complex insurgencies experienced in Iraq and Afghanistan would become the central modality of conflict in this new century.[134] The pivot in planning was borne directly from a perceived necessity to understand the character of the adversary in order to attack the network behind the IEDs. The ensuing need to understand the terrain on a cultural level stood in marked contrast from the hubristic beginnings of Operation IRAQI FREEDOM in which there was "a relative lack of concern by the President and the top military leadership" regarding Iraqi culture and consultation with academic experts.[135] In the HTS in particular, there was an identified requirement to "understand the cloak in which the insurgent wrapped himself in: the population."[136] Focusing on the insurgent would lead to collateral damage and popular support for the insurgency. If the population's needs were met, the insurgents can be exposed and isolated.[137]

Early in his military career, Petraeus ghost-wrote a *Parameters* article for Southern Command commander General John Galvin.[138] In it, Petraeus observed the conditions necessary for a shift in emphasis in military thinking:

> We arrange in our minds a war we can comprehend on our own terms, usually with an enemy who looks like us and acts like us. This comfortable conceptualization becomes the accepted way of seeing things and, as such, ceases to be an object for further investigation unless it comes under serious challenge as a result of some major event — usually a military disaster.[139]

The rapidly expanding IED threat which spread from Iraq to Afghanistan was such a military disaster. But despite U.S.$20.4 million from the JIEDDO—the only funding the HTS could find—the program was not configured to trace IED networks. The MAP-HT was configured for social network analysis, like the CPE before it, in order to identify networks in the area, but it was used "to understand the problem in the AO [area of operations] in all its dimensions, educate the BCT and plan research."[140] Fondacaro had planned to transition the HTS into the Department of State and MAP-HT was a tool which would facilitate that migration. As noted in the Concept of Operations:

> The mission of MAP-HT is to support multi-disciplined Civil, Social analysis through dynamic fusion of data throughout the civil picture that will require interaction between Non-Governmental Organizations, Governmental Organizations, and Interactional Organizations.[141]

The HTS ended as a quasi-nongovernmental organization (NGO) disavowing any assistance to kinetic targeting. The emerging COIN milieu of military thinking quoted in the 2006 FM *Counterinsurgency* as the "graduate level of war" heightened the ability of the HTS to recruit from the civilian sector as it promised smart war, superior tactical thinking in order to conduct more population-centric operations.

In crises, we think anew and act anew.

ENDNOTES - CHAPTER 3

1. American Anthropological Association, *Final Report on the Army's Human Terrain System Proof of Concept Program*, Arlington, VA: American Anthropological Association, p. 3.

2. Christopher J. Lamb *et al.*, *Human Terrain Teams: An Organizational Innovation for Sociocultural Knowledge in Irregular Warfare*, Washington, DC: Institute of World Politics Press, 2013, p. 1.

3. Hugh Gusterson, "Anthropology and Militarism," *Annual Review of Anthropology*, Vol. 36, 2007, p. 164.

4. Patrick Porter, *Military Orientalism: Eastern War through Western Eyes*, London, UK: Hurst and Company, 2009, p. 7.

5. Derek Gregory, "The Rush to the Intimate: Counterinsurgency and the Cultural Turn," *Radical Philosophy*, Vol. 150, 2008, p. 16.

6. *Ibid.*, p. 17.

7. George Packer, *The Assassins' Gate: America in Iraq*, New York: Farrar, Straus and Giroux, 2005.

8. Fred Kaplan, *The Insurgents: David Petraeus and the Plot to Change the American Way of War*, New York: Simon & Schuster, 2013.

9. Ralph Peters, "Progress and Peril: New Counterinsurgency Manual Cheats on the History Exam," *Armed Forces Journal*, February 1, 2007.

10. Janine Davidson, *Lifting the Fog of Peace: How Americans Learned to Fight Modern War*, Ann Arbor, MI: University of Michigan Press, 2010.

11. David Kilcullen, "Countering Global Insurgency," *Small Wars Journal*, November 30, 2004.

12. Montgomery McFate, "The Military Utility of Understanding Adversary Culture," *Joint Force Quarterly*, Vol. 38, 2005, p. 43.

13. David Petraeus, "Learning Counterinsurgency: Observations from Soldiering in Iraq," *Military Review*, Vol. 86, No. 1, 2006, p. 11.

14. Quoted in Vernon Loeb, "Instead of Force, Persuasion," *The Washington Post*, November 5, 2003.

15. Paul Joseph, *"Soft" Counterinsurgency: Human Terrain Teams and U.S. Strategy in Iraq and Afghanistan*, New York: Palgrave Pivot, July 8, 2014, pp. 2-3.

16. *Ibid.*, p. 19.

17. Yvette Clinton *et al.*, *Congressionally Directed Assessment of the Human Terrain System*, Arlington, VA: Center for Naval Analyses, 2010, p. 1.

18. Montgomery McFate, interview with author, Newport, RI, August 1, 2013. For the controversy and debate in DoD over McFate's draft of her section of Chap. 3, see Kaplan, pp. 213-219.

19. Audrey Roberts, "'Embedding with the Military in Eastern Afghanistan: The Role of Anthropologists in Peace and Stability Operations," Walter E. Feichtinger, Ernst M. Felberbauer, and Erwin A. Schmidl, eds., *International Crisis Management: Squaring the Circle*, Vienna, Austria, and Geneva, Switzerland: National Defense Academy and Austrian Ministry of Defense and Sports in cooperation with Geneva Centre for Security Policy, 2011, p. 90.

20. Vanessa Gezari, *The Tender Soldier: A True Story of War and Sacrifice*, New York: Simon and Schuster, 2013, p. 24.

21. Following Thomas Kuhn, I define a "crisis" as constituted by "a pronounced failure in the normal problem solving activity," where "Failure of existing rules is the prelude to a search for new ones." Thomas S. Kuhn, *The Structure of Scientific Revolutions*, 3rd Ed., Chicago, IL, and London, UK: The University of Chicago Press, 1996, pp. 68, 74-75.

22. Thomas Metz, "Defeating the Improvised Explosive Device and Other Asymmetric Threats: Today's Efforts and Tomorrow's Requirements, Joint Improvised Explosive Device Defeat Organization," Hearing Before the Committee on Armed Services, Oversight and Investigations Subcommittee, Washington, DC: U.S. Government, September 16, 2008.

23. Christopher J. Lamb, Matthew J. Schmidt, and Berit G. Fitzsimmons, "MRAPs, Irregular Warfare, and Pentagon Reform," Occasional Paper 6, Washington, DC: Institute for National Strategic Studies, National Defense University Press, 2009, p. 1.

24. *Ibid.*

25. *Ibid.*

26. *Ibid.*, pp. 1-2.

27. Stephen J. Hedges, "U.S. Battles Low-Tech Threat," *Chicago Tribune*, October 23, 2003.

28. Christopher J. Lamb, Matthew J. Schmidt and Berit G. Fitzsimmons, "MRAPs, Irregular Warfare, and Pentagon Reform," *Joint Force Quarterly*, Vol. 55, 2009, p. 77.

29. John P. Abizaid, Commander, U.S. Central Command, Iraqi Reconstruction, Hearing before the Committee on Armed Services, U.S. Senate, 108th Cong., 1st Sess., Washington, DC: U.S. Government Printing Office (USGPO), September 25, 2003.

30. *Ibid.*

31. *Ibid.*

32. *Ibid.*

33. Christopher Sims, "Fighting the Insurgents' War in Afghanistan," *Small Wars Journal*, January 12, 2012.

34. Abizaid, Iraqi Reconstruction, Hearing before the Committee on Armed Services.

35. *Ibid.*

36. "Warfighter Support: Actions Needed to Improve Visibility and Coordination of DOD's Counter-Improvised Explosive Device Efforts," Report to Congressional Committees, GAO-10-95, Washington, DC: U.S. Government Accountability Office (US-GAO), October 2009, p. 9.

37. *Ibid.*, p. 10.

38. *Ibid.*

39. *Ibid.*

40. *Ibid.*

41. Quoted in James J. Lovelace and Joseph L. Votel, "The Asymmetric Warfare Group: Closing the Capability Gaps," *Army Magazine*, Vol. 55, No. 3, 2005, p. 34.

42. *Ibid.*, p. 31.

43. *Ibid.*

44. "Warfighter Support," USGAO, p. 13.

45. Gezari, p. 35.

46. Lamb *et al.*, *Human Terrain Teams*, p. 27.

47. *Ibid.*, p. 29.

48. Cited in Montgomery McFate and Steve Fondacaro, "Reflections on the Human Terrain System during the First 4 Years," *PRISM*, Vol. 2, No. 4, p. 66.

49. McFate interview.

50. Steve Fondacaro, personal communication with author, September 15, 2015.

51. *Ibid.*

52. Lamb *et al.*, *Human Terrain Teams*, p. 32.

53. *Ibid.*

54. *Ibid.*, p. 34.

55. *Ibid.*

56. Lovelace and Votel, p. 30.

57. *Ibid.*

58. *Ibid.*, pp. 31-32.

59. William G. Adamson, "An Asymmetric Threat Invokes Strategic Leader Initiative: The Joint Improvised Explosive Device Defeat Organization," Industrial College of the Armed Forces (ICAF) Research Paper, Washington, DC: National Defense University, 2007, p. 21.

60. Lamb *et al.*, *Human Terrain Teams*, pp. 27-28.

61. *Ibid.*, p. 28.

62. *Ibid.*

63. Montgomery McFate and Andrea Jackson, "An Organizational Solution for DOD's Cultural Knowledge Needs," *Military Review*, Vol. 85, No. 4, 2005, pp. 18-21.

64. McFate interview.

65. *Ibid.*

66. *Ibid.*

67. Montgomery McFate, "Iraq: The Social Context of IEDs," *Military Review*, Vol. 85, No. 3, 2005, p. 37.

68. *Ibid.*

69. *Ibid.*

70. *Ibid.*

71. *Ibid.*

72. *Ibid.*, p. 38.

73. *Ibid.*, p. 39.

74. *Ibid.*

75. McFate interview.

76. *Ibid.*

77. Hedges.

78. National Public Radio, "U.S. Military Works to Combat I.E.D.s in Iraq," November 4, 2005.

79. *Ibid.*

80. "General: Insurgents Upgrading Explosives Used in Attacks," *World Tribune,* June 14, 2005.

81. *Ibid.*

82. Montgomery C. Meigs, "Unorthodox Thoughts about Asymmetric Warfare," *Parameters,* Vol. 33, No. 2, 2003, p. 5.

83. *Ibid.*

84. Adamson, p. 51.

85. George Packer, "Knowing the Enemy," *The New Yorker,* December 18, 2006.

86. *Ibid.*

87. McFate and Fondacaro, p. 66.

88. Fondacaro, personal communication with author, September 15, 2015.

89. "Warfighter Support," USGAO, pp. 13-14.

90. *Ibid.,* p. 14.

91. *Ibid.,* p. 20.

92. *Ibid.,* p. 18.

93. *Ibid.,* p. 19.

94. *Ibid.*

95. Vincent T. Clark, "The Future of JIEDDO—The Global C-IED Synchronizer," Newport, RI: Naval War College, Department of Joint Military Operations, October 31, 2008, p. iii.

96. *Ibid.*, p. 10.

97. Fondacaro, telephone interview with author, September 15, 2015.

98. John P. Abizaid, Commander, United States Central Command, House Appropriations Subcommittee on Defense, U.S. Congress, *Command Posture*, Washington, DC: Government Printing Office, March 15, 2006.

99. *Ibid.*

100. *Ibid.*, p. 55.

101. *Ibid.*, p. 59.

102. John P. Abizaid, Commander, United States Central Command, Iraq and Afghanistan, "Hearing Before the Committee on Armed Services," 109th U.S. Cong., 2nd Sess., Washington, DC: USGPO, November 15, 2006, p. 2.

103. *Ibid.*, p. 3.

104. Lester W. Grau, "Bashing the Laser Range Finder with a Rock," *Military Review*, Vol. 77, No. 3, 1997, pp. 42-48; Lester W. Grau and Jacob W. Kipp, "Urban Combat: Confronting the Specter," *Military Review*, Vol. 79, No. 4, 1999, pp. 9-17.

105. Grau, "Bashing the Laser Range Finder," p. 42. I thank Michael Davies for referencing this early work to me.

106. McFate interview.

107. Fondacaro, telephone interview with author, September 15, 2015.

108. *Ibid.*

109. McFate interview.

110. *Ibid.*

111. Lamb *et al., Human Terrain Teams*, p. 30.

112. *Ibid.*, p. 31.

113. Michael Davies, interview with author, Washington, DC, August 10, 2013.

114. Lamb *et al., Human Terrain Teams*, p. 31.

115. The phrase "left of bang" is a retrospective of a phrase used at that time, but published in 2013 by Michael T. Flynn, James Sisco, and David C. Ellis, "'Left of Bang': The Value of Sociocultural Analysis in Today's Environment," *PRISM*, Vol. 3, No. 4, 2013, pp. 13-21.

116. McFate interview.

117. Fondacaro, personal communication with author, September 15, 2005.

118. *Ibid.*

119. Further limiting the program, the funding was approved by JIEDDO in June 2006 but only half the funds were released, in August 2006, with the remainder provided when progress had been proven. Fondacaro interview.

120. Lamb *et al., Human Terrain Teams*, p. 32.

121. Clinton *et al.*, p. 61.

122. Fondacaro, telephone interview with author, September 15, 2015.

123. McFate interview.

124. Fondacaro, telephone interview with author, September 15, 2015.

125. *Ibid.*

126. *Ibid.*

127. Bob Reuss and Steve Fondacaro, "Human Terrain System (HTS) Update to GEN Wallace," TRADOC/DCSINT, May 17, 2007.

128. Lincoln Group, Baghdad Focus Groups, June 6, 2006.

129. Andrea V. Jackson, "Social Science Research and Analysis: Implementation Plan for Baghdad," Presentation, June 13, 2007.

130. Steve Fondacaro, "EXSUM: HTS Coordination with MG Hahn, DCOS, NATO JFC," January 11, 2009.

131. Quoted in Allan Nevins, ed., *The Strategy of Peace by John F. Kennedy*, New York; Evanston, IL; and London, UK: Harper & Row, 1960, Introduction.

132. DoD, Office of the Assistant Secretary of Defense, Speech as delivered by Secretary of Defense Robert M. Gates, Washington, DC: National Defense University, September 29, 2008.

133. *Ibid.*

134. David H. Petraeus, "Learning Counterinsurgency: Observations from Soldiering in Iraq," *Military Review*, Vol. 86, No. 1, 2006, p. 11.

135. Geoff Emberling, "Archaeologists and the Military in Iraq, 2003-2008: Compromise or Contribution?" *Archaeologies*, Vol. 4, No. 3, 2008, p. 449.

136. Fondacaro, telephone interview with author, September 15, 2015.

137. *Ibid.*

138. Kaplan.

139. John R. Galvin, "Uncomfortable Wars: Towards a New Paradigm," *Parameters*, Vol. 26, No. 4, 1986, p. 2.

140. Fondacaro, personal communication with author, September 15, 2015.

141. Human Terrain System, "Concept of Operations (CONOPS) for the Mapping the Human Terrain (MAP-HT) Joint Capability Demonstration: DRAFT," October 2009.

CHAPTER 4

TRIAL, ERROR, AND AMENDMENT

The Human Terrain System (HTS) began as a start-up program from a proof-of-principle in 2006, with the intention of putting two teams into Afghanistan and three teams into Iraq. Training and recruitment were designed *de novo*, and continually revised as part of an ongoing reflective process.[1] As Janice H. Laurence notes, the:

> HTS was experimental, and thus the whole HTS program, especially training, was meant to evolve. As a learning organization, HTS adjusted to experience on the ground as the organization learned how to serve the military mission better. Training was iterative; the composition of teams was iterative; human capital strategies and program and personnel management practices were iterative. One might even say that the whole war was iterative.[2]

The original concept of operations for the program completed in January 2007 left the role of the embedded team on the brigade staff unspecified because the team was a new tool for the U.S. Army, and it was not known how best to proceed. However, a brigade commander cited in that original concept had envisioned a permanent presence of the embedded team on staff, along with other elements deployed to the forward operating bases (FOBs). This was how AF1 was configured, with team roles being a team leader, cultural analyst, regional studies analyst, research manager, and human terrain analyst.[3]

In April 2007, the concept of operations was refined to provide specific recruitment and new posi-

159

tions for the five Iraq teams, IZ1 to IZ5, which would become the blueprint for the Human Terrain Teams (HTTs). The roles were now: team leader; two social scientists; a research manager; and a human terrain analyst.[4] As a result of lessons learned from AF1, the roles of the HTT were refined and broadly could "improve the human terrain understanding of the brigade staff."[5] The structure of the teams and the identities and functions of those in it had been difficult to deduce from the beginning. Steve Fondacaro had been at Fort Leavenworth, Kansas, from May 2006, and in 2007 took AF1 to FOB Salerno, Italy, for 2 weeks. Despite being immersed, the team roles did not emerge as obvious ones, but the HTS wanted social science research and thus there was a "social scientist" role from the beginning.[6] Instructive in the complexity of recruitment, AF1 team leader Rick Swisher was hired through a BAE Systems subcontractor, Echota.

In a May 2007 brief to outline how HTS filled a "tactical" capability gap, Fondacaro and Bob Reuss note that "COIN [counterinsurgency] and 4th Generation Warfare has clearly identified people as the Center of Gravity in future conflict" and that "at present, no capability exists to research, process and apply information on the local population."[7] To solve the problem, the proof-of-concept objectives as outlined were to provide the brigade combat team (BCT)/regional command team (RCT) commanders with the means to "collect, process, and apply relevant, sociocultural data, information, knowledge and understanding" and to "integrate that understanding into their military decisionmaking process"; enhance continuity of action between units during Relief in Place/Transfer of Authority; provide a support structure to "research, interpret, archive and make readily available cultural data, information and knowledge"; and, "Maximize effectiveness of tactical operations by harmonizing COAs [Courses of Action] with target area cultural context (population)."[8]

The three pillars of support to the brigade were divided into collection, analysis, and application. Collection was subdivided into:

> Patrol Debriefs (U.S./Indigenous); SOF [Special Operations Forces]; NGOs [Non-Governmental Organizations]; PRT [Provincial Reconstruction Team]; LEPs [Law Enforcement Professionals]; CA/PSYOP [Civil Affairs/Psychological Operations]; Survey Data; Local Hires; Special Events.[9]

In order to train recruits in each of the three pillars, the May 2007 brief outlines a 3- to 4-month training program which would include:

> Social Science Field Research Methods Training; Map-Human Terrain (MAP-HT) Toolkit Training; Area Orientation/Study; Counterinsurgency (COIN) Instruction; Capstone Exercise (BCT MDMP); Basic Military Common Skills.[10]

Training was an iterative process. Complex training elements such as the teaching of advanced military tradecraft—for example, behavior in key leader engagements—is "something that HTS in the beginning didn't have time to do," and it continued to be "hard to develop a way to communicate that uniformly throughout the program, coherently, cohesively, over time."[11] The troop surge in Iraq and commensurate expansion of the number of HTTs required in the country to support deployed brigades meant that the pace of, and demands on, the program did not allow opportunities to implement fixes.[12] Of the primary researchers with the teams, the initial focus was on social scientists, the first of which was a cultural anthropologist. The expansion period in 2007 to equip the surge is indicative of the malleable and amorphous identity of the program in its earliest stages, which gained initial funding from both counterterrorism (CT) and counter-improvised explosive device (C-IED) sources.

Under pressure to develop the HTS as a program-of-record and given the expanding numerical requirement for embedded teams, it was difficult to address problematic contours between the program, its contractor, BAE Systems, and its parent, the U.S. Training and Doctrine Command (TRADOC). As a program start-up, financing was the core concern and senior management was working on that aspect. From his perspective as BAE Systems program manager, David Zacharias asserted that Montgomery McFate and Fondacaro were a powerful force, driving the HTS and securing funding.[13] Fondacaro himself notes that McFate was able to produce the theoretical social science frameworks, while he provided the operational knowledge and understood the military enterprise, ultimately tessellating to produce a viable program architecture for the HTS.[14]

The iterative process meant that it became a necessity to formalize lessons learned from the field. These lessons were captured from both within the embedded teams and from feedback from the brigade and the divisions that were using them—U.S. and coalition partners—and examine the best way to train team members specifically and more generally improve the program. Some of these investigations were from program resources and some were externally directed; they included the West Point study, Paul Joseph at

Tufts University, the Center for Naval Analyses and the Institute for Defense Analyses between 2008 and 2010.[15] In addition, the Training and Doctrine Command (TRADOC) found that the HTS had not used "good judgement" on which people "could deploy and live in an austere environment and serve there for 9 months or more."[16]

The problem of hiring was not resolved for the duration of the program's time in Iraq and Afghanistan. It created a serious division between the HTS program management and its parent, TRADOC, which was the recipient of significant funding from both the Army G-2 and the Department of Defense (DoD) for the sociocultural capability. Screening for the program did not involve a specialized team to hire for social science positions. This is problematic because social science itself is "very fluid; there are many ways to be a social scientist. You have to define what the field encompasses."[17] Jennifer Clark explains that the program "did not individually select. If I didn't have the background I did, or the personality I have, I would have failed miserably. So part of that is personality so how do you code for personality? You can't."[18]

Coding for personality is certainly problematic, but rigorous interviews are not. BAE Systems had a thin, *laissez-faire* recruitment process, as related by the majority of HTT social scientists interviewed in the book. There are four requirements for effective HTT social scientists: first, regional area expertise, the knowledge component; second, field experience, the practical component; third, physical ability, the dynamic component; and fourth, mental adaptability, the psychological component. Interview phases grouped around each component in turn would ensure the very highest caliber of recruits to the program. The first three components are self-explanatory and easy to access through examination while the fourth requires further refinement for assessment.

Ultimately, this points to the overriding problem of the application of social science techniques to war-fighting. Unlike a technological solution, social science cannot be taken out of a box and applied in a prescriptive manner to an obvious end.[19] Definition of success in the application of social science is problematic, and, for that reason, demonstrating value over time is arduous, based around unmeasurable dimensions of amorphous notions such as "understanding" or "culture." The problematic application is mirrored in recruiting.

In the summer of 2008, the HTS and TRADOC contacted PDRI, a training solutions company, to assess the recruitment and selection process, partly because of the difficulty in defining jobs which did not previously exist, partly because of contracting issues. Published in February 2009, the report observed that the recruitment process was so dispiriting that it was reasonable to assume self-selection out of the process was continuing out of "frustration with a contractor."[20] As part of that evaluation, PDRI also created a structured interview pilot test on which to evaluate current HTT trainees at Fort Leavenworth. The evaluation highlighted that some personnel in training in all roles, "provided responses that showed they were unable to work effectively with others when dealing with challenging situations."[21] In addition: "Several trainees for all HTT jobs provided responses that indicated they would have problems dealing with individuals from other cultures."[22]

For future research platforms that might address this complex problem, there is a wealth of experience resident in former HTT personnel regarding "what works" when embedded. Assessing feedback from each HTT member regarding every other member of that team and coding thematically would allow a deeper picture of the ideal social science disciplines, ideal level of academic attainment, age, language capability, personality traits, skills, research methods, and gender comments to emerge. For example, female HTT social scientists, especially in Afghanistan, could engage more easily the "forgotten 50 percent" of that society. From that detailed picture of 7 years of HTS across two COIN campaigns, a picture will crystalize of optimum capabilities and psychologies. This will resonate beyond the program itself because personality examination has connotations for all Armed Service components concerned with intrateam dynamics.

To examine what the program management considered to be the optimum HTT social scientist, I investigate the training cycle and its evolution through development groups created by the program. Better understanding of the role of social scientists in Iraq and Afghanistan can be gained by examination of the internal investigation of HTT performance conducted during the period of program revision. This evolutionary process based on lessons learned, feedback from commanders and best practice sheds light on the ways in which the U.S. Army, as the primary customer, wanted to utilize embedded teams and thus goes to the heart of the question.

RECRUITMENT

Why was recruitment for the program problematic? In answering this question, I include material from an interview conducted with Zacharias, BAE

Systems program manager for the HTS between 2008 and 2009. Zacharias, who was the third BAE Systems program manager for the HTS and entered during a period when the relations between the HTS and TRADOC had already deteriorated, explains that recruitment during the early period incorporated a blanket approach, including papers and websites, with most of the applicants citing the website advertisements as being where they first saw the vacancies.[23] From the beginning, starting with AF1 team leader Swisher, private contractors were used for teams because of the difficulty of recruiting from the existing DoD pool. The omni-contractor for TRADOC, BAE Systems, was awarded the contracting role without a tender process.

The recruitment process was *laissez-faire*. During his time with the program, Zacharias estimates that there was approximately an 80 percent success rate of the people accepted for interview.[24] This high success rate was a result of the contract; BAE Systems were given no bonus for the quality of the contractor and were not forced to bid for the contract. The high success rate was also a result of a gulf between the program and the contractor. Social science was an abstract term, and there appears no attempt to refine the selection process for the social scientist. BAE Systems managers were not convinced that the concept of a social scientist held tangible substance.[25] HTS managers were working from a "best guess" about what might work in Iraq and Afghanistan. The HTS management in order to define the role of social scientist had given BAE Systems a list of graduate degrees that management "believed constituted a social science degree."[26] This list included anthropology, sociology, social psychology, cultural geography, political science including International Relations, area studies, and especially expertise sets related to the Middle East or Central

Asia. Moreover, "field experience" was of interest to the HTS management, as was personnel who had qualitative backgrounds; showing that the program was always configured as primarily a qualitative research function.[27]

The Iraq surge requirements prompted BAE Systems to accelerate its use of subcontractors that had their own recruiters, and, as the rapid expansion of the number of teams created hiring tensions, David Zacharias took over the BAE Systems management for the program.[28] The contractor assessment has been largely obscured in recent studies, with the exception of the Center for Naval Analyses investigation and thus has value in investigating further here. Highlighting the amorphous nature of social science and the difficulty of comprehension, Zacharias observes that HTS "needed anthropologists and they needed social scientists, but I would say that it was harder to come by the anthropologists than it was a social scientists, so it turned into a social science hunt."[29] But, from the beginning, the HTS was always configured to employ "social scientists" as noted in the original blueprints for HTT structure. Moreover, both HTT personnel and at least one BAE Systems subcontractor have expressed dissatisfaction at the BAE Systems role and function.

The problematic definition of social science manifests most acutely in the contracting requirement, where the disconnect between the HTS program management and the TRADOC omnibus contractor was pronounced. As Zacharias notes of his time as BAE Systems program manager, "What kind of credentials do you need to be a social scientist? How do you choose a social scientist? I don't know and neither did they."[30] This, however, fails to explain the scope and severity of the contracting missteps. Returning to the four components identified as core to an HTT social scientist — knowledge, practical, physical, and psychological components — the social science component is only one section of the requirement. The program still hired physically ill-suited individuals, personnel who lacked field experience, and personalities which were overtly immiscible in training and when embedded with brigades. The HTS program could not vet hires, only reject them when they arrived at Fort Leavenworth to begin the training cycle. With the urgent requirement to field teams, this created a dangerous situation where there was a necessity to embed personnel, and resulted in the arrangement where many former personnel have related teams becoming dysfunctional when embedded in the brigades.

The dialogue between the program management, TRADOC, and BAE Systems became fraught, having a deleterious impact on any attempt to remedy the fractious relationship. This disconnect may have gone unnoticed in a less visible program, but the HTS was the subject of intense media and academic scrutiny. McFate and Fondacaro were not bureaucrats. Working effectively with BAE Systems to develop improved selection processes would require significant interaction and collaboration. This was a controversial program which embedded civilians into combat brigades, and it would have required sustained dialogue between both parties — BAE Systems and the program management — in order to quickly refine the recruitment process. The opposite occurred, and worsened to the extent that, when the BAE Systems contract for the HTS was offered to tender, TRADOC did not inform the HTS of the process when it began.

The HTS management had minimal ability to set the job skills or influence the hiring process. Further, the dimensions of the Iraq surge of forces amplified the problem by necessitating a large number of contractors to be recruited rapidly and quickly embedded. While the interview process has come in for substantial criticism from former team members interviewed, there were positive endorsements of some contacts regarding subcontractors, which strongly suggest that if the contractor in the first instance had been selected carefully, the net effect of the program may have been altered, perhaps minimally but also perhaps significantly. One social scientist who deployed to Afghanistan noted that the interview process over the phone, the first contact with the program, actually added to his or her motivation to join the program because of the competent, caring nature of the contact. The social scientist at this point already knew of the myriad concerns regarding the program, but the contact gave the individual names of people to talk to who were already in the program, and engaged in substantial conversations about the type of research which would be undertaken, the risks, and the negatives in the program.[31] Ultimately, the contact was lucid about the problems, the serious issue regarding recently issued Status of Forces Agreement, such that the social scientist went into the program "fairly well informed."[32] This conversation was with BAE Systems subcontractor Alion, an employee-owned technology solutions company. The positive feedback is important as it suggests that careful selection of the recruiting contractor could have created more positive feedback of the process and prevented many of the hiring missteps. Indeed, PDRI, in its assessment of recruitment, stated that: "There is substantial variation in the selection procedures used by contractors after the initial resume screen."[33] Moreover, "Several subcontractors noted that it was often unclear what BAE Systems was looking for in a candidate."[34]

In addition, the absence of small-team assessment protocols or personality assessment protocols in the recruitment process meant that there could be myriad problems which crystallized acutely in Iraq and Afghanistan to devastating effect. As one former HTT social scientist explains:

> If you have this very relaxed recruitment process you are going to get a lot of people who don't belong on the program and certainly don't belong in a war zone: and they don't belong in a small-team environment in a war-zone because these are all very stressful things.[35]

Given the poor suitability of many hired personnel, which deleteriously impacted the reputation of the program at best and hindered combat brigades at worst, recruitment issues were a singular problem in HTS throughout the program's lifespan in Iraq and Afghanistan. As one social scientist explains, "It all started with recruitment and selection, and then training, and everything else just piles on top."[36]

In practice, the *laissez-faire* contracting meant that there were a number of recruits in the training cycle who were ill-equipped whether academically, physically, or psychologically to insert into a combat brigade. The idea and passion of Fondacaro drove the program forward, and McFate's intellect provided the pedagogic fabric which conditioned the teams, but there were vast tears in the cloth which resulted in problems in Iraq and Afghanistan, where, embedded in combat brigades with high operational tempo, the deficiencies were magnified. Zacharias notes that he could name more team failures than successful teams.[37] In context, the quantitative assessment is purely anecdotal and based on perception from someone removed from the HTS program management, but it hints at the magnitude of the failing in this critical area. The capability gap was real, but filling it with ill-suited recruits did not provide an effective solution. Insufficient training of military command structures, low standards of recruiting, high pay relative to the military units in which they embedded, lack of operationally relevant products and poor interpersonal skills could contribute to the problem. When AF5 was ordered to leave FOB Shank, Afghanistan, in the winter of 2009-10, to become a battalion support element at FOB Airborne, Afghanistan, it was unprofessionalism in the HTT and poor relationships with the unit which caused the relocation. The absence of a strong HTS bureaucracy or in-country oversight also limited the ability of the program to correct problems when they arose in theater.

Problems in the program's natural evolution thus stem from this contract hiring process. There was not enough oversight of BAE Systems by the program management in the beginning of the program, and the problems were not solved. BAE Systems was a technology corporation, and the services element was new and, as a consequence, underdeveloped. In its infancy with such work, BAE Systems should have been monitored more closely, and there should have been collaboration rather than confrontation. In the end, a "jaundiced eye" marked the relationship which was increasingly detrimental to the program. This continually placed manifestly ill-suited personnel into the training cycle and created this empirically observed five-to-one ratio of functioning to nonfunctioning teams. The successes of AF1 showed it could be done, but they just had to find the right people because, if they did not do so, a brigade would reject the embedded team at first contact.

As Fondacaro notes in a memo written during the surge of forces in Iraq, screening up until that point for HTS had been "somewhat "hand-to-mouth"" and that, while BAE Systems had improved its "responsiveness to HTS with regard to applicant screening and coordination with HTS staff" there was a need for urgent improvement given the expanded scope of the program necessitated by the JUONS.[38] Fondacaro explains that the HTS managers:

> require additional support. In particular, we need people who have appropriate human resource skills to screen resumes, engage candidates, and hire HTT members . . . We must avoid hiring unqualified candidates because of hasty and deficient screening.[39]

As the quality of the candidates arriving at Ft. Leavenworth continued to be highly variable, it was inevitable that the personal relationships between the HTS management, the primary contractor, and the TRADOC parent would deteriorate, with significant implications for the character of the program as a whole.

Nevertheless, according to Zacharias, in 2008, the managers in the BAE Systems team working on the HTS program won one of the Chairman's Awards, an annual prize-giving which rewarded outstanding contributions to the profile of the company.[40] In part, this may have been to capitalize on the intense media publicity surrounding the program after positive reports from outlets including *The New York Times* and the British Broadcasting Corporation. Zacharias, however, remains sceptical of the enterprise today: "It was a prestigious award, given because it was so unique what we were doing. But it was miss-sold [the civilian expertise providing sociocultural capability to BCTs]."[41] Sociocultural capability in war is an abstract concept, one which McFate notes has few historically comparable examples. To create a recruitment process so quickly without detailed guidelines, after the original model for five teams embedded over 2 years had been quickly and inexorably expanded, led to strategic missteps.

By 2009, after the contractor deaths, and negative publicity about the relationship between BAE Systems and the program management, recruitment, and training, the attitude from BAE Systems management hardened irreversibly. For Zacharias, it crystalized around the contractor deaths:

> we had three people killed. And that was the overriding factor for BAE Systems; when you pay out six million dollars for each death, it drives home that this is a very liable system. You get a bunch of people killed, at six million apiece, pretty soon, three hundred million dollar program, doesn't take many people.[42]

Zacharias attended the funeral of Paula Loyd which casts the role of BAE Systems in a strange hue; at once it was a human enterprise, but at the same time, it was a contractor with a bottom line. The HTS, like any other BAE Systems contract, was subject to a cost/benefit ratio analysis despite the immense scale of the personal tragedies unfolding on the program.

Lack of bureaucracy hampered the program in wider ways beyond the contracting. Going from "zero to a hundred miles an hour with no prep time" meant that there was little available time for program structure development.[43] As McFate explains:

> We didn't have the personnel to manage a program that large, and we didn't have the budget; the whole

budget that we had was geared towards teams, not to staffing. So we had no money, we had no manpower, we had no facilities.[44]

The program office was opened in Newport News, Virginia, but the staff was split between Fort Leavenworth, Kansas, and Newport News, with the result that upper management were divided from the training facility, and, put bluntly by McFate, "that just doesn't work."[45] As well as management facilities, an operations cell was created to be staffed 24 hours a day, with space made available from the C-IED Operational Intelligence Center, an underfunded initiative McFarland had created upon his return from the JIED-DTF (showing again, from a different angle, the early relationship between the HTS and C-IED initiatives). The program sat beneath the TRADOC Intelligence Support Activity in the organizational chart, which reported to the G-2. Ultimately, at this time, it was "live and learn."[46] The expansion as part of the Iraq surge of forces, while a "catastrophic success," also enabled a wide number of research initiatives on the experiences of the embedded teams to be conducted; such that the period 2008-10 was about trying to systematize what they had done originally in a way that would ensure success in the future.[47]

The program structure and the status of embedded team members were complicated by the prohibition of private contractors after 2008: The U.S.-Iraq Status of Forces Agreement commenced January 1, 2009, prohibited all U.S. private contractors from operating in Iraq. Consequently, HTT personnel transitioned from contractors to government civilians which exerted a profound impact on program hiring. There was no obvious corresponding government civilian position which had an equivalent remuneration package to the HTT social scientist position as a private contractor. To

174

ensure consistency across both Iraq and Afghanistan, the program management applied the status change to deployed program members in Afghanistan, as well as Iraq at that time.[48] The change in status impacted earnings and posed a significant problem for an already beleaguered recruitment practice.

Because of the Status of Forces Agreement, the Center for Naval Analyses assessment estimated that, at this transition point, the program lost 30 percent of team personnel either because they did not qualify for the government positions or resigned rather than convert to federal civilians.[49] It was also suggested that the problematic attrition rate was exacerbated by "limited staff support" available to assist in the transition.[50] The HTS's own estimate, in a 2010 Congressional Staff Update, was that between April 2009 and January 2010, 256 personnel (89 percent) converted from contractor to Department of the Army Civilians.[51] The discrepancy may be because a large number of personnel had already departed by the beginning of April, such that the HTT core personnel remained, en masse. Regarding the limited staff support, it is instructive that the majority of funding had gone toward team staffing, rather than expanding the number of program managers. In August 2009, HTS calculated that funding requirements would be composed of Army Base Funding, approximately U.S.$18 million to U.S.$20 million between Fiscal Year 2011 and Fiscal Year 2015 as the program transitioned to an enduring concept—but zero before—had to fund training, logistics, the RRC and program management. The majority of the funding, through the DoD share of the Overseas Contingency Fund—requested at between U.S.$93 million and U.S.$133 million per annum, Fiscal Year 2009 through Fiscal Year 2015—was for embedded teams in support of Operations ENDURING FREEDOM and IRAQI FREEDOM, "on a COCOM [combatant command] demand basis."[52]

The departure rate cited by the Center for Naval Analyses, however, is indicative of the significance of the remuneration package in motivating many of the contractors. Those that remained could be argued to be motivated by more altruistic concerns and therefore important to the future prosperity of the program. However, the relatively high remuneration package in the civilian pay scale generated animosity from the government side, asking why HTT personnel were being made federal civilians and, while the program endured, "It was not easy recruiting from then on in."[53] In truth, it had not been easy from the beginning, and the Status of Forces Agreement exacerbated an already significant problem. Crisis had facilitated the creation of the HTS but that febrile atmosphere also facilitated a *laissez-faire* approach from program managers and contractors. In part, this was also due to command of the teams. TRADOC was the training entity for the teams, but when embedded, they were under the authority of the brigade commanders. Hence, after the 4-month training period at Ft. Leavenworth, when the teams entered Iraq or Afghanistan, they were no longer hinged to TRADOC and the brigade commander had to understand how to use them effectively. Crises hinder as much as they enable.

To augment military operations, HTTs were present to:

> Conduct operationally-relevant, open-source social science research, and provide commanders and staffs at the BCT/RCT and Division levels with an embedded knowledge capability, to establish a coherent, analytic cultural framework for operational planning, decisionmaking, and assessment.[54]

For some social scientists, and, tellingly, for the convergence of two cultures, it was a necessary experience to have fused theoretical learning with practical understanding of areas in military conflict. Such areas are a different country: they do things differently there. War creates its own borders. Ryan Evans explains, having recently completed a master's degree at King's College London, United Kingdom (UK), before signing up to HTS, that:

> In my whole career, I had been writing about what other people were doing, instead of doing. And so I thought it was important to experience what I would be devoting my career toward which is conflict and international politics. So I wanted to experience conflict and contribute, so the HTS seemed like a good way to combine my academic interests with that aim.[55]

Another social scientist emphasizes the desire to remedy disconnects between theory and practice; abstract knowledge and concrete experience, observing that "I wanted to get my hands dirty. I felt like if I was going to be a peace fellow, I should know what conflict looked like on a firsthand basis. So that was one of the big attractors for me."[56]

TRAINING

The early training cycles exemplified the ad hoc character of the program. Lamb *et al.* suggest that the first team, AF1, received more than 6 months training, but it was not systematic, essentially making it up as they went along and, in parts, the process was auto-didactic. The only official military phase of the training was the pre-deployment training at the Combat Readiness Center, Fort Polk, Louisiana, conducted with the 82nd Airborne Division of the U.S.

Army.[57] That research, conducted through interviews, elucidates a more accurate version of the first AF1 pre-deployment, as previous material, including an account from the HTS, suggests that AF1 undertook training at Fort Leavenworth from September 2006 to February 2007, which included 3 weeks on social science methods.[58] In the subsequent iteration of training undertaken by the next five teams, training was developed as a 16-week training rotation and shaped to correspond roughly to what commanders should want to understand about the human terrain in their area of operations and the nature of research which could be conducted in insecure and highly insecure environments.

To understand what the HTT social scientists were doing in the fields, towns, and cities of Iraq and Afghanistan, it is necessary to understand the character of the training. The 16-week training cycle involved core courses, and commenced with an "HTT Capabilities Brief" given by Fondacaro and McFate, although at least one social scientist asserts that this did not happen until later in the program and may have been dictated by their availability, given various roles they were performing.[59] Subsequent courses were "Military Culture and Army 101," and "Subversion and Espionage Directed Against the U.S. Army," "Intelligence Oversight," and lessons of Army culture, in addition to courses in radical Islam and population-centric COIN.[60] The training cycle was refined again after returning IZ1-IZ5 teams gave feedback on the process in February 2008 to the Program Development Team, which had been initiated by Fondacaro to study and evolve the proof-of-concept program.[61] Program improvements included: refining the week of in-processing and orientation; 3 weeks of tool training; 3 weeks of COIN, stability operations, and the military decision-making-process; 5 weeks of social science methods; 3 weeks on negotiations, mediation, and debriefing; 1 week for the capstone exercise; and 10 days of Combat Readiness Center training.[62]

Given the ad hoc nature of the training cycle, the inevitable problems, which quickly surfaced, led the program to award Georgia Tech Research Institute a U.S$8 million contract on September 30, 2008, to re-design the training curriculum after it had originally been awarded to BAE Systems subcontractor, Echota, as part of the TRADOC contract with BAE Systems.[63] According to Lamb *et al.* on the basis of interviews conducted as part of their research, program manager Fondacaro had argued that Echota wrongly priori-tized military training by former Special Operations Forces personnel and minimized academic training.[64] In addition, it was believed that Georgia Tech would "increase the credibility of the training program in the academic community and distance the program from McFarland's influence."[65]

In training for the teams developed to meet the requirements specified in the Joint Urgent Opera-tional Needs Statements (JUONS) in 2007, there were classes with cultural anthropologists such as Jeffrey C. Johnson, a cultural anthropologist possessing ex-pertise in research design, research strategies, inter-view research, and social networks. This was focused on team dynamics and basic approaches to cultural anthropology.[66] After this initial baseline knowledge development, there were several weeks of briefs by people within the program, developing the concept of the HTS. In these earliest iterations, this was difficult because only one team, AF1, had embedded. Such a small sample, accompanied by the "rose-tinted sun-glasses version of what that team did from two indi-viduals on that team" and lacking ability to communicate effectively the research AF1 had actually done, along with the functions of the team members, was "detrimental to the program."[67]

This problem with the returning AF1 cohort was indicative of a wider problem which existed through multiple iterations — though not isolated within the HTS but part of a much broader issue — regarding bringing local contextual, relevant timely information back into the training cycle. As one social scientist who began training in April 2009 and deployed to Afghanistan noted, "We didn't read a report or even interact with the Research Reachback Center until the very, very end when all our classes were done."[68] Teams would divide up into Afghan and Iraqi culture classes conducted through contracts with the Center for Afghan Studies at the University of Nebraska and the University of Kansas, for Iraq studies.[69]

There was, however, a problem within these country-wide examinations, being the lack of specificity of geography for the team. As a social scientist that deployed with the Marine Corps to Helmand province, Afghanistan noted the problem was that, at the sub-country level, nobody knew the actual regions they would be assigned, nevertheless, "These guys knew a lot, it was all old, from the 1970s, or whatever, it was still much more relevant than the time spent in class."[70] Lamb *et al.* assert that in this aspect of training there was, indeed, a lack of current knowledge of the areas such that much of the teaching was a "conceptual level," and, while a "popular program," it was dropped due primarily to cost constraints."[71]

One former HTT member that went to the University of Nebraska in Omaha for the Afghan immersion training in December 2009, explains that groups split up for a month based on whether they would go to

Iraq or Afghanistan.[72] In Nebraska, the team members were taught Dari and had culture lessons taught by faculty from the University. Classes consisted of approximately 2 to 3 hours of language and a culture class every day, or some different aspect of it. But these two countries, Iraq and Afghanistan, for the last decade at least, had been largely closed societies. However, a singular problem was that the faculty had last been in Afghanistan in the 1970s, and, while their knowledge of that time was profound, its relevance to the current trajectory was necessarily limited. This problem, returned to in the final chapter, hinted at the difficult nature of sociocultural research, which could be deep and thus distanced from the present situation, or rapid, thus relevant to the present but of limited depth. As one social scientist explains, the lecturers:

> had a lot of information about the politics, pre-Russian invasion, and the politics after that, but it wasn't local cultural information which was useful, especially if you are going to Helmand, so much as it was a great history lesson.[73]

While learning Dari was only of limited utility when deploying to Helmand, it helped when working with the Afghan National Army and Afghan National Police who came from the North, "but going to a Pashto speaking area," the social scientist had to learn that language skill in theater as well as could be managed.[74] The lack of current knowledge of the operating environment—an environment which was subject to rapid change and extremely insecure—was a problem which remained unsolved through the duration of operations in Iraq and Afghanistan.

Retaining Expertise.

There were two issues regarding the systemic failure in the program to retain individual expertise. First, there was no out-processing structure, a problem amplified by the program not being located at the U.S. Army Forces Command level, the element of the United States that deploys operating forces overseas. The HTS lacked its own capability to deploy and reinsert, such that HTTs deployed out of Combat Training Centers and returned to them, geographically away from TRADOC, and the program had no legal or regulatory authority to order them back to Fort Leavenworth.[75] Second, retention vehicles through which to hire returning personnel were absent because the program had no control over contracting. This meant that there was a lack of individuals in possession of experience from the contemporary situations in Iraq and Afghanistan teaching in the classroom.[76]

The transition from contractor to government term employee made it "possible to retain those people and keep them as government employees on the staff, because the term of contract was 3 years."[77] The transition was about money, but it was also logistical, about the number of billets on the organization chart of the program.[78] Government term employees possessed a specific number of billets in the Department of the Army Table of Organization and Equipment and Table of Distribution and Allowances. Contractors could be employed in any number, but in the transition to term government employees, the defined billets proved a problem for the rapidly expanded program.

Training Two Cultures.

Despite these granular aspects inhibiting optimum teaching during the cycle, the central problem throughout remained the difficulty in successfully merging the military and civilian cultures. Tensions would be greatly exacerbated in the theater of war. Returning deployed personnel integrated into the teaching, even if short on the appropriate ethnographic methods used, could be valuable simply for answering very simple questions, such as how in the military "they pee in front of a bunch of people" and other basic elements of life on the functioning military base.[79] But ultimately, many teams deployed with inadequate knowledge of operational requirements and previous reporting methods and processes.[80]

These iterations of the training cycle involved negligible military learning for civilians, while at Fort Leavenworth. This highlighted the tale of two cultures because for those with previous military experience, basic training was needless, while for civilians about to embed with a large-scale military operation engaged in countering an insurgency, it was invaluable. As one social scientist observes of training: "everyone always asks, for the training, "Did you ever go to shooting ranges?" assuming the whole thing is about the military; and there was zero; zero."[81] That social scientist explains that military training at Fort Leavenworth was conducted by trainers informing program recruits that this was necessary — carrying the weight of a rifle, helmet, etc. — yet "there was no sense of military in the sense of being fit, being comfortable around firearms, knowing how to shoot one."[82] Absence of military integration experiences in the training structure "sends a really bad message to the military, if you have people showing up who have had no weapons training, I think it needed to be strong from the start," and likewise the physical element, because it would be necessary in the area of operations to go out on patrols.[83]

Research methods and COIN instructors briefed, in which *Learning to Eat Soup with a Knife,* written by John Nagl was a key text, and there was a discussion on the origins of terrorism and the extremist Muslim ideology of Sayyid Qutb. Theoretical discussions, however, were of limited utility. Rather, one social scientist remembers of great value the talk given by Dr. Christopher King, who would later become Director of the Social Science Directorate, speaking:

> at length about this quantitative study that he had done; he showed us the statistics, showed us the questions, showed us the methods, and this was one of the first times we had really seen what a team was doing and what they might be doing.[84]

The same social scientist remembered an element of the teaching, McFate and Fondacaro discussing the program and what it was—"the Montgomery and Steve show"—and this was a passionate appeal, but as that social scientist notes: "I do feel as if that was the myth, I saw the myth and it took a while to figure out what the reality was."[85] Practice was of more value than theory, but given the *sui generis* nature of the tasks ahead of them, even practical discussion had limited utility when the teams embedded.

Weston Resolve.

Elements of the training cycle are invaluable for understanding why social scientists were introduced into Iraq and Afghanistan because they demonstrate what management hoped would be achieved. After the completion of methods teaching, the capstone event called Weston Resolve commenced (named after the town in Missouri where the exercise was conducted). Over time, the teams in subsequent training cycles branched out into other communities in the Leavenworth area, but continued to combine anthropology research and integrate that into military staff processes with a heavy focus on just the staffing process.[86] Conducting this mock field research was valuable, as was briefing results to a mock brigade staff, which allowed the teams to develop a feel for the military structures and operational tempo. For the first time, the academic intake could interact with experienced, retired military officers who had performed these roles in practice. This was also valuable for developing small team interactions and working out the dynamics within the teams. However, that understanding of the military structures could be lost on academics at the time, as one social scientist explained: "I did not get it at all, I did not get what our point was until I got to Afghanistan, when I got it a little bit more."[87]

Despite the obvious value, there were critics of that mock field research component. Jennifer Clark explains of that "cavalier" time in the program that, for the brief moment during Weston Resolve after the research element, the program management afforded the teams a period of time to prepare for the briefing. However, the teams were advised that they would be allowed only a few minutes to brief because "the operational tempo was really extreme, and you had to be fast."[88] Managers on the exercise gave teams "pointers" on the content and delivery, and military officers who would offer advice: "be quick; don't do this; do this."[89] The problem for Clark was one of ethics: the briefing had to be interlaced with that of the commander's critical information requirements. These requirements were "mostly kinetic in nature," but here the teams were "supposed to read between the lines and try and advise them [the commanders] on the things they would need to know to help them turn into a non-kinetic scenario."[90] However, the team wanted to gain information which could be used for kinetic targeting, while Clark "was the lone anthropologist, saying 'that is not our objective'."[91] Experience of the operational tempo was critical to developing in the social scientist mind the rhythm of military operations on the ground. It was a necessity for civilian social scientists to learn the operational tempo of the combat brigade conducting stabilization and enabling operations. However, prior to the Status of Forces Agreement in Iraq that was enacted on January 1, 2009, HTT members were all contractors and as such were limited by time. In the training cycle, that meant that personnel were only allowed on-site for 8 hours a day, and were between very strict parameters on what could be done. This was a shortcoming of early iterations of the training cycle: "you cannot do an Operational Tempo and learn about that if you are confined to an 8-hour work day."[92]

Pre-Deployment.

Positive experience, when embedded with brigades, was often amplified by earlier initiative taken during training that was focused on developing rapport and relationships with preferred teammates. This was due to reluctant "ruthlessness on our part in the training cycle, effectively paring people out. None of us enjoyed it, it becomes a bit political," but it was necessary because "there were some people in the training program who meant well and were nice people but who didn't have anything obvious to offer to the mission. It wasn't clear what they were going to do once they deployed."[93] Being confident in each other's talents thus ensured that the team leader could be hands off with the research elements of the team. One social scientist highlighted "a lot of horse trading" by a "very proactive" team leader to ensure that he obtained the personnel he wanted in his team, but even that "only came together in the last few weeks of training."[94]

The composition of the team was only known at the end of the training process, and, when the program expanded beyond the original five teams subsequent to AF1, this was also true of the location the teams would be sent to, which inevitably had a deleterious impact on planning. As Evans explains, local politics and local history are the most important aspects of pre-deployment knowledge:

> There were people who didn't know what team they were going to until they were already deploying. And there were people who thought they were going to one place, and by the time they arrived, they ended up going someplace completely different.[95]

This meant that they were often unable to research the location of their deployment to the best of their ability, creating a mindset that training had been inadequate. Clark explains that it "was so bad" that at the end of pre-deployment training, she was supposed to be embedding with IZ10 in the south of Baghdad attached to a U.S. Army unit, and it was only during departure that Clark learned she had been reassigned to the a Marine Corps unit elsewhere in Iraq. So Clark was "literally walking onto the plane" when she received "orders to report to al-Anbar," in effect going

from a Shi'ite community which she had been studying for 4 months "to a Sunni community that was the
heart of the insurgency."[96] Moreover, Clark was going
from envisioning her deployment with the Army, to
embedding with Marine Corps, which is a "whole different bag of beans."[97]

Many embedded team members were sent as individual replacements to existing teams. Even when
entire teams were sent intact, there could be problems
in the training cycle. One social scientist explains that
they were sent to the National Training Center at Fort
Irwin, California, to do a "role-player scenario" with
artificial towns in the desert. The military integration
meant that it was "by far the best" part of the training cycle" where 10-15 members of the training cycle
could feel military equipment, go on patrols in substantial heat, understand the pace of operations, sleep
on the cots, "just the whole thing — getting in and out
of a Humvee, all of it was really key to me for understanding really what we were getting ourselves into."[98]
However, the social scientist was embedded with the
Marine Corps in Afghanistan, whereas the National
Training Center integration was with an Army unit
heading for Iraq. This highlights a broader problem;
that the embedded teams were an inorganic addition
to a brigade which had grown and developed through
pre-deployment training. In the Marine Corps — more
centered on personal relationships than the Army —
this made integration even more arduous. As Ben
Connable explains generally, there was no period in
the pre-deployment phase during which the HTT was
able to:

> build rapport with the staff, to establish its *bona fi-
> des*, to establish its role, and so that led to additional

points of friction when the deployments took place. And rightfully, there were commanders questioning what they were hearing from these people that they did not know.[99]

EVOLUTION

Practical missteps highlighted by deploying members of the program necessitated the creation of two different processes to evolve the HTS. The first, the Program Development Team, was an in-house lessons learned investigation designed to capture what was happening with embedded teams in Iraq and Afghanistan. The results would then be fed back into the organization in order to advance the program iteratively. The second process was the Operational Planning Team, necessary because the program had grown too fast relative to the number of systems and structures in place such that there was no organization chart spelling out individual responsibilities and roles in the program, the character of the training, or control over human resources contracting. This lack of organizational identity and clarity were "enormous problems and very hard for a fledgling entity to deal with especially when you are trying to fight with your upper management for the right to even run your program."[100]

Program Development Team.

Created in 2006, the Program Development Team was a multifunctional research and management group comprised of former embedded team social scientists, senior management and military members, the latter providing important input on the nature of the research required by the primary customer. The development team reporting process was instigated by the HTS program manager as a means to absorb lessons learned. The development team's official mission was to:

> manage organizational transformation through project evaluation and the development of change requirements to ensure HTS remains relevant and continues to meet the needs of a rapidly changing environment; and to expand the understanding of HTS through engagement with external critics to facilitate the institutionalization of the HTS concept.[101]

The development team was required because, while there were historical models which were "somewhat similar" to the program, such as the Civil Operations and Revolutionary Development Support program and the Office of Strategic Services field units (although mission and structures were different), HTS was "basically running an experiment because it wasn't like we had an off the shelf model for what we wanted to do."[102]

In truth, policy-directed information to capture funding was found to be fundamentally disconnected from the realities of the field such that, as McFate observes, "we didn't know what would work, and we had to find out what would work based on empirical evidence not because we made it up in the Pentagon."[103] By 2009, it was apparent that lessons learned from embedded teams had not been adequately captured; a problem exacerbated by the fact that many returning HTT personnel had not been retained in the program, leading to a critical departure of field expertise. Variation between theaters and brigades meant that there was no "one-off solution"; no "plug-and-play" for training and doctrine which could work across the spectrum of embedded teams.[104]

The development team was thus tasked with visiting embedded teams to examine form and function in Iraq and Afghanistan using a Doctrine, Organization, Training, Materiel, Leadership, Personnel and Facilities framework, an assessment used to identify deficiencies in holistic warfighting capabilities. Using this framework, the development team captured a diverse array of problems in the field, from not using zippers in Iraq because of the sand, to emerging issues concerning ethics, to training *foci*, to requirements for extra emphasis on methods teaching.[105] A key finding of the development team linked specifically to training in that "people do what they have been trained for over their lifetime, not what you try to teach them in 2 weeks" (see Appendix L).[106] The decision was made to develop experiential learning opportunities so that future embedded team members in training could apply skill sets already learned to new environments. This meant the requirement to develop highly structured tools for reporting either a long-term research process or a short-term research effort of 1 to 2 weeks. Specifically, these tools were designed to enable social science research as part of a bureaucracy to enable tracking and ethical oversight. The goal was "getting the people to understand this is different from writing your dissertation, this is about simple, quick, structured communication of what it is that you are doing" — in short, operationally relevant reporting.[107]

From inside the organization, the development team's work was not simply about capturing and implementing lessons learned in order to evolve the program. The HTS was encountering myriad difficulties and was the subject of multiple external assessments. To defend the program's record, solidify its existence, and propagate funding streams, the development team was an opportunity from within to generate an empirical record which could demonstrate robust performances, consolidating and amplifying funding requests. According to one member of the team:

> the PDT [Program Development Team] was mostly about trying to provide forms of justification for HTS to exist. It allowed us to go to our primary customer; which were units downrange [in Iraq and Afghanistan] and take their reporting on our performance to congress and everyone else for funding.[108]

The role of the development team as a vehicle to facilitate funding was part of a larger *modus operandi* identified in the detailed congressionally directed Center for Naval Analyses assessment, that the program management devoted most "effort to selling the Project [HTS] at the expense of leadership and effective management."[109]

Operational Planning Team.

A core component of the program was the training cycle because it prepared team members for a role which had no historical analogue. Without prior examples to serve as templates, teaching was based around educated surmising of the needs of a commander in the unique situations presented in Iraq and Afghanistan. Inevitably, then, the training had "mushroomed," based on subjective feedback of idiosyncratic concerns for particular types of training from returning HTT members, such that every iteration of the training cycle had been unique.[110] Comparison between iterations proved futile, given the rapid expansion of the program and unforeseen developments such as the Status of Forces Agreement in

Iraq which led to the termination of the use of private contractors. This situation with each training cycle being *sui generis* was clearly untenable for longitudinal development of the program because it did not allow for any coherent planning. The training restructuring based on evidence could only proceed if it was known what the individuals on teams were supposed to be in terms of role and performance—individual tasks. Individual tasks could only be known if the exact role of the team is known—collective tasks. At this time, McFate moved to Missouri to work on the HTS Operational Planning Team where she could interact closely with Jeff Bowden, who was leading the curriculum review.[111]

During the work of the planning team, two critical problems became apparent which fundamentally affected the performance of HTS as an organization. First, there was no knowledge management system adequate to the requirements of the HTS as a viable program. This vacuum necessitated the development of a knowledge management aspect to be incorporated into the work of the planning team. Second, there were clear inadequacies in the social science component of the training; the overarching concern being how to train social scientists in methods and concepts given that the work of the teams in Iraq and Afghanistan was largely unknown to recruits in the United States who were based in Fort Leavenworth.

Evidence collated from the development team and products which had been provided by HTTs to the Research Reachback Center assisted in this investigation, however, there was no broad knowledge of how these products were changing across areas of operations or across time and which classes of research—economic, political, or social—were proving most valuable to the commander. McFate stated the problem thus:

Are they being asked to give training to military units? Are they being asked to give briefings? Are they just sitting by the commander whispering in his ear? How are they inputting into the Military Decision-Making Process? What kind of analysis are they doing?[112]

In addition, it was necessary to know what research the teams were doing and how they were doing it: "Are they coding their notes? How are they analyzing their notes? Are they doing any statistical analysis?"[113] Ultimately, the task became reflexive: "We cannot even answer the question because we have not analyzed ourselves well enough to know what we need to know in order to train people to do it more effectively."[114]

To do it more effectively, the Social Science Working Group — part of the knowledge management component of the Operational Planning Team — sought to shed light upon these processes. The working group was tasked with assessing, categorizing and tracking information; and structuring knowledge. Core concepts for training were thus identified, along with the principle research methods employed in the field and identification of the types of analysis that different teams were performing (see Appendix L).[115] From there, it was possible "to say these are the actual skills you need on a team to carry out the mission, and here is how we believe the skill sets fall into buckets."[116]

Therefore the Operational Planning Team process was to proceed via 10 steps:

1. development of a vision statement;

2. initiating review of the social science concepts and methods;

3. review of collective tasks (those of the HTTs, Human Terrain Analysis Teams, and Research Reachback Center);

4. identify knowledge management requirements (products and processes);
5. develop the knowledge management plan;
6. develop individual tasks for team members;
7. identify knowledge skills and attributes;
8. develop terminal learning objectives;
9. create enabling learning objectives; and,
10. conduct curriculum design.

In March 2009, the vision statement was developed: "Providing decision makers with sociocultural understanding to enhance achievement of desired outcomes across the spectrum of conflict"; and the mission statement:

> Recruits, trains, deploys, and supports a dedicated, embedded social science capability; conducts operationally relevant research and analysis; and develops and maintains a sociocultural knowledge base, in order to enable culturally astute decision-making, enhance operational effectiveness, and preserve and share sociocultural institutional knowledge.[117]

Despite the difficulty in teasing out a definite character of social science research in Iraq or Afghanistan, part of its categorization of knowledge, the working group separated direct and indirect tasks generated by the commander or staff. Direct tasks were specific information requirements directed by the command; whereas indirect tasks were broad, umbrella concerns, such as the problems posed by entering a new area of operation, without giving the HTT specific guidance for their mission sets, but ascertaining that certain information would be required for the execution of the mission in general and executing tasks to achieve that for the command. The other mode could be termed entrepreneurial and would be where the embedded team discovered "basic knowledge gaps that the brigade didn't have, based on their observations of the unit they were supporting."[118]

A Perfect Storm.

Shaping this research and development was the initial inability to define social science knowledge which as a corollary obfuscated the role that HTTs were designed to perform when embedded in a combat team. The amorphous and poorly understood notion of both social science and sociocultural knowledge meant that many embedded teams could fall back to the lowest common denominator; merely augmenting existing intelligence cells' techniques, falling back on a broad definition of "culture" to explain myriad collection techniques focused on an array of categories of information from the economy, to agriculture, to demographics.

The planning team and development team could resolve a number of issues within that sphere. For example, based on feedback, ideal composition of teams were developed for three-, four-, five-, six-, and seven-person roles, with three and seven then being rejected as too parsimonious and too complicated, respectively. The four-role team would remain the same as those which had deployed previously; five-role teams would allow specialization with the Human Terrain Analyst position, which would separate into two, a research-focused Human Terrain Analyst and a separate bilingual, bicultural advisor, because the problem had been that both types of personnel were being hired to the same broad Human Terrain Analyst position, but they behaved differently and had different skill sets when embedded.[119] The six-role team would allow specialization at the social science level, disaggregating quantitative and qualitative social science analysis, where, "because good quantitative scientists and good qualitative social scientists tend not to come in the same package, even if they think they do."[120] The seven-role team included separating information technology and operations functions in the Research Manager role—with the latter serving as a quasi-assistant to the team leader—but this team was ultimately rejected on the grounds that the differentiation between roles was not pronounced.[121]

Ultimately however, both the development team and planning team failed to resolve who the ideal social scientist might be in terms of discipline, level of field research, level of education, and preferential research modes. The personalities and skill sets of the social scientists that had been embedded were so broad as to be amorphous and indistinct in terms of identification and categorization. Complicating this investigation, many of the personalities conflicted, but each individual still functioned effectively. In short, as a general rule, individuals with excellent interpersonal skills and field research experience might perform well, but there was no black and white answer to the question of what made a successful social scientist. This perfect storm may never be resolved because even assessment of optimal academic achievements is muddied by the broad and changing requirements of stabilization environments. The West Point study, for example, concluded that:

> Limiting academics to only holders of doctorates may be inadvertently missing a talented and eager group of academics with master's degrees who may bring

other needed attributes to the team. While Ph.D.s tend to provide 'deep thinking,' we have observed a civilian team member with only a BA (and some MA level work) providing outstanding analysis and linkages.[122]

"Infinite Opportunity": Curriculum Redesign.

Despite the absence of a black and white solution to the question of the character and content of the ideal social scientist, there was enough research conducted by the program managers finally to redesign the training cycle. The process of curriculum redesign has been traced back to the HTT Handbook, published in October 2008.[123] The handbook, produced by a Doctrine Development Team:

> delineated the Mission Essential Task Lists for the four roles of the HTTs — team leader, social scientist, human terrain analyst, research manager — and presented a list of five contributions embedded teams could make to brigades in Iraq and Afghanistan.[124]

The curriculum redesign process then began more formally with the creation of the Operational Planning Team in December 2008. The team telephoned HTTs in the field and in January 2009 developed a document which posed questions to embedded teams to assess the evolution of research.[125] In order to assist in the development of the planning team, the HTS sent out a survey research tool to all the embedded teams that were currently in the program. This survey used a combination of survey methodology and social network analysis to try and isolate what tools were being used by what teams, where, when, and why.

The sample returned was enough to contribute to the redesign process, but according to one former

HTT member familiar with the process, the problem was that the disparity:

> in terms of what people understood they were doing was so broad, whether you are talking to a social scientist, whether you are talking to a military officer, whether you are talking to this team, that team. That it was very difficult to even code their responses in a meaningful way.[126]

This initiated a series of working groups over the subsequent 6 months, which employed strategies such as pile sorting and focus groups and fed into the mission to Iraq and Afghanistan. The Program Development Team had used a series of interviews on particular issues that were identified on the working group process; the information gathered afforded the opportunity to start developing ideal team structures in the future. As Lamb *et al.* explain as part of their detailed study, at the start of 2010, the HTS had produced a document "Terminal and Enabling Learning Objectives" and the "document provided a de facto roadmap for program reforms."[127] The HTS held a training curriculum review conference from January 26 to February 5, 2010, to assess how much of the HTT research was useful to the commander, and if the research is "incorporated, in a timely fashion, with the unit's decision making process."[128] It was also envisaged that redesign could allow the HTS to integrate into other TRADOC activities such as post-Afghanistan and Iraq Brigade Combat Team road-to-war exercises.[129]

Meanwhile, the first Operational Planning Team meeting took place at Oyster Point in January 2009 focusing on the vision statement and mission statement for the program, led by Colonel Mark Crisci and developed by Robert Holliday, whose position as Director of Doctrine Development began in November 2008. This initial meeting took the U.S. Central Command JUONS and used it to deduce an HTS vision statement, a mission statement, and basic task specialization. The follow-up meeting in March 2009 attempted to generate a collective task list for the program, which is what the individual tasks were that had to be accomplished by organizations within the HTS. The collective task lists composed highlighted that, while there were identifiable bureaucratic tasks for people to execute, there was lacking actual mission-specific tasks that pertained to social science. This was a problematic issue identified by myriad social scientists that embedded in Iraq and Afghanistan. To that end, in early-2010, the rapidly convened Social Science Working Group attempted to bureaucratize social science in the context of the HTS.

In its formation, the Social Science Working Group was intended to review core social science concepts, analyze social science methods used by embedded teams, and redesign two core courses in the HTS curriculum: the "Introduction to Anthropology" and the "Social Science Research Methods." Broadly, the group was convened to attempt to arrive at a common set of methods for what the teams were to do when they embedded with combat brigades.[130] It was found necessary to assess what commanders actually wanted to know from the HTTs, in order to work toward developing the common set of methods for the social scientists. Identification of these core concepts would enable teams to conduct more effective baseline assessments, aggregate data from the brigade combat team to higher units to develop a common operating picture and re-energize social scientist use of the mapping of humain terrain (MAP-HT), the technology tool brought over and developed from the Cultural Preparation of the Environment, but which was a failure like its precursor.

There were two basic questions from which the undertaking could commence. First, answering what the brigade commander wants to know about society and culture in the area of operations. Second, what the commander needs to know about society and culture. The answers were deduced from a pile-sort of requests made by HTTs to the Research Reachback Center for both Iraq and Afghanistan. In developing data categories, the working group examined relevant concepts such as: doctrine in *Field Manual* (FM) *3-24, Counterinsurgency* and FM *3-07, Stability Operations;* and other models maintained in repositories like the Human Relations Area Files at Yale University relating to areas, structures, capabilities, organizations, people, events, political, military, economic, social, information, and infrastructure.

The working group analyzed the main methods through which several teams conducted research, which were centered on three techniques: semi-structured interviews, unstructured interviews and literature reviews. To a lesser extent, research also included social network analysis and rapid ethnography, drive-by reporting, surveys, Research Reachback Center requests, pile sorts, and broad observation. Each data collection method, and the additional methods of key leader engagements, mixed methods and focus groups were assessed according to five criteria: the level of security the method required; the scope; the type of data produced; the strengths of the method; and cautions and caveats. Methods used, however, were not indicative of the brigade needs but rather were the result of team competencies (see Appendix L). In combat zones experts stayed with the skill sets they understood best and the MAP-HT tool did not allow HTT personnel to generate "usable" outputs. This highlights why MAP-HT was so difficult to integrate as a tool into the HTTs, and led to the proliferation of Microsoft Office software to generate research products. The Social Science Working Group produced a list of supported unit deliverables (finished products) which included the structure that different PowerPoint presentations and generic reports should take.

As part of the redesign, an HTS Ontology Working Group was created to produce operationally relevant data taxonomies. The MAP-HT tool based on the Cultural Preparation of the Environment was the most coherent existing attempt to classify data; being by country, ethnic group, confederation (tribal affiliation), and province. Problematic was that many of the sub-branches of each category which were developed in order to add granularity to existing data taxonomies often overlapped with other sub-branches in other levels. It was therefore necessary to redesign these main branches and sub-branches in order to be more discrete and hence prevent overlap. The recommended categorization became: region or geographic area; physical geography; demography; economy; political government; education; crime/justice; history; religion; social organization and relationships; and culture/material culture. After review by the Social Science Working Group, the finalized list became: region/geography; demography; infrastructure; economy; politics and government; security/justice; education; health; history; religion; social organization and identity; and general and material culture.

The individual tasks necessary to perform the collective tasks were developed, which was accomplished from information collected from the Program Development Team, and identified under the team structure those individual tasks, finally bureaucratizing the program in terms of social science: who does it; how they do it; how they work together; and how they communicate. This material became the opening documents to the Knowledge Management Conference in January 2011—and was the final layer of the fundamental question for HTS writ large in its relationship with the military forces in Iraq and Afghanistan: "If this is what we do, how do we train it?"[131]

The Capstone publication, *Joint Publication* (JP), *3-0, Joint Operations*, highlights the necessity for information management because it "is an essential process that receives, organizes, stores, controls, and secures an organization's wide range of data" and is "important for the commander's battle rhythm and the development and sharing of information to increase both individual and collective knowledge."[132] The conference was thus concerned with alloying social science expertise to the customer; specifically the types of technology HTTs were using to enable communication to achieve these tasks set out in the redesign. This involved identification of the customer; data repositories; and future data management strategy. The collective tasks are instructive in how the HTS had developed to that point; the program now defined operationally relevant sociocultural knowledge as focused not on friends or enemies, but on the population and the environment and that "operationally relevant" means that the sociocultural information has utility for the supported unit and their mission, in support of unit requirements and not for personal gain.[133]

The new training curriculum was finally executed in August 2011.[134] Separation of activities occurred such that the process was now divided into three phases: foundation skills and research operations (common training); individual training (specialized); and collective training (combined training in collective environment as part of teams, to understand how they will work in the field).[135] The social science 2-week pre-deployment training configured as part of the redesign was still part of the larger training program in the collective class. The subsequent team break out focused, first, on collective task training as teams; subsequent to that were the individual team training tasks and exercises specific to the job training. The social science 2-week training period relates to that third phase of the training cycle. After this period was a final phase, a team exercise using newly developed skill sets, reconvened as a team in preparation for possible pre-deployment.

The primary problems were two-fold. First, because of the range of social science graduates in the class, from master's graduates to post-doctoral trainees, creating a generic level of teaching was difficult. Questions inevitably arose, such as: was the cohort disposed to quantitative or qualitative methods? Each cohort was thus *sui generis*, in that they had their own identities already formed from considerable academic qualifications and thus teaching them as a whole was problematic. The solution as created by the team was to implement practical exercises which afforded the students an opportunity to contextualize the skills that they already knew, but in the environment that they would be operating in. The work undertaken by the Program Development Team had shown that the training program failed to alter preferred research techniques already central to the social scientist. As one HTS member familiar with the redesign observed:

> even if we tried to teach them new skills, they still wouldn't use them. Because that was one of the key findings in 2009 — people do what they have been trained for over their lifetime, not what you try to teach them in 2 weeks. People will try and pull that in but what is more important is giving them the experiential learning opportunity so that they can take the skills they already know and readily provide those in a new environment.[136]

The training element thus focused on research planning and design tools developed under the auspices of the Program Development Team. Ultimately, in translating the two cultures, it was about emphasizing a type of research which could best be termed "operationally relevant reporting."

Familiarization with tools (resiliency training) was the first section; the subsequent day was the baseline assessment which was a literature review focused on the area, if known, in which the social scientist will operate in. This provided mission-specific training, utilizing academic expertise inherent in the construction of a literature review. It was also considered that this document would be organic; there would be an existing baseline assessment by the embedded HTT, into which this literature review could be integrated, and further research, once in place, could be added. This thus represented an attempt to develop a form of institutional memory, and a coherent central narrative, though this ultimately failed as an attempt and points to a severe challenge in the Army's continual quest to develop institutional knowledge.[137]

The dynamic between language and culture training favored culture training because deep language training was far beyond the time frame of the course; thus Day 3 examined cultural training and included a 1-hour familiarization class with MAP-HT. These 1-hour classes were insufficient to make the equipment central to the team and only the Research Managers got more than 1 hour training with the tool in this resource-constrained curriculum. The remainder of the first week was for the social scientist to develop the baseline assessment. Baseline assessments meant that they had familiarization with at least one area in Afghanistan (combat brigades had by this time departed Iraq), and they could understand where resources exist to get information and further how it would be possible to integrate that information into existing databases using instruction.[138] Despite the high academic standard of the trainees, there were problems discovered, particularly an inability to conduct the literature research or an inability to structure thoughts "in a way that could be simply communicated."[139] These gaps were mitigated by remedial lessons.

The second week focused on research methods. Day 1 discussed quantitative research. Teaching methods in the abstract, it was found that training was facilitated by identifying categories through quantitative analysis rather than entering into a discussion over what categories of analysis could be used and would be necessary for a discussion of qualitative analysis. That class introduced concepts of survey research, but emphasized validity and reliability; in short, the challenges in doing combat research. Those social scientists that were already trained in quantitative methods were then instructed in some of the basic sources in the military, which were unknown to the academic community; military databases that an operational researcher in Iraq and Afghanistan would utilize. Then using the research template generated in the previous week, an exercise focused on attempting to communicate to a commander the goal of the research project to be implemented. At the core of this process was effective communication to a commander about what the social scientist is trying to do; to communicate that HTS is ethically sound in its research proposal; to communicate to the rest of the team what is required of them in the research process.

The subsequent qualitative section created conditions of a conflicted area; to get the social scientists to design qualitative research within constraints based on the information given. The social scientists would then be asked who they would interview, how they would interview them, what they would ask, and what research material they were expecting to get out of the process. Culturally insensitive actions or unrealistic goals could be corrected by the training supervisor. On the third day of the second week, the social scientists continued the qualitative research design, and on the fourth day, they presented papers. The final day capstone project incorporated an information brief for the area they were going to that would replicate a baseline assessment, and then the social scientists were allowed to design a research project as appropriate, without supervision, taking "the training wheels off" and allowing "infinite opportunity," such as that which existed in the operating environment for HTTs when embedded in insecure areas.[140] Various designs for research to be conducted over the subsequent 9 months were created and drafted to support the unit. At this point, the social scientists for the first time developed a baseline assessment in the context of the province, including a background of what qualitative and quantitative methods are possible. Put simply:

> they finally have the opportunity in an Afghan context, real world environment, to say: 'Oh this is what I think my job is supposed to be, this is how I would do it, and this is how I would communicate to the team what my role is'.[141]

ETHICS AT WAR

Due in large part to the absence of historical analogies to the program and the sense of crisis in which it was formed, when the HTS was created, there were no ethical guidelines for the embedded teams. Dr. McFate has noted that the OSS served in some ways as a basic blueprint, and Fondacaro specifically highlighted the Jedburgh teams, as part of the OSS, but beyond those basic ideas there was little information upon which to draw. The HTS personnel in Iraq and Afghanistan were conducting research in highly insecure areas, integrated into the brigade staff, and it was not known how this program would develop. Broadly, the remit of reducing military and civilian casualties was the architecture which would guide actions in an area of operations.[142] As the HTS 2007-08 *Yearbook* explains, social science was a broad church such that a unified ethical architecture beneath which all its social scientists sat was unlikely. In addition, the HTS *Ethics Guidelines* were released in 2009, created by five former HTT social scientists that comprised the Ethics Working Group and incorporated an additional group of social scientists who were deployed in Iraq and Afghanistan. The problem in formation of the ethical guidelines, however, was instructive of the wider problem of homogenization of research and research methods of the broad net of social scientists: "you had an interdisciplinary group, again with different ethical considerations trying to come up with a common set of standards, which of course, doesn't work."[143]

On the academic side, given that AF1's social scientist was a graduate-trained anthropologist and McFate possessed a Ph.D. in anthropology and a juris doctor degree (J.D.), it was most logical to consider the Code of Ethics of the Society for Applied Anthropology, as it related to field research and human participants.[144] On the military side, the beginning of the program was marked by examination of *Title 32, Code of Federal Regulations* (CFR) Part 219, Army regulations pertaining to human subjects.[145] As McFate explains:

> there is a big loophole there; you don't have to do an IRB [Institutional Review Board proposal to the Army Human Research Protections Office] if certain conditions are met. We were in the middle of supporting a war, so the idea that, 'Stop everything we have to do an IRB' was simply not feasible. It is totally impractical and also probably unnecessary.[146]

Unnecessary, because McFate considered that, in the field, social scientists could identify themselves to informants, gain permission to interview, code notes, and not share those notes, or any names with commanders—the exception being public figures already known to the unit—because "you're not going to say "Sheikh X" when the brigade commander was at that meeting and he knows the guy's name."[147]

Criticism by the American Anthropological Association of the program inhibited applications from a top tier of professional anthropologists while master's graduates in anthropology would have fewer concerns, and those outside that specific discipline would see only tangential relevance to their own fields of study. Instructively, as one bio-archaeologist and former embedded social scientist noted, "The cultural anthropologist side was the least side of my concerns, and so it didn't really bother me what the AAA [American Anthropological Association] had to say."[148] Indeed, McFate argued instead that the publicity saw "increased numbers" apply to the program. She used an interesting analogy for the effect of the American Anthropological Association Executive Board's statement, on applications to work for the program, likening the impact to:

> when Google Maps published Barbara Streisand's beach house location, and she sued them. Suddenly everybody was on Google trying to figure out where Barbara Streisand lives. If she had done nothing, then no one would have cared, no one would have noticed: so, thank you AAA.[149]

Social scientists embedded at the patrol level in combat units nevertheless presented a particular problem to the academy because of their consistent proximity to host populations in the presence of coalition soldiers. For Robert Albro, this was a particular problem because the data that is accrued from the embedded teams is going to be uploaded to a shared system at some point, SIPRNet (Secret Internet Protocol Router Network) for example, and from there, the data and information can be used in any way for any purpose, out of the hands of the social scientist who collected and processed it.[150] Highlighting the notion of two cultures, from inside the military architecture such criticism was seen as hypocritical, particularly when:

people in academia underplay from an ethical point of view the number of people who have access to their research information through FOIA [Freedom of Information Act] requests and everything else.[151]

According to the Army Human Research Protections Office (AHRPO), *Department of Defense* (DoD) *Instruction 3216.02* requires the protections office Institutional Review Board to approve DoD-supported human subjects research that is more than minimal risk.[152] In McFate's assessment, however, the first iteration—the first five teams—fell into Title 32 CFR Part 219 exemptions for human research protection and thus did not necessitate approach to the protections office. Research was exempt beneath Title 32 when it involved survey or interview procedures, if the procedures did not allow human subjects to be "identified, directly or through identifiers" or when any disclosure of the subject's "responses outside the research" could endanger them.[153]

In 2007, the program management approached the Office of the Judge Advocate General (JAG) at TRADOC citing the nature of the mission, the broad character of the field work, existing legislation, and asking for an authorizing letter. Jennifer Clark had returned from her role as a Human Terrain Analysis Team social scientist in Iraq to become Deputy Director of the Social Science Directorate to assist in strengthening the ethics aspect of the program. Clark's position with regard to the protections office was that HTT investigations in Iraq and Afghanistan "did not fit the parameters of research as outlined by any of the ethical guidelines."[154] This led Clark to request exemption status because the only position at which research, as defined by the protections office, was being conducted was at the Theater Coordination Element, because they were using surveys from the Social Science Research Agency, a survey capability which employed members of the host population. After 2 years of approaching the Judge Advocate General quarterly, the HTS management received confirmation that the program fell into the exemptions under Title 32.

Information Versus Intelligence.

In March 2011, Major General Michael Flynn called information and intelligence the fire and maneuver of the 21st century.[155] The observation made is one which cuts to the core of the HTS; an apparent discernible difference between information and intelligence in which both are discrete and separate entities. Yet, in practice, is such a conceptualization feasible? One Theater Coordination Element social scientist that deployed to Afghanistan argued: "Everything is intelligence. Everything in the world is intelligence; depending on who analyzes it and for what purposes. But HTS was not designed to provide intelligence in the classical terms."[156] Indicating the propensity for cross-cultural misunderstanding, one social scientist observed that "the term intelligence is special in the academic community" without necessarily being well understood, and that at the level of the Theater Coordination Element, at least they gathered information, but did not collect information.[157] The differentiation is an interesting one: one analogy is of the woodsman collecting firewood; the collector will cut down a tree and chop up the trunk into logs while the gatherer will find broken off branches on the ground and take them away to be used.

The HTTs existed in a grey area physically because there was an unresolved issue by mid-2008 of where to situate the team in the organization of the brigade. The original concept had been broadly composed to allow flexibility in positioning the teams, such that they could be located in any structure deemed appropriate by the brigade staff.[158] This was left at the discretion of the brigade staff, but it posed a unique problem because there were only two possible scenarios. In the first scenario, the brigade commander could integrate the HTT into other intelligence assets at the level of the S-2 (military battalion and brigade level intelligence staff); in that scenario the embedded team would likely devolve into providing sociocultural information that was broadly in line with existing military products, in order to integrate them successfully and gain leverage. In the second scenario, as social science researchers filling a unique gap, they could be isolated from other assets and conduct academic social science research with hypotheses, methodologies, and caveats, but therein would be the risk of an inability to make that research product integrate successfully into the other cells' products, or influence the commander as a consequence. This is a fundamental issue and goes to the heart of both the program's form and function in stabilization operations.

At the program level, the relationship between the HTS and intelligence continually shifted throughout its time in Iraq and Afghanistan. That is to be expected given the sense of crisis which pervaded the U.S. Army which thus permitted some scope for the program in regard to an aspect of research which was tangential at best to operational success. Moreover, war blurs distinctions and refashions borders, not just physical, but social, ethical, and moral. McFate clarified in the training cycle that the HTS was not an intelligence program, and that the job of embedded teams was not to collect information which could be used for lethal targeting. The problem, however, was located in the reality of the conflicted area; being, how far from intelligence does an HTT stay, physically and ethically? Can information from an HTT be given to intelligence assets?

One former HTT member recalls the heated debate in the training cycle over a scenario where intelligence could be used to save American lives but which would imperil its source. The former HTT member draws the analogy of the 1980s television program, *Ethics in America*. In one debate, in 1987, called "Under Orders, Under Fire," a hypothetical scenario is posed to reporter Mike Wallace of *60 Minutes* in which he embeds with a fictional North Kosanese unit which is preparing to ambush American Soldiers; Wallace asserts that, as an impartial journalist, he would cover the story and not warn the Americans of their impending fate, leading to astonishment from other distinguished panelists, including Brent Scowcroft.[159] The HTT member relates that in training, there were several social scientists who wanted such impartiality; similar to the ethical debate in 1987. The training class considered a scenario where you had information on an improvised explosive device (IED): would you tell that unit where the IED was? There were individuals who said "no" and horrified other people in the class, and it made them feel like they were in danger and probably should not embed in Iraq and Afghanistan at that time, bringing up questions such as loyalty and the idea of betraying the most sovereign trust that any soldier could have, of being supported on their left or right.[160]

The ethical dilemma heightened cross-cultural tensions: as the program evolved, its character crystallized such that, while its teams would be doing a different job from that of intelligence assets, it was necessary to partner with intelligence; to use their research as well as to provide them with information in a collaborative process as part of the unit. To that end, and to avoid confusion and make coherent the identity, in 2011, it was made clear that the program was an intelligence asset.[161] The study of society and culture in stabilization and enabling operations cannot be the sole preserve of an HTS; it is also within the remit of myriad intelligence cells. Inevitably however, HTS as a fully fledged intelligence asset pushed the program further away from academic traditions. As a publicly facing asset in its inception, operating in contested spaces continued to compromise the program's identity:

> I think you have to acknowledge that we were in partnership with intelligence, that we provided information to intelligence and drew information from them, but that is no different from private companies in the United States or academics who willingly publish their information in journals which are read by intelligence officers and utilized accordingly. But to label us as intelligence, particularly at the beginning of HTS and even now, I don't think the Army has come to be able to understand what studying society and culture is, to a degree that they are capable of understanding how that could be different from current intelligence functions.[162]

According to one former senior member of the program, developing it as an intelligence asset under Sharon Hamilton meant that the program:

> started to lose its unique identity; where a lot of the tool sets that we could have brought to bear were sim-

ply left by the wayside because we chose to go with a military, bureaucratic version of what intelligence is, you lose that value of social science methodology:

Inevitably, however, the U.S. Army could only allow the new program to do that for an initial period, "but, man, those were the days."[163]

Many Hats.

When the House Armed Services Committee directed the Center for Naval Analyses to investigate the program after journalistic and academic scrutiny, allegations of severe mismanagement, and three contractor deaths, in 2010, the AHRPO contacted the program management formally, requesting a visit to see the managers, as well as requesting specific documentation. The program convened social scientists in DoD from outside and from within the HTS. At the conclusion of that consultation process, the AHRPO, too, considered that the program was exempt from Institutional Review Board checks.[164] This served to confuse the identity of the program further because it had publicly stated it was an information-gathering vehicle, but it was not reporting to AHRPO. In reality, however, a full human subject review process was impossible because many of the turnaround requirements for HTT research in the field were days, even hours, and:

> a full review would have been the equivalent of requiring an anthropology student who is embedded in a village in sub-Saharan Africa to contact his committee every time he wanted to conduct an interview, which doesn't make sense even in academia.[165]

There was still a necessity to develop a level of review appropriate for embedded teams, which required a "process of negotiation" with the AHRPO. As of November 2013, HTS is a full participant with the AHRPO.[166] AHRPO guidelines are met by an HTT in the field developing a research proposal or concept, then sending it to the senior social scientist at HTS to ensure it meets AHRPO guidelines and report that proposal to the office.[167] The ethical alterations affected speed of research in both Iraq and Afghanistan, with implications for the nature of what HTTs could accomplish in the field. The office required "determination for research proposals rather than the entire project," which in form was a questionnaire employed to determine if research was human subject research exempt and took "two minutes to fill out, but it was required before you submitted any proposal to your commanding officer."[168] At this juncture and beyond, compliance with the result of the collaboration with the AHRPO was necessary because Congress had suspended funding, such that diminishing operational speed in contested spaces was secondary to restarting the funding stream.[169]

The dialogue with the AHRPO centered on the character of HTS as either a social science research program or an intelligence function.[170] If the program was a research asset, then it fell under AHRPO guidelines; but if it was an intelligence asset, it did not. How, then, is the program to be defined within the Army architecture? This definition lies at the heart of the program's relationship with the Army and has central relevance to elucidation of the thesis question. In order to afford HTTs maximum flexibility in function, in reality, the character of the program meant it possessed a dual personality, possessing the ability to conduct intelligence or information depending on the decisionmaking process of the individuals and teams in Iraq and Afghanistan. As one anthropologist familiar with the program explains, "There was a fair amount of shenanigans with them trying to keep HTS away from the review board process."[171] This intrigue was necessary in order to allow the fledgling social science research program room to maneuver.

CONCLUSIONS

By 2011, the HTS had evolved to command an annual budget of U.S.$150 million.[172] But the program was beset by problems resulting in a congressionally directed assessment. As one social scientist, who deployed three times with the HTS and also worked at the program management level, felt that, while McFate and Fondacaro were focused on "building the program," by 2010, the HTS "had reached the age where it was time for someone to come in and introduce bureaucratic structure; standard operating procedures; normalization of this weird, new program."[173] Moreover, Fondacaro had ostensibly, if not consciously, resisted the bureaucratization of the HTS into the TRADOC organizational architecture such that significant tensions existed between the program and its parent organization.[174]

To prevent escalation in tension, in 2010, Maxie McFarland's Deputy Colonel Sharon Hamilton was made interim program manager in place of Fondacaro, and subsequently confirmed as the permanent director. McFate also departed the program in September 2010 to be replaced by Dr. Christopher King who had deployed as a social scientist to both Iraq and Afghanistan.[175] Hamilton had scientific training, allowing her to approach this complex problem from a very linear trajectory. The emphasis was on developing a bureaucracy which would enable the program to become much more in line with other elements in the military structure as well as develop a less fraught relationship with TRADOC and the main contractor. In addition, the program would develop a more coherent and concrete identity, such that, in Hamilton's words, it was now firmly in the intelligence architecture.

The evolution of the program allows insight into the function of the social scientist. Examination in detail of training experiences and the work of the program management in restructuring that cycle in order to better instruct program members is valuable in identifying why social scientists were embedded in combat brigades in Iraq and Afghanistan. Aspects of the recruitment deleteriously impacted the quality of the program. This was, in part, a consequence of the need to quickly expand the number of teams after the U.S. Central Command JUONS (see Appendix F); because the contract with BAE Systems did not include a bonus for quality of candidate hired; but also because the idea of the form and function of a social scientist is something amorphous; it was not entirely understood by the program management, as Jennifer Clark has noted, and that incomprehension was larger still in the recruiting apparatus.

Initial training iterations were done on an educated guess about what social science teams might require in order to perform adequately for their customer in stabilization operations in Iraq and Afghanistan. There were no templates and the JUONS expanded the program at such velocity that it was difficult to conduct lessons learned on the training cycles adequately, although eventually this was performed. The Social Science Working Group showed that the HTS was a qualitative research function and that, importantly, social scientists performed in the manner in which they had already been trained. The ethical examination shows that, until at least 2010, social scientists had freedom in both Iraq and Afghanistan to structure the research as they wished and record data captured in myriad forms and for use by intelligence functions. It was beneath this broad umbrella constructed by the program management that embedded teams conducted research in Iraq and Afghanistan.

ENDNOTES - CHAPTER 4

1. Author's telephone interview with Bob Reuss, Colonel Lee Grubbs, and Dr. Susan Canedy, September 16, 2013.

2. Janice H. Laurence, "The Human Terrain System: Some Lessons Learned and the Way Forward," in Montgomery McFate and Janice H. Laurence, eds., *Social Science Goes to War: The Human Terrain System in Iraq and Afghanistan*, London, UK: Hurst, 2015, pp. 294-295.

3. Human Terrain System, "Human Terrain System Yearly Report, 2007-2008," Program Development Team, Prepared for U.S. Army Training and Doctrine Command, Washington, DC, August 2008, p. 7.

4. *Ibid.*, pp. 8-9.

5. *Ibid.*, p. 10.

6. Steve Fondacaro, telephone interview with author, September 15, 2015. The role of "Social Scientists" is highlighted in a May 2007 PowerPoint brief; Bob Reuss and Steve Fondacaro, "Human Terrain System (HTS) Update to GEN Wallace," TRADOC/DCSINT, May 17, 2007. General Wallace was the TRADOC Commander between 2005 and 2008.

7. Reuss and Fondacaro, "Human Terrain System (HTS) Update to GEN Wallace."

8. *Ibid.*

9. *Ibid.*

10. *Ibid.*

11. Former HTT social scientist 1, interview with author, location withheld upon request, July 25, 2013.

12. Reuss, interview.

13. David Zacharias, interview with author, Virginia Beach, VA, July 22, 2013.

14. Fondacaro, telephone interview with author, September 15, 2015.

15. Reuss, interview; Christopher J. Lamb *et al.*, *Human Terrain Teams: An Organizational Innovation for Sociocultural Knowledge in Irregular Warfare*, Washington, DC: Institute of World Politics Press, 2013, p. 20.

16. Reuss, interview.

17. Jennifer Clark, telephone interview with author, October 9, 2013.

18. *Ibid.*

19. I am indebted to Dr. Robert Johnson for this assessment.

20. PDRI, "Human Terrain System: Evaluation of the Human Terrain Team Recruitment and Selection Process," *Technical Report No. 628*, Arlington, VA, February 2009.

21. PDRI, "Results of HTT Structured Interview Pilot Test," February 5, 2009.

22. *Ibid.*

23. Zacharias, interview.

24. *Ibid.*

25. *Ibid.*

26. Montgomery McFate, interview, August 1, 2013.

27. *Ibid.*

28. Zacharias, interview.

29. *Ibid.*

30. *Ibid.*

31. Former HTT social scientist 2, interview with author, Quantico, VA, July 29, 2013.

32. *Ibid.*

33. PDRI, "Human Terrain System: Evaluation of the Human Terrain Team Recruitment and Selection Process," *Technical Report No. 628*, Arlington, VA, February 2009.

34. *Ibid.*

35. Ryan Evans, interview with author, Washington, DC, August 6, 2013.

36. *Ibid.*

37. Zacharias, interview.

38. Steve Fondacaro, "Memo: Human Terrain System Personnel Screening and Tracking Support," n.d.

39. *Ibid.*

40. Zacharias, interview.

41. *Ibid.*

42. *Ibid.*

43. McFate, interview, August 1, 2013.

44. *Ibid.*

45. *Ibid.*

46. Montgomery McFate, interview with author, Newport, RI, August 2, 2013.

47. Former HTT social scientist 1, interview, July 25, 2013.

48. Lamb *et al.*, p. 60.

49. *Ibid.*, pp. 76, 141-142.

50. *Ibid.*, p. 142.

51. Human Terrain System, "Congressional Staff Update," March 2, 2010.

52. Human Terrain System, "FY 09-15 HTS Funding Requirements," August 8, 2009.

53. Zacharias, interview.

54. Nathan Finney, *The Human Terrain Team Handbook*, Fort Leavenworth, KS: TRADOC, 2008, cited in American Anthropological Association, *Final Report on the Army's Human Terrain System*, p. 4.

55. Evans, interview.

56. Former HTT social scientist 2, interview.

57. Lamb *et al.*, p. 221.

58. Human Terrain System, "Human Terrain System Yearly Report, 2007-2008," p. 11.

59. Lamb *et al.*, p. 222; Former HTT social scientist 2, interview.

60. *Ibid.*

61. Human Terrain System, "Human Terrain System Yearly Report, 2007-2008," p. 12.

62. *Ibid.*, p. 11.

63. Lamb *et al.*, p. 50.

64. *Ibid.*

65. *Ibid.*

66. Former HTT social scientist 1, interview, August 11, 2013.

67. Former HTT social scientist 1, interview, July 25, 2013; Clark, interview.

68. Former HTT social scientist 2, interview.

69. Vanessa Gezari, *The Tender Soldier: A True Story of War and Sacrifice*, New York: Simon and Schuster, 2013, p. 163.

70. Former HTT social scientist 2, interview.

71. Lamb *et al.*, pp. 222-223.

72. Former HTT social scientist 1, interview, July 25, 2013.

73. Former HTT social scientist 2, interview.

74. *Ibid.*

75. McFate, interview, August 2, 2013.

76. *Ibid.*

77. *Ibid.*

78. *Ibid.*

79. Former HTT social scientist 2, interview.

80. *Ibid.*

81. Former HTT social scientist 2, interview.

82. *Ibid.*

83. *Ibid.*

84. Former HTT social scientist 2, interview.

85. *Ibid.*

86. Former HTT social scientist 1, interview, July 25, 2013.

87. Former HTT social scientist 2, interview.

88. Clark, interview.

89. *Ibid.*

90. *Ibid.*

91. *Ibid.*

92. *Ibid*; Gezari, pp. 166-167.

93. Nicholas Krohley, telephone interview with author, July 26, 2013.

94. Evans, interview.

95. *Ibid.*

96. Clark, interview.

97. *Ibid.*

98. Former HTT social scientist 2, interview.

99. Ben Connable, interview with author, Arlington, VA, July 15, 2013.

100. McFate, interview, August 1, 2013.

101. Montgomery McFate, Britt Damon, and Robert Holliday, "What do Commanders Really Want to Know? U.S. Army Human Terrain System Lessons Learned from Iraq and Afghanistan," Janice H. Laurence and Michael D. Matthews, eds., *The Oxford Handbook of Military Psychology*, Oxford, UK: Oxford University Press, 2012, p. 110.

102. McFate, interview, August 1, 2013; Zacharias also refers to the Human Terrain System as an "experiment." Zacharias, interview.

103. McFate, interview, August 1, 2013.

104. Clark, interview.

105. McFate, interview, August 1, 2013.

106. Former HTT social scientist 1, interview, July 25, 2013.

107. *Ibid.*

108. *Ibid.*

109. Cited in Lamb *et al.*, p. 72.

110. McFate, interview, August 1, 2013.

111. Lamb *et al.*, p. 71.

112. McFate, interview, August 1, 2013.

113. *Ibid.*

114. *Ibid.*

115. *Ibid.*

116. *Ibid.*

117. Human Terrain System, "Vision and Mission Statements," March 3, 2009. Copy held with author.

118. McFate, interview, August 1, 2013.

119. Former HTT social scientist 1, interview, July 25, 2013.

120. *Ibid.*

121. *Ibid.*

122. Cindy R. Jebb, Laurel J. Hummel, and Tania M. Chacho, "HTT Trip Report: A 'Team of Teams'," West Point, NY: Unpublished report for TRADOC, 2008, p. 8. Copy held by author.

123. Lamb *et al.*, p. 225.

124. *Ibid.*

125. Lamb *et al.*, p. 225.

126. Former HTT social scientist 1, interview, July 25, 2013.

127. Lamb *et al.*, p. 232.

128. *Ibid.*, p. 227.

129. Human Terrain System, "Training Directorate Information Brief," December 11, 2009, Slide 25. Copy held with author.

130. *Ibid.*

131. *Ibid.*

132. *Joint Publication* (JP) *3-0, Joint Operations*, Washington, DC: United States Joint Chiefs of Staff, August 2011, p. III-12.

133. Human Terrain System, "Social Science Working Group: Learning Objective 1.2 Provide Operationally relevant sociocultural knowedge," n.d. Copy held with author.

134. Former HTT social scientist 1, interview, July 25, 2013.

135. Lamb *et al.*, p. 17.

136. Former HTT social scientist 1, interview, July 25, 2013.

137. *Ibid.*

138. *Ibid.*

139. *Ibid.*

140. *Ibid.*

141. *Ibid.*

142. Human Terrain System, "Human Terrain System Yearly Report, 2007-2008," p. 31.

143 . Anonymous, interview with author, location withheld, July 29, 2013.

144. Human Terrain System, "Human Terrain System Yearly Report, 2007-2008," pp. 31-32.

145. McFate, interview, August 1, 2013.

146. *Ibid.*

147. *Ibid.*

148. Clark, interview.

149. McFate, interview, August 1, 2013.

150. Robert Albro, interview by author, Washington, DC, August 14, 2013.

151. Former HTT social scientist 1, interview, July 25, 2013.

152. Army Human Research Protections Office, "Policy and Guidance," Washington, DC: Headquarters of the United States

Army, n.d., available from *ahrpo.amedd.army.mil/Policy-and-Guidance/FAQs.html,* accessed August 16, 2014.

153. Office of the Secretary of Defense, "Title 32—National Defense, Part 219—Protection of Human Subjects," Washington, DC: DoD, n.d., available from *www.tricare.mil/hpae/_docs/32cfr219. pdf,* accessed August 16, 2014.

154. Clark, interview.

155. Michael Flynn, "Sandals and Robes to Business Suits and Gulf Streams: Warfare in the 21st Century," *Small Wars Journal,* April 20, 2011.

156. Zok Pavlovic, interview with author, Alexandria, VA, August 14, 2013.

157. *Ibid.*

158. Human Terrain System, "Human Terrain System Yearly Report, 2007-2008," p. 22.

159. Former HTT social scientist 1, interview, July 25, 2013.

160. *Ibid.*

161. Sharon Hamilton, "HTS Director's Message," *Military Intelligence Professional Bulletin,* Vol. 37, No. 4, 2011, pp. 1-3; Institute for Defense and Government Advancement, Special Operations Summit 2011, Colonel Sharon Hamilton on "Human Terrain Systems, Tampa, FL, available from *www.youtube.com/ watch?v=Tl3rNcbjPJE,* accessed November 8, 2014.

162. Former HTT social scientist 1, interview, July 25, 2013.

163. *Ibid.*

164. McFate, interview, August 1, 2013.

165. Former HTT social scientist 1, interview, July 25, 2013.

166. Reuss, interview.

167. *Ibid.*

168. Clark, interview.

169. *Ibid.*

170. *Ibid.*

171. Anonymous, interview.

172. Montgomery McFate and Steve Fondacaro, "Reflections on the Human Terrain System during the First 4 Years," *PRISM*, Vol. 2, No. 4, p. 63.

173. Former HTT social scientist 3, interview with author, Alexandria, VA, August 1, 2013.

174. Lamb *et al.*, p. 73.

175. *Ibid.*, p. 74.

CHAPTER 5

THEORY AND PRACTICE

In 2008, in Salah ad-Din province, north of Baghdad, a recently deployed Human Terrain Team (HTT) joined the Brigade Commander from the 101st Airborne and his personal security detachment on a mission. This HTT's specific purpose was to collect information on the *Abna al-Iraq* (Sons of Iraq). The Sons of Iraq were a security force, the bureaucratic embodiment of the tribal sheikhs' uprising against al-Qaeda in Iraq. This revolt began in the summer of 2006 in response to the brutality of the al-Qaeda splinter group which had become entrenched in al-Anbar. Understanding the motivation and expectations of the Sons of Iraq, the security force pivotal to stability in the area, was a strategic priority for U.S. forces as they prepared to withdraw from the nation.

The convoy's first visit was to an electrical plant in Bayji, where members of the embedded team went into a side office to interview mid-level plant officials. The research manager of the team had an M16 rifle rather than an M4 (a result of being armed at a Continental United States Replacement Center and not as an infantry soldier) and a pistol. As they walked into the confines of the small office, his first thought in this, his first engagement with the Iraqi population, was that, "This room is way too small for me to shoot someone if I have to pull out my weapon, because the barrel is too long."[1]

Realizing that the rifle was redundant in the confines of the room, the research manager undid the catch on his pistol, thinking that "If someone comes through the door, I have got to be able to draw my

231

weapon within this very small space, totally logistically thinking."[2] The mid-level Iraqi officials in the small room looked stunned, and the research manager realized he had made a mistake of judgement and perception. While those in the room "glossed over" the incident, the research manager observed that there were connotations of the:

> role of the pistol as a status symbol of intelligence officers in the secret police in Iraq during the era of Saddam Hussein. To walk into the government official's office and basically do everything but draw a pistol? It was incredibly culturally insensitive in so many ways, not to mention rude,

such that he realized that this was his "first introduction to "Oh yeah, this is a lot harder to do in practice than in the classroom."[3]

This situation emphasized a gap between theory and practice. It suggests that the experiences of HTT members in the field are a necessity in any examination of the Human Terrain System (HTS). For that HTT member in Salah ad-Din, it highlighted "the importance of experience-based learning"; that:

> even with all the 6 months of training and talking, even knowing intellectually what was right and wrong, the military training and the idea of personal safety somehow made me gloss over all of that for an instant.[4]

Ultimately, in this reading, "it's a reflex that you have to train out or at least develop some understanding of how you use it. It's very subtle tradecraft things like that make all the difference when you are dealing with people."[5]

American anthropologist H. Russell Bernard has written that, "Good ethnography is about the narration of good stories."[6] In the military environment, ethnography is also about developing quickly an understanding how seemingly insignificant body movements can become inflated in the atmosphere of conflict to assume disproportionate problems for researchers. There are limits to what a training cycle at Fort Leavenworth, Kansas, can prepare recruits for, because conflict zones possess their own norms where the social boundaries in the United States no longer exist. The complicated discrepancies between theory and practice as related by a former embedded team member are exacerbated by the change in the character of the military during forward-deployed operations as opposed to training in the United States. As Jennifer Clark notes starkly, "It is a different culture over there [Iraq]."[7]

Theory and practice diverge on two distinct levels. First, at the individual level of the HTTs in the stabilization and enabling operations, there is observable difference between the theoretical architecture constructed during their training and the reality on the ground. Second, a conflict zone is a unique environment. It is a "war culture," where the system is characterized by a tendency toward increasing societal disorder, which has its own reality. Prussian military theorist and practitioner Carl von Clausewitz observed that war, as an absolute, theoretically tends toward chaos because of its intrinsic modality but is constrained from reaching absolute disorder by policy—the goal for which the conflict is waged and hence the method used to achieve it.[8]

There is a notable lack of literature on the actual experiences of HTT social scientists in Iraq and Afghanistan, these "war cultures." I cannot answer why social scientists were required by the Brigade Combat Teams

(BCTs) without investigating their involvement in the brigades, the research they undertook, and the products they created to plug the sociocultural capability gap in operations. This chapter investigates these aspects of the social scientists' experiences in Iraq and Afghanistan. I find that the deep research they undertook was able to augment BCTs' understanding of the battle space.

To varying degrees, the information could influence planning, but this influence was limited by existing policy, which shaped operations, and the duration of research, which by the time it was produced, spoke of a sociocultural picture which was already an artifact from the battle space. Therefore, the best research was in ad hoc operations devoid of overarching strategy, conducted in synchronization with the battle tempo. When that tempo was slow, the deep research had greater probability of influence thinking at the staff level. This investigation thus has value in ascertaining why HTS might have value as a tool for long-range planning, plugged into the strategic level of planning in Army service regional component commands.

IN CONFLICT

The military enterprise embraced intellectual curiosity, as seen in their doctrine, teaching, exhaustive list of publications, and open-source platforms for publication. Those products stem from the desire to arrive at solutions for complex problems faced in the spectrum of threats facing the nation. At first contact, however, civilian academic integration into the military enterprise can suffer from seemingly insignificant elements such as technical language. As Zok Pavlovic, who went through training in the June 2010 cycle and embedded at the Theater Coordination Element level in Afghanistan notes, foremost among these particular differences which create confusion is the aspect of language and terminology, words such as "diffusion, other scholarly terms; our colleagues [in the academy] have to understand that these are not terms the intelligence community would use."[9] For Pavlovic:

> When you bring an academic crowd into a military environment, each side wants to remain in their own domain. The military wants to run things the way they want to and they are the customer. The academic crowd has difficulty adjusting to the customer's needs and that generates issues. It is difficult to adjust that working environment to the planning process, to the decision making process and to address the issues that commanders need.[10]

These clashes were not predetermined, and it is part of the problem with attempts to offer generalization of the HTS that each encounter was *sui generis*. A highly adaptive academic and an engaging brigade staff could mitigate such issues. In adaptation, it could be the reverse, that academic language was integrated into the military decisionmaking process, and valued as part of a highly unique solution set.

The military planner requires objective facts and clear language, and this must be made explicit and understood by the academic. The military is a highly adaptive enterprise because it has to evolve in order to defeat its adversaries. Failure to do so costs lives. As a consequence, there is no doubt that the U.S. military enterprise learns academic concepts extremely well and extremely quickly. There was a deficit of sociocultural knowledge in the military in 2006, however, which meant that the HTTs had to couch their products in military concepts which already existed in order to integrate it into the staff operations process. This strikes upon a wider problem; that existing models such as areas, structures, capabilities, organizations, people, and events (ASCOPE) and political, military, economic, social, infrastructure, and information (PMESII) were ill-suited to the *sui generis* challenges facing each HTT, but they were the concepts which were widely used in the brigades at this time. The adaptive academic sociological requirement of warfighting demanded by the December 2006 *U.S. Army Field Manual* (FM) *3-24/Marine Corps Warfighting Publication* (MCWP) *3-33.5, Counterinsurgency* is yet to be integrated into the military enterprise.[11]

Parsimony was very much required. Verbiage omnipresent in scholarship would obfuscate the findings of granular research conducted by HTTs. Academic orientation toward research for the sake of knowledge rather than for an operational end would require curtailment. Moreover, that end product had to be presented in a concise manner which could integrate into the military decisionmaking process. The tendency in academia was for complex data to be conveyed in complex manners. The HTS was an amendment of that pathway, taking complex sociocultural data and parsing it into intelligible forms.

This transition was not immediate and required the understanding of the brigade while the embedded team adapted to operational demands. For the HTT, that embedded to plug a capability gap, the burden was on that team to adapt to the military customer. That required amelioration of language, simple representation of granular research and development of products that maintained pace with a fast operational tempo. The HTS had to plug into the brigade staff through the team leader, who in the original conception would be a retired or reservist colonel or lieutenant colonel in order to be of an equal military stature to brigade staff, but the HTTs also comprised a field element and, as such, had to attach themselves to military convoys. They had been trained to conduct research in that manner, write up reports, and push them to the staff in order to inform the operating picture. Failure was not inevitable in this reading, but required both excellent HTTs and adaptive brigades. If those two elements united, then there was every reason to expect the HTTs could significantly augment detail of the human terrain.

Consider Dr. Montgomery McFate's use of structural functionalism to model and make resonant the human environment in stabilization and enabling operations. As McFate explains elegantly, the model "is predicated on looking at society as a holistic entity and the view that all parts are all elements of the society at some function" but importantly, it must be thought of as "a heuristic model, not as an accurate description. Some way in which to capture a bit of social reality and make it explicable to people who do not know what these words mean, it is not such a bad approach."[12] Compromise and collaboration are the first steps in enabling the conversation between the academy and military. Academic verbiage would uncouple the synthesis. Incorporating abstract concepts such as "postmodernism" would lead the military to reject the modelling out of hand.[13]

Already, we have visited the fundamental challenge: social scientists had to relate their granular research to a military customer and integrate it into the military decisionmaking process. This required subtle attenuation of academic style. The product had to be of immediate value and not something limited to the work done by the HTTs: every cell in the brigade had to produce coherent products from complex counterinsurgency (COIN) data and present it at a speed that it could influence the planning process. It was difficult to prepare for that tempo at Fort Leavenworth because conflict creates its own norms, and each region at each time was unique. Indeed, this gets to a larger issue in academia in the 21st century; that there is an accelerated need for research to resonate beyond the academy, that knowledge exchange activities are fundamental to the work of the academic.

Underpinning research with theoretical context, for example, complicated the message of the product. Ultimately, it is the "so what" that matters—as much with academic knowledge in general, as with academic research conducted for a nonacademic audience. All knowledge requires that "so what?" element. Here was a paradox of the training, because it necessarily taught theory in order to proceed onto facts, but the theory muddied research products when embedded in brigades. Products had to be direct, balanced, and objective, showing research methods up front and identifying limitations. Embedded teams encountered problems when they delivered a product without research context. As Ryan Evans notes, in that circumstance, the research became "social science as sorcery" and thus difficult to convince the brigade of its utility.[14] There was a delicate balance to be struck that would be successful only with extremely adept HTTs that depended largely on the research ability of the social scientists. Research had to be transparent in terms of how it was created, but the operational tempo did not allow for deep examination of peripheral theoretical concepts which offered little or no added value. Deeply complex information had to be presented clearly and concisely, with the very minimum of qualifications to the findings.

INTELLIGENCE AND INFORMATION IN THE FIELD

Compromise between academic complexity and military clarity was only one distinct aspect of the process of negotiation which was evolving between HTTs and their parent brigades. The debate seeking to clarify the program as an intelligence or information asset lay at the heart of the efficacy of leveraging academic research methodologies in Iraq and Afghanistan for a military customer. In its earliest iterations, the debate was a heated one; one writer, Nathan Hodge, argued that because HTS worked for a unit commander, it was an intelligence asset because any information could be used to improve lethal targeting, and moreover, HTTs were co-located with intelligence cells.[15]

That assertion from Hodge is demonstrably false; most information cannot be used to improve lethal targeting because it fails to capture any atmospherics regarding the insurgents. The certainty of his claim loops back to the entrenched positions of proponents and critics; that it was often difficult to commence and retain a calibrated debate. Ethics were what the individual and, by extension the team, made of them. Information control and personal motivation regarding targeting insurgencies were *sui generis*. In the beginning, the HTS management was uncertain as to where to place HTTs—either in the intelligence cell or in the nonlethal effects cell (the latter composed primarily of Psychological Operations and Civil Affairs units), and in late-2008 ascertained that the effects cell was the best place for the HTT.[16] This made Hodge's argument a moot point. The permanent separation may have been done to preserve the academic profile of the HTS in order to retain appeal among the scholarly community.

The HTT products could be subject to grey pathways which potentially criss-crossed the channels of intelligence and information.[17] Under the direction of McFate, therefore, training stressed information over intelligence, which was one of the "big classroom discussions" for HTS recruits.[18] Instructive in the differing mentalities, from the military-trained presence in the classes, there were arguments that, if information gathered could save lives, it should be used in any way necessary. Ultimately, the academic and military approaches which clashed in training were symptomatic of the character of research conducted in the field. As one social scientist explains:

> that I think was both the most productive and the most impactful parts of the training; the very culture-conflict in class is the same as you experience in the real world, which is not the culture conflict with Afghans it is the military versus the researcher conflict which is like — how to do a research project, the slowness, the care that you take about, you know, privacy or about taking time to understand what somebody says, and none of that fits well with the military pace.[19]

The importance of intelligence versus information was amplified by the population-centric COIN tactics enabled by General David H. Petraeus in Iraq and later endorsed by General Stanley A. McChrystal in Afghanistan. COIN tactics made cooperation and support from the host population "at least as important to our success as combat operations."[20] COIN environments where emphasis is in understanding the population invert the conventional intelligence pyramid, generating the need for a "bubble-up" framework where knowledge gleaned at the tactical level ought to influence operational character and policy direction. Tactical collection of sociocultural information can be amplified by embedded academic experts, whose research methods are outside army capabilities and:

> include classic anthropological and sociological methods such as semi-structured and open-ended interviews, polling and surveys, text analysis, and participant observation. Both qualitative and quantitative methodologies are used, based on the research required.[21]

Those methodologies, now implemented in Iraq and Afghanistan, were subject to scrutiny. Application of models to convey cultural information of the area of operations (AO) is problematic and contributes to the reticence of the military to engage actively and continually the "soft" sciences.[22] For example, PMESII, the most widely used sociological model for warfighting generally, originated from a 2000 wargame, *Unified Quest*, conducted jointly by the U.S. Department of the Army and U.S. Joint Forces Command. It was developed "as a means of enabling kinetic targeting tangible nodes in a network."[23] *Unified Quest* was a year-long annual wargame, the capstone wargame in the U.S. military enterprise, and examined military adaptation in the face of several international crises. Thus the wargame looked at evolution and concepts and models which would most facilitate holistic examination of the changing, complex environment.

Instructively, therefore, PMESII was an analytic sub-component of a concept known as Operational Net Assessment and "meant to provide a holistic view of the environment in which military forces will be operating."[24]

Highlighting the compromise between academy and military, and the limitations of existing models, the PMESII model suffers three principal shortfalls. First, it is over-simplistic, failing to incorporate informal political systems. It is therefore less accurate in modeling weak states where illicit economies are a substantial feature of the societal system. Second, the model is incompatible with social science literature in its definition of government, which implicitly spoke at how far behind the academy the military enterprise was in 2007-13 in their conceptualization of the social domain. Third, it only evaluates physical tangibles, leaving no room for belief systems or other important intangible aspects of human systems.[25] McFate, Britt Damon, and Robert Holliday sum up the COIN environment thus: "Unfortunately, the tail wags the dog far too often in the military-industrial-contractor complex, and systems designed at the joint level rarely aid in the company fight."[26]

This fundamental disconnect between the rarefied doctrinal atmosphere of joint publications and the "company fight" was exacerbated by the unforeseen, *sui generis* character of the insurgencies. Inevitably, the U.S. Department of Defense (DoD) methods, models, and taxonomies spoke to a more regular adversary that competed on a battlefield and used standard munitions. The existing models thus had "limited reference to the lived experience of commanders on the ground that actually used this information in day-to-day planning and execution of operations."[27] In addition, the input to develop the concepts had come from the top level, with little input from the "lowest possible level of the command structure."[28] What this means is that, for instance, culture courses at the U.S. Army Command and General Staff College or the "multi-million dollar simulations" at the Joint Training Counter Improvised Explosive Device Center were not responding accurately to the important lessons derived from on-the-ground experience.[29]

HTTs thus offer a rare glimpse into expert experience of the utility of such models at the lowest level in the conflict zone. HTS follows doctrine codified in FM 2-01.3, *Intelligence Preparation of the Battlefield*, in additionally using ASCOPE to define civil considerations in an AO. The ASCOPE model is broad enough that it has been used by HTTs, most especially as an initial baseline assessment. According to the *Human Terrain Team Handbook*, examination of ASCOPE begins with analysis of available data, including from Provincial Reconstruction Teams (PRTs), Psychological Operations, and information networks.[30] The model is codified into the 2006 *Counterinsurgency* field manual, which was extremely useful for highlighting to BCTs what it was that embedded teams could provide to the staff in terms of sociocultural awareness.[31] The HTT social scientist Marcus Griffin, writing about what he did when embedded in a BCT in Baghdad, noted that he used the ASCOPE model and populated the six categories by visiting the Joint Security Stations, staying several days.[32] The method allowed him to understand better the exact needs of the brigade in terms of knowledge gaps, and research necessary in order to fill them.

While that model was used extensively by HTTs to create baseline assessments, use of the method hints at a particular and paradoxical problem. The HTS was created and developed in order to fill a need which was nonresident in DoD. This particular need was for sociocultural awareness brought in from social scientists who could conduct research in areas of operations to a depth beyond existing military capabilities. Using existing military methods, however, particularly ASCOPE and PMESII, meant that the embedded teams became in effect an integrated part of the existing military intellectual architecture. Given the fluidity of conflict and the *sui generis* nature of the spectrum of challenges facing embedded teams, this preoccupation with existing structural models and taxonomies obfuscates the dynamic character of insurgencies.

The existing models afford a static structure to something which is by definition subject to change over time. How can HTTs expect to replicate research products across *sui generis* operating environments? Is there enough similarity between the city and the village; the key leader engagement in Iraq and the *Jirga* in Afghanistan; the oil refineries and the agricultural fields; Arabic and Pashto? The social scientist in the HTT should be relied upon to develop *sui generis* research products which can speak to all levels of the brigade and relate to their experiences. Abstract models could miss granularity identified by the social scientist. Structural functionalism, ASCOPE, and PMESII were all used by the military already when AF1 embedded in February 2007. Using such models was not new. We are thus left to investigate the research modalities of the social scientists in order to understand if they were merely filling these models or conducting investigations using methodologies which were novel in the military enterprise.

ATTACHÉ AND RESEARCHER

Integration of theory was entwined with a more practical, physical integration. The military enterprise in Iraq and Afghanistan was far from uniform and HTTs largely depended upon any individual brigade commander regarding the level of importance placed on the team and their research. For example, there exists between the Marine Corps and the Army subtly differing group mentalities.[33] This variation in institutional character led to differences in how the two components perceived HTTs.

As early as 2008, Marine Corps feedback on HTTs that had been provided by the Army noted that as individual members these embedded teams had been useful, but that the teams in their entirety could have a net deleterious effect. The Marine Corps "has a lot of experience with bringing on individual augments, and knows how to do that; I think I probably would have been happier with that rather than being saddled with this whole team."[34] Additionally, as Clark explains, in the Marine Corps culture:

> You have 5 minutes to prove yourself. If you are no longer valuable in 5 minutes, you are not value added, and they get you out. You have to have a certain level of toughness, you have to be willing to stand your ground, but also be willing to say when you are wrong.[35]

The difference is not only cultural but organizational. As McFate explains, Marine Corps Regimental Combat Teams operate, and are organized, differently than that of BCTs:

Marines are like a tribal society with their own norms and rules, so we had to select people pretty carefully for those teams. The first team that goes into a unit, the first unit receiving a team, it is always an uphill climb to prove your worth, show what you can do, integrate into their battle rhythm.[36]

Implicit in McFate's statement, and telling from the point of view of the HTS management, is that there was less care in selecting the HTT members for other teams which would not embed with the Marine Corps and goes back to the mutual missteps in hiring between the management and BAE Systems. Interestingly, this comment would suggest that the HTS management did not carefully select embeds for the U.S. Army, and thus apportions at least some of the missteps to the management, rather than the contracting recruiter.

One of the first social scientists to embed with the Marine Corps noted that it is "a whole different animal from the Army" and that:

they are very small, and therefore they do a better job of leveraging whatever resources are available. And so if they have an enabler come in, if that enabler proves that they can be useful then the Marines will leverage them and act upon their information.[37]

Another social scientist found the Marine Corps "very insular" and:

so it really took a lot of effort to prove that you are useful, but the Catch-22 is, in order to get resources in order to conduct missions so that you can produce work, you have to prove you are useful; it's kind of like requiring job experience before you can get a job type-thing.[38]

This was part of the practical problem with the remit of the HTS. It had to plug a sociocultural knowledge gap. That knowledge when the team embedded, by definition, did not exist. To get the requisite knowledge, there was a requirement to get out into the area of operation, but gaining convoy support could be difficult. The ease of gaining convoy support varied according to the unique experiences of the HTT, but by-and-large was proportional both to the resources of the brigade and the perceived value of the research of the team. In the first instance, gaining convoy support required networking, which required interpersonal skills. It also meant researching any or all aspects of the bases on which the teams found themselves. These bases could be petri dishes containing the elements of the wider environment.

To prove worth, one social scientist integrated Marine Corps requirements directly into the questions used for initial team surveys, "getting what the Marines needed but also getting what [the] State department needed, so it was two birds with one stone."[39] It also necessitated an inexhaustible ability to share that information between the Department of State and the Marine Corps, facilitating conversation and collaboration because "there was a surprizing lack of coordination between those two."[40] Absence of coordination between service components was far greater, however:

> The Marines and Army do not communicate in theatre. They even have two different networks which they use. So the Army had TIGR [Tactical Ground Reporting System], CIDNE [Combined Information Data Network Exchange], and the Marines had [other systems].[41]

In practice, this meant that embedded teams across Army and Marine components possessed a horizontal character that the Armed Services lacked at the official level. HTTs could thus communicate between brigades, across different areas of operations, while the Army and Marine Corps "didn't talk to each other and although some of the Marine and Army counterparts would talk to each other, they did not do it frequently and their mission objectives were different."[42]

Organizational and cultural discrepancies were complicated by *sui generis* attitudes to the teams at the brigade staff level. Like other social scientists, Clark worked by integrating her research with information operations and civil affairs, the closest groups resembling her team, networking at every opportunity with teams such as the Iraqi Advisor Task Force, and leveraging language expertise to assist in messaging. The Iraqi Advisor Task Force was created in 2006 and was comprised of former U.S. Army Special Operations Forces (SOF) personnel, host population and Iraqi expatriates, charged with analyzing host media and conducting polls in order to assist the COIN campaign through knowledge of Iraqi society.

Networking was critical to getting the team noticed. Clark went to every command meeting that she was able to, with the result that "more and more people wanted us to do working groups, more people coming in saying, 'Hey, I just want to read through your database, how do I get to it?'" That led to the task force, working on a full assessment of the hospital system in the area requesting assistance with cultural information, specifically asking for Clark.[43] Working on the hospitals explains why that individual, if not the team, became useful; Clark was able to leverage research from the hospital system, including information on gender relations and the nursing college training system, which hinted at larger problems in the community, trading that information with other assets in the brigade and requesting convoy space for further missions.[44]

Differences also existed not just between services, but between nations. This was granular nuance that could not be taught in training because not only could combat unit configuration be amended in theater, but U.S. Army trainers would lack specific knowledge of coalition partner brigade structures, especially their function and arrangement in theater. As a consequence, HTT members were flying blind when initially embedded. For example, Evans noted that British brigade headquarters were ordered differently than U.S. brigades, which, in turn, were similar to the Danish battalion. Having embedded with both coalition partners, Evans observed a lack of communication within the Danish battalion, finding that "the right hand often didn't know what the left hand was doing, and how much information they already knew," and so they had to interview Danes as they would Afghans to develop the information the HTT required in order to perform as per the requirements of the customer.[45] Interestingly, then, such were the unique identities of combat brigades that the first ethnographies necessary to be undertaken were of the coalition forces. War truly recreates societies anew on every level.

Special Operations Forces Augments.

Gathering information at the tactical level, the remit of the HTS meant that some social scientists embedded in smaller units than brigades. Indeed, Lamb *et al.* in their seminal study of HTTs have argued that the program would be best situated within the U.S. Army's Special Operations Command. They note the command's familiarity with small cross-cultural units and the continuing centrality of special operations to irregular warfare.[46] Reinforcing this assessment, according to intelligence officials at the U.S. Army Training and Doctrine Command (TRADOC), the Joint Special Operations Command has expressed interest in HTS assets, but by the end of 2013, there was no formal collaboration between the HTS and the command.

In practice between 2007 and 2014, official HTS collaboration with special operations units was largely limited to Afghanistan, primarily to support Combined Joint Special Operations Task Forces when the Village Stability Operations program began in early-2010. For these operations, it was of special import that the social scientists sent were physically capable of performing the role due to the remote locations, lacking infrastructure and engaged in arduous work as part of a daily routine.[47]

As well as official embeds, there were individual augments to SOF units based on entrepreneurial activity from HTT and Human Terrain Analysis Team members. For instance, Clark worked with SOF in Iraq though she found them "more insular, even than Marines."[48] Clark had originally embedded with II Marine Expeditionary Force division as a Human Terrain Analysis Team social scientist before attaching to Regimental Combat Team 8 in the North of Iraq to concentrate on Sinjar. Indicative of the variety of social scientist experiences, to conduct research, Clark was given convoys that would also deliver supplies.[49] The resources had been provided after a Fragmentary

Order from the II MEF G-2 to fill the sociocultural gap for the division.[50] Approximately half of the locations visited during the work were chosen specifically by Clark and her Human Terrain Analysis Team. During the course of her work with II Marine Expeditionary Force, Clark worked with SOF. It is the insular identity of the SOF and the rigorous physical demands of special operations that may limit HTS integration in the future.

One unnamed social scientist that deployed officially to a SOF unit in Afghanistan found the relationship with the unit they worked with to be much more dynamic than with regular Army units, in terms of the size of the team itself—there were 12 members of the unit—and the demanding character of the tasks. Those tasks included involvement in the Community Defense Initiative (which would migrate to Village Stability Operations and Afghan National Police [ANP]), which both ensured and required constant access to the population. As two other former HTT social scientists and an Army Civil Affairs Officer note of their work with those platforms:

> Stability practitioners that reside at a more local level, such as USASOC [U.S. Army Special Operations Command] teams, may live in a village their entire tour, with near total access to the nonverbal behaviors required to make more substantive judgments of norms and group identity.[51]

The research was of a similar modality to their previous work with the regular Army unit but the scope was reduced because the resources were more limited by the size of the team. As the social scientist explains, it "was a pretty unique setting" camped out in a village, living in an Afghan house, "right on a main road, with mud walls around us."[52]

The austere living conditions and rudimentary security were positive in that:

> You would get folks who would come by and knock on your door each day, so you would get access to a lot more people; but me being by myself was certainly challenging. Being an outsider on those [Special Operations Forces] teams is exceptionally hard, to be accepted within the units themselves.[53]

Integration was achieved by earning the trust and respect of the small unit, and the social scientist recalls an important rule made by one member of the unit for them: "There was a good line when I got there, 'You don't have to do guard duty because you're a civilian, but I want to let you know you cannot stay here unless you help us out with guard duty'."[54] To that end, the social scientist's experience was a wide spectrum of involvement from "hooking a local up to an IV [intravenous drip], filling sandbags, shoveling dirt, constructing houses, to digging holes.[55] The social scientist also found value in their Arabic language skills, translating some of the religious verses for the population. With SOF, reputation and rapport with the population were critical:

> It is a force-multiplier for them when they have that capability to count upon, locals for intelligence, development projects—they need the support of the local community. So, bringing a different, random skill set is not only important for them, because you're capable of doing something that is a little bit unique, a little bit different and in turn you can go into a town and talk and having a language skill set like that which is totally different, but you get into a setting where you're in a mosque, or wherever it may be, and you can talk to Quranic verses [sic]; rapport building; not a lot of

substance behind it but it could be a huge advantage because you are perceived as someone who can un-derstand the community; that can understand the cul-ture a lot better. They are not just seeing someone who is stopping through their villages.[56]

Integration into the unit was critical, because of the small size — there was a central question, as an outsid-er, but also as a civilian, will the social scientist be a li-ability? The difference between SOF and regular units was pronounced, as the social scientist explained:

If you are in a battalion or a company, there are plenty of guys that pick up the slack; but if there are 12 guys, you are out on patrol with six people, they have got to know that you are going to be able to hold your own.[57]

Other social scientists reinforce this view. Two other social scientists that worked on village stability ob-served: "On some of the most remote combat outposts, civilian social scientists can be quickly labeled 'dead weight' if they fail to participate in camp cleanup, solidify defensive positions, or participate in guard duty."[58]

Ultimately, the social scientist interviewed judged his or her efforts and those of the unit as a success, based on the observation that the area had the first successful Afghan Local Police (ALP) team in the country.[59] As "the human terrain guy" attached to the SOF unit, the social scientist had reach-back sup-port from the HTS which was of utility. In addition, "coming from the civilian side you do have that flex-ibility. However, it is very difficult to integrate with those guys, it has to be the right personality, and you just have to be really flexible with the teams."[60] This distinct skill set meant that social science expertise, is

"something that is a little bit vague in lots of ways"
you can still influence outcomes, such as *shuras*, relationships with locals, which is the human terrain, and
is "enormously beneficial" because "most of the time,
we don't know what the hell is going on out there. You
can chip away at that a little bit, and have a positive
impact."[61] Although that was a plus, problematic elements existed because of the team size, perhaps five or
six people on a tactical mission—key leader meetings
with the governor or the mayor were logistically challenging. But a larger team would be a double-edged
sword, which is "too big; it requires too much red tape
and bureaucracy" to do flexible engagement with the
population.[62]

With the Special Operations units:

> you get a really short proposal and you can get buy-in
> from your company commander or the team leader or
> whoever it is and they say, 'okay if that's your call,
> make the call, go for it.' Being on the tactical level like
> that is a pretty beautiful thing to see.[63]

HTS in areas where the incumbent exercises hegemonic or complete control would thus most likely
operate in a similar manner but without the SOF character because of the arduous process of integration.
HTS in this iteration, therefore, would be small teams
in the field, a section of which operate close to local
populations, ensuring integration and collaboration
at the societal level; while the military team leader
would operate in an advisory role, in the "hip pocket"
of a combatant commander. Working for the small
unit will bring with it the inevitable cost of detached
objectivity; however, social scientists "should be an
integral part of the team but at the same time maintain a level of autonomy and independence to conduct

substantive fieldwork. These two prerequisites are not easily met."[64]

OPERATIONALLY RELEVANT REPORTING

In practice in Iraq and Afghanistan, the highly contested character of the spaces in which HTTs operated gave them an entrepreneurial character. This was because of the unique requirements facing each team that led to *sui generis* research agendas. Nicholas Krohley embedded with a BCT managed overall by the 4th Brigade, 10th Mountain Division in southeastern Baghdad in February 2008. As the social scientist, Krohley was broadly responsible within the HTT for research design, the overall management of fieldwork, and the analysis and presentation of collected data. From the early program training cycle, Krohley drew the impression that the social scientist's role would be part of the staff element, possessing a research team of other analysts to fill information requirements as needed; attend meetings and, facilitate reconstruction talks.

But arriving in the eastern edge of Baghdad at the beginning of 2008 and embedded with a brigade which had three districts of the city within its responsibility, the brigade found one of the districts, Tissa Nissan, "in chaos basically—the local government didn't really meet, and when it did meet, nothing really did happen of any use, efforts to develop local relationships weren't going anywhere."[65] Absence of physical security meant that:

> people were getting killed—both Iraqis killing Iraqis, people killing the Iraqi police, and also American soldiers were getting killed, in roadside bombings, par-

ticularly the EFPs [explosively formed penetrators] that were coming in . . . Those were a big deal, in our neck of the woods.[66]

From the classroom at Fort Leavenworth to the combat zone in Baghdad was a sizeable transition. On the ground, instructively, Krohley notes that:

there was no mission, clearly-defined, beyond being 'useful'—in quotes, for Human Terrain Teams at the outset. There was a purpose to fill, but it wasn't clear how you were supposed to do that. It was a case of 'you have these skills, go out and make yourselves useful'.[67]

Because there was only one district which required deciphering at the societal level, the "traditional model of being sort of a meeting-driven, staff-driven asset, wasn't going to work, just because we didn't have answers to the questions that were being asked."[68] Knowledge of complex Iraqi history such as that the social scientist possessed was inadequate in meetings where the problem set was specific, fluid, and contemporary. Put succinctly, the question was why was this one particular neighborhood in conflict, when around it there was relative calm? The team structure was organized to generate an answer; the team leader remaining at the brigade staff level and the remainder of the team dispersing and embedding at the company level; going "neighbourhood to neighbourhood, often alone, but sometimes in pairs, and language ability was the real determinant there" where the "really good Arabic speakers we [Krohley's team] had were effectively turned loose."[69]

How had this arrangement of the team, different from that of the function and roles envisaged in the training cycle, occurred? The military structure is by design a kinetic machine which leverages overwhelming physically destructive assets to compel, coerce, or defeat an adversary by killing. Even within a COIN framework, there may still be present an overwhelming predisposition — through training, belief, and experience — to triumph in combat through kinetic means against an identifiable enemy through that preferred mode. As such, for there to be an appreciation for sociocultural awareness in the high levels of the brigade structure, the "commander has to truly value diversity of ideas, through his actions as well as his words, and he has to truly value the criticality of cultural knowledge and the importance of non-lethal effects in general."[70] Arrangement of the HTT in the command structure, as befitted the operational tempo, pertinent problems, intrateam and interteam relationships and perceptions of mission were therefore fundamental to the character of the research conducted.[71] As Krohley explains generally of leveraging sociocultural experts: "You are told why you were being sent, and why the job existed, and there is a general understanding of the utility of this service, but there were no specific instructions regarding, 'Well, when you get there, what the hell you do'."[72]

Part of the problem was the *sui generis* character of operating environments. As a consequence, there arose different identities which a team could assume when conducting research for the BCT staff, crystallizing around two forms: first, the investigator operating among the population; second, the staff-centered advisor who advised on the base. These identities were mostly shaped by the goal of the commander; an investigator would go out and find answers as part of a field-situated unit — a collection platform — whereas the staff-centered advisory team would influence the hierarchy of the military to ask the right questions, and "seed in" social science thinking of academic character to as many staff functions as possible.[73] In the staff-centered approach, social science thinking would filter downward into the field, through the generation of hypotheses to allow for specific research, through social science elements to written orders, and the tasks given to units in the field.[74] Ultimately, in the early iterations of the program, with teams sent to crisis environments, these heterogeneous characters of embedded teams were not resolved and suggest an inherent difficulty in generating a uniform template for team models across areas of operation or across time.

Despite this core problem, there were broad similarities in research methods between teams, based on the operating environment and the necessity of integration into the brigade structure. In order to enhance the reputation of their HTT and capture information about the operating environment, Krohley's team began by interviewing U.S. Soldiers in the AO, many of whom had been in the AO for nearly 2 years because of the extended surge deployments. There was value in gaining understanding of the customers and their mindset:

> some had insights, many had impressions mostly; it was very interesting. It was essential to view how different aspects of the military viewed the place they were operating in because you had to speak to that when you have answers, when you gave insight and guidance.[75]

Processing and analyzing the impressions and observations of the soldiers allowed the construction of 4-page neighborhood profiles (see Appendix P); simplistic representations intended to clarify the problem faced in the neighborhood.

From that base, more detailed research plans could be compiled which filled gaps in the data: What's wrong? What's missing? Where are the conflicts of opinion? Where do people see different things? Different question sets were thus constructed which formed the research plan tasked ultimately with answering the question as to why the conflict was persisting in Tissa Nissan, which then allowed research to proceed. This account provides a fascinating insight into the construction of a research agenda to answer a question where the baseline of knowledge upon first examination of the human terrain was negligible (see Appendix M). The basic landscape was mapped from initial reconnaissance by the brigade and research on what the Army was doing there—how they were operating—was ascertained. From that, the venues in which it might be reasonable to assume data could be collected were mapped: Were there useful government meetings? Were there civil society groups asking coalition forces for money? Were there locally recruited policeman who are part of the national Iraqi police force that could be engaged? Were there lots of door-to-door searches ongoing, which would allow an avenue for interviewing the population?

This methodology was a binary dynamic between collection requirements and collection opportunities, with a plan built around executing both. Krohley:

> built this out in more detail, probably in more detail than was used. Because in the end reality intercedes and you end up making the most of your opportunities, but it was a useful mental exercise and planning exercise to build this plan; basically to turn a research plan into a collection plan.[76]

Colleagues within the team were only contacted periodically, as little as once a month, via telephone or a SIPRNet email connection, and meetings with the team leader were of a similar frequency—the reason was not a personal one, rather "logistics were challenging enough" without having to take an additional ride in a convoy to sit down in an approximately 30-minute meeting where nothing necessarily might be learned.[77] The structured research plan, even if not strictly adhered to, was specific guidance on what was to be done and how it was to be done, enabling the dispersal of the team to achieve the research goals.

In relatively secure sections of the area, language skills allowed the possibility of deep social research. In 2008 in Baghdad, Arabic language skills afforded the opportunity for those proficient team members in IZ4 to develop substantive, long-term relationships with people, to go into different meetings, sitting down in a room in a chair, sitting across the table from someone, or on the phone, allowing collection from the same source repeatedly over a period of time, cultivating a relationship. At the other end of the spectrum were deeply insecure areas, where the local neighborhood council either would not collaborate because they were overtly hostile to the American presence there, or were dubious research partners in that their information provided would be compromised; mostly because of their desire in "milking the U.S. Defense budget, or whatever the State Department budget was for reconstruction, to feed money to their buddies."[78] Those "dead ends" meant collection opportunities were limited to street-level encounters, dictated by the contemporary, evolving character of mission activities and conducted on an ad hoc basis.

In practice, the character of missions determined the modality of the research. Krohley notes that an important development for him occurred over the summer of 2008 when weapon ownership in residences became illegal for Iraqis as part of the terms of a decree which initiated large numbers of search and seizure missions across Baghdad. Sections of neighborhoods would be cordoned off:

> and you would have a few dozen Iraqi national police, a platoon or two, going to house to house, you know soft knock, 'Hello sir. How are you? Are you aware of the new law? We need your rifle'.[79]

Searching the house allowed an approximately 10-minute conversation — a one off — but over the course of that day, perhaps 30 or 40 conversations in total. Instructively, the research method changed dramatically, first letting the interviewee lead the conversation, which inevitably focused on lack of electricity, or explaining who the social scientist was, which meant that the social scientist would "effectively spend the 10 minutes doing PR [Public Relations] for the Army, and they would say: 'Ah, that's an interesting programme, it's great that they are doing this'."[80]

The absence of structured methods in this situation accomplished little of operational relevance, so the methods developed rapidly to incorporate various lines of questioning routed in specifics which were known about a particular neighborhood and patterns of movement and migration. In this scenario, understanding the chronological context of the place did matter; knowledge of the historical trajectory at the granular level, which expert social scientists possessed, helped frame the research questions, allowing the outsider to relate to the local area (see Appendix O). As Krohley explains, eastern Baghdad:

had been created in the second half of the 20th century in the migration which had occurred of mixing the populations, and knowing something about local history and the dynamics of local settlement was a very useful frame of reference for questioning; for talking to people.[81]

Why was this valuable? Iraq was in the grip of a civil war, and Baghdad was in the middle of a war which had split along sectarian lines. It was fast-moving and complex, requiring deep understanding of the historical fractures and the identities which had crystallized as a result. It also required integrating that expert historical knowledge into understanding of how the demographics of the city had changed as a result of the U.S.-led invasion, for which there was no existing census data as a result of the insecurity (see Appendix M). Capturing the changing character of the districts could only be possible through interviews. These interviews also shed light on the problems and concerns of the citizens and the groups with which they identified. Understanding the units of identity which were forming during the conflict allowed the staff to understand the best way to combat the insurgency.

Personal Choice.

The *laissez-faire* approach to guidance concerning HTT conduct in Iraq and Afghanistan engendered different approaches to ethics. The permissive protocol for team members allowed them to adopt their own idiosyncratic methods. Clark conducted ethically-rigorous research but observes bluntly that there were "plenty of teams that went to the dark side."[82] Clark was brought into the Social Science Directorate on her return from Iraq to recalibrate the ethical modalities of research. Another social scientist stated that it was always possible to pass on information regarding insurgents to the intelligence cell, suggesting that, at times at the discretion of the individual and team, the line between information and intelligence could become blurred.[83]

The truth of ethics in the program in Iraq and Afghanistan is that, in its design and execution, it was perfectly feasible to conduct ethical research from which the resulting information would not compromise the safety of those members of the population they engaged. For example, in gaining information "atmospherics" of eastern Afghanistan, AF1 in 2008 used a broad semi-structured interview template for the population (see Appendix N). In no way do the question sets compromise those interviewed or enable information gleaned to be used for kinetic targeting. Informed consent for research conducted on medical care in Iraq highlights the calibrated character of the research modes used by social scientists in teams and also shows the quasi-nongovernmental organization (NGO) character of the program and a way forward for the HTS should it transition into a more strategically oriented asset; to assist the Department of the Army in sociocultural planning concerns such as healthcare, agriculture, or commerce. As source protection could be ensured, if it was not at any time that was a misstep in the recruitment and training cycles, exacerbated by the psychological burden of conflict which stressed that the primary duty of the HTT social scientist was to the military unit in which they were embedded.

Concerns that the HTS was a clandestine intelligence asset are demonstrably false. Krohley offers a balanced assessment of the program and its activities:

The program itself was not the Phoenix programme—
we were not there to target and kill people, but that
being said there are ethical challenges to doing work
in this kind of environment because you're not impartial: we are on a side, we are not unbiased, neutral
academic researchers looking at conflict; we are paid
servants of the U.S. Army, there to help win a war,
as corny as that may sound. It creates a tension but it
does not, I think, create an impossible contradiction. I
feel very comfortable that I did ethical work.[84]

There is nothing "corny" in that assessment. The
only point of the HTS was to help the U.S. Department
of the Army win a war. The improvised explosive device (IED) crisis had ushered in the program to help
win a war that was being lost, and now in that "anything goes" environment, there was the possibility of
either protecting a source or not.

Bluntly, source protection—which was the core
ethical concern of social scientists in HTTs—could be
accomplished if there was a desire to achieve it. For
instance, in Iraq, individuals in HTTs cultivated long-
term relationships with Iraqis who were typically
already well known to the Army: local government
leaders; prominent civilians, with names and telephone numbers already listed.[85] Generally, the ethical
dimension of the encounter could be controlled by
calibration of the research method which, in practice,
meant the material discussed with the population and
the character of the questions asked of them.[86] Effective team members, possessing good language skills
and rapport with the population, might be sought out
by locals with intelligence information. Such a scenario is "inevitable" without it being "an ethical ca-
tastrophe" because the individual could be referred to
an intelligence officer.[87] In terms of targeting, the character of the information gleaned was largely inappli-

cable. HTS was not about identification and naming of insurgents. Instead, the program was concerned with tribal dynamics and the social conditions of a particular community, truly a complete transition to a COIN tool rather than a counter-IED asset.

HTS as a COIN tool therefore created a *modus operandi* of teams of nonkinetic information gathering. In one-off "house collection," Krohley, for example, never asked for people's names nor did the notes made in the notepads constitute intelligence and helping the military customer in this manner, but with ethical limitations, meant that the relationship with the Army structure was not contested or adversarial:

> The notes we had—when it came time to write these neighbourhood profiles—I had various colleagues email me their field notes that were typed up. Even those that had established long-term relations, they didn't send names with it; it would just have their (the team member's) initials (at the top) and "Source Number 1." There would be a little bit of contextual information of the person insomuch as that helped me understand the background to the information insofar as they were a policeman for example or a government official or a displaced person or whatever. That was that. The military never asked for us for anything that they shouldn't have asked for, and frankly we didn't have much to give them in that respect, in terms of targeting information.[88]

The same conclusion is drawn by the West Point study which observed that the line of demarcation seems to be "running a source"; which is the point where the HTT should hand over the collection to intelligence agents should the team inadvertently uncover a "likely intelligence source."[89] Given the research questions from AF1 in 2008 and the Iraqi hospital research, it is unlikely that, in conducting that research, information on the insurgency allowing targeting would arise. It has become, in essence, a quasi-NGO.

Developing explicit limits regarding the possibility of targeting is a core theme for social scientists concerned with the ethical character of their research. Clark notes that, in her work with a SOF unit, each night they would go through mission objectives, because even though they often aligned, occasionally they were not the same. According to Clark, while there was an implicit understanding that there was a broad need to identify insurgents because that would reduce coalition casualties in the long term, that was not the job the HTT and to do so would thus ethically compromise her as a social scientist.[90] Both Clark and Krohley had the ostensible motivation for their work to facilitate their unit to make more informed choices at the tactical and operational levels in a COIN environment. This mandate allowed ethical research. Ethics, however, are a black and white issue; either a source was protected or it was not. HTS, as a program for COIN, allowed ethical research; if ethical research was not done, that was the compromised ethical stance of the HTT individual or whole team, which could be exacerbated by pressure applied by a unit commander.

Embedding with a unit, particularly a small unit such as many of those used in operations by SOF, in which rapport and obvious, immediate utility were critical to value, meant that loyalty to the customer might come first and outweigh other considerations. In this environment, strength of character could be a critical factor in determining the ethical content of interactions with the population. This is an inevitable occurrence of embedding with a group in a highly contested space prone to violence. As one social scientist in Afghanistan made clear of work with SOF, their primary import was in supporting the unit. The ethical boundary could easily be crossed, in which case you could side with the military or, according to the social scientist:

> say 'I'm just not comfortable with this.' I was lucky in that I had two really great SF (Special Forces) teams, and they would say 'are you okay with this?' 'I'd say I'm not on board with this' And they were very generous and gracious with me backing off, and they'd say 'okay, no problem'.[91]

Despite indications of teams going to the "dark side," in the course of this research, there emerged few indications that any team did so. There is probably a professional reluctance to identify teams that did, or identify that they themselves conducted unethical research. One social scientist that worked in Afghanistan admits that they "ended up doing a lot of intelligence" because of the nature of the questions, which yielded information on Taliban movements, which they passed along to the military, "very quietly and discretely; I would tell them, 'I am not the right person, I will get you in touch with right person'."[92] If intelligence personnel were in close proximity, this referral could be done quickly, but if not, because it was difficult for intelligence personnel to gain convoy support, then contact information would be taken. The questions often yielded intelligence, not something social scientists could easily walk away from, as to do so would be putting American lives at risk, "even though it doesn't go with what we were professionally supposed to be doing."[93]

Function and Acceptance.

The value of embedded teams in stabilization and enabling operations was to provide an understand function which existed outside the traditional bounds of military hierarchy. The team was plugged directly into the brigade staff and could thus facilitate military comprehension. This was an operational need, evidenced by multiple Joint Urgent Operational Needs Statements (see Appendices C-H). The resulting untested proof-of-concept plan developed in 2006 which went operational in 2007 immediately experienced a high operational tempo.

The high operational tempo required a strong ability of any HTT social scientist to communicate granular research in a concise manner with clear, actionable insights attached. As one social scientist observed:

> the military is very focused on succinct, strong communication. Statements must be backed up with solid evidence. If you don't know, admit it. Assumptions are deadly. Using qualifiers such as 'I think' or 'I believe' will get you eaten alive in a briefing.[94]

To that end, early iterations of training marginalized cross-cultural training between academia and the military, but one social scientist notes that by 2011, a large component of training:

> focused on giving briefings to commanders. Retired colonels and generals would tear us apart during presentations, trying to pull us down rabbit holes where a bad presenter would start to conjecture and only dig himself deeper.[95]

This is an example of training evolution bringing important value to the classroom. What had obviously occurred—implicit in this training revision—was a broad inability of HTTs to convey academic knowledge to the military staff in a manner which was coherent, balanced, authoritative, and actionable. This speaks to the problems of academic complexity in that the military encouraged actionable insights based on balanced and nuanced analysis shaped into easily presentable forms. It is implicitly a robust critique of academic presentation rather than a concern about the character of military thought. In conflict zones, there was no room for the "narcissism of minor differences" or "hollow verbiage masquerading as profundity" resident in the academy and academic texts.[96] The HTS thus refined academic expertise into packages which entered the operating cycle and could plug into the military decisionmaking process of the brigade.

In answering the crux question of the book, therefore, the military wanted social scientists for academic research which attached actionable outcomes. Compilation of taxonomies and theoretical context complicated the military decisionmaking cycle. Qualified assessments had utility, if relevant to operational planning. HTS was an ambitious Department of the Army enterprise to integrate academics into that process, funded through the U.S. Government to wed academic praxis to the military cycle. The onus was on the social scientists to make their research relevant. That their research was relevant shows the structural possibility of developing these refined academic research modalities in conflict zones.

Team failure was a result of the inability of the HTT to refine their research to integrate into the operating tempo. As the social scientists with the SOF in Village Stability Operations observed, the burden was on the academic to adapt and prove utility; that was their remit, and they were paid to produce demonstrable utility. If the social scientists failed to recalibrate their expert modality, either through choice or an inability to refine their work, then that was a recruitment and training misstep. The gap requiring an asset which conducted deep sociocultural research existed; it was a question of filling it effectively. Given the *laissez-faire* recruitment and the demands of a conflict zone, some teams failed to fill that gap.

Adapting to demands of the military unit was arduous in the conflict zone. Social scientists found that in order to function effectively and add value, it was necessary to integrate, "becoming much more direct."[97] This speaks to both the challenges of the academic in the conflict zone and the broader direction of academia more generally, as it seeks to ensure relevance in the social sciences in the 21st century. The military was a culture, in the words of one social scientist, "weird and totally antithetical to how I'd grown up—in order to bond, I had to tease and ridicule."[98] This affords insight into the lack of training which the program gave to academics. The carefully delineated boundaries of individuals in academia are unrepresentative of team relationships in the civilian sector more broadly, and the military even more so. There is a question here regarding the core challenges posed in training sets to integrate, both physically and psychologically, from the isolated academic environment to the team environment of the military unit.

To be accepted was to be functional and to be functional was to be accepted; this required an acceptance of military values. At the granular level of the soldiers in the company or platoon, this included respecting a fallen comrade and partaking of menial chores, such as filling sandbags or observation in a Mine Resistant

Ambush Protected vehicle while on a mission. Team members were earning wages much higher than the soldiers and enjoyed more freedom, which could breed tension if not held in check by communal participation in menial work and adoption of the lifestyle; small things such as eating the same food; wearing the same fatigues; and not be seen killing time in relaxing environments such as "the base Green Beans" (U.S. coffee house company with a contract with the U.S. military). "Then maybe you'll get enough goodwill to be able to request convoy support."[99] Deaths of fallen comrades were particularly hard if team members were embedded in small Forward Operating Bases, affecting everyone on the base.

These events could be made harder by the remit of the teams, as explained by a social scientist regarding his or her experience in Afghanistan, because:

> then the next day I went and had to interview the family of the Afghan policeman who had shot the soldier at point blank range. I quickly learned that every commander is going to prioritize the lives of his men over everything—and rightly so. But I had to show that I was factoring it into my mission requests.[100]

The customer was the unit leader, and successful teams were those that contributed to successful missions. To that end, missions or projects developed by the teams had to be conveyed to the commander in a way that showed the social scientist was considering the risk versus the reward, and that assigning soldiers or being granted convoy space were going to be worth the returns. In developing requests, especially in the early stages, the military language was critical because that culture is "so acronym heavy and, just like provincial dialects, every service, every unit, every tiny little team has its own language."[101] Each deployment came with a radically new language set as units moved in and out of a brigade, and the HTT had to adapt to those. Teams were timed to enter the theater of operations during brigade tours so that they could assist in unit transitions. The problem was that they then had to learn the new unit's structure and prove value over again. Certain commonalities existed but even as much as the language is a hurdle, so, too, was adopting the correct mentality.

"A Street Fight They Couldn't Quite Understand."

Part of the remit of the 4th Brigade in which Krohley embedded in 2008 was to re-establish robust governance in Rusafa, Karrada, and Tissa Nissan districts and to that end worked with Iraqi security forces, neighborhood and district councils, the technical and administrative offices of the Baghdad municipality, and civil society in order to accomplish the strategic goal of a transfer of authority for the area to the Iraqi government across 2008 and 2009. Initial assessment highlighted that Tissa Nissan, and particularly its area beyond the Army Canal, possessed much higher levels of insecurity for coalition forces than its neighboring districts, and this district was thus the subject of focus for the team. Juxtaposition to Sadr City meant substantial activity of the *Jaysh al-Mahdi* and other Shia groups in the district. In the Saddam Hussein-era, it was almost entirely a Shia area of the city, poor-to-working class, with pockets of middle-class and minority settlements.

The 2003 U.S.-led invasion and subsequent stabilization efforts fractured the human urban structure in Baghdad which had previously exhibited a degree of structural stability. This is an important point for social science work in conflict zones; qualitative research conducted before a war, no matter how recent, will be rendered largely outdated by forced mobilization of the population induced by systematic acts of violence. If the conflict is characterized by a highly insecure environment, the fluidity of these structural changes to the social fabric makes any deep analysis of the area a cultural relic. By the time the analysis has been rendered into a product, the tempo of violence has reduced the research to an examination of the past. The current of change in eastern Baghdad was pronounced after the invasion, which disrupted and then resulted in the disbandment of the Iraqi Army. The *Jaysh al-Mahdi* formed in an attempt to guarantee the security of Shia populations in the midst of sectarian violence, conducted a campaign of forced displacements such that the population of Tissa Nissan by 2008 was principally Shia, and the insurgency was being countered by Operation FARDH AL-QANOON, begun on February 13, 2007, as part of the surge.

In September 2008, the incoming team leader described the three districts, Rusafa, Karada, and Tissa Nissan as highly heterogeneous and intricate; the team answered operationally relevant questions and the "key is that the research must be operationally relevant. While general in nature, the guidance must be clear enough to allow the team to construct a sound research design."[102] The research conducted by the embedded team in eastern Baghdad had augmented the operational picture of the sociocultural environment (see Appendices O, M, and P). At the higher level, however, the influence and impact of this research was constrained by the strategic picture of the surge in 2008, with plans for the drawdown of forces having already been developed and major operations having already been planned. In addition, the surge of forces was a strategic push which had a distinctly political character and a set narrative: COIN, tribal engagement, and the transitioning of security control to the Iraqi government.[103]

The political dimensions of the COIN mode constrained the HTTs effect in 2008 in Baghdad. U.S. forces had developed a strategic mandate which emphasized the central role of the Sons of Iraq and district councils in developing high enough levels of security that there could be an effective transition. With these plans pinned at the political level, IZ4's (Krohley's team) research on the likely failure of the Sons of Iraq program in Tissa Nissan and the limitations of the district councils was unable to influence the strategic direction of operations. Within these political dimensions, IZ4 could only assist the brigade in understanding why events were unfolding in a particular manner; that understanding could not change the strategic direction of the brigade or the configuration of operations.[104]

Those research methodologies conducted by IZ4 were dictated by the needs of the customer. The problem set as Krohley explained it:

> wasn't Machiavellian politics among competing elites—it was a street fight that they couldn't quite understand and the only way to fix a street fight is to get on the street and figure it out. So it was a different approach, which stemmed a lot from the difference of circumstance.[105]

Research was situational, dictated by the operating environment. If the customer's problem dictated that the street was the answer, then that also avoided lot of the interpersonal issues and intrateam problems which were exacerbated by people in close proximity on base. HTTs were *sui generis* but success—augmenting the brigade's sociocultural picture — was achieved through a combination of adaptive research, team configuration, and a receptive brigade staff. Team configuration was fundamental to success: for instance, to respond to the challenges of Tissa Nissan, IZ4 split the team into deep research components, and only the team leader remained on staff. This suited the expert field research skills of the team members.

Team configuration was an element which could have been better analyzed in the training cycle. A central problem of the HTS had been that it went operational without a proper development phase that would have evolved optimum selection and training procedures for embedded teams. The original Human Terrain System model wove into the design a 24-month proof-of-concept phase based around a handful of teams. Under Fondacaro, bureaucracy was sidestepped, despite the fact that the military itself places enormous emphasis on intrateam compatibility and harmony, selecting teams, pairing individuals and paring certain personality types, as one former HTT social scientist presents it, "focusing a great deal on the team elements of work, particularly when you get into small units doing ambiguous missions."[106]

A small group given an intellectually challenging and ambiguous mission that they are meant to resolve without a particular and explicit reliance on the hierarchical structure around it required detailed planning by the HTS management. Put simply, "HTS didn't do that" and "a lot of it traces back to problems in the hiring places."[107] Krohley once had a colleague offer the opinion that:

> the hardest part of HTS is HTS. The war and the Iraqis are the least of our troubles most days, it's the pro-

gramme management or it's our teammates, and that all stems back to hiring issues and the crafting of the teams, both of which could have been a lot better.[108]

There were limits to the requirement for deep qualitative analysis of the kind offered by HTTs and their bespoke toolkits. In Baghdad during 2008, the IED was among the most pernicious of weapons utilized by the insurgents. IEDs were on the two arterial routes that bisected the AO, and the main access roads to U.S. Army outposts, which was not a complex observation requiring the compilation of social data. IEDs were placed on the major highway which ran north/northeast through Diyala province to Iran, which splits just before Sadr City; and on the other, which ran into the heart of Tissa Nissan. These were obvious sites for insurgent action, due to the volume of traffic, making it a target-rich environment. That analysis was purely qualitative, providing the necessary explanation of the environment.

The centrality of the IED to the military problemset in Iraq had brought the MAP-HT toolkit into existence, because of an "aspiration to build this programme that somehow combined IED incidents with sociocultural demographic information" to enable patterns to emerge, against which to allow the military to predict and plan.[109] Krohley argues that the theory was unlikely to be workable in practice.[110] Instructive for the IED crisis which brought HTS into existence, Krohley suggests that visualizing sociocultural data for the Department of the Army would not impact the IED problem in any discernible way.

In practice, MAP-HT could not augment the qualitative analysis of the operating environment. For example, Krohley notes the investigation of indirect fire sites. These were sites where munitions were launched even though the U.S. targets could not be seen directly. Many of these sites were not located in the militia strongholds themselves but in other areas of the districts with high concentrations of displaced people. Such areas provided an:

> atmosphere of chaos where people didn't really know one another, there was no atmosphere of community, there was no one in charge and there were always a lot of people coming and going, so if a team came in, in a couple of trucks or a pickup, they could come in, shoot a few mortars, and leave.[111]

An understanding of demographics combined with "just a basic idea of line of sight in a district" allows mapping with a great deal of certainty of the locations of indirect fire sites.[112] This comprehension of the sociocultural layer combined with military knowledge was being done well before the entry of the HTS. While the Army may not have appreciated every aspect of the social environment on the ground, they did capture the point of origins for mortar attacks with a great deal of specificity, and they knew where the IED hotspots were, with a great deal of detail.[113]

Instructively for the limitations of population-centered COIN doctrine in practice, the response is limited by the necessity to mitigate collateral damage. The U.S. Army can launch countermortar strikes; firing mortars into uninhabited areas of the city at night, acting on probabilities that there may be a mortar being set up; but that could not be done in a residential dwelling or an internally displaced persons' camp.[114] Kinetic response limited not by ability but by a necessity of responsibility is of import for any wider investigation of responsible parameters when employing

COIN tactics. Here is the dichotomy of the military enterprise conducting population-centered activities, because in preventing mortar strikes, to neutralize a key aspect of the insurgency would require an atrocity; the destruction of the internally displaced persons' camp. Low-intensity conflict expert Thomas Adams has observed that "unless a military force is willing to commit something close to genocide, it cannot destroy the opposing force."[115] Disproportionate use of force beneath the auspices of a narrative which foregrounded justice and humanitarian ideals was never a realistic response. Without a kinetic response approaching something close to genocide, then the military, despite augmented sociocultural knowledge, can only employ tactics which attenuate insurgent activities, lessening the effects, rather than confronting and neutralizing the insurgents themselves, often indistinguishable from the section of the population that has not taken up arms.

A Different Country.

War reshapes societies, fashioning new, warped demographics and propagating fluid shifts in groupings, narratives, and identities. Social layers shift; transitioning more quickly in more environments where selective violence is higher. After the U.S.-led invasion and occupation of Iraq, the power vacuum left by the collapse of the Ba'athist regime and the unpopularity of the incumbent Shia-dominated government generated intense sectarian violence. Religiously centered conflict caused large numbers of Iraqi Christians to flee the country, and by 2008, artificially induced by conflict, the Yezidis, a sect following a pre-Islamic tradition, became the de facto largest non-Muslim minority in Iraq.[116]

Historically, the Yezidis dispersed across various borders when political and administrative boundaries were redrawn in the Middle East as a consequence of the collapse of the Ottoman Empire in the aftermath of World War I. By the time of the U.S.-led invasion in 2003, the largest number of Yezidis was in Iraq, some 400,000, concentrated around the Sinjar region of Nineveh governorate. In Nineveh the Yezidis were outside the jurisdiction of the three Kurdish provinces, but subject to pressures from both the Iraq state and Kurdish political actors, the latter seeing the group as practicing anathema of religion, centered on their worship of a deity with the same name as a Satanic figure in Muslim theology.[117]

The Yezidi belief system draws from both Islam and Christianity, with a central deity being an archangel most closely resembling a peacock. English-language literature on the group is limited, made rarer by the insecurity for researchers during the Ba'ath-era in Iraq and which continued, if not increased, after the fall of the regime. Apparent heretical practices represented apostasy and in the *Hadith*, the sayings of the Prophet, heretics can be punished with death for abandoning their religion. In 2007, the Islamic State of Iraq issued a fatwa for the killing of all Yezidis, which accelerated a refugee crisis. By October 2007, it was estimated that 70,000 Yezidis had left the country.[118] The majority of these were from the cities, leaving many in remote regions of Nineveh still exposed.

In this period of intense population movement centered on identity, Clark was a social scientist researching the Sinjar during 2008. Kurds were pressing for autonomous regions in the north, but the boundary lines were disputed by the Iraqi government, and tense diplomatic negotiations were exacerbated by the presence of oil in the region of Mosul. The Yezidis straddled the Sinjar mountain range, a single ridge, which, according to another social scientist working in the area, was "basically in the zone of conflict of where that line was going to go if they had autonomy and therefore control the oil revenues."[119] Therefore, there was a question regarding the identity of the Yezidis about their inclusion in Iraqi or Kurdish territory and which may have had implications for oil resource allocation. While studying the issue, Clark understood that there was friction in the area, without comprehending the particular granularity, an absence of understanding compounded by the lack of military presence in the Sinjar range.

Clark immediately focused on Sinjar, attaching to convoys which were conducting stabilization missions in the Yezidi area, allowing the team to conduct interviews in towns where the demarcation was under dispute. Through interviews, a picture emerged of the Yezidis pressured by both the Kurds and Iraqi local political structure, which included economic incentives (payment to improve schools and infrastructure) but also coercion through violence in instances, explaining, at least in part, the victimization of the Yezidis during this period.

The Yezidis are clan-oriented and thus insular, rarely marrying outside of their culture, making them an easy, identifiable, and homogeneous group to target. To protect themselves, the Yezidis set up checkpoints around the towns, but physical coercion from both Iraqis and Kurds meant that other military forces were in the area; most particularly the Iraqi Army, Kurdish *peshmurga*, and other paramilitary groups. Research allowed the social scientists to tease apart the details of that conflict. From that research, the Marines deployed additional presence there and may have been responsible for a reduction in violence.[120]

The pace of population change meant that products produced by HTTs were often relics in the sense that the maps or other types of qualitative data captured spoke of a moment in the trajectory of the region which was already in the past. Back-filled team members would often have to conduct research on areas which had already been mapped previously, in order to understand the character of the changed societal environment. In Paktika, Afghanistan, one social scientist's early study was undertaken at the behest of a team leader, to have each district of Paktika province mapped at the socio-economic level, to include information on agriculture and urban settlements. On September 14, 2008, AF2 had requested from the Research Reachback Center a comparison of Iraqi and Afghan tribal structures, because the team had noted that many military units in Afghanistan were trying to transpose Iraqi cultures and tribes into the new AO. The report included a detailed social network analysis of tribal presence in Paktika's government.

This report drew on seminal research conducted by HTTs, including Michael Bhatia with AF1, but was confined to 2007. This 2007 research had been catalyzed and facilitated by Operations ATTAL and SHAM SHAD in the last 2 months of the year, where convoy support allowed the teams to interview the population to map the terrain. In addition, another team member in AF1, Audrey Roberts, based at Forward Operating Base Salerno had contributed to preliminary research and integrated that into the much broader area of Khost, Paktia, and Paktika combined, which was the area of operation for the 4th BCT of the 101st Airborne Division.

The rate of change coupled to the large area under the geographical remit of the team meant that there was continual need for further investigation, often of the same issues. It was the role of the HTT to plug the sociocultural capability gap by repairing holes in military understanding, making abstract complex concepts comprehensible, and integrating information into actionable planning scenarios. A later social scientist in Paktika assessing the needs of the military customer observed broadly the central role of irrigation in the agricultural system. Integrating understanding of the complex role of irrigation in exacerbating situational insecurity was one of the many roles of the HTT. The military staff at that point understood that "water is a very complicated concept" but lacked the tools to explore the issue further and concentrated on other more tangible and understandable aspects of the operating environment.[121]

As the research proceeded, it emerged that the societal structure for co-managing resources had broken down as a result of chronic conflict in the area, and there were no longer governance mechanisms for resource allocation. Government and tribal leaders had been killed, and the small underground well system (*kariz*) had been damaged by both physical movement and ordnance. In addition, ad hoc well digging, to offset the problem, had exacerbated the scope of the issue by lowering the water table, making the *kariz* less functional. Interviews with stakeholders on the canal, principally agriculturalists, allowed the social scientist to brief the military and the Department of State, who had previously been apathetic toward regulation of the *kariz*, seeing it as a problem principally for the local population, with minimal impact on livelihoods. After this research, the Department of State could increase water management projects to improve agriculture and give greater chances of employment for the vulnerable male population who could join the insurgencies.[122]

Granularity was as relevant in this instance for the Department of State as for the principal customer, which was the military unit. This shows the absence of deep sociocultural research across all components of the U.S. Government in conflict zones. While overall, the social scientist knew that the primary customer was the unit in which they were embedded, and that, if the customer was not satisfied, they could "go home now," their embedded team also stressed the need to network extensively with all organizations in the theater of operations.[123] Networking was necessary because of the entrenched stove-piping of organizations: United States Agency for International Development; Department of State, Psychological Operations, Special Operations Forces, Marines, and Army are stovepipe systems; groups which have the potential to share data with each other but choose not to do so. Despite different systems being located on the same base, even in the same building, even in the same room, "they are not sharing their information at the level of fidelity that needs to happen in order to say 'so what?'"[124]

As a broad example of the problem, there is intelligence and information collation required to assess the impact of IED events in an area. If one intelligence cell is collating IED events while another cell is calculating the number of cars crossing roads into the area, unless some entity in the unit is pooling the information, it is largely irrelevant individually. Systems, such as Intellipedia and the Tactical Ground Reporting System, serve to collate information at the ground level, but, in practice, there is nobody designated to pool the data in order to aggregate it into information of value. These disconnected pools of data and knowledge made the research process of embedded social scientists more arduous. Lack of sharing is a common theme in the recollections of social scientists; between armed service components; and between units, cells, and individuals. As such, in order to show value, the social scientists would share team products with any pertinent organizations with presence in the AO.[125]

Granular investigation at the local level had a number of customers who were more receptive to such findings than the military unit in which teams were embedded. As well as the Department of State, HTTs often worked with PRTs in Afghanistan. The creation of the PRTs centralized the role of development organizations in Afghanistan. HTTs could often engage in collaborative research processes, such as that outlined by an HTT member embedded in Ghazni in 2010. At that time, because of the physical scope of the AO, there were multiple districts for which the Research Reachback Center possessed no written material, because no one had been there to write reports previously. The team could use secondary source material—reports written by NGOs and historical documents such as academic articles—but contemporary knowledge of the region did not exist. The first mission of the HTT located there partnered with the PRT in that the governor had residence in the center of the district but would sometimes stay in his home village on the border of an area experiencing violent instability. Effective stabilization operations would require comprehension of these districts as yet unknown; the HTT leased vehicles from the Afghan Police and engaged in ad hoc reporting.

The area of the district was prohibitive to deep analysis, being about half the size of Rhode Island, but the team tried to cover as much as possible in 2 days before returning to the district center.[126] This research was conducted during the September 2010 parliamentary elections; fortuitous as the team analyzed the campaign posters in each village, as a proxy for identifying which candidates could mobilize people and possessed resources. This investigation highlighted key individuals, many of them already known from previous research done before the team deployed.

During the 2-day investigation, the team identified a dam which was cracking, requiring reinforcement. In order to start this process, the team returned to the district center and organized a key leader engagement with the governor. Earlier networking from team members who had been in the HTS for several years facilitated subsequent leveraging of resources required from the PRT. The team met with a local business leader in order to glean a history of the dam project, and a personal history of the individual, and:

> that was one of those moments where you realize, 'Yes, this is so different. This is so different from anything I will have ever been taught as an intelligence officer, that I ever would have been capable of doing, this is valuable, this is important on so many levels, God I wish we could do this more often'.[127]

During the talks, the Afghan related that he had heard of significant flooding in a remote area of the district that the team had not visited, and that those floods were having a significant humanitarian impact. Identification of this secondary, deep problem led to a change of mission, in which the team was broken into two groups, with one group of the HTT taking unarmored civilian vehicles into the mountains, with the governor, a driver, and a small private security detachment, and an engineer. This group examined the impact of the floods from a humanitarian perspective.

Resources were going to Pakistan to respond to the floods there, meaning that the United States had no presence in this area, highlighting that:

> not only do we ignore the people that are in need to some degree because of national interests, which are often driven by the fact that people are trying to blow us up, but our inability to direct assets to areas — to be informed — was shocking. No one knew that there were tens or perhaps hundreds of thousands of people in these upper valley areas whose lives — who were already living on the edge — but their lifestyles had been decimated, simply because no assets were ever applied there. And it points to a failing of the military intelligence process as well as its capacity. If it is not deliberately looking for something, it will never see it. And it simply does not look for things like this humanitarian crisis that was going on.[128]

Identification of the unfolding crisis meant that the HTT coordinated with the World Food Program for the delivery of food aid delivered to that district.

During that period of research, the HTT also visited archaeological sites to attempt to catalogue archaeological theft; they had a Polish archaeologist embedded with the Polish PRT. Archaeological theft was a major source of funding for insurgencies and criminality, though poorly understood by people on the ground and to date in literature: "the military simply overlooks it, because they don't look for it, they don't understand how it works and they don't respond to it."[129] In this area of low operational tempo, when there is not day-in and day-out fighting, civil-military partnerships can make a difference and meaningfully impact societies outside of incredibly violent insurgencies and general warfare.[130]

This is at the heart of the HTS. Meaningful impacts on societies can be made when there is low operational tempo. What would it take? While there is joint planning at the strategic level, this joint execution on the ground in countries would require a complete reconceptualization of the conduct of foreign policy and "some very powerful things would come from it."[131] The U.S. military enterprise has been engaged in a de facto stabilization project since the demise of the Soviet Union. It, however, has been slow to acknowledge that fact or understand how to develop a posture which is optimized for stabilization. While the HTS was a small program, the lessons from it are that civil-military partnerships which stabilize societies in areas of low operational tempo are possible.

Where violence enforced displacement, HTTs were the obvious tool for assessing the novel societal structures, allowing the decoding of both urban and rural environments. This was a common theme across Iraq and Afghanistan; for example, while embedded with a Danish battalion, Evans conducted research on Gereshk, the second largest city in Helmand and poorly understood at the time, which stood out as being particularly valuable to the Danish military structure in which he was embedded. Interviews with various members of the city afforded analysis of the societal structure of the city: From those initial conversations, it was deduced that the urban framework was composed of a number of villages which had bled into each other. Each neighborhood had a *malik*, such that understanding this, it became possible to understand the different populations within the city, geographically, and their adherence to each *malik*. The boundaries also aided understanding:

> the fluid nature of what was going on in the city, in terms of who was moving and who was moving out, and understanding the influence of poppy networks and the narcotics trade on the city, and how the politics of the mujahideen era were still very much relevant to what was happening to current day power struggles in the city.[132]

Fluidity of urban population patterns catalyzed by conflict required and still requires comprehension. The absence of deep knowledge of urban centers was not limited to Gereshk; it is a constant of conflict. Krohley noted the requirement for knowledge of the urban planning history of Baghdad proved critical to understanding insurgency activity; Pavlovic notes that "in a period of 10 years, Kabul grew from about one million, to over five million people; knowing where ethnic boundaries are and how they fit into the stability and security and development was very important to us."[133] War occasions the redrawing of national, regional, and local boundaries, both formal and informal, and the understanding of transformed demographics requires comprehension which recurs in interviews with social scientists that embedded and attempted to decode the alien human terrain.

Deciphering of the social environment on the ground was of a modality characterized by reporting rather than ethnography. Evans explains that the standard mode through which the team members gained access to the population was to walk through villages and fields and enter into conversation:

> there was no sophisticated sampling method, the environment didn't allow for that. We would up and talk

to people, sit down and have a conversation. I would know what data points I wanted to get to and I would try to structure a conversation around that.[134]

While the population was mostly receptive to the team members, Evans sort of "got a sense about when they were holding back about sensitive security issues; that wasn't most of what we were asking about so that was not a big issue."[135] The population was not receptive to the team members if there had been a security issue, which highlights that, with increasing insecurity for incumbent forces, there is an inversely proportional relationship to the fidelity of the data acquired.

Perhaps more than Iraq, Afghanistan presented a series of granular differences: Languages, dialects, and heterogeneity of cultures and identities rendered the human terrain particularly opaque. Ghazni alone had over a thousand villages, each with its own structure of leadership. Blanket generalizations would obscure granular nuance, but that nuance would obscure effective blanket planning. In the midst of this paradox, many effective research projects in Afghanistan were conducted at the atomic level of the village, as explained by one social scientist who worked with SOF in volatile areas where there was an emphasis on establishing the ALP.

The ALP had been created as a stop-gap measure in 2010 to hold security at the level of the village long enough to give the Afghan National Army (ANA) and ANP time to build up capabilities and expand into that area; the U.S. elements of the program were coordinated by the Combined Forces Special Operations Component Command—Afghanistan. The Soviet Union had tried similar programs, as had the International Security Assistance Force previously, but all programs eventually failed, with varying degrees of interim success.[136]

The ALP had the most high profile of several pseudo-militias created by the International Security Assistance Force where the official Afghan National Security Forces were unlikely to permeate for some time. By the middle of 2012, the force was 13,000 in number, with plans to increase to 30,000 by the end of 2014. That surge of ALP is similar to the effort of the Soviets who had raised militias based on the Afghan tribal system to stabilize the country to the extent that they could conduct a phased withdrawal. After the U.S.-led invasion, pseudo-militias such as the Afghan Auxiliary Police, the Afghan Public Protection Program, and the Community Defense Initiative had all been attempted in the regions now occupied by the ALP but Vanda Felbab-Brown, a Senior Fellow with the Brookings Institution indicates that the outcomes of these militias was "cumulatively negative."[137] Given the historical legacy of failure, the social scientist was tasked with examining what was happening in the communities where the ALP was being established; what had happened to it and its history according to academic papers, military histories, and the memories of the local people.

The project conducted by the social scientist was necessary because, given the historical legacy of similar programs, if there were no nuanced corrections offered, then the ALP project was set up for failure before it had commenced.[138] The research was from both secondary (existing literature on previous analogical programs) and primary sources; understanding what the locals remembered of the previous programs. This research was undertaken in combination with analysis of factors in the villages that would cause them to support the ALP and, conversely, factors which might lead to loss of support for the police, as well as examining what was said regarding alleged abuses committed by the police and other security forces.

ACTIONABLE AND INFORMATIVE

Research was only the raw dimensions of the work of embedded social scientists. The research needed to be packaged into a project which was comprehensible and thus actionable. Teams were undoubtedly hampered in their efforts by this lag within the military enterprise in sociological knowledge, and, as a consequence, fell back on rigid frameworks such as ASCOPE and PMESII. Given the flexibility of the successful social scientists, however, I ask exactly how the HTTs produced their research and what effect this research had on the BCT staffs. HTT products:

> are developed through analysing and synthesizing human terrain data gathered in the field and through debriefs/interviews. Products are the documentation of the team's human terrain knowledge of specific topics that are of particular concern to the unit, or should be. Together with input to working groups, this is the primary input to the human terrain team portion of the commander's Common Operating Picture.[139]

An Institute for Defense Analyses study on the HTS observed that human society:

> does not yield to the same type of empirical methods as experimentation that is common in the physical and biological sciences. There is no way to quickly measure changes that take effect over a generation—researchers just don't live that long.[140]

The onus was on the social scientists to conduct research which would then be of value to the commander, rather than having the character of their studies dictated by the commander. Because of the low priority of embedded teams until they proved their worth, they would often have to use transport assets that were used for missions other than their own, and would have to conduct research which fit around the tactical tempo. From that point onward, there was no research plan; no doctrine; no template for fieldwork. Instead, it is called a mission statement "in the corporate sense": go out and be useful, socioculturally: "You know, what the hell does that mean?" Even though procedures and guidelines were incrementally developed by program management, "there were not a set of procedures and guidelines that would have fit every particular experience, you know every type of place that was encountered."[141]

What did social science research in the conflict zone look like? Krohley gives insight into the initial stage of the process:

> to build a rapport with the soldiers—you want to get out and talk to as many of them as possible, particularly those who have been there a long time, to get their perceptions, their thoughts on what is happening, because that is actually the base line for everything.[142]

The methodology was to visit the joint security stations and combat outposts and the forward operating bases to conduct interviews, spending 2 to 3 days there attending ongoing missions, enabling a constant stream of ad hoc interviews with Iraqis. This broad introduction was focused on assessing the tone and lasted for the first 6 weeks. A core limiting factor was the logistics:

The work itself could have been done in three weeks, but you can't always get from one place to the next, you know. That was the biggest operational challenge throughout—it wasn't getting the Iraqis to talk to you, it wasn't finding the right missions to go out on, it was actually getting to the facility you needed to get to in order to get out on the mission that was happening the next day.[143]

The team integrated into existing convoys, rather than attempting to gain their own car service or private security detachment. Integrating into the military structure was important in order to gain acceptance which would optimize the relationship and facilitate research opportunities. As Krohley explains:

for every other hour of the day we weren't doing human terrain work, we would try and contribute, to be soldiers basically. I think that worked very well for us, in terms of the buy-in we got from the Army, people liked us, people liked having us around, we weren't a burden that needed to be looked after.[144]

Initial research conducted by social scientists often simply was broad survey work. This was necessary because team members arrived in the areas of operation with a baseline of knowledge limited to secondary sources and information provided by the Research Reachback Center prior to departure for the relevant theater. Both in Iraq and Afghanistan, this departure from a baseline of knowledge to more valuable information was often made in the same manner. As one social scientist embedded in Afghanistan explains, acute insecurity for coalition forces outside the base— a flare in violence—confined the team to interviewing Afghan nationals that were working on the same forward operating base for the first 3 weeks after the individual embedded.

This survey was comprised of 20-30 interviews to get a better understanding of what respondents' attitudes and perceptions were toward the people that were there, but also toward "fear," "threats," "insults."[145] Questions asked were: "When was the last time you felt threatened?" and "Can you describe it?" The team transcribed each interview and coded it by the frequency of the words that were being used. This was a rudimentary approach, but allowed the construction of a product which could highlight common themes such as how the local nationals perceived the coalition forces operating there. This allowed comprehension of the perception of how the Afghans were being treated by the military forces; answers placed into the categories "'good," "bad," "neutral," "mixed." This in turn facilitated the commander's understanding of how he could engender better relationships with the population. The scope of the survey also assessed perceptions of the Taliban, criminal networks, the extent to which they felt threatened by each, and how the population dealt with grievances. That product was presented, with an executive summary and recommendations, as a PowerPoint presentation "which was a pretty common way of delivering that sort of stuff, to the battalion commander."[146] Ultimately, of that particular product, the executive officer "was not too receptive of it" because:

> a lot of it was quite critical of how they (the Afghan population) were being treated, disrespected, those types of things. The battalion commander saw the utility of it; the XO [executive officer] was providing justification as to why they were wrong, which was certainly kind of troubling.[147]

Such was the broad, diffuse forum of sociocultural knowledge and sociocultural concerns that myriad research methodologies could be developed by teams in Iraq and Afghanistan. For Evans, while every product was different, he made a conscious decision to examine thematic issues developed through interviews, some recorded with audio equipment, others documented by note-taking before returning to base to produce the reports. Evans' team designed interview grids listing a person's name and basic demographic data, such as occupation, gender, age bracket, tribe, grid location, and birthplace, and interviewed each on a variety of topics from agriculture to politics. In the product, that data would be in the appendix of the report so that the customers could check the provenance of the information. This transparency was noted as being useful from at least one customer of the HTT products.[148]

The depth of material offered in the report offered the chance to check the HTT homework, basically so that the military was not under the illusion that the team was "just using social science as sorcery."[149] The British brigade was structured differently than U.S. brigades, with staff groupings under the command of lieutenant colonels designated SO1s. Evans' team was situated within the intelligence, surveillance, targeting, acquisition, reconnaissance (ISTAR) group. The J-2, the intelligence cell, was embedded within that, because they own what the British call the "understand function" and the HTT was tasked with comprehension of the population, situated there but not integrated into the personnel structures tasked with targeting insurgents.[150] Moreover, targeting cells were in a compound that the HTT lacked clearance for, despite being situated in the same command structure, but the team did develop close relations with some of the groups, including Psychological Operations and reported up through that ISTAR unit. The first tier above was the J-2 cell, to which the report would go for review and then subsequently brigade-wide release. During the period that Evans was embedded with Task Force Helmand, he was with two different British brigades, each functioning differently; with the first brigade there could be a brief to the brigadier from the team leader. In the second brigade, with the Royal Marines, there was a more open communication system, in which the embedded could communicate more directly to the chief of staff, the brigadier, and the colonels.[151]

The first several reports conducted were for different battalions, five in total in the AO. In order to assume relevance, the HTT visited each battle group, stating broadly:

> Here are our capabilities, here is what we can do, here is what we can offer. What do you want to know about the population in your Area of Operations?" And we would look at the CCIRs, which are the Commander's Critical Information Requirements and PIRs, Priority Information Requirements, basically their intelligence gaps, what they wanted to know about their AO. And we would look at the ones that had to do with the population. And we would say, "according to your records you wanted to know this, is there anything else you wanted to communicate to me?"[152]

From this identified gap in the brigade knowledge architecture, it was possible to construct a research design. The HTT went into the British systems to examine the institutional information they had collated regarding the AO, and incorporated that information as background into the research design. With objectives and resources required, this request was sent to the battle group for approval and, at this point, the battle group could modify the design if required. As Evans explains:

> that was already a product in and of itself; it was basically a literature review. And then we would go out and execute it in the field; anywhere from a few days to 2 weeks; foot and vehicle patrols where we would conduct semi-structured interviews.[153]

To expand the baseline of knowledge, HTTs would often out of pragmatic necessity conduct surveys as a way to capture a wide range of opinions in a structured manner. HTT IZ9 conducted deep research in 2008, generating one of the first products in which its team was engaged, based around a survey of the Sons of Iraq, the bureaucratic embodiment of the Anbar Awakening which spread through the Sunni-dominated areas in Iraq. The Sons of Iraq was a local community policing initiative paid for by the U.S. military and credited with ushering in stability to al-Anbar and subsequently the rest of Iraq.[154] Because of the militia character of the force, the Sons of Iraq, led by tribal sheikhs, endured a frictional relationship with the Iraqi government. The government, however, was in the process of assuming responsibility for the Sons of Iraq program as part of ongoing integration. The purpose of the survey was to identify their expectations for post-insurgency employment; to ascertain if they were going to be transitioned successfully from militia into the police force or other fields of work. The research was carried out from September 14, 2008, to October 25, 2008, and consisted of 503 interviews carried out in Salah al-Din province and examined the character of the transition of the Sons of Iraq into the elected government. Survey data was recorded at Sons of Iraq checkpoints and salary payment locations, with approximately 100 interviews in five different sections of the BCT's AO, and of the 503 people interviewed, 471 were Sunni.

The research was conducted because the brigade was attempting to transition nearly 3,000 Sons of Iraq from the militia structure into the Iraqi Police. It was thus invaluable that IZ9 work through social science research methods to understand what would happen to the Sons of Iraq that were not integrated into the police force, because there was an assumption that those not transitioned would accept more menial work, rather than take up arms against U.S. forces. Follow-up research was conducted in and around Samarra from December 12 to 16, 2008. The research analysis concluded that the programs offering employment to the Sons of Iraq were imperfect, and some individuals had unrealistic expectations of the positions they could attain because of the Iraqi government's position on reintegrating such individuals. There was a likelihood that a minority for which it was an issue would return to criminal activity or the ongoing multifaceted insurgency if the program was completely stood down.[155] This transition was of primary import to the military customer, and this research proved the value of an HTT in that area. Indicative of the extent of the Sons of Iraq issue, IZ11 also examined the implications of the transition.

The frequency of products was dictated by the frequency of missions. As one team member embedded with U.S. brigades noted, each product from every mission would be emailed out to personnel in the unit as well as posted to SharePoint. Research considered of pertinence to a wider audience would be entered into the Combined Information Data Network Exchange database. Echoing other units whose expertise grew over time, as the tour ended, there was the ability to write major reports, summaries of everything undertaken and achieved, and what was then known about the area. Such was the knowledge gained by the last months of the embedded tour that the content of interviews done previously were then linked to broader themes which were trying to be addressed in these major reports; these were again emailed and added to the SharePoint. As well as this, networking was crucial to ensure the dispersion of the product, such that 2 hours a day were spent walking the base, networking: "Although it was time consuming, it was the way you know it was going to get used."[156] The team member applied a grounded theory approach, using a by-area breakdown of selected sampling based on a stratification of who they believed was in the area, to try and identify key themes and, from that, build a better picture of the human terrain: "a quasi-anthropological approach."[157] Because of the limitations of logistics, this approach was "driven sampling-wise more by targets of opportunity rather than targets of choice in a lot of cases."[158] Largely obscured from existing literature are the differences between Iraq and Afghanistan at both the national and local levels. For instance, in Afghanistan, the same team member found that surveys were unrealistic because there was no way to get access to the sampling size necessary with reliable sampling to do a survey approach.

There were also discrepancies in research dictated by the character of the unit in which the social scientist embedded. Products generated for conventional units were often of a better quality than those produced for SOF because of the greater resources available in the former, more downtime and greater connectivity with information technology. With the regular unit, a product could be produced every 3 weeks while with the SOF team, there would be blending of previously produced products into "teaching lessons" to give them a better understanding of the human terrain.[159] The delivery with SOF was, in one account in Afghanistan, in the form of "fireside chats" given once or twice a week to afford the SOF personnel information on the regional or district issues concerning them and their operations. This could include a breakdown of mosque structure, and key players and important people in the population. Much of this knowledge was drawn from previous research conducted when the social scientist had previously embedded with a conventional unit.

The social scientist identified one problem describing a nomadic people who were removed from the village structure in which they were located. The misnomer for them prevalent among the SOF was *kochi*; which described a large, pre-existing group of mostly ethnically Pashtun nomads. The social scientist, in interviewing them as part of extended research, realized that these people were not nomadic *kochi*, which was in fact used in a derogatory sense, rather they were recently internally displaced peoples. Writing this research up as a product generated valuable information on the chain of events that led to their displacement, including landownership issues and blood feuds.[160]

To be of value, the products had to be tailored to the client's requirements. For the military customer, brevity of content and speed of delivery were of critical importance. One social scientist describes a detailed report which was produced prior to Operation MOSHTARAK. The research had entailed:

trying to get the atmospherics without being there, so we did a lot of atmospherics on reports, and we went to Lashkar Gah, and we tried to interview people there, and we interviewed actual Afghans who had supposedly interacted with the players there.[161]

The report was considered of value from the perspective of the HTT because there were missteps in the planning which were highlighted in the report; but ultimately for the customer "in the end, it was too long."[162] Generating and presenting valuable products on sociocultural analysis absent detailed oversight from the command structure involved a degree of entrepreneurial ability. The HTTs were given "task and purpose" — these were not orders, rather it was a description of a requirement on which to focus, "and the military had no expectation on what we would do or what we were going to give them and how, so we had to figure that out on the fly as well."[163]

The products themselves could be differentiated precisely into two types. The products were unclassified, but their delivery and presentation in the duration of Krohley's deployment were on classified networks, mainly SIPRNet. The first type of product was neighborhood profiles, necessary because of the absence of knowledge of existing demographics (see Appendix M). There was a first version of these profiles which would be mainly for internal consumption, analysis of all the different neighborhoods within Tissa Nissan. These were not shared widely — because it was what the military already knew — and were checked with a number of people in the military and the brigade specifically in order to gain "affirmation effectively" that the teams "were on the right track."[164] Demonstrating how knowledge could increase over time, at the end of the deployment, Krohley:

rewrote those neighbourhood profiles to become 7- to-8-page narratives with maps and pictures, and they were meant to be a legacy document. So the brigade that we had supported left right around the time I left, I think the end of 2008.[165]

These legacy documents allowed the incoming brigade to gain understanding of the neighborhood in a brief, accessible 6- to 8-page document.

Legacy documents were unclassified and did not name individuals in militias or among the general population. These documents, however, did identify government officials, analyzing some of the complexities of those persons: "Public figures are fair game for an unclass(ified) paper, and we weren't making wild allegations, we were just talking about reality."[166] Through the tour, the social scientist conducted a series of briefings, both for brigade staff and for the brigade commanders. It was unnecessary to brief at the company level because this was the level at which they were embedded day-to-day, and therefore talked through the material informally on a daily basis. The second type of product was thematic, produced across the duration of the tour—1-, or at most 2-page write-ups of a particular issue which had relevance to the broad problems seen in the district (see Appendix O). In the thematic products, it was possible to identify and disentangle complex trajectories of issues not readily seen as relevant to the security situation. For example, in the familiar vein of urban planning, there was an investigation of the creation of eastern Baghdad, which became an assessment of city demographics. Rather than growing organically, it evolved as a series of planned communities, grouped around identities and organized by the state, entirely by professions, meaning that pronounced demographic divides were evident from one neighborhood to the next. This result of urban planning resulted in heterogeneous levels of violence across the neighborhoods as well as radically divergent social atmospheres.[167]

This product was the first piece of research presented at the staff level and won goodwill, affording understanding of why there was such variance in violence, discrete by neighborhood. Previous Army understanding of the neighborhoods in eastern Baghdad had characterized them simply as mixed. Other thematic products considered the Sadr family and the Sadrist ideology. There was a concerted effort in the military to look at Iraq as a tribal place; "tribalism" became fashionable in the wake of the Anbar Awakening and the evident successes that were witnessed in western Iraq, where according to the dominant narrative, the U.S. military worked through local tribal groups to turn the tide against al-Qaeda in Iraq, turning the locals away from the foreigners.

If there was any paradigm in the COIN mode dominant in Iraq and later Afghanistan during the period, it was the perceived need to work with the tribes in order to restore stability. This tribal paradigm evolved because of the apparent success of U.S.-sponsored sheikhs in countering complex insurgencies. As Krohley notes:

> The extent to which that (the Anbar Awakening narrative) is true, I don't know, but what came out of that effectively was standing orders for everyone in the U.S. Army to go and find the local tribal sheikh and work with them.[168]

That modeling of the environment as a tribal system had severe limitations, however, and broke down in several geographical sites. In Tissa Nissan, for example, there was no evident tribalism, no sheikh, which was symptomatic of why the U.S. forces were experiencing such problems. Civil society had unraveled; degraded by migration and movement and by Saddam Hussein's government of the area in which he had killed or co-opted key communal leaders.[169]

Krohley thus pushed back against the tribal lens and briefed two papers which attempted to make the Army understand what the community looked like, what had happened to tribes in eastern Baghdad, and their broad interactions over the past 4 to 5 years and also the longer trajectory of the past 50 years. These products "were tricky to write and tricky to brief because you don't want to go too academic, but at the same time these are very smart guys you are talking to; you cannot dumb down."[170] Presentations had to be tailored to the venue, and briefers usually would be afforded 5 minutes (pushed to 7 minutes by the team) at the nightly shift change briefings with the brigade commander and senior staff sitting in the operations center. There would be an audience of 50 people and perhaps seven or eight cared about the research; senior operational commanders, intelligence personnel, and civil affairs personnel. A 1-page narrative was placed in the brigade server for download, and a PowerPoint presentation which would be a maximum of five slides focused on the core issues (see Appendix P). After the presentation, questions would be taken, and then the presenter, usually the team leader, departed, with a target of one such presentation at the night briefing every 2 weeks.[171]

War is entropic; armed conflict increases the disorder of a dynamic system. As such, the problems in identifying the urban plan were exacerbated by the post-invasion movements, where people scattered to avoid communal violence. There remained cohesive elements in Iraq which were identified, such as the tribal sheikhs that led the Anbar Awakening. At worst, however, in the cities, there were no obvious authority figures. Moreover, because of the culture of largesse propagated by profligate coalition forces in the "anything goes" atmosphere of that period, the monies led to various figures identifying themselves dubiously as key leaders at this time. Each area was *sui generis*, possessing its own possibilities for leader engagement.

Because Krohley had rejected the tribal model as irrelevant to his AO, it posed a critical problem. There was minimal social order in any of these neighborhoods that anyone could tap into: "you had a sort of chaos where no one is really in charge and there isn't anyone obvious to work with, and it was a major issue in our work, why this one district wasn't responding to treatment."[172] On the one hand, it had heavy militia activity by virtue of demographics—it had been left after the violence an overwhelmingly poor Shia area, so it was naturally receptive to the security offered by the Mahdi Army. There was excellent connectivity through highways to Iran and to Baqubah in the north, so it was very easy to get explosively formed penetrators and militants in and out of the area. Unlike Sadr City which had the same connectivity, there were Americans to kill in Tissa Nissan.

An upsurge in violence in March 2008 in Sadr City, including rockets fired on coalition forces' positions, had been met with a response from U.S. forces and implementation of a wall building operation in the southern quarter of Sadr City. A ceasefire on May 11 crystallized a May 12 agreement under which U.S. forces would have a presence limited to a southern quadrant of Sadr City, defined by the erected wall. As a result of that agreement, there were no U.S. forces in the northern section of Sadr City and, as a consequence, violent attacks migrated to Tissa Nissan because insurgents from Sadr City could travel to the area, erect an explosively formed penetrator array and leave.

Because of the absence of civil society in Tissa Nissan, winning over the population in order to detract from the insurgency was problematic. Krohley and his team elucidated the chaotic political structure through conversations which were:

> quite mundane and quite simple, talking about community and family, you know: where do you come from? How did you get here? Who are your neighbours? — not who are your neighbours by name — you know, talk to me about your neighbourhood effectively.[173]

Reporting in this environment using key interviews led the team to ascertain that the high level of physical insecurity meant families were taking cover in their houses, which reduced the level and function of civil society. As a corollary, there were no obvious community leaders to engage with for the purposes of COIN, or indeed conversely for the *Jaysh al-Mahdi* to rally a substantive, grass roots campaign. This was the essence of the effective social scientist in the HTT; qualitative analysis through operationally relevant reporting at the company level such that:

> a very simple series of sitting-in-the-living-room 10 minute conversations with people, eventually built into a substantive insight into why certain things were happening. And you could piece all these things together over time based on a lot of data.

Instructively, Krohley also notes the spectrum of approaches possible, based on the security of the AO:

> It goes back to the contrasting approaches I guess, if you are going to be in a more stable area where there are lots of sources you can repeatedly meet with and develop, you can get a depth of information, but that is not achievable in areas of greater insecurity. Instead of having four or five really good sources, you have 70 or 80 or 100 short-term encounters with people, who you weren't going to follow-up with and whose names you didn't know and who were protected by anonymity in their encounters with you. And that works; frankly, I think that works pretty well.[174]

Insecurity for incumbent forces on the ground affecting the ability to report effectively suggests that there were limitations in the field which transformed ethnography into reporting.

CONCLUSIONS

Research was conducted in order to be valuable to the customer, but identification of the particular modes of investigation and subjects of study were the preserve of the HTTs themselves. Methodologies varied by unit, emphatically when the variation was between general purpose and SOF, by place, and by circumstance. Insecurity, or security, meant employment of different methods often based around the ability to get convoy space. The products had to be created in order to fit with the clarity of planning necessary to the customer and, indeed, in harmony with the operational tempo of the unit in the AO.

The sociological requirements of the 2006 FM *Counterinsurgency* entrusted a unique responsibility to the HTTs. As the custodians of academic social science research skills and experience, they were tasked with identifying the sociological dimensions of the battle space. The particular requirements depended on the needs of the commander, but in general, the HTT was tasked with identifying cause or effect in the social domain. Krohley, for example, was tasked with finding the cause of the effect that had left one district, Tissa Nissan, extremely disordered and insecure, while the two other districts were relatively calm. When understanding the causes for known effects were required, this type of research facilitated social science expertise which could test research against several hypotheses. It was these complex causes and effects in disordered societies in conflict zones which necessitated the introduction of HTTs. Civil Affairs and Psychological Operations both were encumbered of limitations on their research abilities.

Beneath the remit of deciphering sociological cause or effect, the product had to be attenuated to the requirements of the operational tempo. In practice that meant theoretical elements of the research were omitted, and the conclusions were stated simply. If the social scientist could not communicate properly the research for the customer, this was the fault of the social scientist, not the military staff. The product also had to fit existing U.S. Department of the Army thinking. The Army is an adaptive enterprise, but the ability to learn current sociological expertise takes years, requiring integration into the training of junior officers who then progress through the ranks.

The cause and effect research explains the remit of the HTTs. The academic bridge to the military customer explains how the research was produced. The "why" and the "how" have thus been investigated, but it leaves us with a further problem. HTTs have delivered research which demonstrates their utility in COIN environments, but after Iraq and Afghanistan, the HTS parent organization, TRADOC, planned to transition the program into a long-range strategic asset in areas where the incumbent exercises complete or hegemonic control, and where, correspondingly, there are relatively low levels of insurgent-initiated violence. If the HTTs were successful in COIN operations, why is such a transition necessary?

The initial concept plan for the HTS included theoretical arrangement for a spectrum of operations in areas where the incumbent exercises are full to negligible control of the environment. However, ongoing operations in Iraq and Afghanistan necessitated focus upon these operations characterized by high levels of insurgent and incumbent violence.[175] According to TRADOC, when the HTS was developed, it was argued that the program's greatest benefit was in the conduct of theater security cooperation at the strategic level, where attempts are made to avoid escalation and where teams would work with combatant commands. When tasked with developing an enduring concept, therefore, TRADOC had to consider what a strategically postured program would look like, post-Iraq and Afghanistan. There would be smaller numbers of teams due to declining resources. But questions also had to be answered about where those teams most likely achieve the greatest benefit in both staff planning but also the ability to deploy forward with Regionally Aligned Forces.[176]

The U.S. Army Concept for Regionally Aligned Forces calls for a division or a brigade or a corps in the Army to be aligned regionally to a specific Army service component command. An HTS pilot took place in 2011 with support to U.S. Army elements in Africa.[177]

Army forces were available to the theater security operation plans, which constituted the team oriented to a strategic posture intended to influence long-range planning rather than brigades at the tactical level. It is in this strategic posture that TRADOC considered the HTS:

> could bring a maximum benefit of not just understanding our partners and how they operate and their professionalism, but also providing further understanding of the operational environment where our partners are operating.[178]

At the end of 2013, the HTS had pilots at four locations that were supporting Army commands for U.S. Central Command, U.S. Africa Command, U.S. Northern Command and U.S. Southern Command (South America and Central America, absent Mexico) at the strategic level. In that iteration of the HTS, social scientists serve at the command and support the planning effort for long-range theater campaign planning. If required, the social scientist could also deploy to the field to support the collection of social science-type information to inform the combatant commander's decisionmaking. To that end, TRADOC has focused on recruiting social scientists with deep regional expertise, a requirement when fulfilling regional-alignment requirements. TRADOC concedes that continent-wide expertise is problematic but recruiting, for example, French speakers, Swahili speakers, or Arabic speakers who have spent a lifetime studying that continent as well as possessing social science expertise, fulfills the mandate of the human capital element of the combatant command concept plan.[179]

Environments where the incumbent exercises full or near complete control with correspondingly high levels of security for aligned forces were noted to be those in which HTTs would be most effective, concluded the authors of the West Point study. In this ideal landscape, teams "help prevent conflict while providing creative tools and ideas to the commander to help build governmental capacity and legitimacy."[180] The authors, with foresight, argued that placing a team at the level of the combatant command level, while violating the currently successful "bubble-up" methodology of HTS at the tactical level in a COIN environment, "would be more effective in this role and environment."[181] HTTs could still contribute at the lower levels within Army service component commands such as U.S. Army Africa, but they must be considered primarily in locations such as U.S. embassies, working with defense attachés and army attachés, only embedding with subsequent deploying ground elements if required by the brigade.[182]

The perceived increased effect of teams at the strategic level means that their effects in COIN operations were deemed to be of a lesser magnitude than the possible benefits to broader theater security. As a corollary of this chapter, therefore, it is necessary to go beyond assessment of the research remits and products. It is a requirement that I examine the limitations of HTTs in operations in Iraq and Afghanistan. The generic conflict zone is both a permissive and a limiting environment for social science research. Conflict legitimates the presence of the social science researcher working as part of the U.S. Department of the Army; it also enables teams to gain convoy support because of the frequency of convoys as part of ongoing operations. Conflict makes a critical need to understand cause and effect in these operations, making the requirement for teams to fill the sociocultural knowledge gap. At the same time, there are inherent limitations in the ability of a human to research society in inherently insecure environments.

ENDNOTES - CHAPTER 5

1. Former HTT social scientist 1, interview, August 11, 2013.

2. *Ibid.*

3. *Ibid.*

4. *Ibid.*

5. *Ibid.*

6. H. Russell Bernard, *Research Methods in Anthropology: Qualitative and Quantitative Approaches*, 4th Ed., Lanham, MD: Alta Mira, 2006, p. 199.

7. Jennifer Clark, telephone interview with author, October 9, 2013.

8. I am indebted to Michael Davies for this observation.

9. Zok Pavlovic, interview with author, Alexandria, VA, August 14, 2013.

10. *Ibid.*

11. See also Ryan Evans, "'The Population is the Enemy': Control, Behaviour, and Counter-Insurgency in Central Helmand Province, Afghanistan," David Martin Jones, Celeste Ward Gventner, and M. L. R. Smith, eds., *The New Counter-Insurgency Era in Critical Perspective*, London, UK: Palgrave Macmillan, 2014, pp. 257-259.

12. Montgomery McFate, interview, August 2, 2013.

13. *Ibid.*

14. Ryan Evans, interview with author, Washington, DC, August 6, 2013.

15. Nathan Hodge, *Armed Humanitarians: The Rise of the Nation Builders*, New York: Bloomsbury, 2011, p. 243.

16. Human Terrain System, "Human Terrain System Yearly Report, 2007-2008," Program Development Team, Prepared for U.S. Army Training and Doctrine Command, Washington, DC, August 2008.

17. Cindy R. Jebb, Laurel J. Hummel, and Tania M. Chacho, "HTT Trip Report: A 'Team of Teams'," West Point, NY: Unpublished report for TRADOC, 2008, p. 6. Copy held by author.

18. Former HTT social scientist 3, interview with author, Alexandria, VA, August 1, 2013.

19. *Ibid.*

20. Bryan N. Karabaich and Jonathan D. Pfautz, "Using Cultural Belief Sets in Intelligence Preparation for the Battlefield, *Military Intelligence Professional Bulletin*, Vol. 32, No. 2, 2006, p. 40; Jennifer Clark, interview.

21. Nathan Finney, *The Human Terrain Team Handbook*, Fort Leavenworth, KS: TRADOC, 2008, cited in American Anthropological Association, *Final Report on the Army's Human Terrain System*, p. 4; Audrey Roberts, "Embedding with the Military in Eastern Afghanistan: The Role of Anthropologists in Peace and Stability Operations," Walter E. Feichtinger, Ernst M. Felberbauer, and Erwin A. Schmidl, eds., *International Crisis Management: Squaring the Circle*, Vienna, Austria, and Geneva, Switzerland: National Defense Academy and Austrian Ministry of Defense and Sports in cooperation with Geneva Centre for Security Policy, 2011; Headquarters Department of the Army and Headquarters U.S. Marine Corps, *Field Manual* (FM) *2-01.3, Intelligence Preparation of the Battlefield*, Fort Huachuca, AZ: U.S. Government, October 15, 2009.

22. Susan K. Numrich, "Human Terrain: A Tactical Issue or a Strategic C4I Problem?" paper presented to the Critical Issues in C4I Symposium, Fairfax, VA, George Mason University, May 20-21, 2008.

23. Montgomery McFate, Britt Damon, and Robert Holliday, "What do Commanders Really Want to Know? U.S. Army Human Terrain System Lessons Learned from Iraq and Afghanistan," Janice H. Laurence and Michael D. Matthews, eds., *The Oxford Handbook of Military Psychology*, Oxford, UK: Oxford University Press, 2012, p. 94.

24. *Ibid.*

25. *Ibid.*

26. *Ibid.*, p. 93.

27. *Ibid.*

28. *Ibid.*

29. *Ibid.*

30. Finney, p. 55.

31. McFate, interview, August 2, 2013.

32. Marcus Griffin, "An Anthropologist among the Soldiers: Notes from the Field," John D. Kelly *et al.*, eds., *Anthropology and Global Counterinsurgency*, Chicago, IL: University of Chicago Press, 2010, pp. 218-220.

33. Paula Holmes-Eber, *Culture in Conflict: Irregular Warfare, Culture Policy, and the Marine Corps*, Stanford, CA: Stanford University Press, 2014; Carl H. Builder, *The Masks of War: American Military Styles in Strategy and Analysis*, Baltimore, MD: Johns Hopkins University Press, 1989.

34. Anonymous, interview.

35. Jennifer Clark, interview.

36. McFate, interview, August 1, 2013; see also Holmes-Eber.

37. Former HTT social scientist 3, interview.

38. *Ibid.*

39. *Ibid.*

40. *Ibid.*

41. Jennifer Clark, interview.

42. *Ibid.*

43. *Ibid.*

44. *Ibid.* See also the more detailed personal account in Jennifer A. Clark, "Playing Spades in Al Anbar: A Female Social Scientist Among Marines and Special Forces," in Montgomery McFate and Janice H. Laurence, eds., *Social Science Goes to War: The Human Terrain System in Iraq and Afghanistan*, London, UK: Hurst, pp. 141-185.

45. Evans, interview.

46. Christopher J. Lamb *et al.*, *HTTs: An Organizational Innovation for Sociocultural Knowledge in Irregular Warfare*, Washington, DC: Institute of World Politics Press, 2013, pp. 216-219.

47. Author's telephone interview with Bob Reuss, Colonel Lee Grubbs, and Dr. Susan Canedy, September 16, 2013.

48. Jennifer Clark, interview.

49. *Ibid.*

50. Jennifer Clark, personal communication with author, October 17, 2014.

51. Matthew P. Dearing, James L. Jeffreys, and Justin A. Depue, "Entry Point: Accessing Indigenous Perspectives During Complex Operations," *Special Operations Journal*, Vol. 1, No. 1, 2015, p. 11.

52. Former HTT social scientist 4, interview with author, Newport, RI, August 1, 2013.

53. *Ibid.*

54. *Ibid.*

55. *Ibid.*

56. *Ibid.*

57. *Ibid.*

58. Dearing *et al.*, "Entry Point," p. 15.

59. *Ibid.*

60. *Ibid.*

61. *Ibid.*

62. *Ibid.*

63. *Ibid.*

64. Dearing *et al.*, "Entry Point," p. 16.

65. Nicholas Krohley, telephone interview with author, July 26, 2013.

66. *Ibid.*

67. *Ibid.*

68. *Ibid.*

69. *Ibid.*

70. Jebb, Hummel, and Chacho, p. 4.

71. Lamb *et al.*

72. Krohley, interview.

73. *Ibid.*

74. *Ibid.*

75. *Ibid.*

76. *Ibid.*

77. *Ibid.*

78. Krohley, interview; also noted by Howard Clark, telephone interview with author, January 25, 2014.

79. Krohley, interview.

80. *Ibid.*

81. *Ibid.*

82. Jennifer Clark, interview.

83. Former HTT social scientist 3, interview.

84. Krohley, interview.

85. *Ibid.*

86. *Ibid.*

87. Former HTT social scientist 3, interview; Krohley, interview.

88. Krohley, interview.

89. Jebb, Hummel, and Chacho, p. 6.

90. Jennifer Clark, interview.

91. Former HTT social scientist 4, interview.

92. Interview notes held with author.

93. *Ibid.*

94. Former HTT social scientist 3, personal communication with author, November 14, 2013.

95. *Ibid.*

96. The phrases are, respectively, from Sigmund Freud and Michael Inwood, Fellow of Philosophy, Oxford University. Inwood was debating the merits of the scholarly texts of the German philosopher Martin Heidegger. I am indebted to McFate for referencing the former, in personal communication with the author.

97. Former HTT social scientist 3, personal communication with author, November 14, 2013.

98. *Ibid.*

99. *Ibid.*

100. *Ibid.*

101. Former HTT social scientist 3, interview.

102. Jonathan D. Thompson, "HTT Operations in East Baghdad," *Military Review*, Vol. 90, No. 4, 2010, p. 78.

103. Nicholas Krohley, personal communication with author, October 2, 2014.

104. I am indebted to Dr. Krohley for this assessment of the operational and strategic pictures in Baghdad during 2008.

105. Krohley, interview.

106. *Ibid.*

107. *Ibid.*

108. *Ibid.*

318

109. *Ibid.*

110. *Ibid.*

111. *Ibid.*

112. *Ibid.*

113. *Ibid.*

114. *Ibid.*

115. Thomas Adams, cited in Jennifer Taw and Robert C. Leicht, *The New World Order and Army Doctrine*, Santa Monica, CA: RAND Corporation, 1992, p. 18.

116. Sebastian Maisel, "Social Change Amidst Terror and Discrimination: Yezedis in the New Iraq," *The Middle East Institute*, Policy Brief, Vol. 18, 2008, executive summary.

117. *Ibid.*

118. Alissa J. Rubin, "Persecuted Sect in Iraq Avoids Its Shrine," *The New York Times*, October 14, 2007.

119. Former HTT social scientist 3, interview.

120. *Ibid.*

121. *Ibid.*

122. *Ibid.*

123. *Ibid.*

124. *Ibid.*

125. *Ibid.*

126. Former HTT social scientist 1, interview, August 11, 2013.

127. *Ibid.*

128. *Ibid.*

129. *Ibid.*

130. *Ibid.*

131. *Ibid.*

132. Evans, interview.

133. Pavlovic, interview.

134. Evans, interview.

135. *Ibid.*

136. Vanda Felbab-Brown, *Afghanistan Trip Report V: The Afghan Local Police: "It's Local, So It Must Be Good" – Or Is It?* Washington, DC: The Brookings Institution, May 9 2012, available from *www.brookings.edu/research/opinions/2012/05/09-afghan-police-felbabbrown*, accessed September 12, 2014.

137. *Ibid.*

138. Former HTT social scientist 4, interview.

139. Finney, p. 86.

140. Numrich.

141. Krohley, interview.

142. *Ibid.*

143. *Ibid.*

144. *Ibid.*

145. Former HTT social scientist 4, interview.

146. *Ibid.*

147. *Ibid.*

148. Evans, interview; Howard Clark, interview.

149. Evans, interview.

150. *Ibid.* For the development of the "understand function" in British military thought at this time, see, for example, Mark Phillips, "Exercise *Agile Warrior* and the Future Development of UK Land Forces," *RUSI Occasional Paper*, May 2011; and, Headquarters, British Chiefs of Staff, *Joint Doctrine Publication 04, Understanding*, Shrivenham, UK: The Development, Concepts and Doctrine Centre, December 2010.

151. Evans, interview.

152. *Ibid.*

153. *Ibid.*

154. See, for example, Stephen Biddle, Jeffrey A. Friedman, and Jacob N. Shapiro, "Testing the Surge: Why Did Violence Decline in Iraq in 2007?" *International Security*, Vol. 37, No. 1, 2012, pp. 7-40.

155. Former HTT social scientist 1, interview, August 11, 2013.

156 . *Ibid.*

157. *Ibid.*

158. *Ibid.*

159. Former HTT social scientist 4, interview.

160. *Ibid.*

161. Former HTT social scientist 2, interview with author, Quantico, VA, July 29, 2013.

162. *Ibid.*

163. Krohley, interview.

164. *Ibid.*

165. *Ibid.*

166. *Ibid.*

167. *Ibid.*

168. Krohley, interview.

169. Nicholas Krohley, *The Death of the Mehdi Army: The Rise, Fall, and Revival of Iraq's Most Powerful Militia*, London, UK: Hurst, forthcoming.

170. Krohley, interview.

171. *Ibid.*

172. *Ibid.*

173. Former HTT social scientist 4, interview.

174. Krohley, interview.

175. Author's telephone interview with Bob Reuss, Colonel Lee Grubbs, and Dr. Susan Canedy, September 16, 2013.

176. Grubbs, interview.

177. Lamb *et al.*, p. 81.

178. Grubbs, interview.

179. *Ibid.*

180. Jebb, Hummel, and Chacho, p. 7.

181. *Ibid.*

182. *Ibid.*

CHAPTER 6

AT THE LIMITS OF KNOWLEDGE

Babaji, Central Helmand, had been under the control of the Taliban in the winter of 2010, but company-level counterinsurgency (COIN) operations in early-2011 had driven the Taliban from the region. The area had been an insurgent stronghold, resisting a significant combined Afghan and British offensive in the summer of 2009. When the COIN initiative proved successful in late-2010 despite other areas remaining insecure, the Human Terrain Team (HTT) social scientist Ryan Evans was tasked by the 2 Scots commander with discovering why those company-level COIN operations had been successful in Babaji over the past 6 months. It was hoped as a consequence of the research in and among the population that Evans would "hit on some lessons or a model that could be learned elsewhere."[1] Evans' hypotheses to be tested were three-fold: first, that operational-level COIN had won hearts and minds; second, that COIN operations had killed, detained, or driven out the insurgents; and third, that COIN operations had changed the decisionmaking calculus of the population to side with the Afghan National Security Forces and the British Task Force. In the study, Evans conducted over 30 semi-structured interviews with residents in Babaji.[2] The result was confirmation of the third hypothesis, that the "main factor determining local behavior was the population's perception of who was in control of the area, which drove their decision-making calculi more than other variables."[3]

Societies disordered by conflict require continued assessment in order to understand the character of the change over time which has been catalyzed by physical insecurity. In more secure environments where the incumbent exercises near full control, more permissive than Afghanistan or Iraq between 2007 and 2014, there is the opportunity for even deeper research which does not just investigate cause but also anticipates effect. It is that ability to examine effect which will allow the Human Terrain System (HTS) to influence planning at the strategic level. Societies must be relatively ordered to do so. Given the Training and Doctrine Command's (TRADOC) preferred application of HTTs to these pre-deployment environments where the program would work at the broad level of theater-wide security, I investigate limitations to those teams that worked in Iraq and Afghanistan. I draw on the experiences of social scientists in both Iraq and Afghanistan to assess the problems encountered. I examine limitations in the field and problems with developing institutional memory of the human terrain. I investigate the dynamic between qualitative and quantitative research in Iraq and Afghanistan, with reference to the spatial turn in the social sciences.

LANGUAGE

When Montgomery McFate wrote eloquently upon the anthropological dimensions of the British COIN experience in Northern Ireland for her doctoral dissertation in 1994, she was considering a conflict in which antagonists and population were united by a common denominating language. Moreover, cultural variation between insurgent and counterinsurgent was minimal. Two decades later, the differences in culture and language which would confront United States and coalition forces in Iraq and Afghanistan were, by contrast, deeply problematic obstacles to overcome in conducting operationally relevant research. Interpreters that accompanied the social scientists were a necessity for conducting valuable research with the population both in Iraq and Afghanistan.

HTTs travel with interpreters, employed independent to HTS but who are "nevertheless vital for successful interactions with the local population."[4] Evans had undergone language training which made him proficient at the basic level, but argued that he could not have accomplished his qualitative research without his interpreter. The interpreter allowed him to hold a sophisticated conversation. As the tour progressed, his understanding of the languages encountered increased, but not so in his speaking, consequently, he relied heavily on the interpreter dedicated to the embedded team. The interpreter for that team was native to the country and had been working with British forces in Helmand for 4 years. While Evans observed that many other interpreters were translating inaccurately, or would summarize too rapidly, he believed that his own specialist, fluent in Dari and Pashto and who fit the physical Army mold as he was in his early-30s, was invaluable.

There was a pool of interpreters on every forward operating base, and it "is sort of a mixed bag whether you get a good one or a bad one—one who is just there for the money."[5] In interviews, it was unanimously observed that the quality of the interpreter helped to define the quality of research in terms of what information could be leveraged from the population. Interpreters could also be used to refine social scientists' research methodology. After the social scientist had formulated a list of questions, the interpreter could be asked about phraseology and formulation, and the questions could then be reconfigured according to the feedback received.

The importance of the interpreter was common to all teams. In Iraq, Jennifer Clark developed a robust professional relationship with one of her interpreters. This enabled the interpreter to know what Clark wanted from her research, the character of the research problems, and the methodology she was employing. Moreover, it allowed the interpreter to know Clark's ethical stance so that research could be conducted appropriately. A second interpreter, female, allowed greater access to Iraqi people in homes because of the ability to talk openly without a foreign male presence, and this atmosphere facilitated deeper information gathering.

After conducting research which spanned both Iraq and Afghanistan, one social scientist found that:

> it is a myth that these cultures won't talk to a women. You have to have a good interpreter, but more so than that, they are just eager to have a voice. They don't care what the venue is for that voice; they just want to be heard.[6]

Clark notes a situation that arose where the women in a village told her about smuggling operations; the information was nonkinetic in nature, because they learned that the reason for the smuggling was to earn money (approximately U.S.$10 a day) to buy clothes for villagers. According to Clark, this was a smuggling culture which was rooted in history and not peculiar to the post-invasion landscape.[7] In lifting this information from the environment, the military gained greater understanding of the illicit networks and the motivations behind peoples' contributions.

Interpreters were not included in the training rotation at Ft. Leavenworth, Kansas, so it was a "pick and mix" for the HTTs when they were sent to Iraq and Afghanistan. This had both positive and negative effects. Positively, picking up an interpreter that has been in the field for months, if not years, to then leverage gives the HTT an expert in the dynamics of the local population.[8] Negatively, it means the embedded team cannot train with the interpreter to build up robust team relationships before entering the area in which the combat brigade operates. Moreover, once embedded after the brigade has already deployed and because they are augments to units, the teams often found they were given the interpreters nobody else wanted.[9] Often, the situation regarding interpreters was political in character; as one social scientist explains: the military had first choice, followed by the Department of State. Even when interpreters are rejected by multiple units, the contracting company wants to keep them hired and so goes to lengths to ensure they have an application, which often meant work with an HTT. Finding interpreters who added value to the HTT, enhancing research, and keeping them in the competitive environment was very much a potentially limiting factor in the work of the team.

One social scientist explains the potential pitfalls. In Iraq, a Kurdish interpreter was taken out to assist in the conduct of research with the Yezidi, during which time he told the social scientists that in the Yezidi dialect, the word for "angel' — *shaytan* — is the Arabic word in the Qu'ran for Lucifer and which formed part of his prejudices against the sect. The interpreter's body language was aggressive to the locals, and, as a result of his personal prejudices, the research conducted during his time with the HTT was so tainted that it was rejected.[10] Effective research which could be treated as objective to a workable degree was based on efficient relationships, key among them being that of the interpreter with the research subject. In Afghanistan, there was a different problem for the same social scientist working in the south of the country: the HTT would enlist the assistance of young men from northern Afghanistan, Kabul, many estimated by the team member to be no older than 18 years of age. These young men spoke fluent Dari but only enough Pashto to pass a very simplistic language test. To add to the complexity, regional dialects are extremely heterogeneous, so that "unless you have an interpreter from that area, he is not going to be able to grasp what is being said. And I say 'he' because 99 percent are men, it is impossible to get women."[11]

The problematic character of the youthful interpreter in this environment was exacerbated by challenging perceived cultural norms. The Afghan culture respects age, particularly, in the words of the social scientist considering a meeting with tribal elders:

> If you don't have facial hair, you can't even sit in the room with the guys. And so here are these super clean shaven young guys, they are with the Americans so they have adopted wearing shiny clothes and sunglasses, hair slicked back and cut short, no beard. And then you expect them to sit down with this tribal elder and be able to convey information appropriately and accurately? No way.[12]

Moreover, Afghans used many proverbs in conversation to illustrate any particular point, and the lack of deep language skills resident in the interpretation rendered the meanings lost in translation. In addition, as with all augments, in insecure environments, interpreters could be scared such that they did not do "enough to build rapport."[13]

ZERO NINE LIMAS

Given the character of the operations conducted in Iraq and Afghanistan and the nature of the human terrain, the military necessarily began to emphasize language capabilities as early as 2004. There is in foregrounding that solution an inherent difficulty in terms of time and expense in building up significant language capability among specific military personnel, for nations and regions which may only possess ephemeral import. One attempt to circumvent this problem was the March 8, 2006, establishment of Lima Company, 111th Military Intelligence Brigade at Fort Huachuca, Arizona. This company was unique in design and character, being the single unit dedicated to culture and language in the Department of Defense (DoD).[14] The company was created to recruit non-American citizens into the U.S. military because of an advantageous cultural background and language proficiency, to then go through training and deployment. On June 1, 2007, the company was renamed the U.S. Army Translator-Aide Detachment, with the army designation of their function being termed Zero Nine Limas. The unit was short lived and was terminated in October 2008 when the members transitioned into the 51st Company at Fort Irwin, California, where the U.S. Army houses its National Training Center.

During the period in which the unit was active, its members were received by HTS, often serving as Human Terrain Analysts, a role which demanded language skills.[15] Zero Nine Limas were assigned to their primary unit and then attached to HTS for a year for their specific mission. The short-lived nature of the unit suggests that it met with as many difficulties as successes, and this is borne out by testimony of team members in the field. One key member of HTS who deployed to both Afghanistan and Iraq was "very impressed with them."[16] This impression was received because they already possessed a degree of U.S. military discipline which facilitates their integration, although there were exceptions which detracted from the overall view of the unit. Problematic were Zero Nine Limas who had no experience of the American system (education and social) to begin with and thus were starting from a disadvantaged point from which it was difficult to make headway.

One research manager observed that the Zero Nine Lima assigned to their team "was the most intelligent, best qualified" he had worked with, "was absolutely amazing in several ways" and "just an absolutely outstanding individual, both in his professional reactions as well as his military behavior. Some of the others were okay, but experiences varied."[17] The Zero Nine Lima that Nicholas Krohley worked with, the only one during his tour, was a brilliant addition to his team; ethnically Sudanese, and had been raised in Egypt, so spoke fluent Egyptian Arabic and had done one or two tours with the Army previously, so was already inculcated into the U.S. military culture.

Institutionalizing language capabilities as nonorganic additions is a difficult process, however. At the brigade and battalion level, when Zero Nine Limas were working for senior staff, there were a number of these translators "who were not all that tactically proficient."[18] U.S. interest in geographies, and therefore languages, is "ephemeral and episodic" (a phrase I have borrowed here from Dr. Kerry Fosher, Director of the Translational Research Group, Center for Advanced Operational Culture Learning, U.S. Marine Corps) such that it becomes problematic to maintain a permanent reservoir of translators when the next threat to face the Department of the Army is so uncertain. Reaching proficiency in a non-native language takes years of work, while military crises can arise in weeks or months. HTTs were often as good as their language skills because, in short, how else does one listen to the population? Outside the scope of this book, but important for future policy-directed research, institutionalization of language skills is an important problematic for the Department of the Army.

MOBILITY

In order to conduct research outside the bases, it was necessary to utilize transport mechanisms: "a commander isn't willing to give up a dismount—which is essentially places we were taking—which is a guy with a gun who can provide protection, because convoys are so limited."[19] For instance, in eastern Baghdad, Krohley observed that he and the Zero Nine Lima conducted research independent of the rest of the team, and, in their area of research in Tissa Nissan, there was no obvious structure to tap into to collect information; there was no obvious set of meetings, events, or government institutions which could be worked through to undertake research. In this environment:

> it was more a case of getting out on the streets and turning over some stones and seeing what we could find and have lots of shorter conversations with people in their houses and on the streets. So we had more of an expeditionary feel to what we were doing.[20]

The method was knocking on doors by Iraqi National Police to interview householders, with U.S. forces present in oversight capacity. The house clearances offered opportunities for research. These environments were calm, uncontested, part of the "mundane realities of occupation and war. It wasn't unusual for an American with a rifle to be in your living room, as weird as that sounds."[21]

These searches for illegal weapons in households — part of Nouri al-Maliki's plan of limiting legal firearms possession to registered guns or those belonging to security forces — that were unfolding across Baghdad were ideal opportunities for research, thus the opportunity was present if transport could be negotiated. The answer for Krohley in this situation was to ride the logistics convoys which would resupply food and water to the various outposts between 2-week intervals and every 10 days. Problematic was the speed of the convoy; it moved extremely slowly and would stop to unload for up to an hour at a time, such that it was:

> a cumbersome, inefficient way to get around. If you were in point A and you wanted to get to point B, point B wasn't necessarily the first stop that the resupply convoy was going to make, so you could be on that thing all day trying to get around.[22]

The other solution was the route clearance convoys; mechanical transport dedicated to improvised explosive device (IED) identification and disposal, particularly focused on the significant explosively formed penetrator threat on the main roads. The two arterial routes in the district were swept for IEDs. The work by nature was dangerous, detecting and neutralizing the main threat to U.S. forces directly, and so space on the convoys was often available, such that:

it was an easy solution to what could have been a big problem of logistics, and they were always happy to have someone ride along and dismount and walk around a lot, talking to people. It wasn't a great collection opportunity but it wasn't a bad one.[23]

When a possible device was spotted, the convoy stopped, and dismounts could further investigate. As Krohley explains:

if you are stopped long enough, Iraqis will start popping out of their shops provided they don't think there is a bomb there and you could talk to people. And that was, you know, a conversation of opportunity every now and then. But it goes to the broader point of our team, as taking a basic philosophy: we were there to be useful at all times.[24]

The mobility was a limiting factor to the most efficient way to conduct the HTS mission, which was to be out on the streets at every possible opportunity, because there can arise spontaneous opportunities to talk to members of the population. The list of people who can be engaged on the forward operating bases or even smaller combat outposts which are in theory embedded in the terrain is limited. All of the myriad land building brigade activities were appropriate times to get outside the forward operating base, but with convoy space as a limiting factor.

Anthropologist Ted Callahan, in his candid account of research in Khost with AF1, observed the difficulty in getting support for research in the province. Moreover, its size meant that to get to a location, it may take as much as 3 hours driving. In all, with preparations accounted for, Callahan calculated that there could be a "ratio of 1 hour of interviews for 10 to 12 hours of effort," and that as a consequence, operationally relevant research was going to be an arduous task.[25] Travel time in large areas had a deleterious impact on the ratio of interviews to effort. As a consequence, and empirically observed, social science in dense urban environments may produce greater volumes of interview data in less time, given the reduced requirement for transport time beyond the military bases.

As a new HTT or new personnel transitioned into a brigade, their worth to the commander had not yet been observed which meant that mobility assets could not be freed up for them, generating a "Catch-22" situation. As one social scientist explains of the U.S. Marine Corps in Iraq, there was no initial convoy support available, therefore it was necessary in such handicapped circumstances to conduct interviews with the local population entering the bases, in this case, hundreds of Iraqi construction workers coming onto the base every day. Each worker had biometric information taken, at which point, in the queue of 5-20 people sitting waiting for this process, it was possible to conduct population surveys, with informed consent and the option not to participate. This survey, designed to prove value, was conducted with both Department of State and U.S. Marine Corps input.

As the social scientist recalls, for a brigade constructing a post-Ba'ath party economic system, information such as traditional money movements, the distribution of farm equipment, and other resource allocation amounted to "bubble up" information of potential worth. Interviewing the population as opposed to the key leader engagements favored at that time through the tribal system model gave the HTT information on what was happening in the actual population.[26] After demonstrating baseline value to both the Department of State and U.S. Marine Corps entities, the brigade could make available space on convoys in order to conduct wider research among the population. From there, the U.S. Marine Corps emphasizing key leader engagements and the Department of State and the United States Agency for International Development emphasizing humanitarian work, convoy support with both necessitated incorporating key concerns into the research structure, to justify convoy support. This was, as all interviewees have suggested, about serving the customer.

Proving initial worth on the base was common across areas of operations and across time. One social scientist in Afghanistan began with a project interviewing all the Afghan drivers coming onto the base. Whilst security procedures were in place to check the vehicles, some of these drivers could be interviewed at length. From this research, which included analysis of tensions between the drivers and those conducting the security checks, the knowledge could be leveraged to gain permissions and resources for off-base projects, and the social scientist argued that the Marine Corps was adept at this, that HTTs:

> were never side-lined, if we figured out how to do it
> we were on. And you know getting on convoys, going
> from patrol base to patrol base, a lot of times battalions,
> when they knew who we were, sort of 'we'll radio in
> to get you guys.' We were never stranded anywhere.[27]

Any deterioration in relationships between members of the HTT and the brigade would commonly lead to blacklisting in the unit, and, as a consequence, convoy space would be more difficult to obtain. Also, the conduct of one team member reflected on the team as a whole, meaning that the group was compromised by any single underperforming individual. Ultimately, across teams, "movement was one of the biggest challenges."[28]

TEAM FUNCTION

Team composition and function could create obvious limitations on the efficacy of research conducted, as noted comprehensively by Lamb *et al.* in their 2013 study.[29] Moreover, a team rarely embedded and left as a complete entity. Typical instead was the experience of one social scientist in Afghanistan in 2009 where the team was composed of a team leader, two social scientists, a research manager, and a Human Terrain Analyst who also worked as the linguist on the team. The team had recently suffered a fatality, and was "in a rebuilding process" when the social scientist arrived.[30] According to the social scientist, this was a "funky setting," where there were problems with personnel integrating within the team, the specific roles of team members within the program, and some issues about where capabilities were best utilized. Over time, the team was able to put different people into research situations for which they were suited.[31] Team size and content fluctuated in all cases; in one example where a team was stood up for the first time, the team leader arrived in Ghazni prior to the rest of the team, followed by a social scientist 2 months later and two further team members, from where the team continued to fluctuate between three and four members.[32] In addition, as noted by one academic expert familiar with the program, it is difficult to communicate to the combat unit the capabilities of the incoming team, given that the teams were so highly variable in terms of peoples' educational and experiential backgrounds.[33]

The team leader was often integral to the success of the team because, possessing military experience, he was a bridge between the two cultures. Evans suggests his own team leader was "vital" because of his military background and his "force of will."[34] The Lamb *et al.* study found that the main strength of the HTT was in its ability to gel as a team.[35] This could be the ability to gel as a whole team, or as split teams. In the case of a well-documented iteration of AF4, Don Ayala, Clint Cooper, and Paula Loyd functioned as a small team, distinct from the rest of that HTT.[36] One social scientist in Afghanistan observed that, while nine members of their team were indicated before deployment, they numbered less upon arrival. Two Human Terrain Analysts, often labelled "interpreters," were Dari speakers from the north of the country, and when they found out they were to be sent to Helmand, they felt unsafe going to a Pashto-speaking area.[37] The social scientist recalls the other team social scientist as having a doctorate in anthropology, and treated the second social scientist as junior, which negatively influenced the team dynamic.

LEADERSHIP

Lamb *et al.* concluded that leadership of the HTT was among the more vital variables that helped to determine the effectiveness of a team internally. Interviews as part of the research conducted in this book with former HTT members reinforce that view of the team leader being vital to the overall efficacy of the team. One social scientist that was embedded in Afghanistan noted that the team leader, a former

Marine, was instrumental in leveraging resources when the team were embedded with the Marines. Because the Marine Corps was more insular than the Army, team leaders were often much more important in a Marine Corps unit than an Army unit, and the ability of embedded teams to be able to work across the spectrum of conventional ground forces was paramount to the concept, such that the team leader was told by the HTS management prior to embedding that "this means a lot, our reputation is staked on our team doing okay."[38]

Another social scientist transitioning into Iraq found a team already in place for nearly a year, which meant that "they had already kind of built their relationships" but that to navigate the integration, the "team leader was very effective at building the relationships, and so that was great."[39] That team had split in two because of a major intrateam conflict before the social scientist arrived; the team leader, one social scientist, and one Human Terrain Analyst conducted research in Fallujah, while one research manager and a Human Terrain Analyst who had decided to break away went to Ramadi. This was made possible because the unit was transitioning from the former to the latter site. The team leader developed a concept for the split, such that the research manager and Human Terrain Analyst would act as a "scout team; get some research going so that when the team arrived, we already had a presence and an understanding of the area."[40]

While that team leader was considered a success by the social scientist after the leader departed, a young Army captain who was originally the research manager became the team leader, and his inexperience led to a deterioration in team cohesion, coupled to two former Special Operations Forces (SOF) personnel joining

338

that were simply there for the remuneration, as was a broader problem with HTS.[41] Leadership quality was even more pronounced toward the end of that social scientist's tour when they joined a team where the two social scientists had left after a dispute. The team as a whole had developed a robust relationship with the brigade command, but there were no longer social scientists to design or conduct studies. In that team, the social scientist who transitioned in praised the team leader, a former Marine and current reservist; he was a colonel, allowing him to approach the colonel of the unit on an equal footing which facilitated procuring resources and transport.[42] Linked to team efficacy was another aspect of successful engagement with the unit in which the team were embedded, the question of acceptable aesthetics: integration was not simply a case of professional expertise.

With the HTTs, integration into that military structure was assisted by "superficial things"; such as "appearance and attitude," levels of fitness, and character.[43] As Krohley asserts of his experiences, many of the team were in their late-20s, and at a physical level similar to the military unit "and that helped — we could talk the talk."[44] Howard Clark, who observed AF7 closely at Camp Dwyer, Garmsir district in 2011, noted that the HTT leader, a reservist major, was an enabler of the rest of the team, facilitating its research by procuring logistical support.[45] Clark has experience of the work of HTTs and thus offers a valuable perspective on the products they produced. As a civilian working for U.S. Special Operations Command in 2009 and 2010, he saw HTT products. When he later embedded with a U.S. Marine Corps regiment conducting research in Southern Helmand, he was working at Camp Dwyer, Garmsir district, based with AF7 from April to September 2011.

"DOTS ON FOREHEADS"

"Culture" is a broad term. In Iraq and Afghanistan, sociocultural research is an amorphous and indistinct concept which has required, and will require, investigation.[46] Beneath its umbrella, specific research could focus on a spectrum of issues, from agriculture to medical aid, all of which influenced, or were influenced by, the cultural environment. The military is a kinetic instrument which is necessarily focused on defeating the enemy through the application of superior strength, despite the COIN tactics which emphasized interaction with the population. In practice, this meant that in Iraq and Afghanistan data which was relevant to kinetic operations was dominant in the concern of the commanders on the ground. In addition, comparative to abstract ideas of culture, kinetic-focused metrics are more easily collected, making them dominant planning modalities.

Familiar with both kinetic and nonkinetic metrics, Richard Heimann, adjunct faculty at the University of Maryland, Baltimore Campus, has worked in Iraq and Afghanistan, most recently returning from a 3-month deployment in Kandahar province where he had worked in a brigade which had an HTT. Heimann argues that, in Iraq and Afghanistan, the data:

> that was easy to measure was being measured. That was the data that was being analyzed as a consequence of measurement being so easy. Anything that wasn't easy to measure in these operations was considered not important.[47]

This data was commonly the size, strength, and whereabouts of enemy personnel. As a consequence, societal aspects of the area of operations were elimi-

340

nated. It is hard to unhinge measurement from data analysis, and little thought was given to what was being measured, and conversely what was not being analyzed as a consequence of not measuring it. Abstract sociocultural analysis with indistinct indicators which did not afford uniform time series was difficult data to prove of value in the kinetic environment.

In a COIN environment where measurement of both kinetic and nonkinetic metrics is considered necessary for successful planning. There is a lot of potential data in the environment, but it is often abstract and consequently difficult to analyze. Moreover, with qualitative analysis, there is a precarious veracity in the conduct of short interviews with members of the populace with which there has been no previous contact by the HTT, when somebody in the vicinity "has an M16, however many feet away from your social scientist they may be, who might be there ambivalently."[48] Problematic security environments were noted by Jennifer Clark in her research in Sinjar after promises were made to military members of units she was attached to, to become a valuable asset:

> The Marines would not let us go further than one boot away from them, so we had to maintain boot contact with a Marine, while interviewing. Essentially, that first mission, I scratched. Although I wrote a report, I put a heavy disclaimer on the report, that this was the security situation, it was extreme, and I am positive that the Iraqis were not being honest with us, apart from the Yezidi, who were open and excited to talk to us, they loved the Marines.[49]

Despite extensive interaction with members of the population who could give detailed accounts of the social terrain and cultural history of the immediate environment, the presence of coalition forces in the vicinity lent an element of doubt to all interview material, while the very interaction between both created a degree of subjectivity. This negatively impacted the fidelity of the data obtained and could be severely compromised in highly insecure environments. As Krohley explains from his research in Baghdad, a pertinent question is: "Can a research team that is an integral part of one of the main parties to a conflict conduct objective research on the roots and dynamics of that violence?"[50] Heimann sums up the problem more generally:

> the goal is non-deterministic interaction with the human terrain with external validity yet at the tactical level HTTs interact and hence impact with the objects they are trying to study; the goal is honest signals and surveys are tenuous at best.[51]

In 2011, HTT AF7 attempted rigorous approaches to their surveys, including random sampling and methodologies which highlighted uncertainties in the data. The team members wore side-arms and noted that:

> firstly, the population are going to be very intimidated, secondly, they are sometimes going to tell you what they want you to hear, thirdly, if somebody wants something out of it, they realise 'hey, the way I answer this question, I may get a project or money.'[52]

This prejudiced the content of the report and Howard Clark, familiar with the products, suggested there was great value in having stated this up front. However, this uncertainty, while it was rigorous social science conducted in highly insecure environments, was very difficult to factor into a high operational tempo in which clarity of judgement would facilitate planning. Condensing rigorous social science research into the battle rhythm is a deep skill. Clark notes that AF7 was able to condense large volumes of data into a 2- to 4-page paper in a manner that the rest of the Marines could use and actually had time to read.[53] This compromise between detail and clarity lies at the heart of the frictional interplay between social sciences and military planning in COIN operations.

OPERATIONAL TEMPO

Operational tempo in Iraq and Afghanistan varied proportionally with the level of insecurity and remained arduous even at brigade headquarters. In Iraq, Jennifer Clark suggested it "was easily an 18-hour work day sometimes less, but, mostly for me, I worked 18-hours a day, 7 days a week, and you were constantly moving."[54] In headquarters, operational tempo was less — 12-hour days — but with added leeway in activities, for instance, down time could involve a movie or a Burger King meal, a work out, or retail purchases, but a 12-hour day was the minimum.[55] Even on base, the operational tempo was frenetic. If not attending working groups, HTT members would create research groups based on the commander's critical information requirements which were produced and disseminated daily.[56] These were reports that were coming back from the field with high frequency because those involved had to complete operation reports after they came back from the missions, but which, according to Jennifer Clark, were "redundant' as sociocultural analysis because they lacked methodology or depth.[57] Indeed, as Howard Clark, who worked with HTT assets in Afghanistan has noted, the research generated by HTTs was of value for one reason — because the methodology was foregrounded, allowing the readers to assess value from the outset.[58]

But robust methodology, creating a research plan, and obtaining a feasible transport arrangement meant that actual ethnographic work was not a continual process. One social scientist in Afghanistan went off base for 2 weeks, before returning to write the report for 2 weeks, which generated substantial products but of a frequency of one every month and noted that other factors, such as rest and recuperation rotations similarly "affected the battle rhythm too, whether or not you were back or not, when you were going to do your next research project."[59]

As the end of the deployment neared in early-2010, the social scientist observed that the monthly duration outside of the base increased. In part, this was because the value of the team had been proved, and the knowledge of the social scientists was reaching its deployed peak. In part, this was dictated by the operations: the Afghan and International Security Assistance Force offensive Operation MOSHTARAK to recapture the strategically important town of Marjah in Helmand from the Taliban was beginning, which increased the number of convoys outside of the base and increased the possible value of all information in the formation of strategy and tactics. As the social scientist explains of the operation: "it was one of the biggest operations that the Marines did while they were in Helmand and so we were out thinking we may help get the ground level information before they even went into Marjah" but ultimately, the HTT spent a protracted period "waiting for them to finish the kinetic stuff" and then the battalion they assumed would ask for the team did not call for them, so their presence in the other battalion was largely superficial.[60] In total, during the 9-month deployment, there were five research periods outside of the base, which generated 20-page reports, but these reports were a compromise between clarity and detail, as the social scientist makes clear:

> we always tried to make it so it was readable from a battalion commander's point of view, which meant that it was difficult though, that kind of research was difficult to sum up. So you could have given a lot more detail that would have made it stronger but you couldn't because you wanted to make it readable.[61]

As the operational tempo increases, the requirement for a deep understanding of the social dimensions of the environment to develop precise planning increases proportionally, but the research capability of the HTT asset is increasingly complicated by the expanding degree of insecurity for incumbent forces on the ground.

AREA OF OPERATIONS

As noted in a variety of existing literature, there is a geographic limitation to the work of HTTs in that a small group cannot cover the entirety of an area of operation. Lamb *et al.* build on interviews with brigade commanders to conclude that for the HTTs in their periods of deployment: "There is simply too much human terrain in a brigade area of responsibility for HTTs to build a comprehensive and current picture."[62] Indeed, even the most able teams could not cover the human terrain in the area of operations "sufficiently well to make a major difference for a brigade commander."[63]

The efficiency gained when splitting a team to cover more ground was confirmed by the first AF1 team from the Foreign Military Studies Office during Operation MAIWAND in Ghazni province in May and June 2007 which was led by the Afghan National Army with Task Force Fury, part of the International Security Assistance Force, in support. The Task Force Fury commander had tasked AF1 with gaining a sociocultural snapshot of the environment to assist maneuver elements and the Provincial Reconstruction Team (PRT). To cover as much of the area as possible, AF1 split, with three members of the team assisting the PRT, while two members worked with Civil Affairs, A Company, 2/508th. During Operation MAIWAND, AF1 tested Rapid Ethnographic Assessment Procedure as a technique. The value of that procedure was in the central role of semi-structured interviews, no formal sampling of participants, and the involvement of a multidisciplinary team allowing different elements of the research to unfold simultaneously, allowing access to more of the population than a single researcher could gain alone.[64]

The Human Terrain Rapid Ethnographic Assessment Procedure was based on this standard applied anthropological methodology and was valuable because it was developed where there was a limited time to conduct research but still allowing a rapid assessment of the sociocultural environment. The AF1 team modified the procedure to the demands of the combat environment and structured the interviews based on Afghan regional-specific taxonomy. During Operation MAIWAND, the part of the HTT with the PRT participated in 16 missions, and the team with Civil Affairs deployed to the area of operations for 16 days and conducted eight missions. These missions included village assessments, participation in organized councils (*Shuras*) and random encounter unstructured interviews with the population.

The rigorous social science research conducted by AF1 during Operation MAIWAND allowed the HTT to reach its full potential. However, more generally, there is an inherent inability to access large volumes of the area of operation which impacted the ability of HTTs to support certain programs. In Afghanistan, this was a tangible limitation of the program; for example, the Village Stability Operations were in remote regions where only local law enforcement and national jurisdiction were weakened by physical distance. For remote areas where HTTs had not travelled, their only products were often summaries of existing literature, focusing broadly on clans and the largest urban centers.[65]

Exacerbating this problem is one of connectivity. In the physical structure of the brigade staff, the S-6 component is tasked with developing and maintaining communications infrastructure and data flows. Given that the broad character of research is interviews with additional secondary source research conducted using the Internet, HTTs with access to the physically positioned brigade structure can produce these qualitative reports with important secondary research which provides valuable context. However, in remote rural regions deployed with, for example, SOFs in support of Village Stability Operations, without access to S-6 resources located on bases, the information highway is absent, and the reports must be produced without the secondary source context. This is a further reason why HTS is so suitable for long-range research in relatively secure environments; absent high operational tempo, interviews can be conducted in remote rural locations, and then the secondary source research can be conducted upon returning to command centers, written up and integrated into long-range planning strategies aimed at conflict mitigation.

ONE YEAR AT A TIME

Across the duration of deployment, the knowledge of an individual, a team, or a unit inevitably increased over time. Part of the problem as social scientist Jennifer Clark explained was in the retention of information in unit transition and exacerbated by absence of synchronicity between service arms and the HTTs themselves; Marine Corps personnel deploy for 7 months; HTT members for approximately 9 months; and Army personnel for 12 months. As noted, for the HTS, at least this was intentional, that team rotations are scheduled not to coincide with the:

> relief in place so that team members on the ground can help new units understand the human terrain in their areas. The team maintains the human terrain databases on separate systems so that information collected year after year is not lost as units transfer and depart.[66]

The result, however, was myriad transfers of authority between units taking place across multiple areas of operation at different times with no structured matrix for the retention and dissemination of information, making the development of homogeneous institutional memory across the entire theater a complex and daunting task. The subsequent absence of social knowledge in the early stages of a rotation could lead to significant missteps. As Fondacaro noted, from the view of a transfer of authority, the loss of engagement with the population was significant: "All the relationships and agreements and tacit understandings you had with those individuals are out of the window."[67] Ultimately, the poor state of the war was "being fed by the unit rotation policy" because "the higher headquarters were rotating on the same schedule. We weren't learning anything."[68]

The results at the tactical level can be explored through teams' insights of their experiences. An HTT member with the 82nd Airborne Division in Iraq demurred on an offer to breakfast during Ramadan with local key Iraqi government officials, which retrospectively was seen to possibly have harmed relationships with the population. As the team member recalls, it "was little things like that which I was supposed to know but I didn't simply because I didn't have the personal experience dealing with that culture and you cannot learn everything."[69] Put simply, "it was just very basic human reactions that really require that personal experience in the area to understand."[70] If knowledge retention had been improved, greater engagement with the population would have been possible from the outset as team members would have been better prepared.

Differing team composition, functional character, and role within a brigade inevitably created heterogeneity of product, both in terms of content and frequency. However, there was a broad template of inquiry which teams followed, shaped by the character of the reporting environment. Initial research conducted by a team would be characterized by rapid mission reporting and "quick turnaround of products' because the information base that the team could work from in the beginning of the deployment was inevitably limited."[71] In these situations, the value-added was often engineered by contacts rather than research skills; occasionally this was from personal relationships with team members who had already embedded in a particular region. Personal relationships, as much with the brigade as with the host community, were critical in that initial period to forging a niche value in the military enterprise.

The goal was to generate a baseline level of knowledge which would allow the construction of deep research plans to be conducted. As such, each product can be modeled as a dissertation; first, constructing a broad literature review to grasp the field and identify gaps in the existing knowledge structure; second, generating a research question and methodology; third, conducting research based around the plan; and finally, completing the dissertation which shows a significant contribution to knowledge thereby demonstrating value to the brigade. Only at the end of the deployment were the dissertations of a depth of understanding that lent themselves to deep research:

> The first part was building a rapport, developing a basic understanding of key personalities, and that is where you see that stuff. It was towards the end where you can build into those long-term products that synchronize everything together.[72]

Such was the evolution of knowledge within the team over the course of even a single deployment that the character of the products could change profoundly. One social scientist noted that from initial iterations of products which were largely generic, eventually his expertise allowed focus on thematic products, such as the problem of corruption across the area of operations and the effect of the counternarcotics programs on the population in the area of operations. This thematic research across a broad geography was only possible through a combination of specific research and data that the team had collected throughout the duration of the period conducting research. In the final iterations of research, it was a sizeable advantage to be able to draw on organized data that had been collated. It was only possible to conduct thematic reports "later in the tour"; battalion-level generic reports may have stayed at the same level of analysis as the tour progresses, but generally "it got better just in terms of every time you do it, you become a little more familiar with local dynamics."[73] Social scientists gathering data in the fluid environment of stabilization operations where information was quickly out of date meant that according to one HTT member who deployed in both Iraq and Afghanistan, "we were so far in the weeds dealing with very specific issues the information that we wanted simply didn't exist in writing, there was nothing that they [the RRC] could use to support us."[74]

THE "LOCAL OPTIC"

Increasing depth of knowledge with prolonged research in the area of operations is inevitable. Therefore, expertise is a function of time. Knowledge and understanding are proportional to time spent in the environment. Value to the brigade similarly increases over time. But, given that conflict zones are, by their nature, harsh and austere environments, deployments are necessarily of limited duration. For that reason, in total an HTT member is deployed for an initial 9-month rotation, with an additional 9 months optional after the first rotation is completed.[75]

As expertise is proportional to the time spent in the operating environment and the rotation is of limited duration, as one social scientist embedded with the Marine Corps in Afghanistan explained, the result is that: "'I finally get it' and you're on the plane out of here."[76] Ultimately:

> it contributes to this whole, '10-year war fought 1 year at a time' thing. Part of that is that nobody gets there understanding what it is the hell they are getting into, so you always have your 2 months of 'What is this? What is going on?'[77]

That social scientist calculated the discrepancy between the operationally relevant reporting of the Human Terrain Team and academic work:

> 'Anthropology takes 2 years in the field usually or at least 1 year in the field, it takes that long to figure out what is going on, you cannot just leave in 6 months.[78]

But in areas of high insecurity, there is a paradox that, with greater time spent in the area, the risks increase. Howard Clark agrees that the ability to look through the "local optic" cannot be achieved in the 9-month rotation but takes years. However, Clark also notes in the the Garmsir district where he observed AF7 between April and September 2011 that it was one of the most dangerous places on earth, and there was the risk of significant psychological trauma to individuals should they remain beyond the 9-months rotation.[79] The HTS capability arose from that observed need to develop institutional memory. Fondacaro had worked on the CPE tool and found that capability gap, the need for humans in possession of social science products plugged directly into the brigade staff that had been in place between rotations, because:

> In reality, for a brigade commander, they'd spend the first three months just finding out where they were, then they'd spend nine months actually doing operations and the last few months of that trying to get out

of there and get accountability for their equipment and without getting anybody else killed or hurt. When you are doing this for a year at a time, the non-thinking status quo becomes the norm and you don't develop a corporate memory to hand off to the new guy; a rich corporate memory.[80]

But the possibility of trauma limits the wide ranging applicability of the program in a conflict zone. This observation allows two important conclusions. First, it shows the suitability of the HTS to long-range planning. The ability to look through the "local optic" takes years, while conflict zones are inherently dangerous and allow only rotations of up to 1 year. In long-range research, social scientists can conduct research for 12-24 months without the risk of psychological trauma. Second, it shows that small size teams such as SOF working on Village Stability Operations are better modalities for research than large footprint units such as brigades. The small units allow researchers that access to the "local optic," permanently embedded with local forces and in and among the population. That physical intimacy increases exponentially the exposure to the society which the researchers are attempting to understand.

The assessment of the social scientist tallies with the broad academic definition of ethnography. Dr. H. Russell Bernard suggests that ethnography of other cultures takes a year or more, and, while focused ethnography study as part of the sub-discipline of applied anthropology can be done more quickly, it would still require 3 months of study and conflicted area research is too broadly focused on the general population to be defined as such.[81] Bernard gives the example of a New York hostel, which during a 3-month period must be visited a minimum of four times a week for 3 hours a day or more each time.[82] However, insecure environments mean that there can be no guarantee that the location will be safe enough to visit, that each visit will allow more than 3 hours of constant interaction and that, finally, the logistics in terms of convoy support will facilitate travel. In Afghanistan, for example, personal relationships are a key modality of transactions, and it is these relationships that take years to build.

In Bernard's reading, good ethnography requires "trustworthy informants who are observant, reflective, and articulate — who know how to tell good stories" and that ethnographers must stay with the informants for a protracted period; in a conflicted area, insecurity makes trust and developing prolonged relationships a difficult endeavor.[83] Indeed, Paula Loyd in Afghanistan "harbored doubts about the validity of the data she and her teammates were gathering. Interviewing Afghans through an interpreter, surrounded by armed soldiers, was far from ideal, and she knew it."[84] If it is not ethnography in stabilization and enabling operations, then what is the research that social scientists undertook? This is operationally relevant reporting, and these were rapid assessments but often ad hoc; after deep research methods were formulated, given the insecurity on the ground there was no way of knowing how the relationship with the as yet undetermined population on the ground would proceed. Jennifer Clark identifies the character of her work clearly:

> Not only was I not acting like an anthropologist but it wasn't research: it was operationally driven reporting. But the distinct difference is that whilst it is operationally driven, we were not directed by anyone to collect a certain thing. There was no one but me telling me what to collect.[85]

Developing ethnographic knowledge based on at least a year in the field and forming longitudinal relationships with the population contrasts with the operational tempo of military operations which requires frequent research products in order to influence operations. An HTT social scientist relates having spent a month in Marjah at a critical period leading to Operation MOSHTARAK. Interviews had allowed the social scientist to gain a greater understanding of the ethnic groups, drugs economy, and key leaders in Lashkar Gah, as well as to produce a map of the area to capture sociocultural research. When the social scientist returned to the Marine Corps regiment, it was anticipated that this information would be of interest at some levels within the staff. However, it became clear that this "information was too granular, it wasn't even a concern for them [the regiment]; they were ten steps ahead, five projects away from what I had seen and from what the information was going to help them decide."[86]

This observation from a social scientist in Afghanistan brings us full circle, tying neatly to Krohley's observation that, at the operational and strategic levels, there was an inability to influence those levels of planning because these big decisions had already been made. HTTs were a tactical asset, connected to the operations and strategy of the Brigade Combat Team staff or Regimental Combat Team staff. To implement a strategy takes time; to plan the operations of a brigade takes time, resources, and planning. These big cogs in the military machine are maneuvered into place slowly, and with difficulty. The HTT's granular research is unlikely to recalibrate that movement.

In addition, research which plugged the sociocultural capability gap took time to collate, process, and disseminate. By the time the work was produced, it spoke of a snapshot of the area that had already changed. The social scientist recounting his or her experiences in Marjah paints the picture bluntly:

> They [the brigade staff] had already made the decision so it wasn't like my information that the farmers are going to react badly to that mattered at all, because it was like 'sorry it's already done, we'll just figure it out as we go'.[87]

Away from the high operational tempos in Iraq and Afghanistan, in environment where strategy is long-range and the necessity for operational planning is limited by relative security, granular research plugged into the combatant command level has a greater likelihood of positively affecting strategic direction.

CONCLUSIONS

A conflict does not stand still, an insurgency changes over time. In consequence, the operational picture can change quickly. Richard Heimann details the daily routine in Kandahar during his tour:

> They [the operational staff] had Sit Reps [Situation Reports] in the morning and in the evening and the commander's brief after those such that ultimately the command structure only 'really care about the last 24 hours.'[88]

The frequency of data required by the commander means that the ability of the HTT to influence the operational tempo is complicated by the operational tempo. Compared to the quantitative work which would analyze a data set every 24-48 hours and move on, the HTT projects were ostensibly long-term and qualitative—"blink type of assessments"—incorporating large amounts of information (and hence multiple variables) and "trying to reconcile it over time."[89] As such, it was difficult for the HTT to influence the "battle rhythm."

When HTS commenced its structural redesign, one of the central aspects was to leverage the research planning and design tools that HTS had standardized in its development and planning team working groups. These were highly structured tools for reporting either a long-term research process or a short-term research effort of approximately 2 weeks in duration. The tools were specifically designed to enable social science research as part of a bureaucracy to enable tracking, ethical oversight, and other facets of the research. The aim here was "to understand this is different from writing your dissertation, this is about simple, quick, structured communication of what it is that you are doing."[90] The aim was to jettison academic theory in order to parse the value of the research for the military customer:

> We didn't actually use social network analysis for it. What we used was just a general survey methodology, one you would see in political science or something like that. Most of the information we reported was just basic descriptive statistics, you know we could have taken it to another level theoretically, but for what we were trying to achieve it was good enough.[91]

Social science research had to be adapted to the battle rhythm: "if it takes 3 months to conduct a study and the deadline is 2 weeks, that automatically makes the person conducting the study irrelevant in the eyes of the commander and in helping the mission."[92] The result, as Ben Connable suggests, is that the extent to which these cultural initiatives had permanence or integral relevance to the day-to-day operations planning was questionable: "It's not bad, it's not irrelevant, it's not non-existent, but it's just questionable."[93]

That makes the research goals of primary importance; if HTT research products serve the commander, then they are tailored to the operational tempo of the mission and must necessarily be rapid reporting. As Heimann explains of the operating environment, "the battle rhythm was important; we were hinged to the operational pace of things. Human Terrain Teams; I saw maybe three briefs during the commander briefings, so maybe at a pace of one a month."[94] This problem experienced by HTTs in the field in Iraq and Afghanistan was captured in the unresolved tension of modeling insurgencies in the 2006 *Counterinsurgency* field manual: "It is important not to oversimplify an insurgency. However, analysts and commanders still require a means of defining and describing the enemy that can be commonly understood."[95]

The changing character of the human terrain is also stated explicitly in U.S. Army doctrine: "Societies are not static, but change over time."[96] Capturing this change with deep qualitative analysis is complicated by the military that "as a customer of social science knowledge, wants to apply whatever they learn to solve problems in a timely, practical manner."[97] The customer ideally learns at the pace of the most valuable asset a command has—its data. As the data evolves, monitoring must capture that evolution in real time. Qualitative research, however, necessarily takes time to develop a plan, conduct the research, write-up the findings, and brief. By that time, what is the state of the original snapshot of the human terrain that was researched?

To model the changing human terrain over time, Heimann uses IBM data scientist Jeff Jonas' analogy of a busy road in a commercial for the company. Jonas argues that, if "all you can do is take a snapshot of how the road looked 5 minutes ago, how would you know when to cross the road?"[98] Out-of-date information can lead to catastrophic decisionmaking. Movement makes basing operations on previous static snapshots of the environment a hazardous approach.

The military fashion is for "fast trajectories," a series of similar data sets at short intervals that can give a good indication of trends.[99] As such, there is a preference in the U.S. military writ large for quantitative over qualitative analysis. While social science expertise is certain to continue to assume a role in the spectrum of warfighting operations, the question becomes what form of social science will be favored by the military. As one social scientist explains:

> anything with numbers on it is seen by Americans as sacred, so there was a lot of polling done by the SSRA [Social Science Research and Analysis], and we saw how invalid these results were when we came to know Helmand.[100]

One social scientist provides an example of an Afghan who is illiterate and received no formal education being polled as to the legitimacy and security of the national government. "Legitimacy" and "security" are not innate concepts, but abstract concepts learned through childhood education, and with increasing sophistication as that education continues; therefore understanding is contingent upon being educated. Asking that Afghan about security, to which they reply "great" reflects as "good" in the poll. But if you talk to the Afghan for 30-40 minutes, talking to him for as long as you can, you find that the Taliban physically abused him last week or has stolen his phone; that for him is security because he is not being killed, and from an International Security Assistance Force perspective that is not security, and for what the poll is trying to measure, that is also not security.[101] The result is polling data which has emerged from Afghanistan which, lacking qualitative assessment, can be highly misleading.

From this perspective, mixed methods would win out over a purely quantitative understanding of the tactical and operational pictures.[102] In that social scientist's view, it is dangerous to draw a Link Chart, and say "we are mapping their telephone calls." You also have to understand the social relationships and personal histories of the people involved, in order to bring valuable context. This means that you have to "sit down and have lengthy conversations with people and get to know them; you have to dig deep and quantitative methods don't allow for that sort of digging."[103] Thus, while the promise of big data is shifting the military emphasis toward quantitative analysis, in the words of data scientist Heimann, "quantitative is going to take the charge with a lot of the data analysis. It is not really a criticism of qualitative analysis. I think when done well, both have utility."[104]

When done well and with a responsive staff command, HTT research augmented the picture of the battle space. To satisfy the military consumer, the social scientist must capture granular detail quickly and enter the battle rhythm to brief the commander on its significance. So too, the research itself requires significant expertise to resolve within its myriad complexities. As Seymour Deitchman noted of the complexities of social science work undertaken during the

Cold War, "The fact of the study, its subject, and the presence of the researchers all affect the social system being studied, in ways that are uncertain and difficult to assess."[105] As such, HTTs will always fight against the military preference for kinetic modalities in operations—DoD exists primarily because of a need to apply force—but it is a fight that is crucial to a more granular understanding of combat, a more nuanced comprehension of the links between societies and war.

ENDNOTES - CHAPTER 6

1. Ryan Evans, personal communication with author, October 18, 2014. See also Ryan Evans, "'The Population is the Enemy': Control, Behaviour, and Counter-Insurgency in Central Helmand Province, Afghanistan," David Martin Jones, Celeste Ward Gventner, and M. L. R. Smith, eds., *The New Counter-Insurgency Era in Critical Perspective*, London, UK: Palgrave Macmillan, 2014.

2. Evans, "'The Population is the Enemy'," p. 258.

3. *Ibid.*, p. 259.

4. Yvette Clinton *et al.*, *Congressionally Directed Assessment of the Human Terrain System*, Arlington, VA: Center for Naval Analyses, 2010, p. 19.

5. Michael Davies, interview with author, Washington, DC, August 10, 2013.

6. Former HTT social scientist 3, interview with author, Alexandria, VA, August 1, 2013.

7. Jennifer Clark, telephone interview with author, October 9, 2013.

8. Former HTT social scientist 3, interview.

9. *Ibid.*

10. *Ibid.*; Jennifer Clark, interview.

11. Former HTT social scientist 3, interview.

12. *Ibid.*

13. *Ibid.*

14. Bill Hess, "Unit of linguists says goodbye to fort," *The Sierra Vista Herald*, October 18, 2008.

15. Former HTT social scientist 1, interview, August 11, 2013.

16. *Ibid.*

17. *Ibid.*

18. Nicholas Krohley, telephone interview with author, July 26, 2013.

19. Former HTT social scientist 3, interview.

20. Krohley, interview.

21. *Ibid.*

22. *Ibid.*

23. *Ibid.*

24. *Ibid.*

25. Ted Callahan, "An Anthropologist at War in Afghanistan," in Montgomery McFate and Janice H. Laurence, eds., *Social Science Goes to War: The Human Terrain System in Iraq and Afghanistan*, London, UK: Hurst, p. 116.

26. Former HTT social scientist 3, interview.

27. Former HTT social scientist 2, interview with author, Quantico, VA, July 29, 2013.

28. Krohley, interview.

29. Christopher J. Lamb *et al.*, *Human Terrain Teams: An Organizational Innovation for Sociocultural Knowledge in Irregular Warfare*, Washington, DC: Institute of World Politics Press, 2013.

30. Former HTT social scientist 4, interview with author, Newport, RI, August 1, 2013.

31. *Ibid.*

32. Former HTT social scientist 1, interview.

33. Anonymous, interview.

34. Ryan Evans, interview with author, Washington, DC, August 6, 2013; Clinton *et al.*, pp. 175-176.

35. Lamb *et al.*

36. Davies, interview.

37. Former HTT social scientist 2, interview.

38. *Ibid.*

39. Former HTT social scientist 3, interview.

40. *Ibid.*

41. *Ibid.*

42. *Ibid.*

43. Krohley, interview.

44. *Ibid.*

45. Howard Clark, telephone interview with author, January 25, 2014.

46. Paul Joseph, *"Soft" Counterinsurgency: Human Terrain Teams and US Military Strategy in Iraq and Afghanistan*, New York: Palgrave Pivot, 2014; Montgomery McFate and Janice H.

Laurence, eds., *Social Science Goes to War: The Human Terrain System in Iraq and Afghanistan*, New York: Oxford University Press, forthcoming.

47. Richard Heimann, interview, August 11, 2013.

48. *Ibid.*

49. Jennifer Clark, interview.

50. Nicholas Krohley, *The Death of the Mehdi Army: The Rise, Fall, and Revival of Iraq's Most Powerful Militia*, London, UK: Hurst, 2015, p. 191.

51. Heimann, interview, August 11, 2013.

52. Howard Clark, interview.

53. *Ibid.*

54. Jennifer Clark, interview.

55. *Ibid.*

56. *Ibid.*

57. *Ibid.*

58. Howard Clark, interview.

59. Former HTT social scientist 2, interview.

60. *Ibid.*

61. *Ibid.*

62. Lamb *et al.*, p. 185.

63. *Ibid.*

64. Frank Fischer and Gerald J Miller, eds., *Handbook of Public Policy Analysis; Theory, Politics, and Methods*, Boca Raton, FL: CRC Press, 2007, p. 449.

65. Howard Clark, interview.

66. Jonathan D. Thompson, "Human Terrain Team Operations in East Baghdad," *Military Review*, Vol. 90, No. 4, 2010, p. 81.

67. Steve Fondacaro, telephone interview with author, September 15, 2015.

68. *Ibid.*

69. Former HTT social scientist 1, interview.

70. *Ibid.*

71. *Ibid.*

72. *Ibid.*

73. Evans, interview.

74. Former HTT social scientist 1, interview.

75. *Ibid.*

76. Former HTT social scientist 2, interview.

77. *Ibid.*

78. Howard Clark, interview.

79. *Ibid.*

80. Fondacaro, telephone interview with author, September 15, 2015.

81. H. Russell Bernard, *Research Methods in Anthropology: Qualitative and Quantitative Approaches*, 4th Ed., Lanham, MD: Alta Mira, 2006, p. 72.

82. *Ibid.*

83. *Ibid.*

84. Vanessa Gezari, *The Tender Soldier: A True Story of War and Sacrifice*, New York: Simon and Schuster, 2013, p. 89; Jennifer Greanias, "Assessing the Effectiveness of the US Military's Human Terrain System," unpublished master's thesis, Washington, DC: Georgetown University, 2010, p. 11.

85. Jennifer Clark, interview.

86. Former HTT social scientist 2, interview.

87. *Ibid.*

88. Heimann, interview.

89. *Ibid.*

90. Former HTT social scientist 1, interview.

91. *Ibid.*

92. Zok Pavlovic, interview with author, Alexandria, VA, August 14, 2013.

93. Ben Connable, interview with author, Arlington, VA, July 15, 2013.

94. Heimann, interview.

95. Headquarters, Department of the Army, and Headquarters, U.S. Marine Corps, *Field Manual* (FM) *3-24/Marine Corps Warfighting Publication* (MCWP) *3-33.5, Counterinsurgency*, Washington, DC: U.S. Government Printing Office, December 2006, pp. 3-33.

96. *Ibid.*, pp. 3-4.

97. Montgomery McFate, Britt Damon, and Robert Holliday, "What do Commanders Really Want to Know? U.S. Army Human Terrain System Lessons Learned from Iraq and Afghanistan," Janice H. Laurence and Michael D. Matthews, eds., *The Oxford Handbook of Military Psychology*, Oxford, UK: Oxford University Press, 2012, p. 102.

98. IBM Commerical, *The Road*, undated, September 9, 2014, available from *www.bing.com/videos/search?q=jeff+jonas+the+road+ commercial&view=detail&mid=9FFA07C708193BDF95A99FFA07C7 08193BDF95A9&FORM=VIRE4.*

99. *Ibid.*

100. Evans, interview.

101. *Ibid.*

102. Connable, interview; Evans, interview; Heimann, interview

103. Evans, interview.

104. Heimann, interview.

105. Seymour J. Deitchman, *The Best-Laid Schemes: A Tale of Social Research and Bureaucracy*, Cambridge, MA: Massachusetts Institute of Technology Press, 1976, p. 348.

CONCLUSIONS

At the height of summer in Baghdad, the tempera-
ture can reach upwards of 110 degrees Fahrenheit. In
this environment devoid of rain, waterproof "Rite in
the Rain" notepads were essential to Human Terrain
Teams (HTTs). These notepads, A5-size flipcharts,
were required to be waterproof in Baghdad because
the intensity of the heat meant that sweat soaked
through the cumbersome military fatigues of personnel. Items carried in pockets, including important research aids such as notepads and incidentals such as
cigarettes, would inevitably become saturated in per-
spiration. The consequences of the drenched fatigues
and soaked cigarettes could be unforeseen and far-
reaching:

> You'd wind up having to smoke the Iraqi menthols,
> which are just disgusting. These guys smoked men-
> thol 100s, the big fat ones. I'm going to die in 5 years,
> bro. I'm not much of a smoker but I'm sure that stuff
> will kill me.[1]

Seemingly unrelated phenomena such as perspi-
ration and paper notebooks can, in the height of a
Baghdad summer, combine in the disorder of conflict
to form significant hurdles to social science research.
Armed conflict in essence is the disordering of society
and social values. There is unpredictability at every
turn, requiring amendment, revision, and adaptation
across the spectrum of military operations, from policy to operations to tactical maneuvers down to the
waterproofing of a notebook. Observing such cause
and effect in late-18th and early-19th century Europe,
Prussian military practitioner and theorist Carl von
Clausewitz wrote eloquently about the fog of war.[2]

The human terrain in war is always shifting in subtle and sometimes illusory ways. As a consequence, it requires constant deciphering in order to focus military operations.

At the same time, by virtue of necessity, the unpredictable character of war means that it forges new alliances. Threats necessitate amendment to the prevailing architecture of knowledge where surmounting such obstacles to progress requires adopting the peripheral and remarkable which, in turn, becomes the convention and normal. The crisis which crystalized in the Iraqi adventure fomented an intellectual insurgency in the military architecture, laying siege to prevailing military thinking. Uncertain of the threat faced, the academic was taken from the blackboard to the battlefield; in the deep weeds of conflict, the scholar shaped military thought not from the policy-level downward, but from the tactical-level upward; not from the blackboard, but between rifles in villages and townships, feeding information directly to brigade staffs, because the language of war requires the addition of a social grammar before it can be accurately translated.

In the book, three key findings have been presented. First, the crisis caused by the improvised explosive device (IED) allowed a competing theory associated with low-intensity conflict to gain emphasis in planning. The conclusion is that there are myriad military theories that wax and wane against the backdrop of ephemeral concerns in the Department of Defense (DoD). Human Terrain System (HTS) was, in principle, a counter-IED (C-IED) function. Dr. Montgomery McFate, through her role in the counterinsurgency (COIN) field manual, was able to create an explicit doctrinal need for an HTS capability which was thus emplaced in the context of countering insurgencies. McFate's section of the COIN field manual so plainly stressed the need for nonorganic additions to the U.S. intelligence enterprise in order to succeed in countering the Iraqi insurgency that her drafted sections of chapter 3, "Intelligence," led to a confrontational meeting on September 13, 2006. The meeting took place at the Institute for Defense Analyses where Mc-Fate was working, and also included Conrad Crane, who was the lead author of the drafted field manual; two personnel from the Army Intelligence Center; a member of the Joint Staff's intelligence branch; and Kyle Teamey, lead author of the "Intelligence" chapter.[3] Objections were raised that McFate's sections took the job of intelligence gathering away from the intelligence professionals and placed it into the hands of the Army and Marine units on the ground.[4] The controversial nature of this transition shows just how far McFate was shifting the idea of what the intelligence- and information-gathering tools should be in COIN operations. It also shows how she used *Field Manual* (FM) *3-24, Counterinsurgency*, to demonstrate a need for the HTS. With the COIN field manual ascendant in DoD planning, the HTS could legitimately obtain significant monies from the Overseas Contingency Fund, enabling it to expand to meet the requirements of the dimensions of the surge of forces in Iraq.

The program's divorce from the C-IED enterprise was abrupt and decisive. The first embedded teams in Iraq may have been aware of the origins of the program, but there was no training on aspects of detecting IED networks. In that regard, therefore, the program was peculiar in that, while it ushered forth as a C-IED enterprise, in form and function it was a COIN tool to understand civilian populations. The prominent notion in the literature that the program was formed solely as a device to understand the population eliminates important aspects of its evolution. The Joint Urgent Operational Needs Statement (JUONS) supplied by Combined Joint Task Force-82 in April 2007 noted the requirement of an embedded team capability to identify IED cells (Appendix D). On the ground, however, of the hundreds of pages of embedded team products seen by the author, only one contained any reference to IEDs. That reference was tangential and related to a mine-clearing camp. On June 22, 2009, members of an embedded team north of Lashkar Gah, Afghanistan, learned from a mine-clearing group that red rocks denoted that there was danger from unexploded IEDs in the minefield.[5]

That abrupt divorce is to the detriment of the longevity of the program. In *Out of the Mountains* published in 2013, David Kilcullen noted that use of the IED has become a chronic, global problem with particularly important application as a space denial weapon in urban environments.[6] If the HTS had systematically examined, at least in part, civilian attitudes to IEDs — the devices often caused civilian casualties — there would at least have been something concrete that the program had worked toward. A kernel of knowledge built around the impact of the IED on civilian populations is something that the program should contemplate if it transitions into a theater security asset intended to influence strategic-level planning and activities.

Second, I find that the program training cycle suffered in its initial iterations from a "best guess" process permitted by the *laissez-faire* attitude of an "anything goes" period in U.S. military affairs. However, evolution of teaching in the program was rapid after the return of embedded members into the program management. With implications beyond the HTS, it suggests the value of integrating the experience of combat veterans in the student curriculum. That said, there is no evidence to support the notion that teams in 2012 were of more value than teams in 2008, despite a gap of 4 years, with all the commensurate improvement in training. The training may have had incremental, limited impact, but the teams appear only as efficient as the people on them, suggesting that future attempts to code for knowledge, practicality, physicality, and psychology in recruitment will be at least as important as the training.

Third, I find that embedded social science research in Iraq and Afghanistan was hindered by a series of limiting factors. These factors were the complexity of embedding civilians into the military unit: the limited initial knowledge the social scientists embedded with; the challenge of creating a timely, robust social science product which influenced the military decisionmaking cycle; and often making abstract and complex concepts resonate with brigade staff seeking clarity of information. High operational tempo in deeply insecure environments inhibits social science research capabilities at the tactical level, which, instead, are ideally suited to studies intended to inform and influence long-term planning in more secure regions of strategic importance to the U.S. Army.

When embedded, social scientists conducted research using the tools and techniques that they had learned in academia. This meant that the HTS was not confined to ethnographies and anthropology, with implications for the scholarly debate which focused on that element of the program. Nor did the program militarize anthropology. The high operational tempo of brigades necessarily hastened research processes and created something new; a social science reporting platform which was never standardized through 2007-14 because of the difficulty of integrating *sui generis* experiences at Fort Leavenworth, Kansas, under a program management engaged in an ad hoc working pattern. A baseline research template for applied social science may facilitate future integration of the research into staff planning.

Success was defined by the militarization of the civilian, by personality and adaptability. Integrating personnel into the unit was pivotal if they were to be considered a valuable addition to the array of personnel and could contribute not just research capabilities but a number of functions from erecting HESCO barriers to guard duty when attached to Special Operations Forces (SOF) units. Academics therefore had to become military personnel, in function if not in form. As Bob Reuss notes, probably the most prominent item of training and from lessons learned:

> was that you had to spend more time on militarising those folks that we took from all the civilian walks of life and bringing them into an organisation that is not necessarily one you have down on Main Street.[7]

The cross-cultural divide is pronounced, complicating uniformly robust value-added social science capability to brigades in stabilization operations, as seen by the heterogeneous performance of embedded teams in Iraq and Afghanistan. Effective social scientists all successfully made the transition.

Neither is the long-term training of military personnel, as suggested by Ben Connable, a particularly viable route. True, the military researcher could "speak the same language [as the Brigade Combat Team staff], have the assets, the procedures; and lines of authority are already established."[8] But the high turnover rate of young officers in the U.S. Armed Services and the difficulty and length of a doctoral studentship in the best social science departments in United States universities means that there is no guarantee that social science research expertise will be resident in the military enterprise when the next crisis unfolds. Ben Connable, a brilliant thinker and decorated U.S. Marine Corps officer, is now retired from the military and working at the RAND Corporation. As a consequence, the civilian sector will again in times of crises be sought out and recruited into the military enterprise. The continuation of the program after Iraq and Afghanistan will allow a crucial line of sight between academia and the DoD to remain open.

Problematic is that the program between 2007 and 2014 gained such negative media attention. The U.S. Army is a results-focused enterprise that rewards success, whether at the individual, unit, or organization level. In the HTS, successful individuals could often be rendered impotent by a badly functioning team. Each embedded member was different; team social scientists possessed dissimilar academic skills and various favored modalities of research. There could be no true uniform training blueprint because in the heat of the battle rhythm, these academics conducted research in the ways in which they had been trained to do so by the academy. Reverting to type thus did not allow formulation of a one-size-fits-all training program. Nor was it a case that the post-doctoral embeds made the best researchers; because they had been trained to the highest degree by the academy, they were often the most difficult to transition to a military mindset and their writing style could be verging on the unintelligible to the military customer. In addition, personalities were not coded nor was it known which personality would function well in areas exposed to high levels of selective violence against the incumbent forces. It could be guessed, but the transition from Fort Leavenworth to combat conditions on different continents carried with it various unknowns. As a suggestion of the author, future research could include examination of each team's feedback on every individual within the team allowing construction of a matrix determining positive and negative attributes against frequency cited.

One of the many unknowable variations was in individuals' approaches to the ethical dimension of their research which was simply a binary outcome where ethical research was conducted, or it was not. Often the broad array of social science expertise meant that ethics carried more or less emphasis, depending on the social scientist's own discipline's proximity to anthropology. In addition, conflict creates its own rules beneath the blurring of boundaries in insecure environments. Despite the arguments of the American Anthropological Association, research profiles and products seen by the author and interviews conducted strongly suggest that ethical research could be conducted, by calibrating the character of the interaction with the population. There was a persistent and unresolved dilemma as social scientists were there serving a military customer, a priority which could obfuscate ethical requirements in research and engagement with the population.

This ethical quagmire, which is exacerbated by increasing incumbent insecurity in an operating environment, would be substantially reduced in strategic research modalities away from conflict zones. In addition, in more secure environments, the incumbent exercises hegemonic control allowing for measured, careful, and protracted dialogue between the academy and military. It is in the strategically oriented articulation of the HTS where deep social science research with hypotheses and systematic approaches of the type envisaged by the program management can be realized; where experts in disciplines can conduct deep research and develop a proper social science platform for the U.S. Army.

However, there is a significant issue with the capability were it to transition to a strategic asset at the level of theater security. Countering insurgencies in Iraq and Afghanistan gave embedded teams a reason for being among the population. Researching the population was necessary to mitigate the cause and effects of pronounced, highly visible insurgencies. Embedded teams were present in COIN roles; that much was clearly understood. In relatively calm environments in the Philippines, for example, the population will less likely understand the presence of researchers that identify themselves as a U.S. Department of the Army asset. This would actually exacerbate concerns as to the ethical function of the program because long-range research would transition the character of products from operationally relevant reporting to ethnographies conducted for a military customer. In such a strategic articulation, therefore, analogies to entities with covert character such as the Office of Strategic Services and Central Intelligence Agency gain greater credence. Dr. Nicholas Krohley, for example, argues that, in a strategic articulation, U.S. Army social scientists may struggle to do research because of the distrust of the population and the magnified scrutiny of critical academics.[9]

Fundamentally, however, the remit of embedded teams in a theater security role has not changed. It is, simply, to listen. The U.S. Department of the Army is engaged in a global stabilization operation, which has as much relevance at the strategic level as tactical planes. In theater security, long-term issues such as food security, natural hazards, and institutional capacity building are fundamental to the well-being of societies. In September 2014, DoD deployed its military to assist in the fight against the spread of Ebola virus in West Africa under Operation UNITED ASSISTANCE; increasingly, it is a tool to safeguard livelihoods. The HTS would represent a very human face to this mission.

Greater collaboration between the program and academia in a rearticulation to the strategic level may alleviate certain of these problems. To influence long-range planning and macroscopic activities, the Human Relations Area Files (HRAF) are a historical analogy worthy of consideration and mentioned by McFate as being relevant in shaping her ideas on the HTS.[10] The files were created in the late-1940s when behavioral scientists at Yale University initiated an interuniversity, nonprofit organization which developed into the HRAF at Yale, becoming the preeminent archive of anthropological research, containing more than a million pages of ethnographical analysis collated from nearly 8,000 books and articles, assessing approximately 400 different cultural groups.[11] The HRAF has developed categories for archived research with indexing based on the Outline of Cultural Materials to organize field research around anthropological taxonomies which can be subsequently used to research cultural data to build social science research platforms.[12]

Developing typologies for data archived from existing and future research conducted under the auspices of HTS is therefore a plausible reality. HTT products would be more easily digested by a combat unit over time if they were presented in a standardized template.[13] A central database would allow any military personnel to search by keyword, category, or area. The problem encountered by Howard Clark in Afghanistan is instructive: for him it was "like pulling teeth trying to get HTS products."[14] Products from 1 to 2 years previous to the point of inquiry were often no longer on SIPRNet, suggesting a problem in the data management of the military regarding the retention of social science products.[15] Neither was there, to Clark's knowledge, an HTS portal on any of the information-sharing systems available to the U.S. military, instead, in Clark's experience, getting team products was personality-dependent based on social relationships with embedded teams. The problematic sharing of HTS research permeated all levels of the coalition effort in Afghanistan. In a 2009 brief with John Salvatori, Deputy Under Secretary of Defense for Intelligence—which had come at the request of Major General Michael Flynn—Program Manager Forward-Afghanistan Mike Warren noted that, during the positive reception, the issue of sharing of products was raised. Instructively, the program manager observed that despite shortcomings in that area, it was a broader issue, that "complete integration" within the "ISAF system was imperative."[16]

A recommendation of the author as a consequence is that the U.S. Army convene a panel of experts to forge a set of recommendations for theater security research plans. This could develop a new path for open-access research and propagate new categories of analysis for social science products, developed under the auspices of the U.S. military. Public access to social science research information aggregated in theater security research would lead by default to greater engagement with the academy and deliver on the broad call of the U.S. Government's Office of Science and Technology to make all federal agencies with research budgets of U.S.$100 million or above develop plans to make that research open access.[17] Increasing the existing level of academic engagement, principally through the Cultural Knowledge Consortium, would enable an important conversation which would speak at once to issues such as ethics, civil-military relations, and intelligence.

These recommendations would bring it closer in practice to the original model of the program conceived by the Foreign Military Studies Office. In that conception, research analysts would collate information to be categorized in an open-source database. Some of the best work of the social scientists represents invaluable contributions to scholarship. Krohley's research in Baghdad during the surge of forces in 2008 is likely to represent the acme of academic understanding of the *Jaysh al-Mahdi* during that time. His knowledge has been gleaned from on the ground interviews, lending significant authority to his findings. This must be the ultimate aim of the HTS, and an idealistic one: to inform both military planning and ultimately for that expertise to inform scholarship. The program, in transitioning to a theater security asset in more stable areas would therefore be part of a valuable suite of tools which continue to examine critically and to evolve understanding of sociocultural dimensions of irregular warfighting.[18]

The HTS was brilliantly conceived but hindered by rapid expansion and an incongruous home at TRADOC. In addition, bureaucracy may be a necessary requirement. As one social scientist notes: "Steve Fondacaro and Montgomery McFate were visionaries in that they saw the need for this programme; but the visionary that has the idea and can start it is not always the best person to run it."[19] For his part, and with legitimacy, Fondacaro can point to the problematic interactions with the parent organization, as he wrote in a memo:

> Mistrust in the HTS leadership extends to the leadership of TRADOC G2 as well. Much, not all, of the turmoil we are dealing with daily in terms of managing the myriad of pay and administrative personnel issues, and with internal issues and attitudes within the workforce both team members and staff, result from frustration over issues not created in HTS.[20]

Hampered by the contracting issues and in a deeply fractured relationship with TRADOC, management of the program in retrospect should have been given more personnel and hence expertise in recruitment, selection and pay. In the future, social science research programs should evolve to become a long-range Army component, integrated into the architecture of the combatant commands at a strategic level rather than combat brigades, facilitating deep learning of environments with a more explicit and concerted transfer of knowledge to military staff, to thus inform foreign policy.

Ultimately, war reshapes borders and positions populations in new patterns onto the geographic landscape. The sociocultural domain in stabilization operations is malleable, prone to rapid transformations, manipulated through violent means for uncertain ends. Pre-conflict societies are torn, and traditional relations of reciprocity between the government and the governed are suppressed. Parochial, ideographic interests of combatants literally engaged in life or death battles press the population from a state of civility to one of Hobbesian nature. It is for this reason that sociocultural analysis in conflict will be required in the future and continue to be identified as a paramount consideration in U.S. Army requirements. Here, the greatest hindrance to effective analysis of the rapidly transforming sociocultural terrain by qualitative field work will always be the high operational tempo of commanders in the field.

Ethnographic research requires considerable time and focus. Quick research, by contrast, can require only a week and can cover wide areas, but the knowledge gained can be superficial and its production environment — done in the chaotic environment of a conflicted area without establishing deep rapport — inevitably leads to questions regarding the fidelity of the research findings. The greater the operational tempo, the lower the security; and the greater the possible error in the research results obtained by the sociocultural moment. Complicated by the "fog of war," language barriers, team schisms, and coupled with the a military preference for quantitative research that can fit into fast operational tempos that increases physical risk and is conducted in insecure areas, all complicate embedded team effectiveness. As McFate observed in her doctoral dissertation, "Effective war-fighting depends, at the most basic level, on the ability to cope with disorder."[21] Ethnography in disordered environments has many limitations not least because, in the words of one embedded team member:

> Conflict zones really suck to live in. It's incredibly dangerous and it's incredibly violent and there is no guarantee that the knowledge and understanding and capacity that you develop there will carry you on into your future career. So when a human being takes a

long perspective, it is very difficult to incentivize developing the type of knowledge that the Army says that they want.[22]

On the one hand, conflict zones facilitate the work of embedded teams because in that disordered environment "anything goes," and the work of the team has obvious legitimacy in the eyes of the population, whether or not they accept their presence. On the other hand, the caliber of research that the team can achieve in a conflict zone is open to interpretation. It is a new form of social science-based research and poorly understood. Compromised by the tensions of conflict, the level of fidelity of qualitatively derived data must be questionable.

As a strategic articulation in theater security, there is the reverse scenario for the program. There is no overt reason for an embedded team presence, but the level of security makes prolonged interaction possible. The program would still have to orient even more toward academia, becoming a tangible link between the two cultures. Given the lack of immediate insecurity, there would also be no guarantee that the embedded team would not simply be stuck at the combatant command, unable to get travel room because without crisis, there was no need to embed a team. This paradoxical formulation of the HTS between strategic pre-deployment arenas and population-centric COIN environments is the crux of the problem going forward for applied social science research and worthy of larger discussion.

As a fundamental requirement, the embedded team's job is to satisfy the commander on the ground, whether that is the battalion, brigade, or the company. Arguably, it can most satisfy the requirements of the combatant commander in a strategic articulation. The HTS was designed with the spectrum of arenas under consideration. To that end, the program experimented with two pilot projects between 2011 and 2012. The first deployed a two-person team to U.S. Army Africa elements between June 2011 and September 2011 which generated 28 reports on multiple countries, focused on long-term planning needs.[23] There is no known record of a possible second two-person team that embedded with Northern Command in April 2012 for a proposed 6-month pilot program funded by the Office of the Under Secretary of Defense for Intelligence.[24] In February 2010, the HTS drafted a mission analysis for Special Operations Command, Pacific, which would be composed of a 5-person Theater Coordination Element team and a 9-12 person Human Terrain Analysis Team, which could be split into three HTTs. The proposed arrangement also included a dedicated Research Reachback Cell, composed of two people in Virginia and one person at Special Operations Command (SOCOM).[25] These were, in theory if not in reality, theater security proof-of-concept teams, which led to subsequent social scientist presence at the Southern, Northern, Central and African Army service regional component commands by late-2013.[26]

COINs are *sui generis* — painfully so. Iraq and Afghanistan were characterized by heterodox communities and posed significant language hurdles. Each brigade faced different challenges in areas in which they operated. Little recent field research existed on the politics, economics, society, or infrastructure of either country at the time of the U.S.-led invasions. The language hurdles and risk of cultural miscommunication amplified the possible inaccuracy of information gathered in the combat environment. There is thus the requirement to relearn, address, and revise military failures in Iraq and Afghanistan; and to maintain social science approaches to combat operations because war is a human enterprise, inextricably linked at the granular level to social dimensions of civilization such as economics, agriculture, and politics. Ignoring these complex interrelationships is certain to suppress the important aspects of the operating environment that allow an enemy to function.

There is scope for institutionalizing social science research capabilities if the home for the HTS would be in the planning phase of military strategy. However, the program envisaged as a strategic articulation was improperly conceived. Colonel Lee Grubbs at the TRADOC G-2 notes:

> When we talk about phase 0 [theater security], we are talking about in its current form from four social scientists at our Army service component commands. We are talking very small numbers at a headquarters. And when they deploy for a specific mission, go and embed with a force, going forward with a force for 3 weeks, 4 weeks, for however long a discrete mission is and returning. Nothing as permanent or as direct as what you are talking about what we did in Afghanistan to support the Village Stability concept.[27]

What Colonel Grubbs is saying is that research at the strategic level will be more superficial than at the tactical levels in Iraq and Afghanistan. The opposite is required. For example, the social scientist in the Village Stability Operation embedded in a village for months, and contributed physically to the well-being of the villagers. Instead of 3 or 4 weeks, the team involved in theater security must go into the field for several months. The program can function as a quasi-nongovernmental organization, supporting capacity building. Repositioning the capability as a strategic asset would be prudent. As the sense of the Afghanistan military crisis recedes from memory, there is a sense of unlearning the conflict. Just as the Office of Strategic Services, which emerged in the existential threat faced in World War II, faded in the embers of peacetime, so too there is the challenge social science research faces to reformulate and refocus to prolong relevance, after the last HTTs departed Afghanistan in 2014. Fondacaro had planned to transition the tool to the Humanitarian Information Unit at the Department of State; he saw the HTS as a tool for long-term research and planning. In the "Human Terrain System Information Briefing" from January 2009 given by Fondacaro and McFate, they include a slide showing that ideally, instead of in Phase 4 and Phase 5 operations in Iraq and Afghanistan, the HTS would be used as a Phase 0 asset; "Where we should be," in their assessment.[28]

Steven Metz of the Strategic Studies Institute, in supporting a continuation of the program's capability and function, notes that the Chairman of the Joint Chiefs of Staff's 2015 U.S. *National Military Strategy* includes a requirement for cultural knowledge; for support teams and building partner capacity.[29] The global landscape is one where, more broadly, inequality creates resistance to any established status quo, which in severe examples can foment armed rebellion. Such insurgencies as they occur, where they coincide with regions or ideologies of interest to the United States, will require comprehension in order to create intelligent responses which may utilize political, and economic tools in collaboration with military efforts.

Often, our own obvious and understandable positions can elide important observations of phenomena and in so doing propagate policies and prescriptions which are at best impotent and at worst deleterious. When Islamic State captured Mosul, Iraq, in June 2014, this "extreme manifestation" of law and order and protection from persecution by Shia-dominated security forces meant the group's arrival was met with some semblance of hope, manifest in footage of small crowds cheering their convoys as they entered the city.[30] As capture and change give way to governance and stagnation, the inexorable realities of limited civic duty and a draconian penal code mean that discontent may burgeon. Yet, this emerging civilian antipathy is offset by continued popular concern within the urban center at the possible actions of the Iraqi national security forces should they recapture the city. Islamic State does not need to create a utopian ideal in Mosul to ensure relations of reciprocity between itself and those it governs; the group only needs to continue to be viewed as a preferential ruling polity to the national government in a city in which years of war has created an atomized social structure incapable of coherent civil dissent.

Military solutions aimed at recapture in such situations are only one element of the answer to U.S. foreign policy questions at both the strategic and tactical levels. Understanding the historical trajectory of a region through social, economic, and political lenses, including as much engagement with communities as security allows, can create powerful platforms for policy formation. The output of research conducted in and around Sadr City, Iraq, by HTTs for example, has afforded a deeper understanding of the position of the population regarding the violent actors than previously existed, by investigating popular sentiment and the relation of civilians to these actors. As one social scientist notes of the prevailing tendency to obscure the host nation in studying the Iraq conflict, there has been a systematic neglect of any:

> detailed examination of the localized dynamics of violence (instead, more commonly dismissing the viability of such exploration by presenting Iraq as hopelessly divided and impenetrably complex), the country and its people have received only token attention from authors whose central focus has lain elsewhere.[31]

The HTS embedded field social scientists throughout 8 years in Iraq and Afghanistan, and their research explored these "localized dynamics of violence" through a myriad of heterogeneous methodologies. The ongoing effect is an aggregation of research, insights, and experiences borne from a program which, at its height in 2009, had more than 40 HTTs deployed and embedded an estimated 700 people between 2007 and 2010.[32] The public output of this research is already considerable, including in its sweep several academic presses and multiple scholarly journals. The compelling story of the program means that their work receives robust levels of engagement across military and academic communities upon publication. This is an important second-order effect of the program; a long-term result of conducting research in contested spaces as paid servants of the U.S. Army; and a continuing and aggregating effect which appears to have outlasted the duration of the HTS itself.

Throughout this book I have recorded the recollected experiences of former HTT social scientists in Iraq and Afghanistan. The HTS saw a number of social scientists whose professional development and subject matter expertise have been accelerated in conflict working for the military enterprise. Many of them are now dispersed into the broader DoD enterprise. Those individuals have since qualified the character of the HTS; critiqued their participation in it, and assessed the possibilities and limitations of social science research during military operations. Former program members now weigh both academia and the military from the vantage point of invaluable experience, understanding the structure and limitations of each discipline, speaking both languages. Regardless of the future of social science research in the military, in possession of esoteric knowledge, robust credibility and legitimacy from their work in Iraq and Afghanistan affords immense value to the expertise of these individuals that embedded as part of the program. In conclusion, it suggests that an enduring legacy of the U.S. Army's HTS will be an altogether human one.

ENDNOTES - CONCLUSIONS

1. Nicholas Krohley, telephone interview with author, July 26, 2013.

2. Carl von Clausewitz, Michael Howard and Peter Paret, eds. and trans., *On War*, Princeton, NJ: Princeton University Press, 1976, pp. 119-120.

3. Fred Kaplan, *The Insurgents: David Petraeus and the Plot to Change the American Way of War*, New York: Simon & Schuster, 2013, pp. 213-219.

4. *Ibid.*

5. Human Terrain System, "HTT AF6 Patrol Report—Refugee Camp," June 22, 2009. Copy held with author.

6. David Kilcullen, *Out of the Mountains: The Coming Age of Urban Guerrilla*, London, UK: Hurst, 2013, pp. 288-293.

7. Author's telephone interview with Bob Reuss, Colonel Lee Grubbs, and Dr. Susan Canedy, September 16, 2013.

8. Former HTT social scientist 3, interview with author, Alexandria, VA, August 1, 2013.

9. Nicholas Krohley, personal communication with author, October 4, 2014.

10. Montgomery McFate, interview, August 1, 2013.

11. H. Russell Bernard, *Research Methods in Anthropology: Qualitative and Quantitative Approaches*, 4th Ed., Lanham, MD: Alta Mira, 2006, p. 515.

12. *Ibid.*

13. Howard Clark, telephone interview with author, January 25, 2014.

14. *Ibid.*

15. *Ibid.*

16. Human Terrain System Program Manager Forward-Afghanistan, "HTS Briefing for Mr. John Salvatori Deputy Under Secretery [sic] of Defense for Intelligence; AAR (After Action Review) Submission," n.d.

17. Cited in Carol Ember and Robert Hanisch, "Sustaining Domain Repositories for Digital Data: A White Paper," *Human Relations Area Files*, New Haven, CT: Yale University, 2013, pp. 1-2.

18. Christopher Sims, "Both Sides of the Coin: Theory Versus Practice," *Foreign Affairs*, Vol. 91, No. 1, 2012, pp. 178-180.

19. Ryan Evans, interview with author, Washington, DC, August 6, 2013.

20. Steve Fondacaro, Memorandum to the Director, TRADOC G-2 Intelligence Support Activity, n.d. (copy held with author).

21. Montgomery Cybele Carlough (McFate), "Pax Britannica: British Counterinsurgency in Northern Ireland, 1969-1982," unpublished Ph.D. dissertation, New Haven, CT: Yale University, 1994, p. 97.

22. Former HTT social scientist 1, interview, August 11, 2013.

23. Christopher J. Lamb *et al.*, *Human Terrain Teams: An Organizational Innovation for Sociocultural Knowledge in Irregular Warfare*, Washington, DC: Institute of World Politics Press, 2013, p. 81.

24. *Ibid.*

25. Human Terrain System, "TCE-HTAT—Task Force SOPAC," February 2010.

26. Bob Reuss, interview.

27. Grubbs, interview.

28. Steve Fondacaro and Montgomery McFate, "Human Terrain System Information Briefing," January 9, 2009.

29. Steven Metz, "Pentagon's Decision to Cut Human Terrain System Short-Sighted," *World Politics Review*, July 10, 2015.

30. Atwan, Abdel Bari, *Islamic State: The Digital Caliphate*, London, UK: Saqi, 2015, p. 44.

31. Krohley, Nicholas, *The Death of the Mehdi Army: The Rise, Fall, and Revival of Iraq's Most Powerful Militia*, London, UK: Hurst, 2015, p. xii.

32. Montgomery McFate and Janice H. Laurence, "Introduction: Mind the Gap," in Montgomery McFate and Janice H. Laurence, eds., *Social Science Goes to War: The Human Terrain System in Iraq and Afghanistan*, London, UK: Hurst, 2015, pp. 20-21.

BIBLIOGRAPHY

PRIMARY MATERIAL

Unpublished Works.

Official Documents and Other Government Publications.

Headquarters, Multi-National Corps-Iraq, Memorandum: Joint Urgent Operational Needs Statement for Human Terrain Teams, Baghdad, Iraqi, APO AE 09342, April 7, 2007.

Partially redacted document made available by U.S. Central Command (USCENTCOM), Office of the Chief of Staff in response to USCENTCOM Freedom of Information Act request case numbers 14-0046 and 14-0052 made by the author. The document calls for real time knowledge of host populations; as much as any document, it perhaps highlights the limitations of social science research in the Iraq and Afghanistan theaters, with real time social science research being unfeasible in the insecure environments.

Joint Urgent Operational Needs Statement for Cultural Operations Research — Human Terrain Systems, Combined Joint Task Force-82, April 17, 2007.

Partially redacted document made available by USCENTCOM, Office of the Chief of Staff in response to USCENTCOM Freedom of Information Act request case numbers 14-0046 and 14-0052 made by the author. The document details the requirement for a Human Terrain Systems (HTS) capability to ensure effectively knowledge transfer between outgoing and incoming units.

Memorandum, Helms to Rostow, February 17, 1967, folder "Vietnam memos (A). Vol. 66," Box 41, National Security File: Vietnam, Lyndon B. Johnson Library, Austin, Texas.

Multi-National Corps-Iraq, Joint Urgent Operational Needs Statement for Human Terrain Team Support to Operation IRAQI FREEDOM Surge, n.d.

Partially redacted document made available by USCENTCOM, Office of the Chief of Staff in response to USCENTCOM Freedom of Information Act request case numbers 14-0046 and 14-0052 made by the author. This document makes a request for teams to support the surge: 13 HTTs and four Human Terrain Analysis Teams.

Headquarters, Multi-National Force-Iraq, Memorandum for Commander, USCENTCOM: Joint Urgent Operational Need for Human Terrain Teams, Baghdad, Iraq, APO AE, 09342-1400, April 19, 2007.

Partially redacted document made available by USCENTCOM, Office of the Chief of Staff in response to USCENTCOM Freedom of Information Act request case numbers 14-0046 and 14-0052 made by the author. This is the Multi-National Force-Iraq's endorsement for the Joint Urgent Operational Need for HTTs and links HTT knowledge of host populations to successful counterinsurgency (COIN) operations.

Perry, Walter, "An Assessment of the Sociocultural Capabilities Required to Accomplish Military Missions: Final Briefing," Santa Monica, CA: RAND Arroyo Center, June 15, 2011.

This study was commissioned by the U.S. Army to assess the character and content of sociocultural analysis which could be undertaken across the spectrum of military operations. The final report was not released but is cited here with permission of the author.

U.S. Central Command, Office of the Chief of Staff, Memorandum for Director for Force Structure, Resources, and Assessment J8, Subject: Joint Urgent Operational Needs Statement for Human Terrain Teams (U) (CC-0197) (U), 7115 South Boundary Boulevard, MacDill Air Force Base, FL 33621-5101, May 23, 2007.

Partially redacted document made available by USCENTCOM, Office of the Chief of Staff in response to USCENTCOM Freedom of Information Act request case numbers 14-0046 and 14-0052 made by the author. The document shows that, although forwarded, it was at that time unclear if an HTT capability met the strict definition of a Joint Urgent Operational Needs Statement (JUONS).

U.S. Department of Defense, Headquarters, "Memorandum for Commander, U.S. Central Command: Endorsement of Joint Urgent Operational Need for Cultural Operations Research—Human Terrain System," Combined/Joint Task Force-82, Bagram Airfield, Afghanistan, APO AE 09354, April 21, 2007.

Partially redacted document made available by USCENTCOM, Office of the Chief of Staff in response to USCENTCOM Freedom of Information Act request case numbers 14-0046 and 14-0052 made by the author. The document content expresses the requirement understanding of social, cultural and political factors at the local level for success in COIN and stability operations, and the "war on terror."

Private Correspondence.

Zacharias, David, letter to BAE Systems TSS Leadership, December 1, 2008.

A 4-page typed letter written by the BAE Systems Project Manager for HTS outlining the significant liabilities that both BAE Systems and the U.S. Government are exposed to by their roles in the program. The letter provides detailed analysis of problems with specific personnel in the program and that continued problems without resolution should lead to BAE Systems terminating the contract. This letter is therefore an important evaluation of the program from the perspective of the primary contractor.

Human Terrain System Documents Cited.

Finney, Nathan, *The Human Terrain Team Handbook*, Fort Leavenworth, Kansas: U.S. Army Training and Doctrine Command (TRADOC), 2008.

Fondacaro, Steve, "EXSUM: HTS Coordination with MG Hahn, DCOS, NATO JFC," January 11, 2009.

_____, "Memo: Human Terrain System Personnel Screening and Tracking Support," n.d.

Fondacaro, Steve, and Montgomery McFate, "Human Terrain System Information Briefing," January 2009.

Human Terrain System, "HTT AF6 Patrol Report—Refugee Camp," June 22, 2009. Copy held with author.

Human Terrain System Program Development Team, "Human Terrain System Yearly Report, 2007-2008: Introduction and Executive Summaries," Prepared for TRADOC, August 2008. Copy held with author.

This document is important to understanding the formation, deployment, and experiences of AF1, and comprehension of the program's trajectory up to 2008. Prepared as part of research conducted by the Program Development Team (PDT), according to one PDT member, the report was valuable in demonstrating the value in the HTS as part of a shift in military emphasis to COIN tactics in Afghanistan, and by extension, Iraq.

Human Terrain System Program Manager Forward-Afghanistan, "HTS Briefing for Mr. John Salvatori Deputy Under Secretery [sic] of Defense for Intelligence; AAR Submission," n.d.

Human Terrain System, "Concept of Operations (CONOPS) for the Mapping the Human Terrain (MAP-HT) Joint Capability Demonstration: DRAFT," October 2009.

_____, "Congressional Staff Update," March 2, 2010.

_____, "FY 09-15 HTS Funding Requirements," August 8, 2009.

_____, "Social Science Working Group: Learning Objective 1.2: Provide Operationally relevant sociocultural knowledge," n.d. Copy held with author.

Spreadsheet demarcating tasks and responsibilities for each individual role within an HTT, revised as part of the remit of the Social Science Working Group in 2009-10.

_____, "TCE-HTAT – Task Force SOCPAC," February 2010.

_____, "Training Directorate Information Brief," December 11, 2009. Copy held with author.

A document delineating the structure and tasks within the program's training directorate.

_____, "Vision and Mission Statements," March 3, 2009. Copy held with author.

Jackson, Andrea V., "Social Science Research and Analysis: Implementation Plan for Baghdad," June 13, 2007.

Lincoln Group, Baghdad Focus Groups, June 6, 2006.

PDRI, "Human Terrain System: Evaluation of the Human Terrain Team Recruitment and Selection Process," *Technical Report No. 628*, Arlington, VA, February 2009.

_____, "Results of HTT Structured Interview Pilot Test," February 5, 2009.

Reuss, Bob, and Steve Fondacaro, "Human Terrain System (HTS) Update to GEN Wallace," TRADOC/ DCSINT, May 17, 2007.

Interviews.

Albro, Robert, interview with author, Washington, DC, August 14, 2013.

Anonymous, interview with author, location withheld, July 29, 2013.

Clark, Howard, telephone interview with author, January 25, 2014.

Clark, Jennifer, telephone interview with author, October 9, 2013.

Connable, Ben, interview with author, Alexandria, VA, July 15, 2013.

Davies, Michael, interview with author, Washington, DC, August 10, 2013.

Evans, Ryan, interview with author, Washington, DC, August 6, 2013.

Fondacaro, Steve, telephone interview with author, September 15, 2015.

Former HTT social scientist 1, interview with author, location withheld, July 25, 2013.

_____, interview with author, location withheld, August 11, 2013.

Former HTT social scientist 2, interview with author, Quantico, VA, July 29, 2013.

Former HTT social scientist 3, interview with author, Alexandria, VA, August 11, 2013.

Former HTT social scientist 4, interview with author, Newport, RI, August 1, 2013.

Heimann, Richard, interview with author, McLean, VA, July 12, 2013.

_____, interview with author, Washington, DC, August 11, 2013.

Krohley, Nicholas, telephone interview with author, July 26, 2013.

McFate, Montgomery, interview with author, Newport, RI, August 1, 2013.

_____, interview with author, Newport, RI, August 2, 2013.

Pavlovic, Zok, interview with author, Alexandria, VA, August 14, 2013.

Reuss, Bob, U.S. Army Colonel; Lee Grubbs, and Susan Canedy, telephone interview with author, September 16, 2013.

Zacharias, David, interview with author, Virginia Beach, VA, July 22, 2013.

PUBLISHED WORKS

Official Documents and Other Government Publications.

American Anthropological Association, *Executive Board Statement on the Human Terrain System Project*, Arlington, VA: American Anthropological Association, October 31, 2007.

_____, Commission on the Engagement of Anthropology with the U.S. Security and Intelligence Communities: *Final Report*, Arlington, VA: American Anthropological Association, November 4, 2007.

_____, Commission on the Engagement of Anthropology with the U.S. Security and Intelligence Communities, *Final Report on the Army's Human Terrain System Proof of Concept Program*, Arlington, VA: American Anthropological Association, October 14, 2009.

Baker, James A. and Lee H. Hamilton, *The Iraq Study Group Report*, Washington, DC: United States Institute for Peace, 2006.

Clinton, Yvette, Virginia Foran-Cain, Julia Voelker McQuaid, Catherine E. Norman, and William H. Sims, *Congressionally Directed Assessment of the Human Terrain System*, Alexandria, VA: Center for Naval Analyses, Analysis and Solutions, November 2010.

DeTeresa, Steven J., Michael W. McErlean, Noah B. Bleicher, Thomas E. Hawley, Sasha Rogers, and Lorry M. Fenner, *The Joint Improvised Explosive Device Defeat Organization: DOD's Fight Against IEDs Today and Tomorrow*, U.S. House of Representatives, Committee on Armed Services, Subcommittee on Oversight and Investigations, Washington, DC: U.S. Government, November 2008.

Government Accountability Office, *Warfighter Support: DOD Needs Strategic Outcome-Related Goals and Visibility over Its Counter-IED Efforts*, GAO-10-95, Washington, DC, October 29, 2009.

_____, Counter-Improvised Explosive Devices: Multiple DOD Organizations are Developing Numerous Initiatives, GAO-12-861R, Washington, DC: United States Government, August 1, 2012.

_____, *Warfighter Support: Actions Needed to Improve Visibility and Coordination of DOD's Counter-Improvised Explosive Device Efforts*, GAO-12-280, Washington, DC: U.S. Government, February 22, 2012.

Headquarters, British Chiefs of Staff, *Joint Doctrine Publication 04, Understanding*, Shrivenham, UK: The Development, Concepts and Doctrine Centre, December 2010.

Headquarters, Department of the Army, *Field Manual (FM) 3.04.401, Civil Affairs Tactics, Techniques and Procedures*, Washington, DC: U.S. Government, 2003.

Headquarters, Department of the Army and Headquarters, U.S. Marine Corps, *Field Manual, Interim*

(FMI) *3-34.119/Marine Corps Information Publication* (MCIP) *3-17.01, Improvised Explosive Device Defeat,* Washington, DC: U.S. Government, September 2005.

_____, FM *3-24/Marine Corps Warfighting Publication* (MCWP) *3-33.5, Counterinsurgency,* Washington, DC: U.S. Government, December 2006.

Headquarters, Department of the Army, *Terrorism Handbook,* Fort Leavenworth, KS: U.S. Government, 2007.

_____, FM *3-07, Stability Operations,* Washington, DC: U.S. Government, October 2008.

Headquarters Department of the Army and Headquarters United States Marine Corps, FM *2-01.3, Intelligence Preparation of the Battlefield,* Fort Huachuca, AZ: U.S. Government, October 15, 2009.

Headquarters, Department of the Army, *U.S. Army Functional Concept for Engagement,* Fort Eustis, VA: U.S. Government, February 24, 2014.

Headquarters, Department of the Army, *Policy and Guidance,* Arlington, VA: Army Human Research Protections Office, n.d., available from *ahrpo.amedd.army. mil/Policy-and-Guidance/FAQs.html,* accessed August 16, 2014.

Hearing before the Committee on Armed Services, U.S. Senate, 108th Cong., 1st Sess., John P. Abizaid, Commander, USCENTCOM, *Iraqi Reconstruction,* Washington, DC: Government Printing Office, September 2003.

_____, U.S. Cong., Statement of General John P. Abizaid, U.S. Army, Commander, USCENTCOM, *Command Posture*, Washington, DC: Government Printing Office, March 3, 2004.

_____, U.S. Cong., John P. Abizaid, Commander, USCENTCOM, *Command Posture*, Washington, DC: Government Printing Office, March 1, 2005.

_____, U.S. Cong., John P. Abizaid, Commander, USCENTCOM, *Iraq and Afghanistan*, 109th Cong., 2nd Sess., Washington, DC: Government Printing Office, November 15, 2006.

_____, U.S. Senate, Michael D. Maples, Director, Defense Intelligence Agency, *Iraq and Afghanistan*, 109th Cong., 2nd Sess., Washington, DC: U.S. Government, November 15, 2006.

_____, Oversight and Investigations Subcommittee, 110th Cong., 2nd Sess., Martin Schweitzer, *Hearings on the Role of Social and Behavioral Sciences in National Security*, Washington, DC: U.S. Government, April 24, 2008.

_____, Oversight and Investigations Subcommittee, U.S. Cong., 110th Sess., 2nd Sess., Montgomery McFate, *Hearings on the Importance of Sociocultural Knowledge to the United States Military*, Washington, DC: U.S. Government, July 9, 2008.

_____, Oversight and Investigations Subcommittee, Thomas Metz, *Defeating the Improvised Explosive Device and Other Asymmetric Threats: Today's Efforts and Tomorrow's Requirements*, Joint Improvised Explosive

Device Defeat Organization, Washington, DC: U.S. Government, September 16, 2008.

House Appropriations Subcommittee on Defense, U.S. Congress, John P. Abizaid, Commander, USCENTACOM, *Command Posture*, Washington, DC: Government Printing Office, March 15, 2006.

Jebb, Cindy R., Laurel J. Hummel, and Tania M. Chacho, *Human Terrain Team Trip Report: A "Team of Teams,"* West Point, NY: Unpublished Report for TRADOC, 2008.

Office of the Secretary of Defense, *RDT&E BUDGET ITEM JUSTIFICATION (R2 Exhibit), R-1 Shopping List Item 36*, Washington, DC: Government Printing Office, February 2007.

Schwartz, Moshe, *Department of Defense Contractors in Iraq and Afghanistan: Background and Analysis*, Congressional Research Service Report, Washington, DC: U.S. Government, December 14, 2009.

U.S. Department of Defense, *Defense Science Board, 21st Century Strategic Technology Vectors — Vol. 1*, Main Report, 2006 Summer Study, Washington, DC: Office of the Under Secretary of Defense for Acquisition, Technology, and Logistics, 2007.

_____, Directive 2000.19, *Joint Improvised Explosive Device (IED) Defeat*, Washington, DC: Government Printing Office, June 27, 2005.

_____, Directive 2000.19E: *Joint Improvised Explosive Device Defeat Organization (JIEDDO)*, Washington, DC, February 14, 2006.

_____, *Speech as Delivered by Secretary of Defense Robert M. Gates*, Washington, DC: Association of American Universities, April 14, 2008.

_____, Office of the Assistant Secretary of Defense, *Speech as Delivered by Secretary of Defense Robert M. Gates*, Washington, DC: National Defense University, September 29, 2008.

U.S. House of Representatives, Committee on Armed Services, *Building Language Skills and Cultural Competencies in the Military: DOD's Challenge in Today's Educational Environment*, Subcommittee on Oversight and Investigations, Washington, DC: Committee Print 110-12, November 2008.

United States Joint Chiefs of Staff, *Irregular Warfare: Countering Irregular Threats, Joint Operating Concept, Version 1.0*. Washington, DC: U.S. Joint Chiefs of Staff, September 11, 2007.

_____, *Joint Publication (JP) 1-02, Dictionary of Military and Associated Terms*, Washington, DC: U.S. Joint Chiefs of Staff, November 8, 2010, amended November 15, 2012.

_____, *JP 3-0, Joint Operations*, Washington, DC: U.S. Joint Chiefs of Staff, August 11, 2011.

United States House of Representatives, to authorize appropriations for fiscal year 2015 for military activities of the Department of Defense and for military construction, to prescribe military personnel strengths for such fiscal year, and for other purposes, 113th Cong., 2nd Sess., H. R. 4435, April 9, 2014, amended May 13, 2014.

U.S. Office of the Secretary of Defense, *Title 32 – National Defense, Part 219 – Protection of Human Subjects,* n.d., available from *www.tricare.mil/hpae/_docs/32cfr219.pdf,* accessed August 16, 2014.

Private Correspondence.

Helbig, Zenia, 'Memorandum: Human Terrain System Program; U.S. Army Training and Doctrine Command,' letter to Representative Ike Skelton, Chairman of the House Armed Services Committee; and Representative Henry Waxman, Chairman of the House Committee on Oversight and Government Reform, September 13, 2007.

LATER WORKS

Books and Book Chapters.

Albro, Robert, Marcus George, Laura A. McNamara, and Monica Schoch-Spana, eds., *Anthropologists in the Security Scape: Ethics, Practice, and Professional Identity* (Walnut Creek, CA: Left Coast Press, 2012).

Atwan, Abdel Bari, *Islamic State: The Digital Caliphate* (London, UK: Saqi, 2015).

Bale, Jeffrey, *Jihadist Cells and I.E.D. Capabilities in Europe: Assessing the Present and Future Threat to the West* (Monterey, CA: Monterey Institute of International Studies, 2009).

Bar-Tal, Daniel, *Group Beliefs* (New York: Springer-Verlag, 1990).

Barber, Pauline Gardiner, Belinda Leach, and Winnie Lem, eds., *Confront Capital: Critique and Engagement in Anthropology* (New York: Routledge, 2012).

Barnard, Alan and Jonathan Spencer, eds., *The Routledge Encyclopedia of Social and Cultural Anthropology*, 2nd Ed. (London, UK, and New York: Routledge, 2012).

Bernard, H. Russell, *Research Methods in Anthropology: Qualitative and Quantitative Approaches*, 4th Ed. (Lanham, UK: AltaMira, 2006).

Bhatia, Michael V., *Contemporary Peace Operations: Issues for Contemporary Peace Operations* (Bloomfield, CT: Kumarian Press, 2003).

Bohannan, Paul, *Social Anthropology* (New York: Holt, Rinehart and Wilson, 1961).

Bryman, Alan, *Quantity and Quality in Social Research* (London, UK: Routledge, 1988).

_____, *Social Research Methods* (Oxford, UK: Oxford University Press, 2004).

Builder, Carl H., *The Masks of War: American Military Styles in Strategy and Analysis* (Baltimore, MD: Johns Hopkins University Press, 1989).

Campbell, David, *Writing Security: United States Foreign Policy and the Politics of Identity* (Minneapolis, MN: University of Minnesota Press, 1992).

Cardinalli, Anna-Maria, *Crossing the Wire: One Woman's Journey into the Hidden Dangers of the Afghan War* (Havertown, PA: Casemate, 2013).

Clausewitz, Carl von, Michael Howard and Peter Paret, eds. and trans., *On War*, (Princeton, NJ: Princeton University Press, 1976).

Davidson, Janine, *Lifting the Fog of Peace: How Americans Learned to Fight Modern War* (Ann Arbor, MI: University of Michigan Press, 2010).

Davis, Paul K. and Kim Cragin, eds., *Social Science for Counterterrorism: Putting the Pieces Together* (Santa Monica, CA: RAND Corporation, on behalf of the National Defense Research Institute, Washington, DC, 2009).

Deitchman, Seymour J., *The Best-Laid Schemes: A Tale of Social Research and Bureaucracy* (Cambridge, MA: Massachusetts Institute of Technology Press, 1976).

Dockery, J. T., and A. E. R. Woodcock, eds., *The Military Landscape: Mathematical Models of Combat* (Cambridge, UK: Woodhead Publishing, 1993).

Douglas, Mary, *How Institutions Think* (London, UK: Routledge and Kegan Paul, 1987).

Enloe, Cynthia, *Ethnic Soldiers: State Security in Divided Societies* (London, UK: Penguin Books, 1980).

Evans, Ryan, "The Population is the Enemy': Control, Behaviour, and Counter-Insurgency in Central Helmand Province, Afghanistan," David Martin Jones, Celeste Ward Gventner and M. L. R. Smith, eds., *The New Counter-Insurgency Era in Critical Perspective*, (London, UK: Palgrave Macmillan, 2014), pp. 257-277.

Farrell, Theo and Terry Terriff, *The Sources of Military Change: Culture, Politics, Technology* (Boulder, CO: Lynne Rienner, 2002).

Ferguson, Brian R., "Plowing the Human Terrain: Toward Global Ethnographic Surveillance," Laura A. McNamara and Robert A. Rubenstein, eds., *Dangerous Liaisons: Anthropologists and the National Security State,* (Santa Fe, NM: School for Advanced Research Press, 2011), pp. 101-126.

Firth, Raymond, ed., *Man and Culture: An Evaluation of the Work of Bronislaw Malinowski* (London, UK: Routledge and Kegan Paul, 1957).

Fischer, Frank and Gerald J. Miller, eds., *Handbook of Public Policy Analysis; Theory, Politics, and Methods* (Boca Raton, FL: CRC Press, 2007).

Galula, David, *Counterinsurgency Warfare: Theory and Practice* (Westport, CT: Praeger Security International, 2006).

Gezari, Vanessa, *The Tender Soldier: A True Story of War and Sacrifice* (New York: Simon and Schuster, 2013).

Gonzalez, Roberto, *American Counterinsurgency: Human Science and the Human Terrain* (Chicago, IL: Prickly Paradigm Press, 2009).

_____, *Militarizing Culture: Essays on the Warfare State* (Walnut Creek, CA: Left Coast Press, 2010).

Gusterson, Hugh, "Militarizing Knowledge," Union [sic] of Concerned Anthropologists, *The Counter-Counterinsurgency Manual* (Chicago, IL: Prickly Paradigm Press, 2009), pp. 39-55.

Hamilton, Peter, *Talcott Parsons* (Chichester, UK: Ellis Horwood, 1983).

Harris, Charles H. and Louis R. Sadler, *The Archaeologist was a Spy: Sylvanus G. Morley and the Office of Naval Intelligence* (Albuquerque, NM: New Mexico University Press, 2003).

Hodge, Nathan, *Armed Humanitarians: The Rise of the Nation Builders* (New York: Bloomsbury, 2011).

Holmes-Eber, Paula, *Culture in Conflict: Irregular Warfare, Culture Policy, and the Marine Corps* (Stanford, CA: Stanford University Press, 2014).

_____, Patrice M. Scanlon, and Andrea L. Hamlen, eds., *Applications in Operational Culture: Perspectives from the Field* (Quantico, VA: Marine Corps University Press, 2009).

Joseph, Paul, *Soft "Counterinsurgency": Human Terrain Teams and US Military Strategy in Iraq and Afghanistan* (New York: Palgrave Pivot, 2014).

Kaldor, Mary, *Old and New Wars: Organized Violence in a Global Era* (Oxford, UK: Polity Press, 1999).

Kalyvas, Stathis N., *The Logic of Violence in Civil War* (Cambridge, UK: Cambridge University Press, 2006).

_____, "Promises and Pitfalls of an Emerging Research Program: The Microdynamics of Civil War," Stathis N. Kalyvas, Ian Shapiro, and Tarek Masoud, eds., *Order , Conflict, and Violence* (Cambridge, UK: Cambridge University Press, 2008), pp. 397-421.

Kaplan, Fred, *The Insurgents: David Petraeus and the Plot to Change the American Way of War* (New York: Simon and Schuster, 2013).

Katzenstein, Peter J., ed., *The Culture of National Security* (New York: Columbia University Press, 1996).

Keesing, Roger M. and Andrew J. Strathern, *Cultural Anthropology: A Contemporary Perspective*, 3rd Ed. (New York and London, UK: Harcourt Brace, 1998).

Kelly, John D., Beatrice Jauregui, Sean T. Mitchell, and Jeremy Walton, eds., *Anthropology and Global Counterinsurgency* (Ann Arbor, MI: University of Chicago Press, 2010).

Kilcullen, David, *The Accidental Guerrilla: Fighting Small Wars in the Midst of a Big One* (Oxford, UK: Oxford University Press, 2009).

_____, *Counterinsurgency* (Oxford, UK, and New York: Oxford University Press, 2010).

_____, *Out of the Mountains: The Coming Age of Urban Guerrilla* (London, UK: Hurst, 2013).

Klotz, Audie, and Cecelia Lynch, *Strategies for Research in Constructivist International Relations* (Armonk, NY: M. E. Sharpe, 2007).

Krasner, Stephen, *Defending the National Interest* (Princeton, NJ: Princeton University Press, 1978).

Krohley, Nicholas, *The Death of the Mehdi Army: The Rise, Fall and Revival of Iraq's Most Powerful Militia* (London, UK: Hurst, 2015).

Kuhn, Thomas S., *The Structure of Scientific Revolutions*, 3rd Ed. (Chicago, IL, and London, UK: The University of Chicago Press, 1996).

Kuper, Adam, and Jessica Kuper, eds., *The Social Science Encyclopedia*, 2nd Ed. (London, UK, and New York: Routledge, 1999).

Lamb, Christopher J., James Douglas Orton, Michael C. Davies, and Theodore T. Pikulsky, *Human Terrain Teams: An Organizational Innovation for Sociocultural Knowledge in Irregular Warfare* (Washington, DC: Institute of World Politics Press, 2013).

Lapid, Yosef, and Friedrich Kratochwil, eds., *The Return of Culture and Identity in IR Theory* (Boulder, CO: Lynne Rienner, 1995).

Long, Austin, *On "Other War": Lessons from Five Decades of RAND Counterinsurgency Research* (Santa Monica, CA: RAND Corporation, 2006).

Lowie, Robert H., *The History of Ethnological Theory* (New York and London, UK: Holt, Rinehart and Winston, 1938).

Lucas, George R., Jr., *Anthropologists in Arms: The Ethics of Military Anthropology* (Walnut Creek, CA: AltaMira Press, 2009).

Malefyt, Timothy de Waal, and Robert J. Morais, *Advertising and Anthropology: Ethnographic Practice and Cultural Perspectives* (New York: Berg, 2012).

Malinowski, Bronislaw, *The Dynamics of Culture Change* (New Haven, CT: Yale University Press, 1945).

_____, *A Scientific Theory of Culture* (Oxford, UK: Oxford University Press, 1960).

Martin, Mike, *An Intimate War: An Oral History of the Afghan Conflict* (London, UK: Hurst, 2014).

McFate, Montgomery, "The 'Memory of War': Tribes and the Legitimate Use of Force in Iraq," Jeffrey Norwich, ed., *Armed Groups*, (Newport, RI: Naval Institute Press, 2008), pp. 187-202.

McFate, Montgomery, Britt Damon, and Robert Holliday, "What do Commanders Really Want to Know? U.S. Army Human Terrain System Lessons Learned from Iraq and Afghanistan," Janice H. Laurence and Michael D. Matthews, eds., *The Oxford Handbook of Military Psychology*, (Oxford, UK: Oxford University Press, 2012), pp. 92-113.

McFate, Montgomery, and Janice H. Laurence, eds., *Social Science Goes to War: The Human Terrain System in Iraq and Afghanistan* (London, UK: Hurst, 2015).

McFate, Sean, *The Modern Mercenary: Private Armies and What They Mean for World Order* (New York: Oxford University Press, 2014).

Nagl, John, *Learning to Eat Soup with a Knife: Counterinsurgency Lessons from Malaya and Vietnam* (New York: Praeger, 2001).

Network of Concerned Anthropologists, *The Counter-Counterinsurgency Manual* (Chicago, IL: Prickly Paradigm Press, 2009).

Nevins, Allan, ed., *The Strategy of Peace by John F. Kennedy* (New York, Evanston, IL, and London, UK: Harper & Row, 1960).

Packer, George, *The Assassins' Gate: America in Iraq* (New York: Farrar, Straus and Giroux, 2005).

Paparone, Chris, *The Sociology of Military Science: Prospects for Postinstitutional Military Design* (New York: Continuum, 2012).

Parsons, Talcott, *The Structure of Social Action* (New York: Free Press, 1937).

Pew, R. W. and A. S. Mavor, *Modeling Human and Organizational Behavior: Application to Military Simulations* (Washington, DC: National Academy Press, 1998).

Porter, Patrick, *Military Orientalism: Eastern War through Western Eyes* (London, UK: Hurst, 2009).

Priest, Dana, *The Mission: Waging War and Keeping Peace with America's Military* (New York: Norton, 2003).

Pye, Lucian W., "The Roots of Insurgency," Harry Eckstein, ed., *Internal War: Problems and Approaches* (New York: Free Press, 1964).

Radcliffe-Brown, A. R., *Structure and Function in Primitive Societies* (London, UK: Cohen and West, 1952).

Rhode, Joy, *Armed with Expertise: The Militarization of American Social Science Research during the Cold War* (Ithaca, NY: Cornell University Press, 2013).

Rid, Thomas, and Marc Hecker, *War 2.0: Irregular Warfare in the Information Age* (Westport, CT: Praeger Security International, 2009).

_____, and Thomas Keaney, eds., *Understanding Counterinsurgency: Doctrine, Operations, and Challenges* (Oxford, UK, and New York: Routledge, 2010).

Roberts, Audrey, "Embedding with the Military in Eastern Afghanistan: The Role of Anthropologists in Peace and Stability Operations," Walter E. Feichtinger, Ernst M. Felberbauer, and Erwin A. Schmidl, eds., *International Crisis Management: Squaring the Circle*, (Vienna, Austria, and Geneva, Switzerland: National Defence Academy and Austrian Ministry of Defence and Sports in cooperation with Geneva Centre for Security Policy, 2011).

Rosen, Stephen Peter, *Winning the Next War: Innovation and the Modern Military* (Ithaca, NY, and London, UK: Cornell University Press, 1991).

Rubinstein, Robert A., Kerry Fosher, and Clementine Fujimura, eds., *Practicing Military Anthropology: Beyond Expectations and Traditional Boundaries* (West Hartford, CT: Kumarian Press, 2012).

Salmoni, Barack A. and Paula Holmes-Eber, *Operational Culture for the Warfighter: Principles and Applications* (Quantico, VA: Marine Corps University Press, 2008).

Satia, Priya, *Spies in Arabia: The Great War and the Cultural Foundations of Britain's Covert Empire in the Middle East* (New York: Oxford University Press USA, 2008).

Schaffer, Barbara, ed., *The Limits of Culture: Islam and Foreign Policy* (Cambridge, MA: Massachusetts Institute of Technology Press, 2006).

Schubert, Hiltmar and Andrey Kuznetsoz, *Detection and Disposal of Improvised Explosives* (New York: Springer, 2006).

Schweiller, Randall L., *Maxwell's Demon and the Golden Apple: Global Discord in the New Millennium* (Baltimore, MD: John Hopkins University Press, 2013).

Sen, Amartya, *Identity and Violence: The Illusion of Destiny* (New York: W. W. Norton, 2006).

Simpson, Christopher, *Science of Coercion: Communication Research and Psychological Warfare, 1945-1960* (Oxford, UK: Oxford University Press, 1994).

Sims, Jennifer E., and Burton Gerber, eds., *Transforming U.S. Intelligence* (Washington, DC: Georgetown University Press, 2005).

Strauss, Anselm, *Qualitative Analysis for Social Scientists* (Cambridge, UK, and New York: Cambridge University Press, 1987).

Tashakkori, Abbas, and Charles Teddlie, eds., *Handbook of Mixed Methods in Social and Behavioral Research* (Thousand Oaks, CA, London, UK, and New Dehli, India: Sage, 2003).

Tetlock, Philip E., and Aaron Belkin, *Counterfactual Thought Experiments in World Politics: Logical, Methodological, and Psychological Perspectives* (Princeton, NJ: Princeton University Press, 1996).

Ucko, David H., *The New Counterinsurgency Era: Transforming the US Military for Modern Wars* (Washington, DC: Georgetown University Press, 2009).

Weiss, Carol H., *Evaluation: Methods for Studying Programs and Policies*, 2nd Ed. (Upper Saddle River, NJ: Prentice Hall, 1998).

Wendt, Alexander, *Social Theory of International Politics* (Cambridge, UK: Cambridge University Press, 1999).

Wohlstetter, Roberta, *Pearl Harbor: Warning and Decision* (Stanford, CA: Stanford University Press, 1962).

Young, Marilyn "Lost in the Desert: Lawrence and the Theory and Practice of Counterinsurgency,"

David Ryan and Patrick Kiely, eds., *America and Iraq: Policymaking, Intervention and Regional Politics* (New York: Taylor and Francis, 2009), pp. 76-91.

Articles.

Adams, Thomas K., "L.I.C. (Low-Intensity Clausewitz)," *Small Wars and Insurgencies*, Vol. 1, No. 3 (1990), pp. 266-275.

Andrade, Dale, and James H. Willbanks, "CORDS/ Phoenix: Counterinsurgency Lessons from Vietnam for the Future, *Military Review*, Vol. 86, No. 2 (2006), pp. 9-23.

Ansorge, Josef, "Spirits of War: A Field Manual," *International Political Sociology*, Vol. 4, No. 4 (2010), pp. 362-379.

Avenier, Marie-José, "Shaping a Constructivist View of Organizational Design Science," *Organization Studies*, Vol. 31, No. 9-10 (2010), pp. 1229-1255.

Barker, Alec D., "Improvised Explosive Devices in Southern Afghanistan and Western Pakistan, 2002-2009," *Studies in Conflict and Terrorism*, Vol. 34, No. 8 (2011), pp. 600-620.

Barnes, Trevor J., "Geographical Intelligence: American Geographers and Research and Analysis in the Office of Strategic Services 1941-1945," *Journal of Historical Geography*, Vol. 32 (2006), pp. 149-168.

Barnett, Michael, "Institutions, Roles and Disorder: The Case of the Arab States System," *International Studies Quarterly*, Vol. 37 (1993), pp. 271-296.

Baumann, Andrea Barbara, "Clash of Organisational Cultures? The Challenge of Integrating Civilian and Military Efforts in Stabilisation Operations," *Royal United Services Institute Journal*, Vol. 153, No. 6 (2008), pp. 70-73.

Biddle, Stephen, Jeffrey A. Friedman, and Jacob N. Shapiro, "Testing the Surge: Why Did Violence Decline in Iraq in 2007?" *International Security*, Vol. 37, No. 1 (2012), pp. 7-40.

Busch, P., T. Heinonen, and P. J. Lahti, "Heisenberg's Uncertainty Principle," *Physics Reports*, Vol. 452 (2007), pp. 155-176.

Carroll, Katherine Blue, "Not Your Parent's Political Party: Young Sunnis and the New Iraqi Democracy," *Middle East Policy*, Vol. 18, No. 3 (2011), pp. 101-121.

_____, "Tribal Law and Reconciliation in the New Iraq," *Middle East Journal*, Vol. 65, No. 1 (2011), pp. 11-29.

Checkel, Jeffrey T., "The Constructivist Turn in International Relations Theory," *World Politics*, Vol. 50, No. 2 (1998), pp. 324-348.

Connable, Ben, "All Our Eggs in a Broken Basket: How the Human Terrain System is Undermining Sustainable Military Cultural Competence," *Military Review*, Vol. 89, No. 2 (2009), pp. 57-64.

Cox, Dan G., "Human Terrain Systems and the Moral Prosecution of Warfare," *Parameters*, Vol. 41, No. 3 (2011), pp. 19-31.

Craig, Susan, "Reflections from a Red Team Leader," *Military Review*, Vol. 87, No. 2 (2007), pp. 57-60.

Cukier, Kenneth and Viktor Mayer-Schoenberger, "The Rise of Big Data: How It's Changing the Way We Think About the World," *Foreign Affairs*, Vol. 92, No. 3 (2013), pp. 28-40.

Davies, Michael, "The Truth About Human Terrain Teams: An Evidence-Based Response to Gian Gentile," *E-International Relations*, September 21, 2013, available from *www.e-ir.info/2013/09/21/the-truth-about-human-terrain-teams-an-evidence-based-response-to-gian-gentile/* (August 18, 2015).

Davis, Rochelle, "Culture as a Weapon," *Middle East Report*, Vol. 255 (2010), pp. 8-13.

Dearing, Matthew P., James L. Jeffreys, and Justin A. Depue, "Entry Point: Accessing Indigenous Perspectives During Complex Operations," *Special Operations Journal*, Vol. 1, No. 1 (2015), pp. 7-18.

Diana, Ron, and John Roscoe, "The Afghanistan TCE and TSO: Administrative and Logistical Support to HTS Teams and Knowledge Management of HTS Information," *Military Intelligence Professional Bulletin*, Vol. 37, No. 4 (2011), pp. 21-23.

Dobriansky, Paula J., and Henry A. Crumpton, "Tyranny and Terror: Will Democracy in the Middle East Make Us Safer?" *Foreign Affairs*, Vol. 85, No. 1 (2006), pp. 135-137.

Edwards, David B., "Counterinsurgency as a Cultural System," *Small Wars Journal*, (2010), pp. 1-19.

Eikenberry, Karl W., "The Limits of Counterinsurgency Doctrine in Afghanistan: The Other Side of the Coin," *Foreign Affairs*, Vol. 92, No. 5 (2013), pp. 59-74.

Eisenhardt, K. M., "Building Theories From Case Study Research," *Academy of Management Review*, Vol. 14 (1989), pp. 532-550.

Eisenstadt, Michael, "Tribal Engagement: Lessons Learned," *Military Review*, Vol. 87, No. 5 (2007), pp. 16-31.

Emberling, Geoff, "Archaeologists and the Military in Iraq, 2003-2008: Compromise or Contribution?" *Archaeologies*, Vol. 4, No. 3 (2008), pp. 445-459.

Farrell, Theo, "Figuring Out Fighting Organizations: The New Organizational Analysis in Strategic Studies," *Journal of Strategic Studies*, Vol. 19, No. 1 (1996), pp. 122-135.

_____, "World Culture and Military Power," *Security Studies*, Vol. 14, No. 3 (2005), pp. 448-488.

Fearon, James, "Counterfactuals and Hypothesis Testing in Political Science," *World Politics*, Vol. 43, No. 2 (1991), pp. 169-195.

Flynn, Michael T., "Sandals and Robes to Business Suits and Gulf Streams: Warfare in the 21st Century," *Small Wars Journal*, April 20, 2011.

_____, James Sisco, and David C. Ellis, "'Left of Bang': The Value of Sociocultural Analysis in Today's Environment," *PRISM*, Vol. 3, No. 4 (2013), pp. 13-21.

Forte, Maximilian C., "The Human Terrain System and Anthropology: A Review of Ongoing Public Debates," *American Anthropologist*, Vol. 113, No. 1 (2011), pp. 149-153.

Freedman, Lawrence, "Writing of Wrongs: Was the War in Iraq Doomed From the Start?" *Foreign Affairs*, Vol. 85, No. 1 (2006), pp. 129-134.

Gallagher, Sean, "Taming the Terrain: U.S. Human Terrain System adds more mapping software," *C4ISR Journal* (May 2009), pp. 28-30.

Galvin, John R., "Uncomfortable Wars: Towards a New Paradigm," *Parameters*, Vol. 26, No. 4 (1986), pp. 2-8.

Gentile, Gian P., "A Requiem for American Counterinsurgency," *Orbis*, Vol. 57, No. 4 (2013), pp. 549-558.

Gill, Paul, John Horgan, and Jeffrey Lovelace, "Improvised Explosive Device: The Problem of Definition," *Studies in Conflict and Terrorism*, Vol. 34, No. 9 (2011), pp. 732-748.

Gonzalez, Roberto J., "'Human Terrain': Past, present and future applications," *Anthropology Today*, Vol. 24, No. 1 (2008), pp. 21-26.

_____, "Anthropology and the Covert: Methodological Notes on Researching Military and Intelligence Programmes," *Anthropology Today*, Vol. 28, No. 2 (2012), pp. 21-25.

Gough, K., "Anthropology: Child of Imperialism," *Monthly Review*, Vol. 19, No. 11 (1968), pp. 12-27.

Grau, Lester W., "Bashing the Laser Range Finder with a Rock," *Military Review*, Vol. 77, No. 3 (1997), pp. 42-48.

_____, and Jacob W. Kipp, "Urban Combat: Confronting the Specter," *Military Review*, Vol. 79, No. 4 (1999), pp. 9-17.

Gregory, Derek, "The Rush to the Intimate: Counterinsurgency and the Cultural Turn," *Radical Philosophy*, Vol. 150 (2008), pp. 8-23.

Gruber, T. R., "A Translation Approach to Portable Ontologies," *Knowledge Acquisition*, Vol. 5, No. 2 (1993), pp. 199-220.

Gusterson, Hugh, "Anthropology and Militarism," *Annual Review of Anthropology*, Vol. 36 (2007), pp. 155-175.

_____, "Human Terrain Teams by Any Other Name?" *Critical Asian Studies*, Vol. 42, No. 3 (2010), pp. 441-443.

Hamilton, Sharon, "HTS Director's Message," *Military Intelligence Professional Bulletin*, Vol. 37, No. 4 (2011), pp. 1, 3.

Heinrich, Thomas, "Cold War Armory: Military Contracting in Silicon Valley," *Enterprise & Society*, Vol. 3, No. 2 (2002), pp. 247-284.

Hempel, Carl G., "The Function of General Laws in History," *Journal of Philosophy*, Vol. 39 (1942), pp. 35-48.

Heuser, Beatrice, "The Cultural Revolution in Counter-Insurgency," *Journal of Strategic Studies*, Vol. 30, No. 1 (2007), pp. 153-171.

Hill, Mike, "'Terrorists are Human Beings': Mapping the U.S. Army's 'Human Terrain Systems' Program," *Differences*, Vol. 20, No. 3 (2009), pp. 250-278.

Howard, Michael, "The Forgotten Dimensions of Strategy," *Foreign Affairs*, Vol. 57, No. 5 (1979), pp. 975-986.

Huntington, Samuel P., "Clash of Civilizations?" *Foreign Affairs*, Vol. 72, No. 3 (1993), pp. 22-49.

Jean, Grace V., "Army's Anthropology Teams Under Fire, But in Demand," *National Defense*, Vol. 95, No. 675 (2010).

_____, "Culture Maps Becoming Essential Tool of War," *National Defense*, Vol. 95, No. 675 (2010).

Kalyvas, Stathis N., "The Ontology of 'Political Violence': Action and Identity in Civil Wars," *Perspectives on Politics*, Vol. 1, No. 3 (2003), pp. 475-494.

Kaplan, Fred, "The End of the Age of Petraeus: The Rise and Fall of Counterinsurgency," *Foreign Affairs*, Vol. 92, No. 1 (2013), pp. 75-90.

Karabaich, Bryan N., and Jonathan D. Pfautz, "Using Cultural Belief Sets in Intelligence Preparation for the Battlefield," *Military Intelligence Professional Bulletin*, Vol. 32, No. 2 (2006), pp. 40-49.

Kilcullen, David, "Countering Global Insurgency," *Small Wars Journal*, November 30, 2004.

_____, "Twenty-Eight Articles: Fundamentals of Company-level Counterinsurgency," *Military Review*, Vol. 83, No. 3 (2006), pp. 103-108.

_____, "Counterinsurgency *Redux*," *Survival*, Vol. 48, No. 4 (2006/2007), pp. 111-130.

_____, "Comment: Ethics, Politics and Non-State Warfare," *Anthropology Today*, Vol. 23, No. 3 (2007), p. 20.

King, Christopher, "Managing Ethical Conflict on a Human Terrain Team," *Anthropology News*, Vol. 50, No. 6 (2009), p. 16.

Kipp, Jacob, Lester Grau, Karl Prinslow, and Don Smith, "The Human Terrain System: A CORDS for the 21st Century," *Military Review*, Vol. 85, No. 5 (2006), pp. 8-15.

Kiszely, John, "Learning about Counterinsurgency," *Military Review*, Vol. 87, No. 2 (2007), pp. 5-11.

Kusiak, Pauline, "Sociocultural Expertise and the Military: Beyond the Controversy," *Military Review*, Vol. 86, No. 6 (2008), pp. 65-76.

Lafaye, Christophe, Alicia Paya Y Pastor, and Mathias Thura, eds., "La pratique des sciences sociales en milieu militaire: une une opération spéciale?" ("The practice of social sciences in the military: a special operation?") *Les Champs de Mars* (*The Champs of Mars*), Vol. 27 (2015).

Lamb, Christopher J., Matthew J. Schmidt, and Berit G. Fitzsimmons, "MRAPs, Irregular Warfare, and Pentagon Reform," *Joint Force Quarterly*, Vol. 55 (2009), pp. 76-85.

Lauder, Matthew, "Red Dawn: The Emergence of a Red Teaming Capability in the Canadian Forces," *Canadian Army Journal*, Vol. 12, No. 2 (2009), pp. 25-36.

Lebow, Richard Ned, "Thucydides the Constructivist," *American Political Science Review*, Vol. 95, No. 3 (2001), pp. 547-560.

_____, "Counterfactual Thought Experiments: A Necessary Teaching Tool," *The History Teacher*, Vol. 40, No. 2 (2007), pp. 153-176.

Lichtenstein, Bronwen, "Beyond Abu Ghraib: The 2010 APA Ethics Code Standard 1.02 and Competency for Execution Evaluations," *Ethics and Behavior*, Vol. 23, No. 1 (2013), pp. 67-70.

Lovelace, James J., and Joseph L. Votel, "The Asymmetric Warfare Group: Closing the Capability Gaps," *Army Magazine*, Vol. 55, No. 3 (2005), pp. 29-34.

Mack, Andrew, "Why Big Nations Lose Small Wars: The Politics of Asymmetric Conflict," *World Politics*, Vol. 27, No. 2 (1975), pp. 175-200.

Mahoney, James, "Path Dependence in Historical Sociology," *Theory and Society*, Vol. 29 (2000), pp. 507-548.

McFate, Montgomery, "Anthropology and Counterinsurgency: The Strange Story of their Curious Relationship," *Military Review*, Vol. 85, No. 2 (2005), pp. 24-38.

_____, "Iraq: The Social Context of IEDs," *Military Review*, Vol. 85, No. 3 (2005), pp. 37-40.

_____, "The Military Utility of Understanding Adversary Culture," *Joint Force Quarterly*, Vol. 38 (2005), pp. 42-48.

_____, "Manipulating the Architecture of Cultural Control: A Conceptual Model for Strategic Influence Operations in North Korea," *Journal of Information Warfare*, Vol. 4, No. 1 (2005), pp. 21-24.

_____, "Cultural Intelligence: 'Far More Difficult than Counting Tanks and Planes'," *American Intelligence Journal*, Vol. 24 (2006), pp. 16-26.

McFate, Montgomery, and Andrea Jackson, "An Organizational Solution for DoD's Cultural Knowledge Needs," *Military Review*, Vol. 85, No. 4 (2005), pp. 18-21.

_____, "The Object Beyond War: Counterinsurgency and the Tools of Political Competition," *Military Review*, Vol. 86, No. 1 (2006), pp. 13-26.

_____, and Steve Fondacaro, "Reflections on the Human Terrain System During the First 4 Years," *PRISM*, Vol. 2, No. 4 (2011), pp. 63-82.

McKenna, B., "A Good Military Education is Hard to Find: If I Taught Anthropology at the US Army War College, I'd Ask, 'What Would Smedley Butler Do?'" *Newsletter of the Society for Applied Anthropology*, Vol. 19, No. 2 (2008), pp. 13-18.

Medina, Richard, M., "From Anthropology to Human Geography: Human Terrain and the Evolution of Operational Sociocultural Understanding," *Intelligence and National Security*, 2014, pp. 1-17.

Meigs, Montgomery C., "Unorthodox Thoughts about Asymmetric Warfare," *Parameters*, Vol. 33, No. 2 (2003), pp. 4-18.

Meinshausen, Paul and Shaun Wheeler, "Tribes and Afghanistan: Choosing More Appropriate Tools to Understand the Population," *Small Wars Journal*, June 11, 2010.

Mirzoeff, Nicholas, "War is Culture: Global Counterinsurgency, Visuality and the Petraeus Doctrine," *PMLA*, Vol. 124, No. 5 (2009), pp. 1737-1746.

Onwuegbuzie, Anthony J. and Nancy L. Leech, "On Becoming a Pragmatic Researcher: The Importance of Combining Quantitative and Qualitative Research Methodologies," *International Journal of Social Research Methodology*, Vol. 8, No. 5 (2005), pp. 375-387.

Ouchi, William G., "A Conceptual Framework for the Design of Organizational Control Mechanisms," *Management Science*, Vol. 25, No. 9 (1979), pp. 833-848.

Petit, Sandra Charreire, and Isabelle Huault, "From Practice-based Knowledge to the Practice of Research: Revisiting Constructivist Research Works on Knowledge," *Management Learning*, Vol. 39, No. 1 (2008), pp. 73-92.

Petraeus, David H., "Lessons of History and Lessons of Vietnam," *Parameters*, Vol. 16, No. 3 (1986), pp. 43-59.

Petraeus, David H., "Learning Counterinsurgency: Observations from Soldiering in Iraq," *Military Review*, Vol. 86, No. 1 (2006), pp. 2-12.

Pierce, Peter W. and Robert M. Kerr, "The Human Terrain System in Northeast Baghdad: The View from the Team Level," *E-International Relations* (August 20, 2012), available from *www.e-ir.info/2012/08/20/the-human-terrain-system-in-northeast-baghdad-the-view-from-the-team-level/* (accessed August 17, 2014).

Price, David, "Lessons from Second World War Anthropology: Peripheral, Persuasive and Ignored Contributions," *Anthropology Today*, Vol. 18, No. 3 (2002), pp. 14-20.

_____, "Past Wars, Present Dangers, Future Anthropologies," *Anthropology Today*, Vol. 18, No. 1 (2002), pp. 3-5.

_____, "America the Ambivalent: Quietly Selling Anthropology to the CIA," *Anthropology Today*, Vol. 21, No. 5 (2005), pp. 1-2.

Renzi, Fred, "Networds: Terra Incognita and the Case for Ethnographic Intelligence," *Military Review*, Vol. 86, No. 5 (2006), pp. 16-22.

Roberts, Audrey, "A Unique Approach to Peace-keeping: Afghanistan and the Human Terrain System," *Journal of International Peace Operations*, Vol. 5, No. 2 (2009), pp. 24-25.

Robinson, Sarah-Ann, "SfAA Board Resolution Concerning the HTS Project," *Newsletter of the Society for Applied Anthropology*, Vol. 19, No. 2 (2008), pp. 11-13.

Satia, Priya, "The Defense of Inhumanity: Air control and the British idea of Arabia," *American Historical Review*, Vol. 111, No. 1 (2006), pp. 16-51.

Scales, Robert H., "Adaptive Enemies: Achieving Victory by Avoiding Defeat," *Joint Force Quarterly*, Vol. 23 (1999/2000), pp. 7-14.

Simons, Anna, "War: Back to the Future," *Annual Review of Anthropology*, Vol. 28 (1999), pp. 73-108.

Sims, Christopher, "Both Sides of the Coin: Theory Versus Practice," *Foreign Affairs*, Vol. 91, No. 1 (2012), pp. 178-180.

_____, "Fighting the Insurgents' War in Afghanistan," *Small Wars Journal*, January 12, 2012.

431

_____, "The Insurgents: General Petraeus and the Plot to Change the American Way of War," *Journal of Strategic Studies*, Vol. 37, No. 1 (2014), pp. 167-169.

Spencer, Emily, and Tony Balasevicius, "Crucible of Success: Cultural Intelligence," *Canadian Military Journal*, Vol. 9, No. 3 (2009), pp. 40-48.

Strauss, Barry, "Military Education Models From Antiquity," *Academic Questions*, Vol. 21 (2008), pp. 52-61.

Swanson, Scott, "Viral Targeting of the IED Social Network System," *Small Wars Journal*, May 8, 2007.

Thompson, Jonathan, D., "Human Terrain Team Operations in East Baghdad," *Military Review*, Vol. 90, No. 4 (2010), pp. 76-84.

Tilman, Robert O., "Non-lessons of the Malayan Emergency," *Military Review* (1966), pp. 62-71.

Weinberger, Sharon, "The Pentagon's culture wars," *Nature*, Vol. 455 (2008), pp. 583-585.

Wendt, Alexander, "Anarchy is What States Make of it: The Social Construction of Power Politics," *International Organization*, Vol. 46, No. 2 (1992), pp. 391-425.

Zehfuss, Maja, "Targeting: Precision and the Production of Ethics," *European Journal of International Relations*, Vol. 17, No. 3 (2011), pp. 543-556.

_____, "Culturally Sensitive War? The Human Terrain System and the Seduction of Ethics," *Security Dialogue*, Vol. 43, No. 2 (2012), pp. 175-190.

Theses, Conference Papers and Briefs.

Adamson, William G., "An Asymmetric Threat Invokes Strategic Leader Initiative: The Joint Improvised Explosive Device Defeat Organization," ICAF Research Paper, Washington, DC: National Defense University, 2007.

Belcher, Oliver Christian, "The afterlives of counterinsurgency: postcolonialism, military social science, and Afghanistan 2006-2012," unpublished Ph.D. dissertation, Vancouver, Canada: University of British Columbia, 2013, available from *https://circle.ubc.ca/bitstream/handle/2429/45520/ubc_2014_spring_belcher_oliver.pdf* (September 1, 2015).

Blascovich, James, and Christine R. Hartel, eds., *Human Behavior in Military Contexts: Committee on Opportunities in Basic Research in the Behavioral and Social Sciences for the U.S. Military, Board on Behavioral, Cognitive, and Sensory Sciences; Division of Behavioral and Social Sciences and Education*, Washington DC: National Research Council of the National Academies, September 17, 2007.

Carlough [author's note: McFate], Montgomery Cybele, "Pax Britannia: British counterinsurgency in Northern Ireland, 1969-1982," unpublished Ph.D. dissertation, New Haven, CT: Yale University, 1994.

Chandler, Jennifer V., "Why Culture Matters: An empirically-based pre-deployment training program," Master of Arts Thesis, Monterey, CA: Naval Postgraduate School, 2005.

Clark, Vincent T., "The Future of JIEDDO—The Global C-IED Synchronizer," Department of Joint Military Operations, Newport: Naval War College, October 31, 2008.

Corum, James S. "Fighting Insurgents—No Shortcuts to Success," Carlisle, PA: U.S. Army War College, 2004.

Delp, Benjamin T., "Ethnographic Intelligence (ETHINT) and Cultural Intelligence (CULINT): Employing under-utilized strategic intelligence gathering disciplines for more effective diplomatic and military planning," IIIA Technical Paper 08-02, April 2008.

Eldridge, Erik B., and Andrew J. Neboshynsky, "Quantifying Human Terrain," unpublished master's thesis, Monterey, CA: Naval Postgraduate School, 2008.

Ellis, Richard, F., Richard D. Rogers, and Bryan M. Cochran, "Joint Improvised Explosive Device Defeat Organizaton (JIEDDO): Tactical Successes Mired in Organizational Chaos; Roadblock in the Counter-IED Fight," Norfolk, VA: Joint Forces Staff College, 2007.

Ember, Carol, and Robert Hanisch, "Sustaining Domain Repositories for Digital Data: A White Paper," Human Relations Area Files, New Haven, CT: Yale University, 2013.

Ferguson, R. Brian, "Full Spectrum: The Military Invasion of Anthropology," paper prepared for *Vir-*

tual War and Magical Death: Technologies and Imaginaries for Terror and Killing, Neil Whitehead and Sverker Finnstrom, eds. (Durham, NC: Duke University Press, 2011).

Flynn, Michael T., Matt Pottinger, and Paul D. Batchelor, "Fixing Intel: A Blueprint for Making Intelligence Relevant in Afghanistan," Working Paper, Washington, DC: Center for a New American Security, 2010.

Gray, Colin S., "Recognizing and Understanding Revolutionary Change in Warfare: The Sovereignty of Context," Monograph, Carlisle, PA: U.S. Army War College, 2006.

Greanias, Jennifer "Assessing the effectiveness of the US military's Human Terrain System," unpublished master's thesis, Washington, DC: Georgetown University, 2010.

Grubb, Lee K., "Achieving Peace in Afghanistan: Obstacles and Recommendations," Strategy Research Project, Carlisle, PA: U.S. Army War College, 2012.

Gusterson, Hugh, "Human Terrain Teams and the militarization of the anthropological conscience: A meditation of the futility of ethical discourse," Paper presented at the Annual Convention of the International Studies Association, Montreal, Quebec, Canada, March 16-19, 2011.

Helbig, Zenia, "Personal Perspective on the Human Terrain System Program," Paper presented to the American Anthropological Association's Annual Conference, Washington, DC, November 29, 2007.

Hoffman, Bruce, "Insurgency and Counter-Insurgency in Iraq," Occasional Paper, Santa Monica, CA: RAND Corporation, 2004.

Institute for Defense and Government Advancement, Special Operations Summit 2011, "COL Sharon Hamilton on Human Terrain Systems," Tampa, FL, available from *www.youtube.com/watch?v=Tl3rNcbjPJE* (accessed November 8, 2014).

International Crisis Group, "In Their Own Words: Reading the Iraqi Insurgency," Brussels, Belgium: International Crisis Group, 2006.

Jackson, Andrea V., "Cultural Training and Intelligence for OIF," Conference paper, Naval Industry Research and Development Conference, August 5, 2004.

Jager, Sheila Miyoshi, "On the Uses of Cultural Knowledge," Monograph, Carlisle, PA: U.S. Army War College, 2007.

King, Christopher, "Human Terrain System and the Role of Social Science in Counterinsurgency," Colloquim Presentation to the University of Hawai'i, Manoa, September 20, 2011.

Lamb, Christopher J., Matthew J. Schmidt, and Berit G. Fitzsimmons, "MRAPs, Irregular Warfare, and Pentagon Reform," Occasional Paper 6, Institute for National Strategic Studies, Washington, DC: National Defense University Press, 2009.

McMillin, Eric, and Bryan N. Karabaich, "Cultural Operating Environment IPB: Important Local Knowledge for Tactical Leaders," Fort Leavenworth, KS: Center for Army Lessons Learned, 2005.

Numrich, Susan K., "Human Terrain: A Tactical Issue or a Strategic C4I Problem?" paper presented to the "Critical Issues in C4I Symposium," Fairfax, VA: George Mason University, May 20-21, 2008.

Odierno, Raymond, James F. Amos, and William H. McRaven, "Strategic Landpower: Winning the Clash of Wills," Fort Leavenworth, KS: U.S. Army Training and Doctrine Command, 2013.

Page, Julia, "Human Terrain Teams," unpublished master's thesis, Blacksburg, VA: Virginia Polytechnic and State University, February 3, 2012.

Peters, Ralph, "Progress and peril: New counterinsurgency manual cheats on the history exam," *Armed Force Journal*, February 1, 2007.

Phillips, Mark, "Exercise *Agile Warrior* and the Future Development of UK Land Forces," *RUSI Occasional Paper*, May 2011.

Price, David, "Soft Power, Hard Power, and the Anthropological 'Leveraging' of Cultural 'Assets': Distilling the Theory, Politics, and Ethics of Global Counterinsurgency," Conference Paper, Anthropology and Global Counterinsurgency, University of Chicago, April 25-27, 2008.

Simpson, Erin Marie, "The Perils of Third-Party Counterinsurgency Campaigns," unpublished Ph.D. dissertation, Cambridge, MA: Harvard University, 2010.

Smith, Andrew, "Improvised Explosive Devices in Iraq, 2003-2009: A Case of Operational Surprise and Institutional Response," Carlisle, PA: Strategic Studies Institute, U.S. Army War College, 2011.

Taw, Jennifer, and Robert C. Leicht, "The New World Order and Army Doctrine," Santa Monica, CA: RAND Corporation, 1992.

Thompson, Loren B., "Iraq: Stop the Bombers, Win the War," Issue Brief, Arlington, VA: Lexington Institute, June 10, 2005.

Wilson, Clay, "Improvised Explosive Devices in Iraq: Effects and Countermeasures," Washington, DC: Congressional Research Service, 2005.

Woods, Kevin M., and James Lacey, "Iraqi Perspectives Project A View of Operation Iraqi Freedom from Saddam's Senior Leadership, Volume 1, Redacted," Quantico, VA: Joint Center for Operational Analysis, Institute for Defense Analyses, November 2007.

Newspaper Articles and Other Media.

AAA Blog, "AAA Applauds Decision to End Controversial HTS Program," *American Anthropological Association*, July 2, 2015, available from *blog.aaanet. org/2015/07/02/aaa-applauds-decision-to-end-controversial-hts-program/* (accessed September 10, 2015).

Albro, Robert and Hugh Gusterson, "Commentary: 'Do No Harm'," *C4ISR Journal*, April 25, 2012, available from *www.defensenews.com/article/20120425/ C4ISR02/304250001/Con* (accessed September 14, 2014).

Anderson, Claudia, "Getting to Know You: The U.S. Military Maps the Human Terrain of Afghanistan," *Weekly Standard*, January 18, 2010.

Atkinson, Rick, "When 'Physics Gets in the Way'," *The Washington Post*, October 2, 2007.

Behn, Sharon, "US Watchdog Slams Afghanistan Aid Waste," *Voice of America*, August 12, 2013.

Belt, Mike, "Three Questions with . . . Brit Damon, Civilian Analyst with the Army," *Lawrence Journal – World and 6News*, November 19, 2007.

Boot, Max, "Navigating the 'Human Terrain'," *The Los Angeles Times*, December 7, 2005.

Dearing, Matthew, and Jim Lee, "Research Returns from War,"*Foreign Policy*, July 23, 2015.

DeYoung, Karen, "U.S. Moves to Replace Contractors in Iraq," *The Washington Post*, March 17, 2009.

Doubleday, Justin, "Controversial Army Social-Science Program Morphs Into 'Reach-Back' Office," *Inside the Army*, Vol. 27, No. 27 (2015).

Evans, Ryan, "The Seven Deadly Sins of the Human Terrain System: An Insider's Perspective," *Foreign Policy Research Institute*, July 13, 2015, available from *www.fpri.org/geopoliticus/2015/07/seven-deadly-sins-human-terrain-system-insiders-perspective* (accessed September 7, 2015).

Forte, Maximilian, "A SPY IN OUR MIDST: Montgomery Sapone/Montgomery McFate," *Zero Anthropology*, available from *zeroanthropology.net/2008/07/31/a-spy-in-our-midst-montgomery-sapone:montgomery-mcfate/* (September 14, 2014).

Felbab-Brown, Vanda, "Afghanistan Trip Report V: The Afghan Local Police: 'It's Local, So It Must Be Good' — Or Is It?" Washington, DC: The Brookings Institution, May 9, 2012, available from *www.brookings. edu/research/opinions/2012/05/09-afghan-police-felbab-brown* (September 12, 2014).

Fox News, "Afghan Men Struggle with Sexual Identity, Study Finds," January 28, 2010.

Garamone, Jim, "Threat of Terrorist IEDs Growing, Expanding, General Says," *Armed Forces Press Service*, September 21, 2012.

Geller, Adam, "One Man's Odyssey from Campus to Combat," *Army Times*, March 16, 2009.

"General: Insurgents Upgrading Explosives Used in Attacks," *World Tribune*, June 14, 2005.

Gezari, Vanessa, "The Quiet Demise of the Army's Plan to Understand Afghanistan and Iraq," *The New York Times*, August 18, 2015, available from *www.nytimes.com/2015/08/18/magazine/the-quiet-demise-of-the-armys-plan-to-understand-afghanistan-and-iraq.html?_r=0* (accessed September 10, 2015).

Glenn, David, "Former Human Terrain System Participant Describes Program in Disarray," *Chronicle of Higher Education*, December 5, 2007.

González, Roberto J. "We Must Fight the Militarisation of Anthropology," *The Chronicle of Higher Education*, February 2, 2007.

_____, "The Rise and Fall of the Human Terrain System," *Counterpunch*, June 29, 2015, available from *www.counterpunch.org/2015/06/29/the-rise-and-fall-of-the-human-terrain-system/* (accessed September 10, 2015).

Grossman, Elaine, "Army To Create 'Asymmetric Warfare Group' To Prepare For New Threats," *Inside the Pentagon*, July 8, 2004.

Hayden, Tom, "Meet the New Dr. Strangelove," *The Nation*, July 7, 2008.

Hedges, Stephen J., "U.S. Battles Low-Tech Threat," *Chicago Tribune*, October 23, 2004.

Hess, Bill, "Unit of Linguistics Says Goodbye to Fort," *The Sierra Vista Herald*, October 18, 2008.

Hulse, Carl, and Marjorie Connelly, "Poll Shows a Shift in Opinion in Iraq War," *The New York Times*, August 23, 2006.

IBM Commercial, *The Road*, u.d., available from *www.bing.com/videos/search?q=jeff+jonas+the+road+commercial&view=detail&mid=9FFA07C708193BDF95A99FFA07C708193BDF95A9&FORM=VIRE4*.

Jaschik, Scott, "Embedded Conflicts," *Inside Higher Ed*, July 7, 2015, available from *https://www.insidehighered.com/news/2015/07/07/army-shuts-down-controver-*

sial-human-terrain-system-criticized-many-anthropologists (accessed September 2, 2015).

Kagan, Robert, "We're Not the Soviets in Afghanistan: And 2009 isn't 1979," *Weekly Standard*, August 21, 2009.

Kassel, Whitney, "The Army Needs Anthropologists," *Foreign Policy*, July 28, 2015.

Kavanaugh, Lee Hill, "Army Takes Human Terrain to Heart," *Kansas City Star*, October 14, 2008.

Loeb, Vernon, "Instead of Force, Persuasion," *The Washington Post*, November 5, 2003.

Luttwak, Edward, "Dead End: Counterinsurgency Warfare as Military Malpractice," *Harper's Magazine*, February 2007.

Marlowe, Ann, "Anthropology goes to war: There are some things the Army needs in Afghanistan, but more academics are not top of the list," *Weekly Standard*, November 26, 2007.

Maas, Peter, "Professor Nagl's War," *The New York Times*, January 11, 2004.

Metz, Steven, "Pentagon's Decision to Cut Human Terrain System Short-Sighted," *World Politics Review*, July 10, 2015.

Milbank, Dana and Claudia Deane, "Poll Finds Dimmer View of Iraq War," *The Washington Post*, June 8, 2005.

Motlagh, Jason, "Should Anthropologists Help Contain the Taliban?" *Time*, July 1, 2010.

"National Affairs: Professor at the Blackboard," *Time*, February 24, 1961.

National Public Radio, "U.S. Military Works to Combat I.E.D.s in Iraq," November 4, 2005.

Packer, George, "A Reporter at Large: Knowing the Enemy," *The New Yorker*, December 18, 2006.

Porter, Gareth, "How the US quietly lost the IED war in Afghanistan," *The Nation*, October 11, 2012.

Rogers, Rick, "Taste of the Culture: Marines Learning Iraqi Customs, Language before Deployment," *The San Diego Union-Tribune*, September 12, 2007.

Rohde, David, "Army Enlists Anthropology in War Zones," *The New York Times*, October 5, 2007.

Rubin, Alissa J., "Persecuted Sect in Iraq Avoids Its Shrine," *The New York Times*, October 14, 2007.

Shachtman, Noah, "Army Anthropologist's Controversial Culture Clash," *Wired*, October 2008.

Stockman, Farah and Bryan Bender, "Afghan Plan Adds 4, 000 US Troops: Obama to Include Hundreds of Civilian Advisors," *The Boston Globe*, March 27, 2009.

Swire, Nathan "McFate explains Human Terrain Teams," *The Dartmouth*, September 26, 2008.

Tyrrell, Marc W. D., "The Human Terrain System: Clashing Moralities or Rhetorical Dead Horses," *E-International Relations*, February 5, 2012 available from *www.e-ir.info/2012/02/05/the-human-terrain-system-clashing-moralities-or-rhetorical-dead-horses/* (August 12, 2014).

Udris, David, James Der Derian, and Michael Udris, Dirs., *Human Terrain: War Becomes Academic*, Oley, PA: Bullfrog Films, 2010.

Vanden Brook, Tom, "IEDs go beyond Iraq, Afghanistan," *USA Today*, May 13, 2008.

_____, "Army Kills Controversial Social Science Program," *USA Today*, June 29, 2015.

Vine, David, "Enabling the Kill Chain," *Chronicle of Higher Education*, November 30, 2007.

Wilson, Scott, "A Different Street Fight in Iraq: U.S. General Turns to Public Works in Battle for Hearts and Minds," *Washington Post Foreign Service*, May 27, 2004.

APPENDIX A

SEMI-STRUCTURED INTERVIEW QUESTIONS TO FORMER HUMAN TERRAIN TEAM SOCIAL SCIENTISTS

Recruitment.

How did you first learn about the Human Terrain System?
Why did you enlist with the Human Terrain System?
Can you describe the recruitment process?

Training and Pre-Deployment.

Can you describe the training process?
Can you describe your experiences during pre-deployment?

Team Composition.

Can you describe the team dynamics?
Can you describe the team relationship with the unit in which you were embedded?

Logistics.

How did you gain transport for research projects among the civilian population?

Research.

Did language capabilities matter?

In your opinion, which was the best research project you conducted?

Which piece of research did you think had most effect on the unit in which you were embedded?

What was the frequency of the reports generated by the team?

Relationship to Continental U.S.-Human Terrain System.

Did you use the Research Reachback Center during your time in theater?

Products.

How did you create the product from the research? How did you disseminate the product to the embedded unit?

APPENDIX B

US HOUSE OF REPRESENTATIVE, 113TH CONGRESS, 2ND SESS., H. R. 4435 [REPORT NO. 113-446], APRIL 9, 2014, AMENDED MAY 13, 2014, pp. 333-335

333

1   (b) *APPLICABILITY.*—*The amendments made by sub-*
2   *section (a) shall apply with respect to a claim arising after*
3   *the date of the enactment of this Act.*

4   **SEC. 1074. PILOT PROGRAM FOR THE HUMAN TERRAIN SYS-**
5   **TEM.**

6   (a) *PILOT PROGRAM REQUIRED.*—*The Secretary of the*
7   *Army shall carry out a pilot program under which the Sec-*
8   *retary uses the Human Terrain System assets in the Pacific*
9   *Command area of responsibility to support phase 0 shaping*
10   *operations and the theater security cooperation plans of the*
11   *Commander of the Pacific Command.*

12   (b) *LIMITATION.*—*Not more than 12 full-time equiva-*
13   *lent personnel, or 12 full-time equivalent personnel for*
14   *reach back support, may be deployed into the Pacific com-*
15   *mand area of responsibility to support the pilot program*
16   *required by subsection (a). The limitation under the pre-*
17   *ceding sentence shall not apply to training or support func-*
18   *tions required to prepare personnel for participation in the*
19   *pilot program.*

20   (c) *REPORTS.*—

21   (1) *BRIEFING.*—*Not later than 60 days after the*
22   *date of the enactment of this Act, the Secretary of the*
23   *Army shall provide to the congressional defense com-*
24   *mittees a briefing on the plan of the Secretary to*
25   *carry out the program required by subsection (a), in-*

334

1 cluding the milestones, metrics, deliverables, and re-
2 sources needed to execute such a pilot program. In es-
3 tablishing the metrics for the pilot program, the Sec-
4 retary shall include the ability to measure the value
5 of the program in comparison to other analytic tools
6 and techniques.

7   (2) INITIAL REPORT.—Not later than one year
8 after the date of the enactment of this Act, the Sec-
9 retary of the Army shall submit to the congressional
10 defense committees a report on the status of the pilot
11 program. Such report shall include the independent
12 analysis and recommendations of the Commander of
13 the Pacific Command regarding the effectiveness of
14 the program and how it could be improved.

15   (3) FINAL REPORT.—Not later than December 1,
16 2016, the Secretary of the Army shall submit to the
17 congressional defense committees a final report on the
18 pilot program. Such report shall include an analysis
19 of the comparative value of human terrain informa-
20 tion relative to other analytic tools and techniques,
21 recommendations regarding expanding the program
22 to include other combatant commands, and any im-
23 provements to the program and necessary resources
24 that would enable such an expansion.

1   *(d) TERMINATION.—The authority to carry out a pilot*

2 *program under this section shall terminate on September*

3 *30, 2016.*

APPENDIX C

CJTF-82 ENDORSEMENT TO JOINT URGENT OPERATIONAL NEED FOR HUMAN TERRAIN SYSTEMS

Released as a part of a Freedom of Information Act request by the author, the endorsement was signed on April 21, 2007, by Brigadier General Rodney O. Anderson, Deputy Commanding General—Support of the Combined Joint Task Force (CJTF). The memorandum notes that understanding of social, cultural, and political factors at the local level is critical to success in counterinsurgency and stability operations, and more broadly, the war on terror. At this stage in the evolution of the program, it was noted by the commanding officer that Human Terrain System could "identify Al Qaida Associated Militants leaders operating among the population."

DEPARTMENT OF DEFENSE
HEADQUARTERS, COMBINED/JOINT TASK FORCE (CJTF)-82
BAGRAM AIRFIELD, AFGHANISTAN
APO AE 09354

REPLY TO
ATTENTION OF

CJTF-82-DCG-S   21 APR 2007

MEMORANDUM FOR Commander, United States Central Command (CENTCOM),
MacDill Air Force Base, FL 33621-5101

SUBJECT: Endorsement of Joint Urgent Operational Need (JUON) for Cultural
Operations Research - Human Terrain System (COR-HTS). (U)

1. (U) Reference: JUONS for Cultural Operations Research - Human Terrain System
(COR-HTS)

2. (S//REL) Detailed knowledge of local cultural, political, and social factors is crucial to
successful counter-insurgency and stability operations and, ultimately, to success in the
war on terror.

The operational impact of not resolving
this capability gap is a continued cycle of local cultural knowledge

the complex interaction between tribes, and identify Al Qaida Associated Militants
(AQAM) leaders operating among the population.

4. (U) The CJTF-82 JUONS point of contact (POC) is
NIPRNET: @swa.army.mil; SIPRNET:
76.centcom.smil.mil.

RODNEY O. ANDERSON
Brigadier General, USA
Deputy Commanding General-Support

Encl

Classified by CJTF-82, R.O. Anderson, DCG-S

APPENDIX D

CJTF-82 JOINT URGENT OPERATIONAL NEED FOR HUMAN TERRAIN SYSTEMS

Released as a part of a Freedom of Information Act request by the author, the original Joint Urgent Operational Needs Statement for Human Terrain System is dated April 17, 2007. More detailed than the previous endorsement, it notes that an inability to translate "hard won local cultural social knowledge" to newly arriving units had operational impact, the breakdown of which is redacted. Importantly for the supposition of this thesis, it explicitly links Human Terrain Teams to analyzing "the complex interaction between tribes, identify Al Qaida Associated Militants leaders and Improvised Explosive Device cells operating among the population."

(U) Title: Joint Urgent Operational Need Statement (JUONS) for Cultural Operations Research - Human Terrain System (COR-HTS)

(U) Submitted by: CJTF-82

(U) Date Certified/Prioritized by Combatant Commander: 17 APR 2007

(U) Relative Priority: 1

(S//REL TO USA AND GCTF) General Description: Detailed knowledge of local cultural, political, and social factors is crucial to successful counter-insurgency and stability operations, and ultimately, to success in the war on terror. [redacted]

U.S. Forces generally develop an understanding, albeit topical, of these factors via extensive interaction with tribal elements and governmental figures throughout their areas of operation. [redacted] Additionally, there is limited capability in place to effectively transfer these hard won local socio-cultural knowledge gains to newly arriving units who operate in a cultural vacuum until they improve their understanding through extensive patrolling and interaction the same areas.

The operational impact of not resolving this capability gap includes:

-
-

-

-

This deficiency exists at the Battalion, Brigade and CJTF level. [redacted]

SECRET // REL TO USA AND ISAF

The rapid funding and fielding of the Cultural Operations Research-Human Terrain System (COR-HT) is required. It consists of three primary elements:

a. Human Terrain Team (HTT): a five-person element of military and civilian personnel specifically trained in Denied Area Ethnographic and other research and analysis techniques who are deployed with the unit, report to the unit Executive Officer or Chief of Staff, and serve as the Commander's human terrain advisory team. HTTs will primarily serve within each Brigade staff to assist the S2 and Effects Coordinator with socio-cultural and ethnographic information collection and consolidation, visualization, and analysis as it relates to and supports unit operations, intelligence, planning, targeting, and assessment. The HTT will also provide specific support to psychological operations, information operations, and civil affairs operations.

b. Human Terrain Visualization and Analysis Tool and underlying Knowledge Base (Map-HT): a socio-cultural factors collection, visualization and analysis toolkit that allows HTTs and Reachback Research Cells (RRC) to develop human terrain analysis products and populate a human terrain database with operationally relevant cultural information. The database will be accessed through SIPRNET by commanders and staffs as they operate in the various border provinces enabling the search for tribal and cultural information using specific parameters such as tribe, village, or specific names and positions. The database includes a secret version, as well as an unclassified version to facilitate information sharing with host nation and NATO elements.

c. Reach Back Capability: a nine-person element of military and civilian personnel specifically trained in Denied Area Ethnographic, socio-cultural, open source, quantitative, and qualitative research and analysis techniques. The cell will be based in CONUS, report to the COR-HT Unit Commander, and provide dedicated support via a network of subject matter experts (the Human Terrain SME-Net) able to conduct focused research on cultural topics, secure unique socio-cultural information and address queries from commanders in the Afghanistan theater.

The HTTs will support the CJTF HQ and Task Forces that control battlespace. The Map-HT ("mapping" human terrain toolkit) and the dedicated support Reachback Research Cell will be initially accessible to company level via SIPR and NIPR networks supported by Joint Network Node (JNN) satellite network architecture.

(S//REL TO USA AND GCTF) Mission and Threat Analysis: [REDACTED]

[REDACTED]

(b)(1)1.4a (b)(1)1.4g

(b)(1)1.4a (b)(1)1.4g The rapid fielding of the Cultural Operations Research-Human Terrain System with its HTTs, RRC and MAP-HT Toolkit will enable U.S. Forces in Afghanistan to assess and analyze the complex interaction between tribes, identify Al Qaida Associated Militants (AQAM) leaders and Improvised Explosive Device (IED) cells operating among the population, and therefore conduct more effective operations in these challenging environments.

(b)(1)1.4a (b)(1)1.4c (b)(1)1.4g

c. Desired Date: Immediately.   (b)(1)1.4a (b)(1)1.4g
(b)(1)1.4a (b)(1)1.4c (b)(1)1.4g

d. Impacts to Safety, Survivability, Personnel, Training, Logistics or Communications: The architecture of the CONUS reach back capability in this system needs to be developed. The reach back capability should be designed to access information via a Web portal construct. This would limit both the bandwidth of the system, as well as the amount of potentially classified information that would be stored in a less than secure environment.

(U) Non-Materiel Alternatives: No non-materiel options or alternatives were considered.

(S//REL TO USA AND GCTF) Potential Materiel Alternatives: (b)(1)1.4a (b)(1)1.4c (b)(1)1.4g

(b)(1)1.4a (b)(1)1.4c (b)(1)1.4g

(U) Potential Resource Tradeoffs: None identified.

(U) Constraints: No known constraints.

SECRET // REL TO USA AND ISAF

(U) Points of Contact (POCs):

(U) Authorized by: RODNEY O. ANDERSON, Brigadier General, Deputy Commanding General- Support, CJTF-82.

Classified by CJTF-82, REF: This Subject
Declassify: 17 APR 2017

~~SECRET // REL TO USA AND ISAF~~

APPENDIX E

MNC-I (MULTI-NATIONAL CORPS-IRAQ) ENDORSEMENT TO JOINT URGENT OPERATIONAL NEED FOR HUMAN TERRAIN TEAMS

Lieutenant General Raymond T. Odierno, commander of Multi-National Corps-Iraq signed the endorsement for Human Terrain Teams to support Operation IRAQI FREEDOM-SURGE on April 7, 2007. "Detailed knowledge of the host populations" in "real time" is critical to counterinsurgency operations in the country.

HEADQUARTERS
MULTI-NATIONAL CORPS - IRAQ
BAGHDAD, IRAQ
APO AE 09342

REPLY TO
ATTENTION OF

07 APR 07

FICI-GT-C2

MEMORANDUM THRU Commander, Multi-National Force-Iraq, APO AE 09342-2001

FOR Commander, United States Central Command, CCJ8, 7115 South Boundary Blvd, MacDill AFB, Florida 33621-5101

SUBJECT: Joint Urgent Operational Need Statement for Human Terrain Teams

1. Reference: Joint Urgent Operational Need Statement for Human Terrain Team Support to OIF Surge

2. Detailed knowledge of host populations is critical in areas where U.S. forces are being increased to conduct counterinsurgency and stability operations in Iraq. U.S. forces continue to operate in Iraq without real-time, detailed knowledge of the drivers of behavior within the host population. This greatly limits Commanders' situational awareness and creates greater risks for forces. This human terrain knowledge deficiency exists at all command echelons.

3. Recommend [(b)(5)   ]

4. The point of contact is [b)(6), 10 USC §130b. (b)(6)] C2 Operations, DSN: [(b)(6)], email: [b)(6), 10 USC §130b. (b)(6)]

RAYMOND T. ODIERNO
Lieutenant General, USA
Commanding

APPENDIX F

MNC-I (MULTI-NATIONAL CORPS-IRAQ) JOINT URGENT OPERATIONAL NEEDS STATEMENT FOR HUMAN TERRAIN TEAMS

The undated Joint Urgent Operational Needs Statement (JUONS) also signed by Lieutenant General Odierno gives additional reasoning for the request for Human Terrain Teams, stressing a need for a "social science expert" in an Iraqi theater which is "complicated by a number of human factors." The JUONS notes that five teams of four personnel each would be in Iraq by mid-2007 and that, to support the surge, there was a requirement for an additional 13 Human Terrain Teams and four Human Terrain Analysis Teams. This shows the concept of the Human Terrain Analysis Team existed from at least mid-2007 and before any Human Terrain Teams had embedded in Iraq. The teams would increase knowledge of the population and tribal systems, and institutionalize this knowledge, decreasing "both coalition and local national casualties."

Title: Joint Urgent Operational Need Statement (JUONS) for Human Terrain Team Support to OIF Surge

Submitted by: Multi-National Corps – Iraq (MNC-I)

Date Certified/Prioritized by COCOM:

Relative Priority: 1

General Description: Detailed knowledge of host populations is critical in areas where U.S. forces are being increased to conduct counterinsurgency and stability operations in Iraq. U.S. forces continue to operate in Iraq without real-time knowledge of the drivers of behavior within the host population. This greatly limits Commanders' situational awareness and creates greater risks for forces. These human terrain knowledge deficiencies exist at all command echelons in the Iraqi Theater of Operations (ITO).

To address this lack of knowledge, Commanders need social science experts who are focused full-time on conducting research and analysis of the human dynamics in localized areas of operations. This research and analysis must produce a human terrain knowledge base with visualization tools that enable Commanders to quickly understand the behavior and motivations of key local leaders and sub-groups within the host population.

Mission and Threat Analysis: The current operational environment in the ITO is complicated by a number of human factors, including an ancient and complex tribal system, historic religious allegiances, political schisms along sectarian lines, and the presence of al-Qaeda and other foreign-based terrorist organizations. Adversaries trying to defeat Iraqi government and Coalition forces take advantage of their superior knowledge of local power structures and religious affiliations. Commanders need much more detailed knowledge of the human terrain in order to beat the insurgents at their own game – the following framework is suggested to provide Commanders that necessary information.

    Mission Deficiency: The MNC-I requirement is for 18 Human Terrain Teams (HTTs) for the MNC-I BCTs and 4 Human Terrain Analysis Teams (HTAT) for the MNC-I MND/Fs to support surge operations. These teams of social scientists can be composed of civilian and/or military, but must have a current secret clearance.

    Initial Operating Capability (IOC): A Concept of Operations (CONOP) for the Human Terrain Initiative will be completed by mid-April 07. Twenty analysts should be trained during April and May 07 on the CONOP, the common analytic framework for conducting operationally-relevant social science analysis, and the available collection, analysis and visualization tools. The MAP-Human Terrain JCTD will accelerate to provide the toolkit. By mid-June 07, five (4 per HTT) human terrain teams should be available to deploy into the ITO as directed by MNC-I.

Expanded requirement An additional 13 HTTs and 4 HTATs will be formed, trained, and deployed to the ITO in the quantities indicated below
    MND-B - 3 HTT, 1 HTAT (on top of the 5 HTT deployed for the IOC)
    MNF-W - 3 HTT, 1 HTAT
    MND-C - 3 HTT, 1 HTAT
    MND-N - 4 HTT, 1 HTAT

Delivery Date: Immediately The original 1CD Operational Needs Statement (ONS) for the theater main effort required capability was signed and forwarded on August 2006 [Note In response to this operational need (ONS), TRADOC is currently executing a JIEDDO funded, OSD-supported HTS Proof of Concept For OIF, this preliminary capability is five teams for Multi-National Division-Baghdad (MND-B) This JUON will increase the capability for MND-B, as well as expand it to encompass the other Major Subordinate Commands (MSCs) throughout Iraq]

Requirement:

The required capability should be enabled by the following key components

(1) Comprehensive social science field research that provides statistically significant indicators of the attitudes and proclivities of various segments of the population, and not just anecdotal information This information will feed an analytic framework that brings coherency to the data structure and will identify key motivators of population behavior A richer understanding of the drivers of behavior will result in better operational decisions with respect to interactions with the local community

(2) Human Terrain analysts with social science and regional and/or operational experience in the area of operations These analysts must be able to analyze and interpret data collected through field research, troops in the field, and Open Source information in a way that translates into valuable advice to the Commander These analysts should be deployed forward in support of the BCT/RCT commanders and staff to ensure up-to-the-minute synthesis of information as it comes in from the field

(3) This analytic capability must be supported by effective data management, analytic and visualization tools The data structure should use a common analytic framework mentioned above to organize and synthesize data gathered in field research, troop collection and through Open Sources The data must be tagged with geospatial and temporal metadata It must be maintained in an unclassified repository which future commanders and their staffs can use and build upon, and which can be shared with other mission partners The data will be fed into the Commanders' planning process through intelligence directorates for fusion with formal intelligence sources to enable the staff to provide a full picture of the human terrain to the Commander The COR-Human Terrain System (COR-HT) Project is the foremost example of an analytic and visualization tool set being developed for this capability

(4) The HTKB must be integrated into the theater information architecture to provide two way access both vertically and horizontally. Human Terrain Teams (HTT) must be able to reach back to CONUS for supplementary information from subject matter experts outside the AOR. Additionally, the reach back capability should be designed to access information via a Web portal construct if possible. This would limit both the bandwidth of the system, as well as the amount of potentially classified information that would be stored in a less than secure environment.

Impact. Immediate satisfaction of this JUONS will:

- Improve operational decisions and chances for mission success in the ITO through:
  - Increased understanding of Iraqi citizens' physical and economic security needs at local/district resolution
  - Increased understanding of local ideological, religious, and tribal allegiances
  - Avoidance of unintended second order effects resulting from a lack of understanding of the local human terrain

- Decrease both coalition force and local national casualties

- Institutionalize human terrain knowledge — Avoid needless loss of life that has occurred due to lack of a systematic process and systems to enable transfer of human terrain knowledge during unit Relief in Place/Transition of Authority (RIP/TOA)

Non-Materiel Alternatives: Non-materiel alternatives were not considered

Potential Materiel Alternatives: None known

Potential Resource Tradeoffs: None identified

Constraints: Key to success is hiring the right personnel. These individuals should have operational experience and also have social science and/or regional expertise in the area into which they are being deployed to support the Brigade. Getting the right people hired fast enough to train them before a June deployment will be a challenge, but TRADOC has already hired 20 and has already started training. But most of these people were not in the pipeline to go to Baghdad, so training needs to be altered somewhat to support the Surge and the focus on Baghdad as the initial priority.

The COR-HTS program is not included in the Program Objective Memorandum, it is still a "proof-of-concept" funded by JIEDDO at $20.4M for FY07. The initial estimate to field HTTs and the HTAT for Baghdad is estimated at $30.7M. Costing for the expanded requirement is TBD.

The MAP-HT Toolkit is a CENTCOM and U.S. Army (TRADOC and G2) sponsored 2007 Joint/Advanced Concept and Technology Development (J/ACTD) program candidate with SOCOM, JFCOM, EUCOM, U.S. Marine Corps supporting. Funding is provided by OSD AT&L/Advanced Systems and Concepts (AS&C), Army G2, FMSO, and Marine Corps Warfighting Lab. PM DCGS-A is the transition manager for the MAP-HT Toolkit.

The Joint Rapid Acquisition Cell (JRAC) has previously recommended submission of a JUONS for this capability from the COR-Human Terrain Project of the Foreign Military Studies Office.

Points of Contact (POCs):

Authorized by: Raymond T. Odierno, LTG, Commanding

010

463

APPENDIX G

MNF-I ENDORSEMENT TO JOINT URGENT OPERATIONAL NEED FOR HUMAN TERRAIN TEAMS

This short endorsement by Multi-National Force-Iraq notes that the teams can supply "real time host nation intelligence to commanders on the ground."

HEADQUARTERS
MULTI-NATIONAL FORCE – IRAQ
BAGHDAD, IRAQ
APO AE 09342-1400

REPLY TO
ATTENTION OF

MNFI-CG   19 APR 2007

MEMORANDUM FOR Commander, United States Central Command, ATTN: CCJ8, South
Boundary Boulevard, MacDill Air Force Base, Florida 33621-5101

SUBJECT: (S/REL) Joint Urgent Operational Need (JUON) for Human Terrain Teams

1. (S/REL) Reference: Memorandum, Headquarters, Multi-National Corps – Iraq (MNC-I),
SUBJECT: Joint Urgent Operational Need for Human Terrain Teams.

2. (S/REL) MNF-I endorses the requirement of ___ Human Terrain Teams. The teams are
capable of providing real time host nation intelligence to commanders on the ground. This is of
great importance when fighting an insurgency.

3. (U) The MNF-I point of contact is _____ (b)(3), (b)(6) _____ e-mail
_____ (b)(3), (b)(6) _____ | The MNC-I point of contact is ____ (b)(3), (b)(6) ____
_____ (b)(6) _____

FOR THE COMMANDER:

THOMAS L. MOORE, JR.
MajGen, USMC
Chief of Staff

APPENDIX H

U.S. CENTRAL COMMAND ENDORSEMENT TO JOINT URGENT OPERATIONAL NEED CC-0197

Major General Timothy F. Ghormley, U.S. Marine Corps, signed the memorandum and in doing so, observes that USCENTCOM views Human Terrain Teams as not meeting the strict definition of a JUONS, but is nevertheless "forwarding to Joint Staff to assess and determine the best approach to fulfilling this capability gap."

UNITED STATES CENTRAL COMMAND
OFFICE OF THE CHIEF OF STAFF
7115 SOUTH BOUNDARY BOULEVARD
MACDILL AIR FORCE BASE, FLORIDA 33621-5101

CCJ8   23 May 07

MEMORANDUM FOR DIRECTOR FOR FORCE STRUCTURE, RESOURCES &
ASSESSMENT J8, ATTN: DDRA, 8000 DEFENSE
PENTAGON, ROOM 1E962, WASHINGTON, D.C.
20318-8000

SUBJECT: Joint Urgent Operational Need (JUON) Statement for
Human Terrain Teams (U) (CC-0197) (U)

REF: CJCSI 3470.01, dtd 15 July 2005, Subject: Rapid Validation
and Resourcing of Joint Urgent Operational Needs (JUON) in the
Year of Execution

1. (U) USCENTCOM endorses the MNC-I and CJTF-82 requirements
(enclosed) for Human Terrain Teams (HTT).

2. (U) CJCSI 3470.01 limits the scope of a JUON to "addressing
urgent operational needs that: (1) fall outside of the
established Service processes; and (2) most importantly, if not
addressed immediately, will seriously endanger personnel or pose
a major threat to ongoing operations." Although USCENTCOM does
not view the enclosed subject as meeting the strict definition
of a JUON, we are forwarding to Joint Staff to assess and
determine the best approach to fulfilling this capability gap.

3. (U) Human Terrain Teams represent a significant force
multiplier to existing national, theater, and tactical-level
efforts to characterize the human terrain, filling a critical
gap in current analytical and production capabilities. As such,
CENTCOM endorses this MNC-I and CJTF-82 request in order to
assist the Office of the [(b)(3) 50 USC 403g   ]
in developing and finalizing a funding strategy. This
requirement is further supported by Department of the [(b)(3) 50 USC 403g   ]
and [   ].

4. (U) USCENTCOM point of contact is the CCJ8-ARC, [(b)(6)   ]
[(b)(6)   ], the CCJ2-OCR point of co [(b)(6)   ]
[(b)(6)   ]

TIMOTHY F. GHORMLEY
Major General, USMC

Encls
as

DERIVED FROM: CJTF-82 HTT JUON, 21 Apr 07
DECLASSIFY ON: 20170421

Regrade UNCLASSIFIED when separated from enclosures

467

APPENDIX I

SUPERVISORY SOCIAL SCIENTIST, TASK LIST, COMPLETE TASK LIST 20090808

Unique ID	Supervisory Social Scientist		Roles and Responsibilities	
16	1.2.1.1.6.3 Determine Methodological Feasibility of Research Efforts	Research Plan	Team Mission Statement	Conduct operationally relevant research and analysis in order to enable culturally astute decision-making, enhance operational effectiveness, and preserve and share socio-cultural institutional knowledge.
22	1.2.1.1.2.2 Define the Research Objective	Research Plan		
23	1.2.1.1.2.3 Formulate Research Questions	Research Plan		
27	1.2.1.1.2.5 Analyze Knowledge Gap	Research Plan		
31	1.2.1.1.6.3 Evaluate Methodological Aspects of the Research Environment	Research Plan		
34	1.2.1.1.2.9 Select Methods	Research Plan		
36	1.2.1.2.10.1 Supervise the Design of the Collection Protocol	Research Plan	Supervisory Social Scientist Position Description	The supervisory social scientist leads all aspects and functions of the research and analysis process.
37	1.2.1.2.10.2 Develop the Instrument	Research Plan		
40	1.2.1.2.11.1 Design the Analysis Protocol	Research Plan		
48	1.2.1.1.2.2.2 Identify Research Process Assessment Requirements	Research Plan	Research Planning	The supervisory social scientist plans and designs research projects, including long-term and short-term projects. Planning of research projects includes determining the methodological feasibility of research efforts, defining the research objective, formulating the research questions, analyzing knowledge gaps, selecting collection and analysis methods, and developing appropriate research instruments such as interview protocols and surveys.
67	1.2.1.1.5.2 Conduct Mission Specific Methodological Training	Research Execution		
69	1.2.2.1.6 Review / Refine Research Design	Research Execution		
94	1.2.2.3.7 Manage Research	Research Execution		
95	1.2.2.3.2.1 Analyze Requirements	Research Execution	Roles and Responsibilities 1	
96	1.2.2.3.2.2 Refine Requirements	Research Execution		
97	1.2.2.3.2.3 Task Organize for Research	Research Execution		
100	1.2.2.3.3.2 Evaluate Research Products	Research Execution	Research Execution	The supervisory social scientist oversees the collection of primary and secondary-source data to develop a common operating picture of the socio-cultural environment. The supervisory social scientist oversees the qualitative or quantitative analysis of data.
104	1.2.3.1.1 Supervise Integration of Research Products	Research Execution		
107	1.2.3.2.1 Supervise Aggregation of Research Products	Research Execution	Roles and Responsibilities 2	
127	1.2.5.2 Conduct Research and Analysis Process Assessment	Research Assessment	Research Assessment	The supervisory social scientist oversees the assessment of research processes and methods.
			Roles and Responsibilities 3	

APPENDIX J

FIELD SOCIAL SCIENTIST, TASK LIST, COMPLETE TASK LIST 20090808

Unique ID	Field Social Scientist	Roles and Responsibilities	
16	1.2.1.1.6.3 Determine Methodological Feasibility of Research Efforts	Research Plan	
22	1.2.1.1.2 Define the Research Objective	Research Plan	
23	1.2.1.2.3 Formulate Research Questions	Research Plan	Team Mission Statement
27	1.2.1.2.5 Analyze Knowledge Gap	Research Plan	
31	1.2.1.2.6.3 Evaluate Methodological Aspects of the Research Environment	Research Plan	
34	1.2.1.2.9 Select Methods	Research Plan	
36	1.2.1.2.10.1 Supervise the Design of the Collection Protocol	Research Plan	Field Social Scientist Position Description
37	1.2.1.2.10.2 Develop the Instrument	Research Plan	
40	1.2.1.2.11 Design the Analysis Protocol	Research Plan	
48	1.2.1.2.13.2.2 Identify Research Process Assessment Requirements	Research Plan	
67	1.2.2.1.5.2 Conduct Mission Specific Methodological Training	Research Execution	
69	1.2.2.1.6 Revise / Refine Research Design	Research Execution	
94	1.2.2.3.2 Manage Research	Research Execution	
95	1.2.2.3.2.1 Analyze Requirements	Research Execution	
96	1.2.2.3.2.2 Refine Requirements	Research Execution	
97	1.2.2.3.2.3 Task Organize for Research	Research Execution	Roles and Responsibilities 1
100	1.2.2.3.3.2 Evaluate Research Products	Research Execution	
104	1.2.3.1.1 Supervise Integration of Research Products	Research Execution	
107	1.2.3.2.1 Supervise Aggregation of Research Products	Research Execution	Roles and Responsibilities 2
127	1.2.5.2 Conduct Research and Analysis Process Assessment	Research Assessment	Roles and Responsibilities 3

Team Mission Statement
Conduct operationally relevant research and analysis in order to enable culturally astute decision-making, enhance operational effectiveness, and present and share socio-cultural institutional knowledge.

Field Social Scientist Position Description
The field social scientist conducts all aspects and functions of the research and analysis process.

Research Planning
The field social scientist assists in planning and designing research projects, including long-term and short-term projects. Planning research projects includes determining the methodological feasibility of research efforts, defining the research objective, formulating the research questions, analyzing knowledge gaps, selecting collection and analysis methods, and developing appropriate research instruments such as interview protocols and surveys.

Research Execution
The field social scientist assists in the collection of primary and secondary source data to develop a common operating picture of the socio-cultural environment. The field social scientist assists in the qualitative or quantitative analysis of data.

Research Assessment
The field social scientist assists in the assessment of research processes and methods.

APPENDIX K

REVISED POSITION DESCRIPTION FOR SOCIAL SCIENTIST, JANUARY 14, 2009

Position Description

PD#: ST302454   Replaces PD#: NEW

Sequence#: VARIES

SOCIAL SCIENTIST
GG-0101-15

Servicing CPAC: CIVILIAN INTELLIGENCE PERS – CENTRALIZED, FORT HUACHUCA, AZ

Agency: VARIES
MACOM: VARIES
Command Code: VARIES

Region: WEST

Citation 1: OPM SERIES DEF., GS-101, AUG 2002

Citation 2: CIPMS PGS, PART 2 FOR NON-SU-PERVISORY POSITIONS, JUN 90

Citation 3: CIPMS, APP G, GUIDE-SERIES NOT CVRD BY SPECIFIC AOG, JAN 95
PD Library PD: NO
COREDOC PD: NO

Classified By: MAXIE L. MCFARLAND
Classified Date: 01/14/2009

FLSA: EXEMPT Drug Test Required: VARIES
DCIPS PD: YES

This description is to be used for Title 10 Excepted Service, Defense Civilian Intelligence Personnel System positions only.

Career Program: 35   Financial Disclosure Required: NO   Acquisition Position: NO

Functional Code: 00   Requires Access to Firearms: VARIES   Interdisciplinary: NO

Competitive Area: VARIES   Position Sensitivity: VARIES   Target Grade/FPL: 15

Competitive Level: VARIES   Emergency Essential:

[ ]

Career Ladder PD: NO

Bus Code: VARIES   Personnel Reliability Position: VARIES Information Assurance: N

PD Status: VERIFIED

Duties:

This is a DCIPS position.

The Social Scientist designs and executes social science research and analysis based on the Commander's concept of operation. The Social Scientist oversees the research and analysis process in coordination with the Team Leader and Research Manager.

Conduct Research:

The Operations Manager supports a Human Terrain System team in all phases and types of sociocultural research and analysis conducted by the team in a combat environment. This includes both primary and secondary source research. Primary source research is data collected directly by a Human Terrain System team utilizing knowledgeable local sources. Sociocultural research is not focused primarily on either friendly or enemy actions, instead, it focuses on people, their perceptions, identities, social organization, and interdependencies, all of which tend to be dynamic and contextually specific. The conduct of primary source research includes the movement to and from research sites in conjunction with military units and the data collection activities conducted by teams at unsecured data collection locations in austere environments.

Research Planning:

The Social Scientist plans and designs research projects, including long-term and short-term projects. Planning research is a process that includes the creation of an overarching research plan that guides the research efforts of the team and research designs that guide the research effort for discrete issues and projects. The research design process focuses on specific research objectives that address implicit or explicit requirements of the supported command and contribute to the expansion of the knowledge base. Research designs should be nested within the overall research plan. Both research planning and design are continuous processes and should be reviewed as requirements and resources change over time. When successfully executed, research planning and design provides a framework for collection and analysis that is driven by supported unit requirements and aids in the production of sociocultural understanding. Planning of research projects includes determining the methodological feasibility of research efforts, defining the research objective, formulating the research questions, analyzing knowledge gaps, selecting collection and analysis methods, and developing appropriate research instruments such as interview protocols and surveys.

Data Collection:

The Social Scientist oversees the collection of primary and secondary-source data to develop a common operating picture of the sociocultural environment. The conduct of research encompasses all actions necessary to collect primary and secondary sociocultural information. Research should be conducted to fulfill the unit's sociocultural knowledge requirements, whether that requirement is explicit or implicit. Collected data will be used by supported military units and Human Terrain System teams to develop common operating pictures of the sociocultural environment, which will be aggregated at progressively higher echelons. Data collection must be systematic, empirical, complete, reliable, and valid. Human Terrain System collection methodologies include: direct observation, visual ethnography, key leader engagement, participant observation, depth interviewing, group or focus group interviewing, surveying, secondary source research, and mixed methods approaches.

Data Analysis:

The Social Scientist oversees the qualitative or quantitative analysis of data. Once data is collected, it is subjected to analysis using a variety of tools. Each form of analysis has its own strengths, limitations, and potential outputs. The type of research question to be answered will guide the selection of the appropriate analytical tool. Analytical tools include structural analysis, cultural domain analysis, text analysis, quantitative analysis, and mixed method analysis.

Research Assessment:

The Social Scientist oversees the assessment of research processes and methods. Assessing research activities is an ongoing process which includes assessing the relevance and outcomes of the research for the supported unit. Assessing research activities also includes identifying procedural improvements to facilitate future research, analysis, and products. Process assessments on research and analysis methodologies provide input on effective methodologies to improve future research activities.

Producing Outcomes:

In conjunction with other members of the team, the Social Scientist produces documents, products, and briefings for the military unit as required and presents them at to the supported unit and other audiences. The Social Scientist provides unit specific sociocultural training as requested. The Social Scientist reviews products for accuracy, relevance, timeliness, soundness of analysis and adherence to both commander's intent and the broad guidelines of national policy.

Support to Military Decisiomaking.

In conjunction with other members of the team, the Social Scientist provides support to unit decision-making in the operations and the military decision-making process. Throughout this process, teams aid commanders and staff by providing insight into first, second, and third order effects, providing situational awareness and developing mitigation strategies. The Social Scientist assists in identifying known support-ed unit sociocultural information requirements, the most effective way to integrate into the military deci-sionmaking process and the most effective products to communicate research findings and recommenda-tions. The Social Scientist participates during work-ing groups and mission planning. The Social Scientist coordinates within the command and with staffs at all applicable levels as guided by the Team Leader.

Performs other duties as assigned.

Job Qualifications (Mandatory)

Ability to communicate effectively, both verbally and in written form, in English.

Ability to use relevant presentation software (e.g., Microsoft Office).

Possess and maintain a level of physical fitness which enables them to operate in conditions where they may have to, at a minimum:
1. Tolerate heat well in excess of 110 degrees in the summer and cold or freezing conditions during the winter.

2. Traverse rough and uneven terrain.

3. Endure hostile environment to include persons that may cause bodily harm, injury or loss of life.

4. Work with little sleep or rest for extended periods of time in support of physically and mentally challenging projects.

5. Travel extended distances by foot, military ground vehicles, and air transport into mountainous or desert regions.

6. Sleep on the ground in environmentally unprotected areas from the elements and animals.

7. Carry 40-75 pounds of gear and personal protective equipment for 10-16 hours a day.

8. Conduct a variety of tactical maneuvers in personal protective gear, which may include: entering and exiting a combat vehicle, conducting a security halt, and responding to direct and indirect fire.

M.A./M.S. or Ph.D. in Social Science (Anthropology, Political Science, Sociology, Criminology, Economics, Geography, Government), Behavioral Science (e.g., Psychology), Humanities (e.g., Folklore, History, Middle Eastern Languages and Literature, Religious Studies), Regional Studies (e.g., Mediterranean Studies, Middle Eastern Studies, Near Eastern Languages & Cultures, Central Eurasian Studies), Language and Linguistics (e.g., Arabic, Pashtu, Dari), Public Policy/ International Relations (e.g., International Policy Studies, Diplomacy, Statecraft and Security Affairs, International Affairs, Security Policy, Foreign Service, Strategic Intelligence, Military Studies).

Conducted research design and execution:
- Designed data collection instruments (e.g. surveys, interview protocols)

- Conducted data collection activities (e.g. interviews, focus groups, and participant observation)
- Prepared a variety of in-depth reports and other written material.

Factors.

FACTOR A. ESSENTIAL KNOWLEDGES

Recognized in the social science community as a technical subject matter expert on social science (e.g., has presented papers at conferences, has written peer reviewed publications in academic journals and non-peer reviewed papers in professional journals, and has presented technical briefings and reports to professional and academic audiences).

MA/MS or Ph.D. in Social Science (Anthropology, Political Science, Sociology, Criminology, Economics, Geography, Government), Behavioral Science (e.g., Psychology), Humanities (e.g., Folklore, History, Middle Eastern Languages and Literature, Religious Studies), Regional Studies (e.g., Mediterranean Studies, Middle Eastern Studies, Near Eastern Languages & Cultures, Central Eurasian Studies), Language and Linguistics (e.g., Arabic, Pashtu, Dari), Public Policy/ International Relations (e.g., International Policy Studies, Diplomacy, Statecraft and Security Affairs, International Affairs, Security Policy, Foreign Service, Strategic Intelligence, Military Studies).

Conducted research design and execution:
- Designed data collection instruments (e.g. surveys, interview protocols).

- Conducted data collection activities (e.g. interviews, focus groups, participant observation).
- Prepared a variety of in-depth reports and other written material.

Ability to apply experimental theories and new developments to problems not susceptible to treatment by accepted methods.

Makes decisions or recommendations significantly changing, interpreting, or developing important policies and programs.

Comprehensive understanding of applied research methods and expert knowledge of how to configure research projects to answer questions related to practical matters.

Record of publications in academic or professional journals or newspapers.

Extensive field research experience in a cross cultural environment.

Has managed or supervised research projects and research teams (i.e. principal investigator).

Knowledge of personnel management and administration requirements, procedures, and techniques to supervise personnel and programs.

FACTOR B. GUIDELINES

The nature of the guidelines available for the conduct of human terrain research and analysis varies greatly depending on the research, operational, or planning mission that is being undertaken. Some of the tasks performed enter uncharted areas of social science research and applications. Basic guidance comes from the commander of the supported unit and the activity. Often there is limited guidance regarding how vaguely stated requirements are to be translated into concrete recommendations for courses of action in support of military operations. There are recurrent requirements for supervision of the research portion of extremely sensitive and creative programs in support of national policy. Judgment, ingenuity, and originality are required to adapt mission to foreign policy objectives.

FACTOR C. SCOPE OF AUTHORITY AND EFFECT OF DECISIONS

Social Scientist makes authoritative determinations regarding research findings and advises on technical social science issues. Decisions and commitments often involve large expenditures of resources and have a strong impact on important programs. Work consists of broad functions with enduring requirements and duration of effort that often requires phasing. Incumbent must plan for multiple lines of operation and consider multiple courses of action and potential conflict and cooperation with internal elements and external agencies. Developing and supervising research requires coordination and development of contacts across a wide range of scientific, academic, commercial and government agencies.

FACTOR D. WORK RELATIONSHIPS

With respect to research and analysis, incumbent represents the Activity in all forms and at all levels as required. Assessment of the Activity's capabilities in those spheres is authoritative. Once a position is settled upon internally, incumbent is expected to win support from outside agencies for the Activity's programs. Regular person-to-person work contacts are maintained with officials within the Activity and with staff officers and planners at the theater command, Department of Defense, and National Agency levels. The last category includes meetings and liaison with officials at the Department of State, Defense Intelligence Agency, and the Central Intelligence Agency. Contacts with general officers and their civilian equivalents are not infrequent. When called upon, helps to develop and present the Activity's position to bodies as high as the National Security Council, and to high officials, both American and foreign, in the United States and abroad. Maintains regular contact with nationally recognized members of the academic community.

FACTOR E. SUPERVISION RECEIVED

The supervisor (the Team Leader) generally provides only administrative direction, with assignments only in terms of broadly defined missions or functions. The Social Scientist has responsibility for planning, designing, and carrying out programs, projects, studies or other work independently. The Team Leader is kept informed of significant developments. Completed work is reviewed only from an overall standpoint in terms of feasibility, compatibility, effectiveness or expected results, and for its contribution to the advancement of the teams' research objectives.

FACTOR F. SUPERVISION EXERCISED

The Social Scientist is responsible for the technical aspects of research process and products of an independently functioning professional research team. Supervises research functions and sets quality standards for the research, analysis, and writing of the team. In conjunction with the Team Leader, recommends approval or returns for revision all studies and other documents produced by the team for distribution. Incumbent has substantial responsibility for the technical soundness of all studies, which involve specialized research of an extremely high intellectual level. Has authority to alter the organization of work within the team in order to accomplish research objectives, and guides subordinates in the achievement of assigned research tasks.

FACTOR G. COMPLEXITY OF WORK SUPERVISED.

The highest level of nonsupervisory work supervised in subordinate work units is GS-14.

TOTAL POINTS:
POINT RANGE: = GG-15

Knowledge, Skills, and Abilities.

KNOWLEDGE

Professional level knowledge in social science or related discipline. This can be demonstrated by M.A./M.S. or Ph.D. in Social Science (Anthropology, Political Science, Sociology, Criminology, Economics,

Geography, Government), Behavioral Science (e.g., Psychology), Humanities (e.g., Folklore, History, Middle Eastern Languages and Literature, Religious Studies), Regional Studies (e.g., Mediterranean Studies, Middle Eastern Studies, Near Eastern Languages & Cultures, Central Eurasian Studies), Language and Linguistics (e.g., Arabic, Pashtu, Dari), Public Policy/ International Relations (e.g., International Policy Studies, Diplomacy, Statecraft and Security Affairs, International Affairs, Security Policy, Foreign Service, Strategic Intelligence, Military Studies).

Knowledge of research design and execution:
- Data collection instruments (e.g. surveys, interview protocols)
- Data collection activities (e.g. interviews, focus groups, participant observation)
- Data preparation (e.g., in-depth reports and other written material).

Comprehensive understanding of applied research methods and expert knowledge of how to configure research projects to answer questions related to practical matters.

Knowledge of management practices for supervising research projects and research teams (i.e. principal investigator).

Knowledge of personnel management and administration requirements, procedures, and techniques to supervise personnel and programs.

SKILLS

Software:

Ability to use relevant presentation software (e.g., Microsoft Office).

ABILITIES

Character and Integrity:

Displays a high standard of ethical conduct and can be trusted in all work situations; chooses an ethical course of action and does the right thing, even in the face of opposition; encourages others to behave accordingly; demonstrates core organizational values and honesty; acts in a principled manner that instills trust and confidence; is honest and straightforward when presenting data, conclusions, and recommendations.

Judgment and Decisionmaking:

Demonstrates good judgment by making sound, timely, and well-informed decisions without deferring actions when decisions need to be made; considers the impact and implications of decisions; commits to action and follows through on decisions.

Communication:

Conveys written information and ideas in a clear, concise, and well-organized manner; written communication is targeted to the level of the audience; uses correct spelling, grammar, and punctuation when preparing written materials; conveys oral information in a clear, concise, and well-organized manner taking into account the audience and the nature of the information (e.g., technical, controversial); speaks clearly, convincingly, and confidently using proper grammar, tone, and pace; tracks audience responses and reacts appropriately to those responses. Receives, attends to, interprets, understands, and responds appropriately to verbal messages and other cues such as body language and other nonverbal communication; pays close attention, listening attentively and seeking additional clarifying information when necessary.

Initiative and Responsibility:

Sets well-defined and realistic personal goals; displays a high level of initiative, effort, and commitment towards completing assignments in a timely manner; works with minimal supervision; is motivated to achieve; demonstrates responsible behavior and determines responsible behavior; takes the lead in getting tasks done with limited prompting or direction; seeks opportunities to begin new lines of inquiry or investigation in order to solve problems; accepts responsibility for one's own actions and words and/or those of the group or team; takes responsibility for accomplishing work goals and meeting deadlines; reliably completes tasks and assignments in a timely manner; follows through on commitments and does what it takes to get the job done; goes beyond the call of duty to meet deadlines.

Interpersonal Competency:

Demonstrates fairness, professionalism, and tact when interacting with others; understands and interacts effectively with a variety of people to include those who are difficult, hostile, or distressed; adjusts interpersonal style, as needed, to interact with differing individuals, new teams, co-workers or customers; performs effectively in different cultures learning new languages, values, traditions and politics.

Handling Work Stress:

Remains calm under pressure, handles frustration, and acts as a calming influence; demonstrates a positive outlook and persistence, even under adverse or difficult situations; persists at a task or problem despite interruptions, obstacles, or setbacks; reacts appropriately and decisively to life threatening or dangerous situations; adjusts and deals with unpredictable situations, shift focus and take reasonable action.

Physical Fitness:

Social Scientists must achieve and maintain a level of physical fitness which enables them to operate in conditions where they may have to, at a minimum:

1. Tolerate heat well in excess of 110 degrees in the summer and cold or freezing conditions during the winter.

2. Traverse rough and uneven terrain.

3. Endure hostile environment to include persons that may cause bodily harm, injury, or loss of life.

4. Work with little sleep or rest for extended periods of time in support of physically and mentally challenging projects.

5. Travel extended distances by foot, military ground vehicles, and air transport into mountainous or desert regions.

6. Sleep on the ground in environmentally unprotected areas from the elements and animals.

7. Carry 40-75 pounds of gear and personal protective equipment for 10-16 hours a day.

8. Conduct a variety of tactical maneuvers in personal protective gear; this may include: entering and exiting a combat vehicle, conducting a security halt, and responding to direct and indirect fire.

Logical Reasoning and Synthesis — Analyzes and integrates information to identify trends, rules, and relationships, draw appropriate conclusions, make recommendations, and address issues or problems; identifies and uses principles, rules, and relationships to construct arguments or interpret facts, data, or other information; dissects problems into meaningful parts and uses logic and judgment to determine accuracy and relevance of data; identifies and reconciles gaps, uncertainties, and key assumptions of data; integrates information, evaluates and prioritizes alternatives, and assesses similarities and differences in data to develop findings and conclusions; and understands potential implications of these findings or conclusions.

Service Orientation:

Works with others (i.e., anyone who receives or uses a product or service that you or your work unit provides) to understand their needs, set expectations, and provide timely, flexible, and responsive products or services; applies knowledge of relevant customer organizations or operations, including how to translate requirements to provide appropriate output or response to meet customer needs.

Team Leadership:

Directs, coordinates, and monitors group activities to ensure timely and effective completion of work; provides coaching, mentoring, and timely and constructive feedback to staff to develop their full potential; motivates staff, inspires work ethic and dedication, and obtains cooperation and commitment toward the group's goals; encourages creative tension and differences of opinions; anticipates and takes steps to prevent counterproductive confrontations; manages and resolves conflicts and disagreements in a constructive manner; develops and maintains collaborative working relationships with others; works with others to achieve goals; encourages and facilitates cooperation and group identity; develops and maintains effective networks, coalitions, and liaison relationships with others to create an authentic foundation for developing trust and respect by bridging personal, professional, team, military, and multinational cultures; respects, understands, and values differences (e.g., technical, demographic, occupational or educational diversity) to achieve the vision and mission of the HTS and supported unit; utilizes diversity of talents to achieve goals.

CONDITIONS OF EMPLOYMENT
1. Must be able to obtain and maintain a Secret security clearance.
2. Performs temporary duty (TDY) travel UP TO 100% of the time.

Evaluation:
Not Listed

APPENDIX L

SOCIAL SCIENCE WORKING GROUP, SESSION 2, MARCH 16-27, 2009, OUTBRIEF 5, SLIDES 41-42

Slide 41

Synopsis of Findings
Teams and Methods

- The network map on the following slide shows the methods used by each team. Key aspects of this map are:
  - Some teams use a lot more methods than others (more lines coming from some teams than others)
  - Methods that a widely used, such as literature reviews, semi-structured and unstructured interviews are in the center of the map
  - Some teams never use some methods – such as surveys
- This suggests that in some cases the methods used may be a result of team preferences/competence rather than driven by brigade needs.

Slide 42

Teams By Methods Used

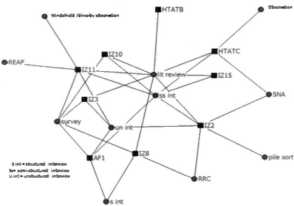

HUMAN TERRAIN TEAM IZ4, 'PROPORTIONS BRIEF SECTARIAN BREAKDOWNS,' POWERPOINT PRESENTATION, 2008, SLIDES 2-5

Slide 2

Disclaimer

- Has been no true census in Baghdad in past ten-years. Most data available is based on rough estimates gathered in 2003 and 2007. These estimates are still being verified for accuracy

- Therefore what we have done is to try and extrapolate backwards based on historical data and existing population estimates

Source: *gulf2000.columbia.edu/maps.shtml*

Slide 3

Ethnic-Religious Neighborhoods in Metropolitan Baghdad, Early-2007

Source: *gulf2000.columbia.edu/images/maps/Baghdad_Ethnic_2007_early_sm.jpg*

Slide 4

Sectarian Distribution by Muhalla in Strike AO in 2007

Source: *gulf2000.columbia.edu/maps.shtml*

Slide 5

**Ethnic-Religious Neighborhoods in
Metropolitan Baghdad, 2003**

Source: *gulf2000.columbia.edu/images/maps/Baghdad_Ethnic_2003_
sm.jpg*

APPENDIX N

GOVERNMENT DOMAIN QUESTIONS, AF1, 2008

Government Domain Questions:

Explanation: *I am interested in learning about government in Afghanistan. I do not know much about it, and was wondering if you would help me understand it. For me to better understand government in Afghanistan, I will have to learn about all the types of government that exist. Please tell me how you would normally refer all the different types of governments in Afghanistan.*

Domain Discovery:
 1. Can you tell me all the different types of governments in Afghanistan you can think of?

Ok, that is great. You mentioned several types of government for me which is very helpful. Now, I would like to go over the list, and have you describe each of the types of government.

 1. <Included Term> Would you please describe this type of government for me?

Thank you very much for helping me understand all of this. I know it is a lot, and I appreciate you taking the time to teach me. So, now I have a list of many types of government in Afghanistan, and a description for each. Now, if we could go through the list again and this time give me examples of each type of government this will help me understand how each type of government exists.

1. Can you please give me an example of <included term>

Domain expansion via inclusion:
 Now you mentioned several words/phases I am not familiar with, earlier. Would you please help me to understand these new things for me?

 1. You mentioned <included term>. Would you please describe to me how you or most people would use describe or refer to <included term>?

Thank you. All of this is very helpful to me. You have taught me a lot today. I am now wondering if you could give me examples of good government and examples of bad government. Let us start with the examples of good government first.

 1. Would you please give me examples of what you think good government is?
 2. Would you please give me examples of what you think bad government is?

Thank you very much for your help today. I have learned so much. I know this has taken a lot of your time, but I am very appreciative. I hope that we have the opportunity to spend more time together so you can teach me more about Afghanistan. Thank you.

APPENDIX O

IZ4 PRODUCT, "ISOLATING SADR CITY," 4TH BCT, 10TH MOUNTAIN DIVISION, FALL 2008

Isolating Sadr City — Anticipated Cultural and Political Consequences.

In an effort to isolate Jaish Al-Mahdi (JAM) activity and apply pressure to Muqtada al-Sadr's political movement, the Government of Iraq and Coalition Forces (GoI and CF) have erected a series of walls to cut Sadr City off from the rest of Baghdad. The following paper anticipates likely consequences of this action in the context of Sadr City's history and the growth of the Sadrist political movement therein. CF can expect extremely negative reactions from both Sadrist leadership and elements of Sadr City's population, but an understanding of the cultural and political background from which these protests stem may enable CF to anticipate, understand and possibly mitigate fallout.

The City of the Revolution.

The area now known as Sadr City was built at the order of General Abdul Karim Qassim in the immediate aftermath of the 1958 revolution. It was the centerpiece of his widely-heralded national initiative to bring "social justice" to Iraq and better the lives of the poor, and was created to replace the sprawling, disease-ridden slums that had developed in East Baghdad during previous decades of uncontrolled urban migration from the rural South. It was named Madinat ath Thawra, "City of the Revolution," and was intended to stand as a symbol of the new egalitarian ethic that would characterize Iraq's future.

The ambitious building project suffered from poor follow-through and subsequent negligence, however, and by the mid-sixties it had become an extraordinarily densely populated slum to which Shi'a tribesmen from southern Iraq continued to flock in search of work. Madinat ath Thawra became a fertile recruiting ground for radical opposition movements like the Iraqi Communist Party and the Da'wa Islamists, experiencing continued neglect from the government while cementing a national reputation as a turbulent, overcrowded, crime-ridden slum of poorly educated Shi'a. Referred as "the stronghold of heroes" in Shi'a Islamist literature, the area developed a localized pride in response to the hardships (often self-inflicted) its inhabitants endured.

Saddam City.

Saddam Hussein renamed the area in his own honor after seizing power, but few benefits were extended to the President's namesake community thereafter. Despite the Ba'th Party's impressive nationwide development of public infrastructure and expansion of government services (facilitated by the oil-boom of the 1970s), the entire area lacked paved roads or a sewage system. Conditions deteriorated as the Iraqi economy neared collapse during the latter years of war with Iran, while its well-deserved reputation for crime, corruption and poverty earned it the continued scorn and derision of the broader Iraqi population. The sanctions regime established after the 1991 Gulf War further crippled the ability of the Iraqi government to extend basic services to its subjects, and the

494

residents of Saddam City were largely left to fend for themselves.

It was in this atmosphere that Mohammed Sadiq al-Sadr (aka Sadr II, father of MAS) built his constituency in Saddam City. Operating with the blessing of Saddam Hussein, Sadr II built a network of charities in the crowded slum which represented the first substantive, organized effort to care for the local population since General Qassim ordered the city's construction. Sadr II was a political figure as much as a religious one, however, and his radical Islamist-populist rhetoric blamed both Western imperialism and government negligence for the plight of his followers. He rallied enormous support among the destitute Shi'a of Saddam City in the process, but his shift from client of Saddam to critic led to his killing at the order of the Iraqi president.

Sadr City.

Sadr II's name lives on—the area was renamed in his honor after Saddam Hussein's removal, and the Office of the Martyr Sadr refers to him as well—and localized pride has further solidified around his legacy. The slums of Sadr City now stand in many ways as a glaring reminder of the failures of successive Iraqi governments to deliver the "social justice" promised by General Qassim, and the Sadrist movement is now seen by significant elements of Baghdad's impoverished Shi'a as the vehicle through which this downtrodden, ridiculed, and neglected constituency will finally find its voice in national politics. A sense of vengeance is evident in the political rhetoric of the movement as a result, and this has fueled the intensity of the Sadr-GoI rivalry because the better-educated, wealthier Shi'a of Da'wa and Supreme Islamic Iraqi Council (SIIC) will be the primary targets of Sadrist retribution.

The Wall and Its Consequences.

The construction of a wall to isolate Sadr City from the rest of Baghdad has met with approval among much of the Iraqi population, which despises JAM and furthermore thinks very little of MAS's constituents.[1] It remains to be seen whether the wall's continued presence will enable the Sadrists to breathe renewed life into the area's perceived historical legacy of neglect and oppression at the hands of both the West and the Iraqi government, however, around which Sadr II originally built his following. These themes interweave seamlessly with traditional Shi'a narratives of injustice and persecution, and it can be expected that related propaganda will resonate among the population of Sadr City. The wall will invite comparisons to Israel's "security barriers," and will be depicted in Sadrist propaganda as yet another iteration of the locals' oppression at the hands of an uncaring central government and malicious Western imperialists. The Sadrists will strive to re-enforce their role as the only organization ever to meet the needs of the people in the area, and the wall may enable the Sadrist movement to rebuild support among its traditional constituents.

Historical Comparisons.

The example of the Berlin Wall has been cited in discussion as a model for the wall that will encircle Sadr City. The argument posits that the wall will punish Sadr City's inhabitants for their facilitation of criminal and militia activity in their neighborhoods, while at the same time enable them to "look over the wall" to see the benefits of cooperation with GoI. The problem with the comparison to Çold War Germany, however, is that, in its application to Sadr City, the United States takes on the role of the Union of Soviet Socialist Republics, and GoI that of the German Democratic Republic. Historically, the builder of a wall is the party blamed for its existence and the suffering that ensues, as anger is typically directed toward the party directly responsible for a barrier as opposed to the more abstract concepts used to justify its existence.

ENDNOTE - APPENDIX O

1. The feelings of many Iraqis verge on hatred for the people of Sadr City. In a recent Human Terrain Team interview, an IA intelligence officer suggested that CD "seal off Sadr City and [use chemical weapons to] gas everyone inside" to solve current problems with JAM.

IZ4 4-SLIDE POWERPOINT PRESENTATION, 4TH BCT, 10TH MOUNTAIN DIVISION, FALL 2008

HTT Culture Brief

Isolating Sadr City – Cultural & Political Consequences

OVERVIEW:
- Brief history of Sadr City

- Likely JAM & local population responses to "the wall" in the context of local history and culture

---

KEY QUESTION:
What are the likely effects upon Patriot OE from walling in Sadr City, given the context of the city's history and sources of Sadrist support in the area?

HTT Culture Brief

- "The City of the Revolution" - 1958
  - Centerpiece of Qassim's national program for "social justice"
  - Replaced disease-ridden slums of East Baghdad
  - Follow through problems... Became radical recruiting ground

- Saddam City
  - Renamed by Saddam upon taking power
  - Few services provided, crime and poverty drew nationwide infamy & scorn
  - The rise of Mohammed Sadiq al-Sadr & local solidarity

- Sadr City
  - Sadrist movement now serves as the political "voice" for the long-neglected Shi'a poor, Sadr & JAM capitalize on the absence of government services
  - Slum conditions a reminder of the failure of successive Iraqi governments to deliver the social justice promised by Qassim

HTT Culture Brief

The Wall and Its Consequences

- Majority of Iraqi Population vs. the Sadrist Movement

- JAM propaganda will reinforce historical theme of government persecution and "Western imperialism" to draw loyalty from local residents

- Ties in perfectly with Shi'a narratives of oppression and injustice

 # HTT Culture Brief

- ## Historical Comparisons
  - Berlin Wall?
  - Israel?

ACRONYMS, ABBREVIATIONS, AND GLOSSARY

AAA	American Anthropological Association
AO	Area of Operations
ASCOPE	Areas, Structures, Capabilities, Organizations, People, Events
AWG	Asymmetric Warfare Group
CA	Civil Affairs
CALL	Center for Army Lessons Learned
CAOCL	Center for Advanced Operational Culture Learning
CENTCOM	United States Central Command
C-IED	Counter-Improvised Explosive Device
CIDNE	Combined Information Data Network Exchange
CKC	Cultural Knowledge Consortium
CNA	Center for Naval Analyses
COIN	Counterinsurgency
CONUS	Continental United States
CONOPS	Concept of Operations
COR-HTS	Cultural Operations Research–Human Terrain System

DISCC	Defense Intelligence Sociocultural Capabilities Council
DoD	U.S. Department of Defense
DOTMLPF	Doctrine, Organization, Training, Materiel, Leadership, Personnel, Facilities
DOTMLPF-P	Doctrine, Organization, Training, Materiel, Leadership, Personnel, Facilities-Policy
FM 3-24	*U.S. Army Field Manual* (FM) *3-24, Counterinsurgency*
FMSO	Foreign Military Studies Office
G-2	Military Intelligence staff element commanded by a general officer
GAO	Government Accountability Office
HTAT	Human Terrain Analysis Team
HTS	Human Terrain System
HTT	Human Terrain Team
HRAF	Human Relations Area Files
IED	Improvised Explosive Device
IRB	Institutional Review Board
IQATF	Iraqi Advisor Task Force
JIEDDTF	Joint Improvised Explosive Device Defeat Task Force

JIEDDO	Joint Improvised Explosive Device Defeat Organization
JUONS	Joint Urgent Operational Needs Statement
MAP-HT	Mapping the Human Terrain
NIPRNet	Non-Classified Internet Protocol Router Network
NGA	National Geospatial-Intelligence Agency
NGO	Nongovernmental Organization
OCO	Overseas Contingency Operations
ONS	Operational Needs Statement
OPT	Operational Planning Team
OUSDI	Office of the Under Secretary of Defense for Intelligence
PDT	Program Development Team
PMESII	Political, Military, Economic, Social, Infrastructure and Information
PSYOP	Psychological Operations
RRC	Research Reachback Center
S-2	Military Intelligence Staff
SfAA	Society for American Anthropologists
SIPRNet	Secret Internet Protocol Router Network

SME-Nets	Subject Matter Expert-Networks
SOCOM	Special Operations Command
SSRA	Social Science Research and Analysis
SSWG	Social Science Working Group
TIGR	Tactical Ground Reporting System
TRADOC	Training and Doctrine Command
TRISA	Training and Doctrine Command Intelligence Support Activity
TCE	Theater Coordination Element
TDA	Table of Distribution and Allowances
TOE	Table of Organization and Equipment
TSO	Theater Support Office

U.S. ARMY WAR COLLEGE

Major General William E. Rapp
Commandant

*****

STRATEGIC STUDIES INSTITUTE
and
U.S. ARMY WAR COLLEGE PRESS

Director
Professor Douglas C. Lovelace, Jr.

Director of Research
Dr. Steven K. Metz

Author
Dr. Christopher Sims

Editor for Production
Dr. James G. Pierce

Publications Assistant
Ms. Rita A. Rummel

*****

Composition
Mrs. Jennifer E. Nevil